14 95
Sch

Miniature
Emergency Vehicles

by Dr. Edward Force

Schiffer Publishing Ltd
Box E. Exton, Pennsylvania 19341

Highway Models #8 **Leyland-Metz 1935 Ladder Truck,** #15 **Dennis 1954 F17 Fire Engine,** and #13 **AEC-Merryweather 1951 Fire Engine.** *(Photo courtesy of Highway Models).*

Library of Congress Catalog Number: 85—50878

Printed in the United States of America.
ISBN: 0-88740-031-0
Published by Schiffer Publishing Ltd., 1469 Morstein Road, West Chester, Pennsylvania 19380
This book may be purchased from the publisher.
Please include $1.50 postage.
Try your bookstore first.

CONTENTS

ACKNOWLEDGEMENTS

Profound thanks to everyone who contributed models or data to this volume, especially to The Rev. Charles W. Gelbach and his daughter Ellen, and to Nelson H. Adams, without whose help both the listings and the photographs would offer much less information than they do, and to all the other collectors, dealers and manufacturers who helped, including John Alden, John Amundson, Robert S. Brennen of Miniature Toys, Richard Bringloe, Edward Bruening, Spielwaren Danhausen, Donald Elliott, David Finkelstein, D. C. Fuller of Corgi Toys, John Gay, Highway Models, Julio Holst, Ralph Horton, Gerhard Klarwasser of Toys For Collectors, Lee Town Model Service, Eugenie Nelson, Peter Retelstorf, Mike and Sue Richardson, David Spencer of Peover Model Productions, Eric Van Caillie, Penny Van Wart, Rod Ward of Model Auto Review, James Wieland of Jim's Miniature Auto Sales, and everyone I've neglected to mention, and certainly not least, thanks to Ron Coleman and Ray Russell for inspiring me to write this book, and to Peter and Nancy Schiffer, Judith Riddell and all the Schiffer Publishing family for helping to make a dream come true.

INTRODUCTION

It is said that every boy, at some time in his life, wants to be a fireman, and therefore every boy likes toy fire trucks. This is certainly true in my case; of the few toys that survived my childhood to become part of my collection, most are fire trucks. In addition, my father drove an ambulance in my younger days, another link with emergency vehicles. But stereotypes notwithstanding, one doesn't have to be a boy (of whatever age) to collect miniature emergency vehicles. My favorite collector of them, in fact, is thoroughly feminine Ellen Gelbach, and I would like to thank Ellen and her father, The Rev. Charles W. Gelbach, for all their help in gathering information and finding models. Nelson H. Adams also deserves special thanks for putting his large collection at my disposal so as to make this book as nearly complete as possible.

One must say "nearly complete", for I am sure I must have omitted many items that deserve to be mentioned, simply because I do not know of them. As for what is in the book, I planned at first not to venture too far afield from the area I know best, 1/40 to 1/100 scale diecast metal miniatures and related (such as plastic) readymade scale models. But where does one draw the line between models and toys? I decided not to draw it at all, so you will find numerous toys included that are not scale models. If I could stand to have it in my collection, or thought you might want to know about it, I included it, and I bought many items that I wouldn't have been caught dead paying good money for before I decided to write this book, just so I could include their data.

In writing this book I naturally moved into ground covered by the two volumes of the Coleman-Russell *FIRE TRUCK TOYS FOR MEN AND BOYS*. These books, a labor of love by two devoted hobbyists, include not only such models and toys as are included here, but also items such as large-scale sheet metal toy fire trucks and non-vehicular fire toys. The present book not only includes other types of emergency vehicles, but also offers as thorough a list of 1/40 and smaller scale diecast and similar miniatures as I, who specialize in such miniatures, can offer, as well as whatever data I could gather on fields such as cast iron toys. Messrs. Coleman and Russell have realized the limitations of their books and voiced a wish for a really thorough book on the subject. I am grateful to them for information I otherwise would not have, and regret only that I have had to correct some of their data.

When I speak of emergency vehicles, I include not only fire trucks, chiefs' cars and ambulances, but also rescue vehicles and the like. Some of them include boats or aircraft, but I did not list an item unless it included at least one vehicle, or a home for one, as I thought model fire

Highway Models #8 **Leyland-Metz 1935 Ladder Truck,** #15 **Dennis 1954 F17 Fire Engine,** and #13 **AEC-Merryweather 1951 Fire Engine.** *(Courtesy of Highway Models).*

Horton T6 **Bedford 1979 TM Crash Tender.** *(Courtesy of Ralph Horton).*

stations would be of interest. The vehicles include those of the Danish Falck and Zonen organizations, now merged, which provide equipment for various municipal services, and of the German Technisches Hilfswerk agency, which deals with many kinds of non-fire emergencies: electric and gas line accidents, explosions, rubble clearing, transporting people and supplies, etc. Many thanks to Peter Retelstorf for an enlightening account of what THW does.

The models and toys listed are now or have been on the retail market. They include conversions of commercially produced models, if the conversions have been sold to the public, but no one-off "chops". A few items that were announced but never put into production have been listed, simply so you will know that they were not actually made.

The length of each model is given in millimeters when I know it, or approximated when my data were not exact. I chose millimeters because they are universally understood and include no fractions or decimal points. As for scale, miniature cars are, with all too many exceptions, made to one of three basic scales, known to model railroaders as O, S and HO gauges. Here O gauge will include roughly 1/40 to 1/50 scale, S gauge 1/60 to 1/70 and HO gauge 1/80 to 1/90. The exact scale is given if the manufacturer stated it, not that the stated scale is always to be trusted! Some models fall between two of these scales, and numerous toys, not being scale models of real vehicles, could not be listed by scale at all.

The details given are meant to be a general description, not an exhaustive one. At times it was not easy to find things to mention, and you may get tired of reading of model after model "with dome light and labels"; at other times I had to be brief so my publisher could get all the data into one book that you can afford.

The year of issue has been stated when I know it; otherwise I have tried to give a general idea: Fifties, early postwar, prewar, etc. Some models may have come on the market earlier than I thought; if you know data that I don't, I'd be happy if you'd tell me. I've tried to make the data as factually correct as possible, but I don't know everything about every one of the 2400 or so items listed.

References to the Coleman-Russell books, including volume and page number, have been included when they were my only source of information. This will help you find pictures of numerous models not pictured in this book, plus a few in more complete condition. But most of the items listed are shown in the photographs, the great majority from my own collection, the rest from the Adams and Gelbach collections.

The order of the photos is basically that of the listing chapters, running from Dinky Toys to Other Asian Models. Since only 32 pages of color photos could be used because of financial considerations, the order had to be applied twice, with the lucky 32 running from Dinky to Other French and the black and white photos starting from the beginning again. The models are shown in side views, which was our most practical way of including as much as possible.

And now I have run out of time to gather models and data, and must stop at the end of 1984 and let Peter Schiffer publish the book as it stands. Fortunately, 1984 was a superb year for collectors of model emergency vehicles, and we surely have much to look forward to in 1985.

You are always welcome to write, offer additions or corrections, or even better, spare models, or just chew the zamak, plastic or cast iron fat. I hope you'll find this book informative and interesting. Happy hobbying to you all!

Horton T7 **Dennis 1939 Fire Pump Trailer.** *(Courtesy of Ralph Horton).*

Horton T8 **Crossley 1918 Fire Tender.** *(Courtesy of Ralph Horton).*

Horton T9 **Ford 1930 Model A Chemical Fire Engine.** *(Courtesy of Ralph Horton).*

Horton T10 **Barton Pump and Ladder Conversion.** *(Courtesy of Ralph Horton).*

Horton T11 **1976 Land Rover Angloco Emergency Tender.** *(Courtesy of Ralph Horton).*

A conversion of a Matchbox Yesteryear **Model T Ford.** *(Courtesy of Robert Shortell).*

Tekno, Horton and Can-Am **Fire Pump Trailers.** *(Courtesy of Model Auto Review).*

Taylor & Barrett **Fire Pump Trailer.** *(Courtesy of Model Auto Review).*

Taylor & Barrett **Ladder Truck, Fire Truck with 4 Firemen,** and **Turntable Fire Escape Truck.** *(Courtesy of Model Auto Review).*

Taylor & Barrett **Fire Truck with 4 Firemen.** *(Courtesy of Model Auto Review).*

Taylor & Barrett **Turntable Fire Escape Truck.** *(Courtesy of Model Auto Review).*

Gasquy-Septoy **Mercury Ambulance** with windup motor. *(Courtesy of Eric Van Caillie).*

Tekno #341 tinplate **Ladder Truck.** *(Courtesy of Model Auto Review).*

Tekno **Falck Fire Station.** *(Courtesy of Model Auto Review).*

Tekno tinplate 341 **Ladder Truck,** 361 **Searchlight Truck,** 351 **Ambulance** and **Falck Fire Station.** *(Courtesy of Model Auto Review).*

Tekno 321 **Fire Truck.** *(Courtesy of Model Auto Review).*

Tekno tinplate #361 **Searchlight Truck.** *(Courtesy of Model Auto Review).*

Tekno tinplate #371 **Generator Truck.** *(Courtesy of Model Auto Review).*

Tekno 480 **Ford Zonen Dump Truck.** *(Courtesy of Model Auto Review).*

Tekno 481 **Ford Zonen Wrecker.** *(Courtesy of Model Auto Review).*

Old Cars #1003 **Fiat Cometto Fire Department Low Loader** and **Shovel Loader.** *(Courtesy of Model Auto Review).*

Elegance **Cadillac** 86 **Hearse and Military, Fire Department** and **Civilian Ambulances.** *(Courtesy of Model Auto Review).*

Bill Barnes **Merryweather Musketeer Fire Tender.** *(Courtesy of Model Auto Review).*

Pyracar **Cournil LWB Forest Fire Truck, LWB Covered** and **SWB Covered Fire Trucks.** *(Courtesy of Model Auto Review).*

MVI **Guinard Fire Truck.** *(Courtesy of Model Auto Review).*

Annecy **Laffly Fire Truck.** *(Courtesy of Model Auto Review).*

Idem **Citroen 45 Fire Truck.** *(Courtesy of Model Auto Review).*

M.O.B. Super Toy **Land Rover** and **Fire Pump Trailer.** *(Courtesy of Model Auto Review).*

MVI #005 **Citroen C4 Fire Tender.** *(Courtesy of Model Auto Review).*

Mini Racing K18 **Peugeot Dangel Forest Fire Truck.** *(Courtesy of Model Auto Review).*

Mini Racing K11 **Fire Department Land Rover.** *(Courtesy of Model Auto Review).*

Mini Racing K3 **Peugeot 203 Fire Department Ambulance.** *(Courtesy of Model Auto Review).*

Mettoy 604A **Fire Chief Car.** *(Courtesy of Corgi Toys).*

Mettoy 633 **Fire Engine.** *(Courtesy of Corgi Toys).*

Mettoy 725 **Fire Engine with Pump.** *(Courtesy of Corgi Toys).*

Mettoy 726 **Fire Engine with Siren.** *(Courtesy of Corgi Toys).*

Mettoy 752 **Fire Chief Car.** *(Courtesy of Corgi Toys).*

Mettoy 909/2 **Fire Chief Car.** *(Courtesy of Corgi Toys).*

Mettoy 850 **Mechanical Fire Engine.** *(Courtesy of Corgi Toys).*

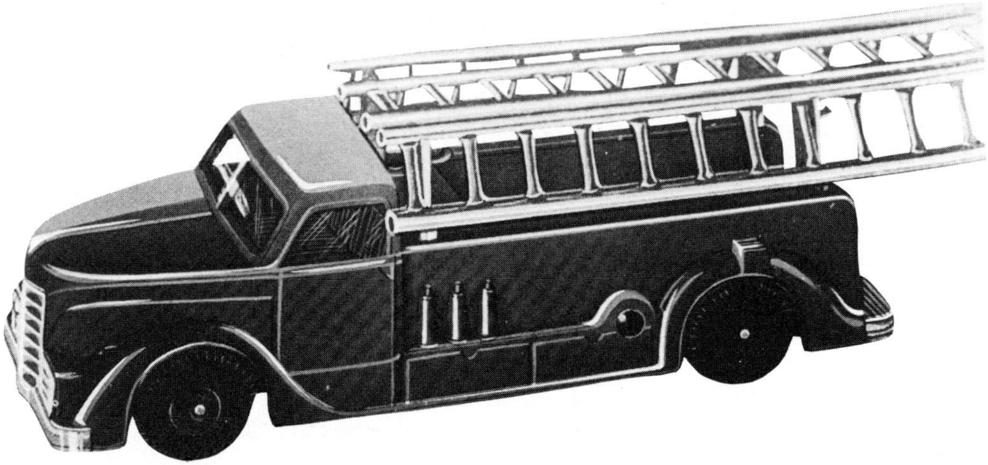

Mettoy 3102/3 **Fire Engine.** *(Courtesy of Corgi Toys).*

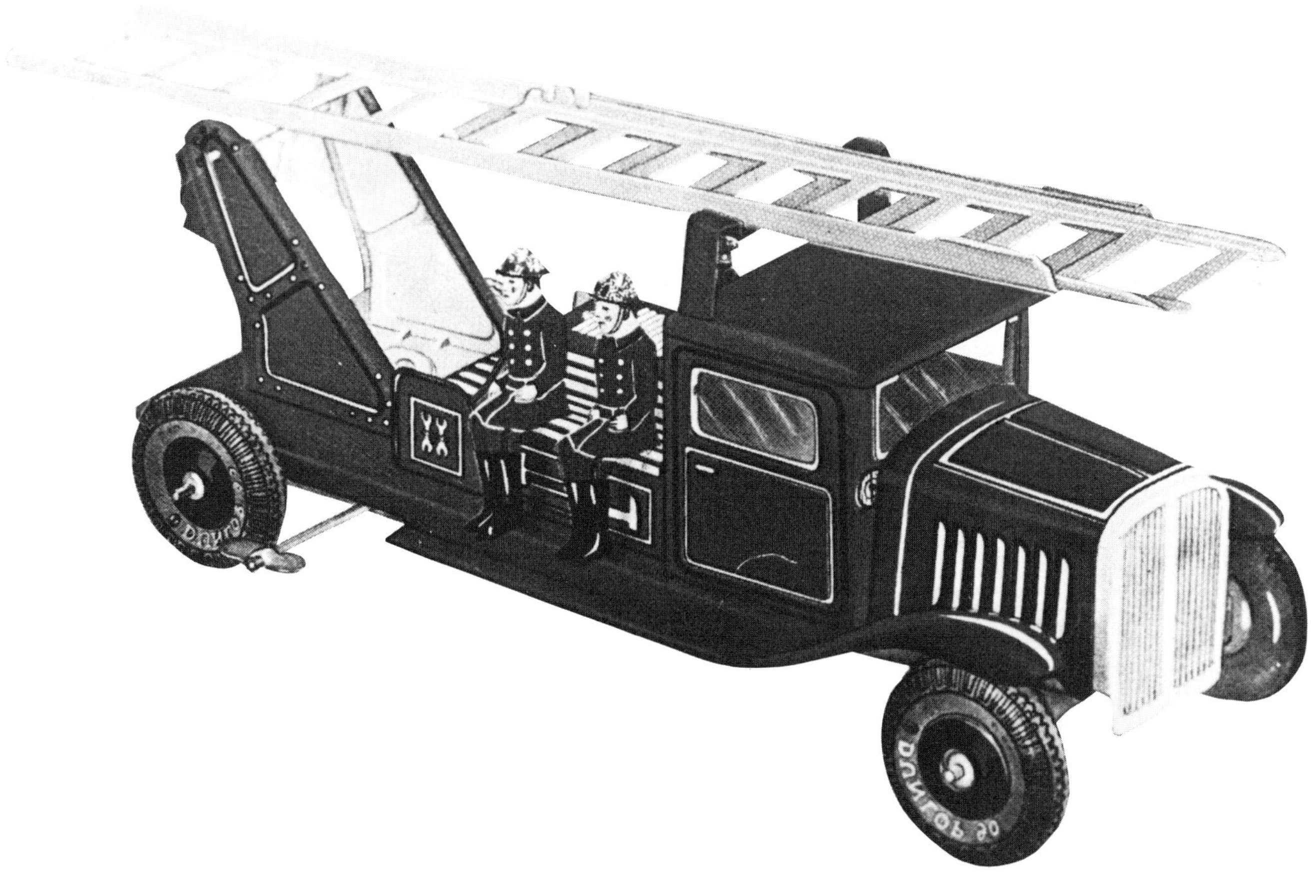

Mettoy 3104 **Fire Engine with Ladder.** *(Courtesy of Corgi Toys).*

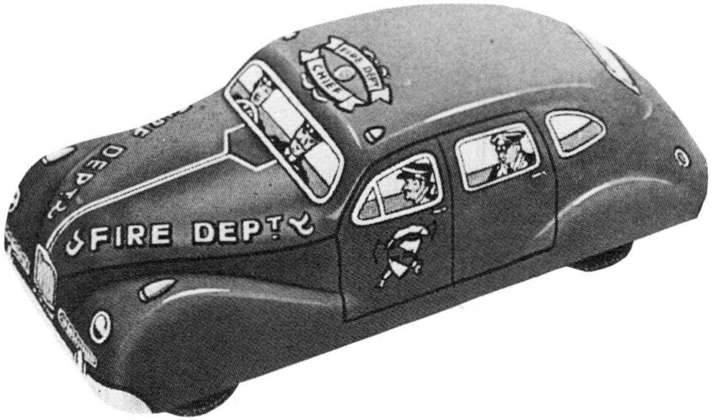

Mettoy 3307 **Fire Chief Siren Car.** *(Courtesy of Corgi Toys).*

Mettoy 3110 **Fire Engine.** *(Courtesy of Corgi Toys).*

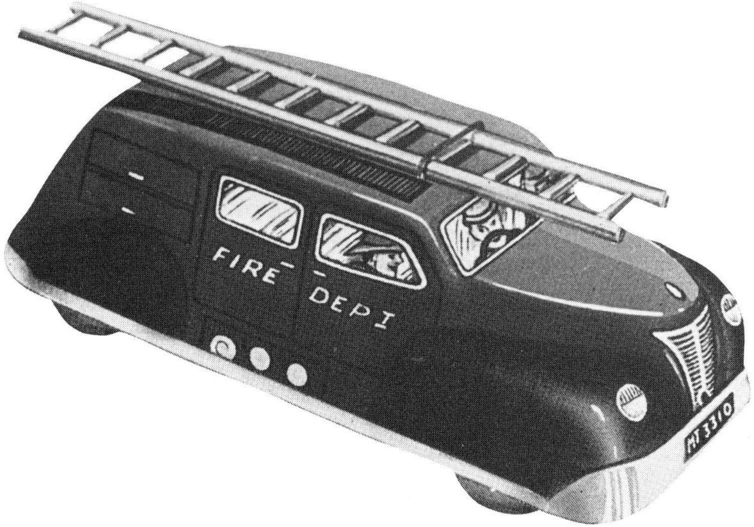

Mettoy 3321 **Fire Tender.** *(Courtesy of Corgi Toys).*

3322
FIRE CHIEF CAR

Metal body decorated as Fire Chief Car. Friction flywheel mechanism operates siren. Rubber tyres. Individually boxed.

6¼″ x 3″ x 2¼″ 7 ozs.
160 x 75 x 55 mm. 200 gms.

Mettoy 3322 **Fire Chief Car.** *(Courtesy of Corgi Toys).*

Mettoy 8287 **Fire Escape.** *(Courtesy of Corgi Toys).*

Mettoy 8288 **Pumping Fire Engine.** *(Courtesy of Corgi Toys).*

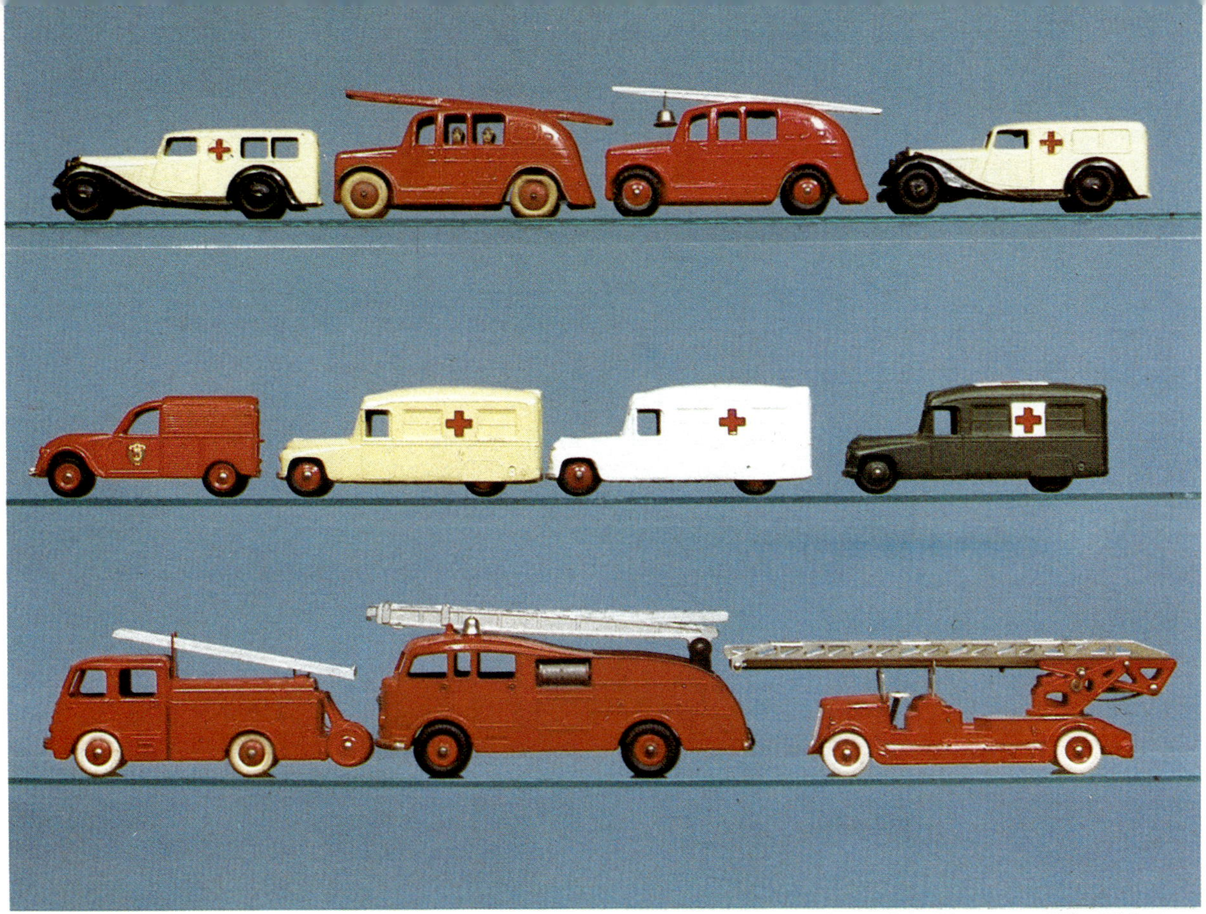

Row 1: Dinky Toys 30f **Ambulance** (prewar type), 25k **Streamlined Fire Engine** with Firemen, 25h/250 **Streamlined Fire Engine,** 30f **Ambulance** (postwar type).
Row 2: Dinky Toys 25d/562 **Citroen 2cv Fire Tender,** 30h (cream) and 253 (white) **Daimler Ambulances,** 30hm/624 **Daimler Army Ambulance.**
Row 3: Dinky Toys 32e/583 **Berliet Fire Engine,** 555/955 **Fire Engine,** 32d/899 **Delahaye Ladder Truck.**

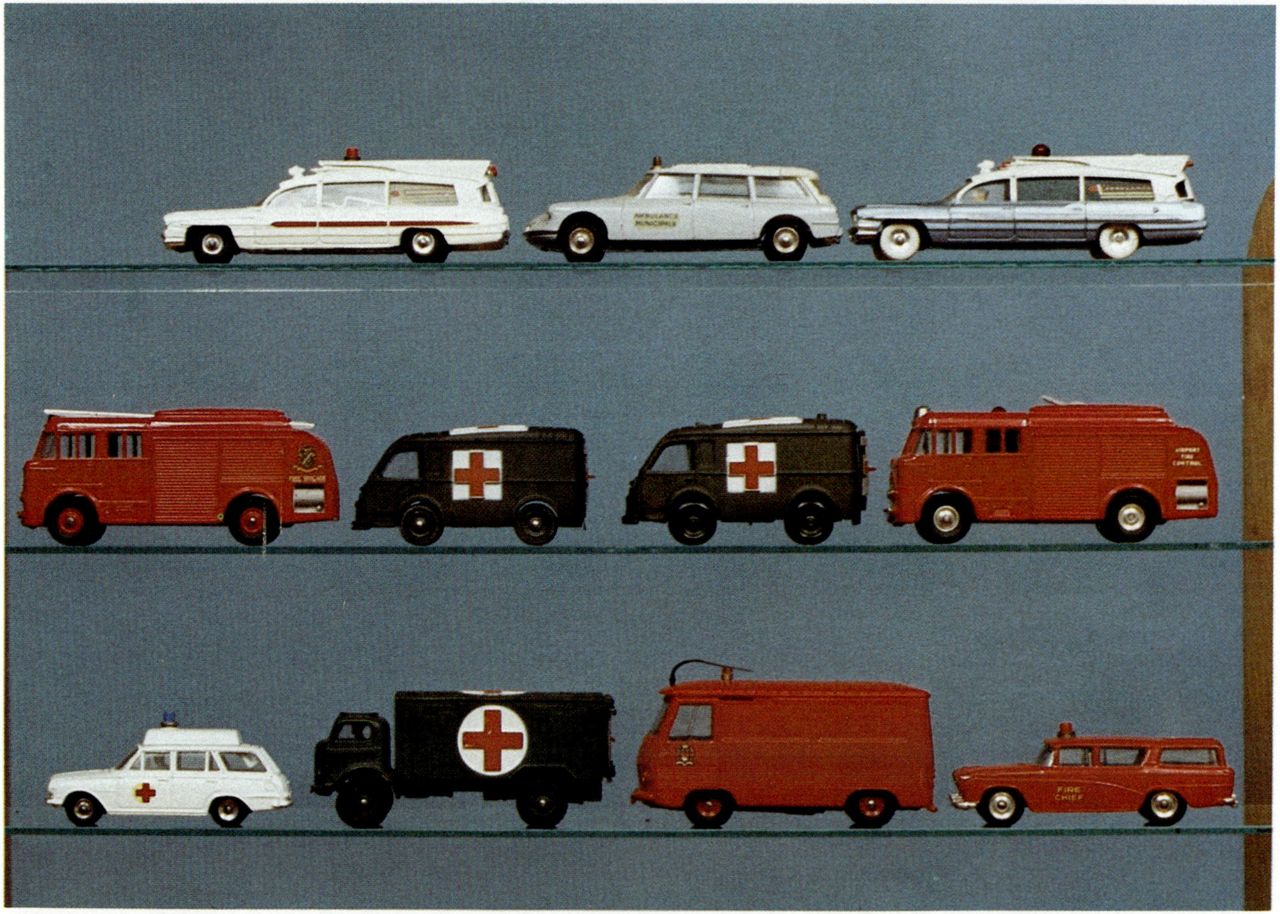

Row 1: Dinky Toys 263 **Superior Ambulance,** 556 **Citroen ID19 Ambulance,** 277 **Superior Ambulance.**
Row 2: Dinky Toys 259 **Fire Engine,** 80f/820 and 807 **Renault Military Ambulances,** 276 **Airport Fire Tender.**
Row 3: Dinky Toys 278 **Vauxhall Ambulance,** 626 **Ford Military Ambulance,** 570p **Peugeot Fire Department Van,** 257 **Rambler Fire Chief.**

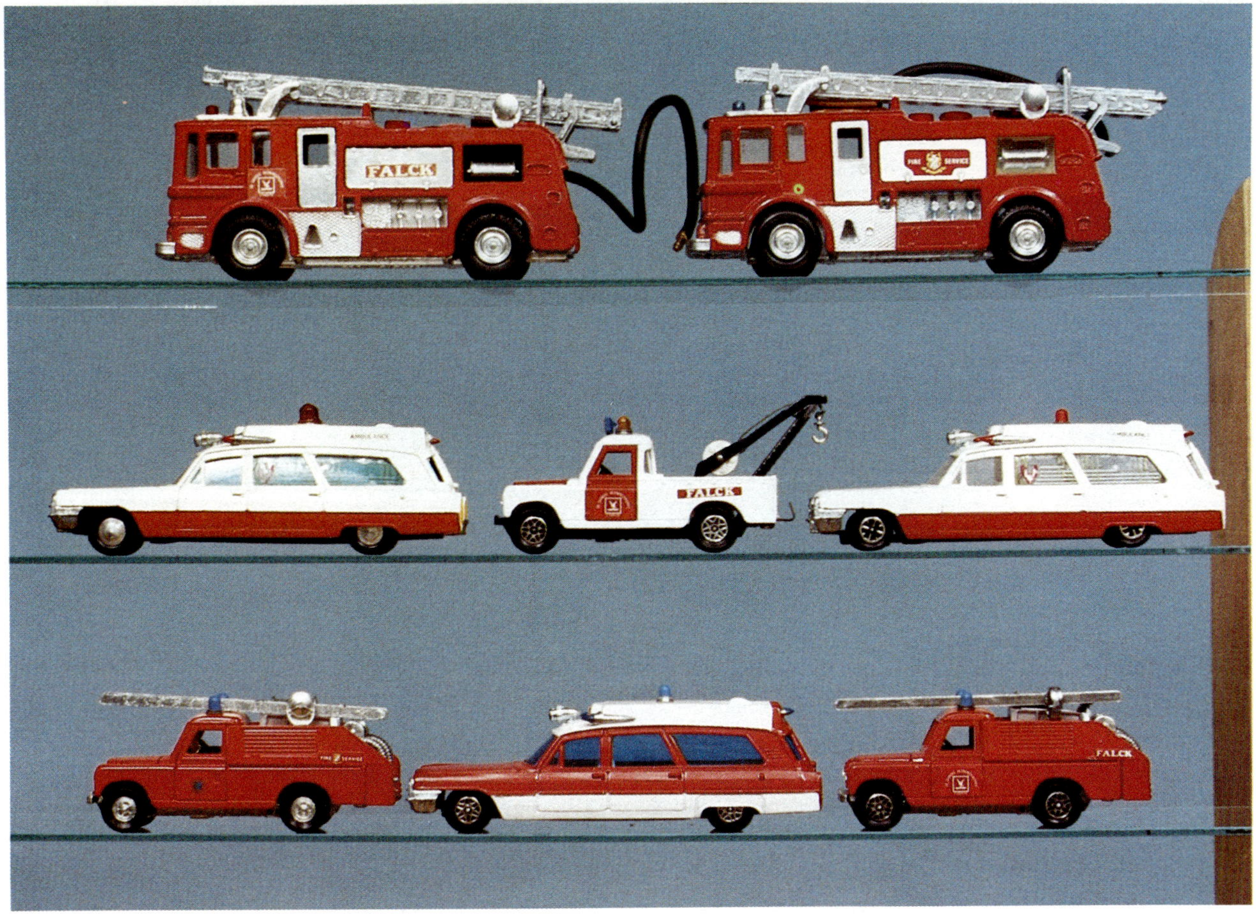

Row 1: Dinky Toys 285 **Falck** and regular issue **Merryweather Marquis Fire Engine.**
Row 2: Dinky Toys 267 **Superior Ambulance,** 442 **Falck Land Rover Wrecker,** 288 **Superior Ambulance.**
Row 3: Dinky Toys 282 **Land Rover Fire Appliance,** 288 **Falck Superior Ambulance,** 282 **Falck Land Rover Fire Appliance.**

Row 1: Dinky Toys 956-2 and 568 **Berliet Ladder Truck** (British and French versions).
Row 2: Dinky Toys 195 **Range Rover Fire Chief,** 956-1 **Turntable Fire Escape,** 268 **Range Rover Ambulance.**
Row 3: Dinky Toys 263 **Airport Fire Tender,** 266 **E.R.F. Fire Tender.**

Row 1: Corgi Toys 405M (red) and 405 (green) **Bedford Fire Tenders,** 412 **Bedford Ambulance,** 414 **Bedford Military Ambulance,** 423 **Bedford Fire Tender.**
Row 2: Corgi Toys 213 **Jaguar 2.4 Fire Chief,** 439 **Chevrolet Impala Fire Chief** (two types), 482 **Chevrolet Impala Fire Chief.**
Row 3: Corgi Toys 437 **Superior Ambulance** (blue and white), 463 **Commer Ambulance** (two types), 437 **Superior Ambulance** (red and cream).

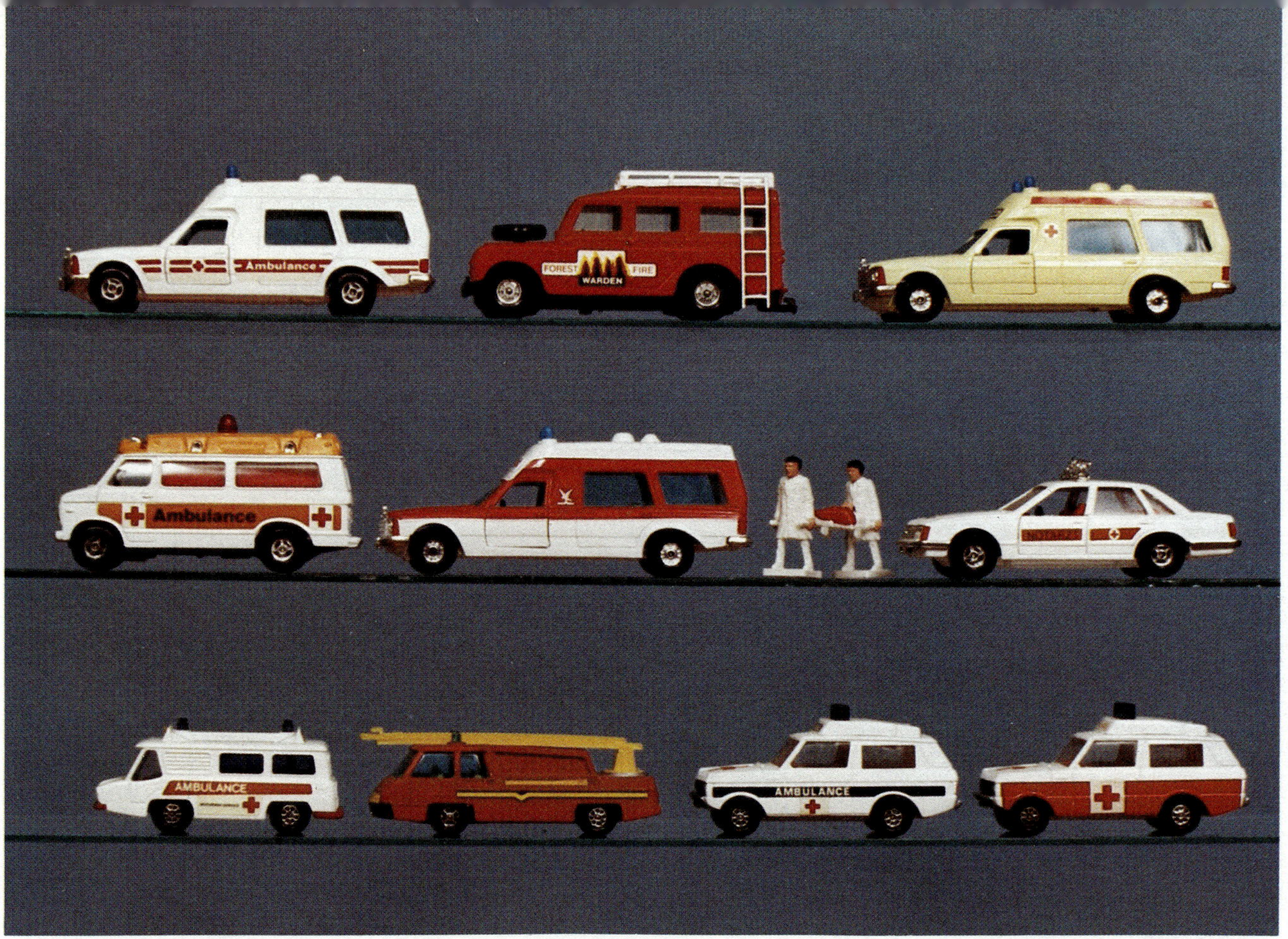

Row 1: Corgi Toys 406 **Mercedes-Benz Ambulance,** 421 **Forest Fire Land Rover,** 4061 **Mercedes-Benz Ambulance** (German issue).
Row 2: Corgi Toys 405 **Chevrolet Ambulance,** 406 **Mercedes-Benz Falck Ambulance,** 332 **Opel Senator Doctor's Car.**
Row 3: Corgi Toys 700 **Motorway Ambulance,** 703 **Hi-Speed Fire Engine,** 482 **Range Rover Ambulance** (two types).

Row 1: Matchbox K67 yellow **Dodge Fire Chief,** K53 **Hot Fire Engine,** K67 red **Dodge Fire Chief.**
Row 2: Matchbox K6, K26 and K63 **Mercedes-Benz Ambulances,** K62 **Citroen Doctor's Car.**
Row 3: Matchbox K15 **Merryweather Fire Engine,** BK112 **DAF Military Ambulance, K9 Fire Tender.**

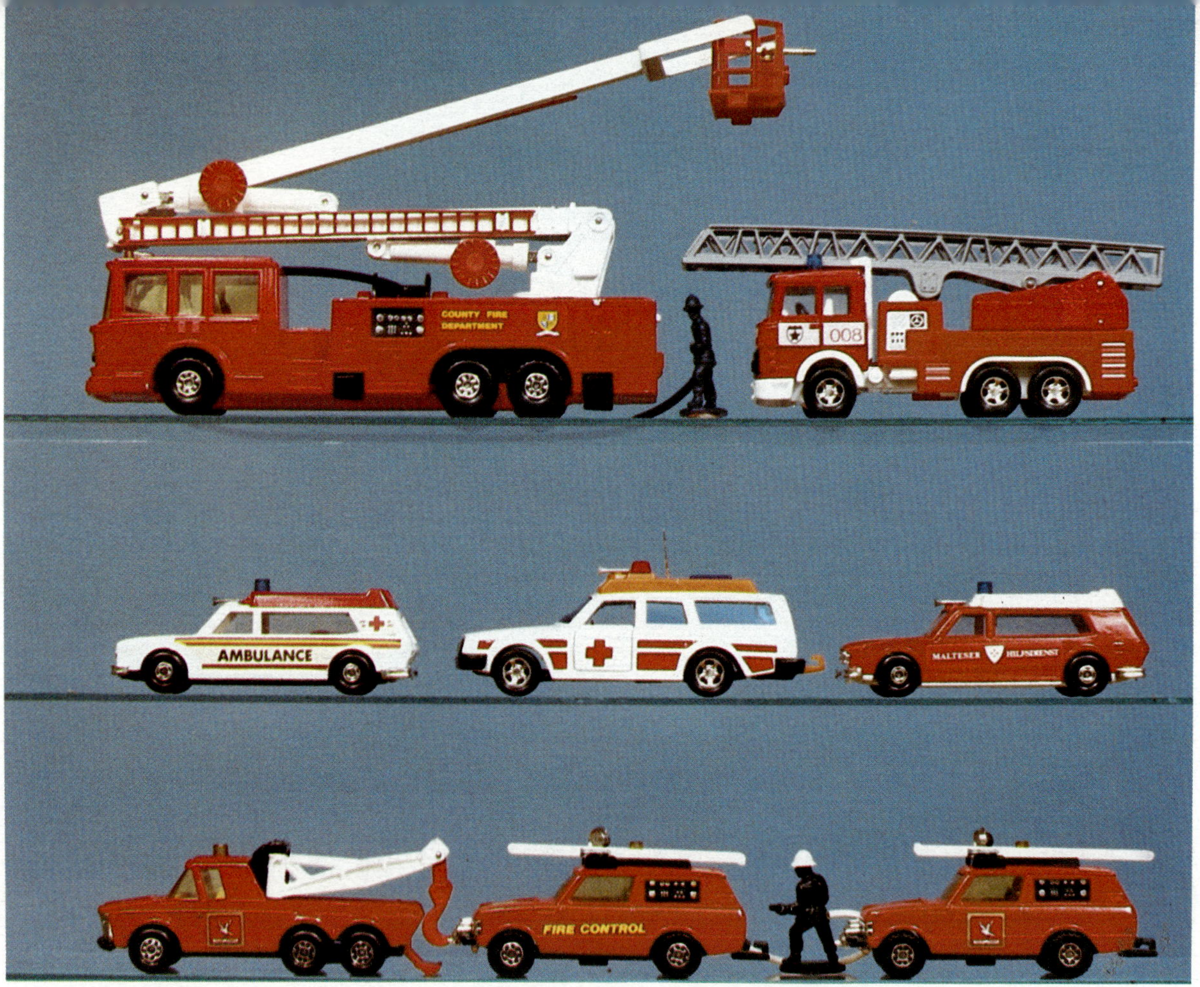

Row 1: Matchbox K39 **E.R.F. Snorkel Fire Engine,** K110 **Fire Tender.**
Row 2: Matchbox K49 **Ambulance,** K96 **Volvo Ambulance,** K49 **Malteser Ambulance.**
Row 3: Matchbox K11 **Falck Wrecker,** K64 regular and **Falck Fire Range Rovers.**

Row 1: Matchbox K75 **Airport Fire Tender**, K40 **Blaze Trailer**, K75 **Flughafen-Feuerwehr.**
Row 2: Matchbox K77 **Highway Rescue**, **Secours Routier** and **Strassen-Service Trucks.**
Row 3: Matchbox K65 **Emergency Rescue Truck**, WD1 **Mickey Mouse Fire Truck**, K65 **Mountain Rescue Truck.**

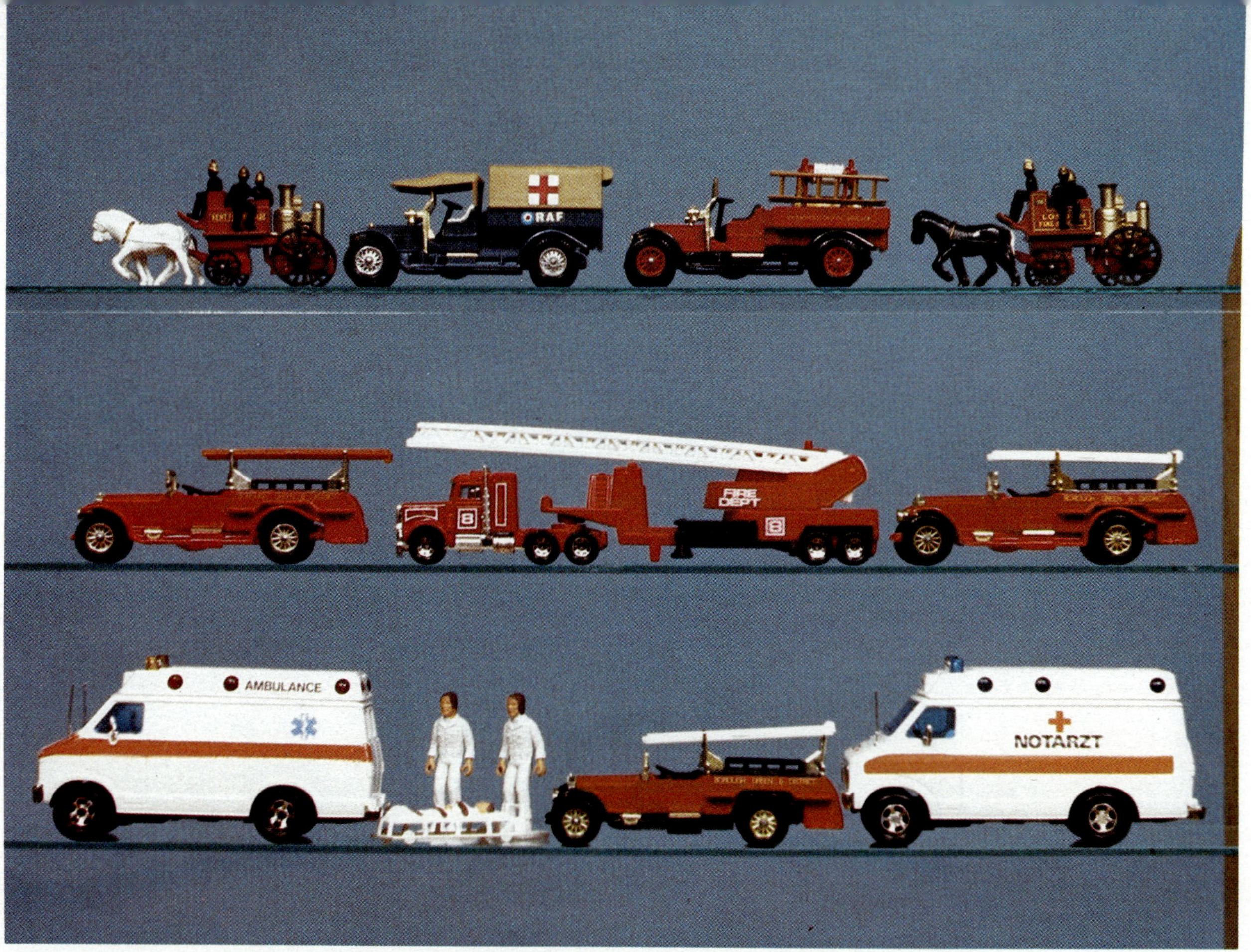

Row 1: Matchbox Y4 **Kent Fire Brigade Shand-Mason Steamer,** Y13 **Crossley R.A.A. Ambulance,** Y13 **Crossley Fire Truck** (conversion), Y4 **London Fire Brigade Shand-Mason Steamer.**
Row 2: Matchbox Y6 **Rolls-Royce Fire Engine** (first type), CY12 **Fire Truck,** Y6 **Rolls-Royce Fire Engine** (second type).
Row 3: Matchbox K38 **Dodge Ambulance,** Y6 **Rolls-Royce Fire Engine** (third type), K38 **Dodge Notarzt Van.**

Row 1: Lledo DG5 **London, Guildford, Hong Kong** and **Chicago Fire Engines**
Row 2: Philadelphia Bureau of Fire Set: **Chief's Car, Ambulance, Steamer, Rescue Van** and **Tank Truck.**
Row 3: DG12 **Dennis Cardiff Fire Engine,** DG5 **BIFBAC II, Lake City** and **GWR Fire Engines,** DG12 **Luckhurst Fire Engine.**

Row 1: Castle Art **Fire Engine,** Lone Star 1296 **Fire Engine,** Morestone **Fire Engine.**
Row 2: Benbros 27 **Daimler Ambulance,** Sopt-On 316 **Land Rover Fire Truck,** Morestone and Budgie 258 **Daimler Ambulances.**
Row 3: LDCW **Streamlined Fire Engine,** Charbens 15 **Fire Truck,** Budgie 298 **Alvis Crash Tender,** Timpo **Dennis Fire Engine.**

Row 1: Chad Valley 9231 **Fire Engine,** Minic **L.C.C. Ambulance** and **Fire Engine.**
Row 2: Unknown **Bentley Ambulance,** Spot-On 207 **Morris Wadham Ambulance,** Johillco **Dennis Fire Engine,** unknown slushmold **Ambulance.**
Row 3: Taylor & Barrett **LWB Ambulance, Fire Engine, Army Ambulance** and **SWB Ambulance.**

Row 1: Brooklin 16 **Ford Fire Van,** Sun 205 **Studebaker Fire Truck,** Brooklin 16 **Philadelphia Fire Van.**
Row 2: Brooklin 9 **Ford Ambulance,** Lledo DG6 **London Police Ambulance,** Pirate **Leyland Fire Control Unit,** Brooklin 9 **Philadelphia Ambulance.**
Row 3: Brooklin 5 **Ford Fire Chief,** Airfix **Emergency Ambulance** and **Fire Truck,** Brooklin 5 **Philadelphia Fire Chief.**

Row 1: Peover 2 **Bedford Fire School, Hydrant Service** and **Breathing Apparatus Vans.**
Row 2: Peover 1 **Bedford Limerick Fire Van,** 3 **Ford Escort Fire Van,** 5 **Land Rover Fire Truck.**
Row 3: Peover 30 **Peugeot Ambulance** (short logo), 4 **Renault Fire Chief,** 30 **Peugeot Ambulance** (long logo).

Row 1: Peover 9a, 9b and 9c **Ford Sharon, Metropolitan and Rockdale Fire Trucks.**
Row 2: Peover 8 **Crossley Fire Tender,** 10 **Ford Irish Hills Fire Truck,** 10b **Talbot Fire Truck.**
Row 3: Peover 32 **Crossley Ambulance,** 31 **Talbot Dorking** and **Welshpool Ambulances.**

Row 1: Märklin 5521/35 **Krupp Ladder Truck,** Cursor 470 **Daimler 1896 Fire Truck,** Märklin 8023 **Magirus Ladder Truck.**
Row 2: Märklin 1809 **VW Variant Ambulance,** 8030 **VW Ambulance bus,** Schuco 637 **BMW Doctor's Car.**
Row 3: Märklin 1807 **VW Variant Fire Chief,** Ziss 400 **Ford Kombi Ambulance,** Schuco 631 **VW Passat Fire Chief.**

Row 1: Siku 339/2212 **Mercedes-Benz Rescue Van,** 2914 **Faun Rescue Crane,** 357/2214 **Mercedes-Benz Rescue Van.**
Row 2: Siku 261/2815 **Mercedes-Benz Ladder Truck,** 2218 **Red Cross Unimog,** 2819 **Mercedes-Benz Ladder Truck.**
Row 3: Siku 2913 **Unimog Fire Truck** and **Trailer,** 332/3411 **Metz-Faun Airport Crash Truck.**

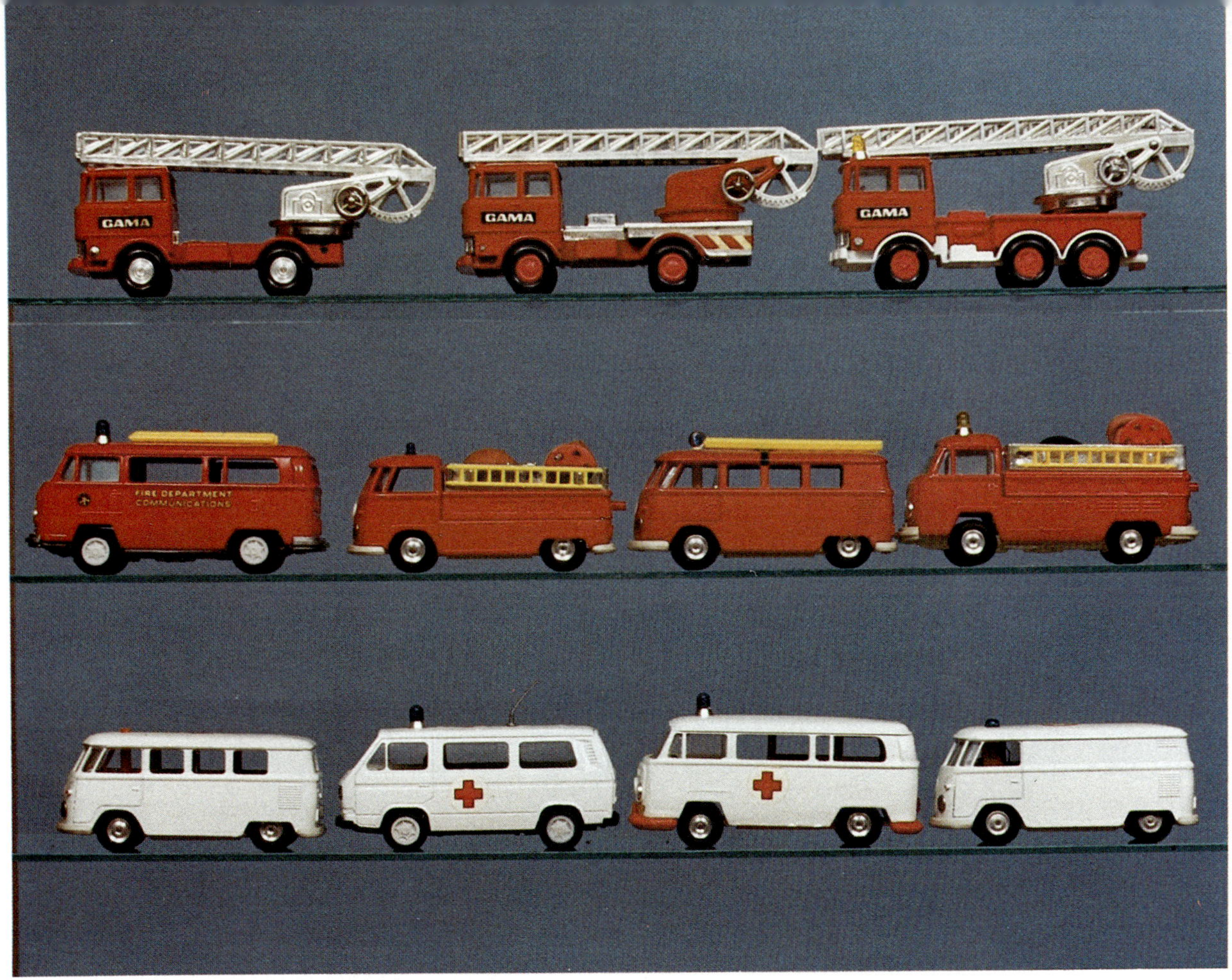

Row 1: Gama 9121, 9122 and 9123 **Faun Ladder Trucks.**
Row 2: Gama **VW Fire Department Bus,** 948 **VW Fire Truck,** 9487 **VW Fire Department Bus,** 9575 **VW Fire Truck.**
Row 3: Gama 954 **VW Red Cross Bus,** 9532 **VW Kombi Ambulance,** 9547 **VW Ambulance,** 9541 **VW Red Cross Van.**

Row 1: Gama 912-1 **Mercedes-Benz Ladder Truck,** 9406 **Krupp Fire Truck,** 912-2 **Faun Ladder Truck.**
Row 2: Gama 916 **VW Fire Chief,** 95477 **VW Army Ambulance,** 9047 **Medical Corps Jeep,** 816 **VW Fire Chief.**
Row 3: Gama 8932 **Opel Rekord Doctor's Car,** 1172 **Opel Ascona Fire Chief,** 1165 **BMW 528i Fire Chief,** 1156 **BMW 528i Doctor's Car.**

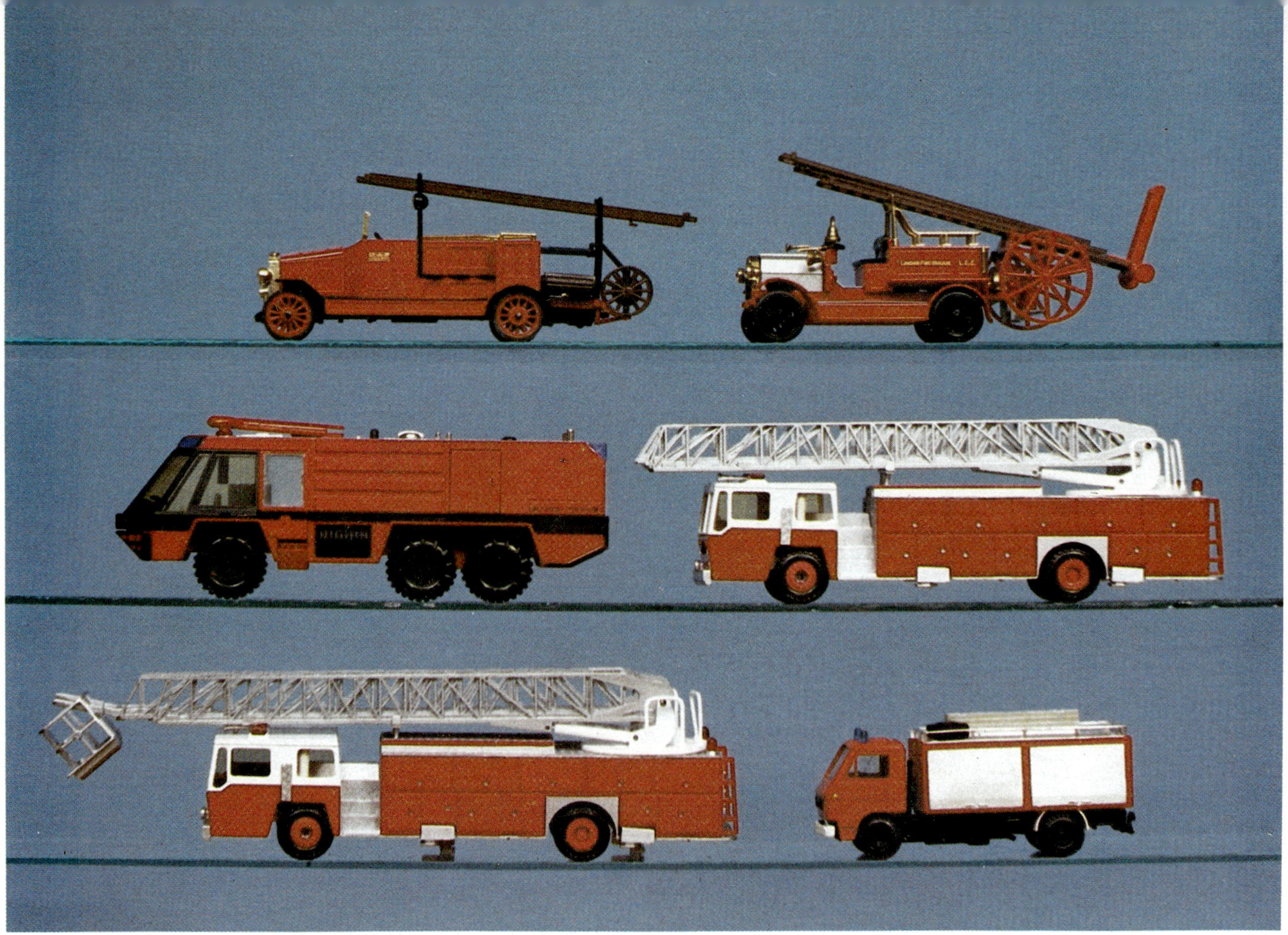

Row 1: Conrad 1018 **Gräf und Stift Fire Truck,** 1025 **Dennis 1914 Fire Engine.**
Row 2: Conrad 5501 **Rosenbauer Simba,** 5503 **Emergency One.**
Row 3: Conrad 5502 **Emergency One,** 3191 **M.A.N.-VW Fire Truck.**

Row 1: Conrad 5504 **Emergency One,** 3090 **Mercedes-Rosenbauer Fire Truck.**
Row 2: Conrad 5505 **Emergency One,** 3490 **Steyr-Rosenbauer Fire Truck.**
Row 3: Conrad 5506 **Emergency One,** 5506 **Emergency One Airport Crash Trucks.**

Row 1: Tekno 486 **Triangel Fire Truck,** 485 **Triangel Ladder Truck,** 486 **Triangel Zonen Fire Truck** and 487 **Fire Pump Trailer.**
Row 2: Tekno 481 **Ford Zonen Wrecker,** 725 **Mercedes-Benz 220SE Fire Chief,** 764 **Harley-Davidson Falck Motorcycle** and **Sidecar,** 483 **Mercury Loudspeaker Car.**
Row 3: Tekno 415a **Ford Taunus white Ambulance,** 415r **Ford Taunus Fire Van,** 415a **Ford Taunus black and white Ambulance,** 414 **VW Ambulance.**

Row 1: Tekno 408 **VW Fire Truck,** 409 **Ladder Trailer,** 814 **Falck Jeep,** 404 **VW Ladder Truck.**
Row 2: Tekno 733 **Dodge Ambulance** (white), 730 **Mercedes-Benz Ambulance** (white), 732 **Dodge Ambulance** (red).
Row 3: Tekno 731 **Mercedes-Benz Ambulance** (red and black, 730 **Mercedes-Benz Ambulance** (black), 731 **Mercedes-Benz Ambulance** (red).

Row 1: Tekno 445 **Scania Ladder Truck,** 459 **Volvo Fire Engine.**
Row 2: Tekno 956 **Dodge Searchlight Truck,** 952 **Dodge Military Ambulance,** 957 **Dodge Ladder Truck.**
Row 3: Tekno 920 **Ford Zonen Car Carrier,** 437 **Falck Flat Trailer.**

Row 1: Tekno sheet metal 341 **Fire Truck** and 351 **Ambulance.**
Row 2: Birk Copy? **Ambulance, Tekno 331 Falck Wrecker,** Gasquy-Septoy **Mercury Ambulance.**
Row 3: H. Langes Legetoj (pre-Tekno) 731 **Buick Ambulance,** Lion Cars **Commer Rutland Fire Service Van,** Tekno 835b **Volvo Fire Chief.**

Row 1: Solido 92 **Fire Escape Truck** (forward control cab), 196 **Ford Ambulance,** 96 **Aerial Ladder Truck** with firemen from 95.
Row 2: Solido 350 **Berliet Fire Engine,** 353 **Richier Rescue Crane,** 352 **Berliet Ladder Truck.**
Row 3: Solido 225 **Army Crash Tender,** 351 **Airport Crash Tender,** 227 **AMX Armored Ambulance.**

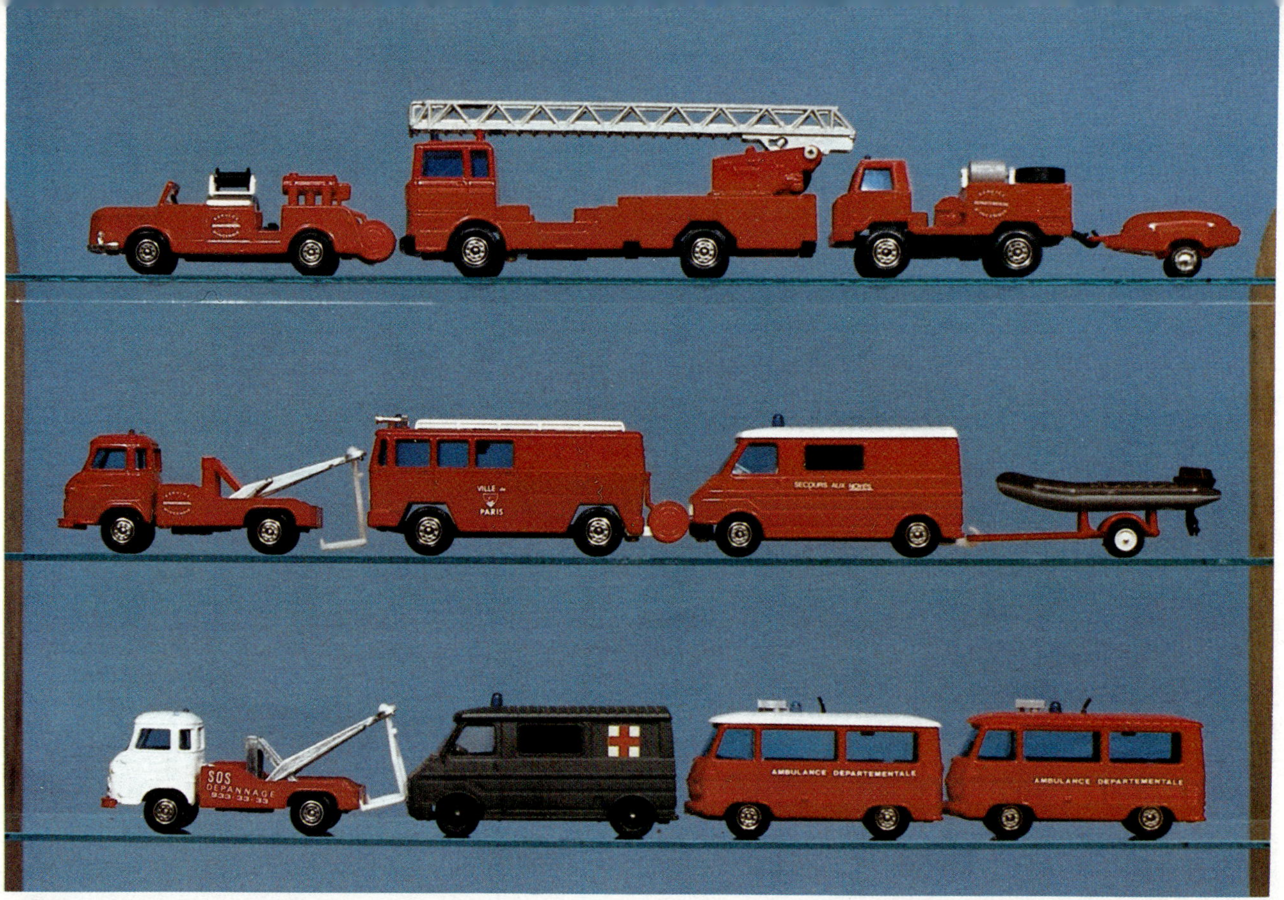

Row 1: Solido 362 **Hotchkiss Fire Truck,** 361 **Mercedes-Benz Ladder Truck,** 354 and 360 **Forest Fire Truck** and **Fire Pump Trailer.**
Row 2: Solido 366 **Saviem Fire Department Wrecker,** 375 **Berliet Fire Truck,** 368 and 371 **Citroen Fire Department Van** and **Lifeboat Trailer.**
Row 3: Solido 366 **Saviem SOS Wrecker,** 259 **Citroen Army Ambulance,** 380 **Peugeot Fire Department Ambulance** (red and white and all red).

Row 1: Solido 23 **Peugeot Ambulance,** 4038 **Cadillac Fire Department Ambulance,** 23d **Peugeot Fire Department Wagon.**
Row 2: Solido 4403 **Citroen Fire Engine,** 4411 **Citroen Ambulance,** 3303 **Saviem Fire Engine,** 1322 **Fire Department Jeep.**
Row 3: Solido 3304 **Fire Department Jeep** and **Fire Pump Trailer,** 1034 **Fire Department Land Rover,** 4033 **Citroen 15 Fire Chief.**

Row 1: Eligor 1014p **Renault 1938 Fire Chief,** 1081 **Ford Ambulance,** 1079p **Ford Sir Alan Cobham Ambulance,** 1016p **Peugeot 201 Fire Chief.**
Row 2: Eligor 1082 **Ford Trenton,** 1083 **San Francisco** and 1084 **Washington Fire Trucks.**
Row 3: Eligor 1091a **Ford Trenton Tanker,** 1087p **Ford Fire Department Wrecker,** 1091b **Ford Washington Tanker.**

Row 1: Eligor 1056 **Citroen 5cv Fire Truck,** 1020 and 1028 **Citroen Fire Trucks,** 1095 **Opel Fire Van.**
Row 2: Eligor 1033 **Citroen 11cv Fire Chief,** 1021 **Citroen Ambulance,** 1049 **Renault Fire Truck,** 1109 **Renault 4cv Fire Chief.**
Row 3: Dubray 21 **Citroen 11bl Fire Chief,** 29a **Citroen C4 Fire Chief,** 29d **Citroen C4 Fire Van,** 4 **Peugeot 402b Fire Chief.**

Row 1: CIJ 3/41 **Citroen ID19 Ambulance,** 3/46e **Peugeot 403 Secours Routiers Car,** 3/55 **Renault Colorale Ambulance,** 3/53a **Renault Ambulance.**
Row 2: CIJ M6 and 3/61 **Renault 1000kg Ambulance,** 3/95 **Renault Fire Truck,** 3/61m and M10 **Renault 1000kg Army Ambulance.**
Row 3: JRD 117 **Citroen Secours Routier Van,** 107 **Citroen Red Cross Van,** 133 **Berliet Fire Truck,** 109 **Citroen Fire Tender.**

Row 1: Dinky Toys 276 **Ford Transit Ambulance** (type 1), 286 **Ford Falck Fire Van** (type 1) and 274 **Ford Transit Ambulance** (type 2).
Row 2: Dinky 271 **Ford Transit Fire Van** (type 2), 286 **Ford Transit Fire Van** (type 1), 271 **Ford Falck Fire Van** (type 2).
Row 3: Dinky 385 **Los Angeles Fire Truck,** 267 **Paramedic Truck,** 384 **Convoy Fire Rescue Truck.**

Row 1: Dinky Toys 304 **Fire Rescue Set.**
Row 2: Dinky 410 **Bedford City,** 412 **Los Angeles** and 410 **Los Angeles Fire Vans.**
Row 3: Dinky 410 **Bedford London, Manchester and Metropolitan Fire Vans.**

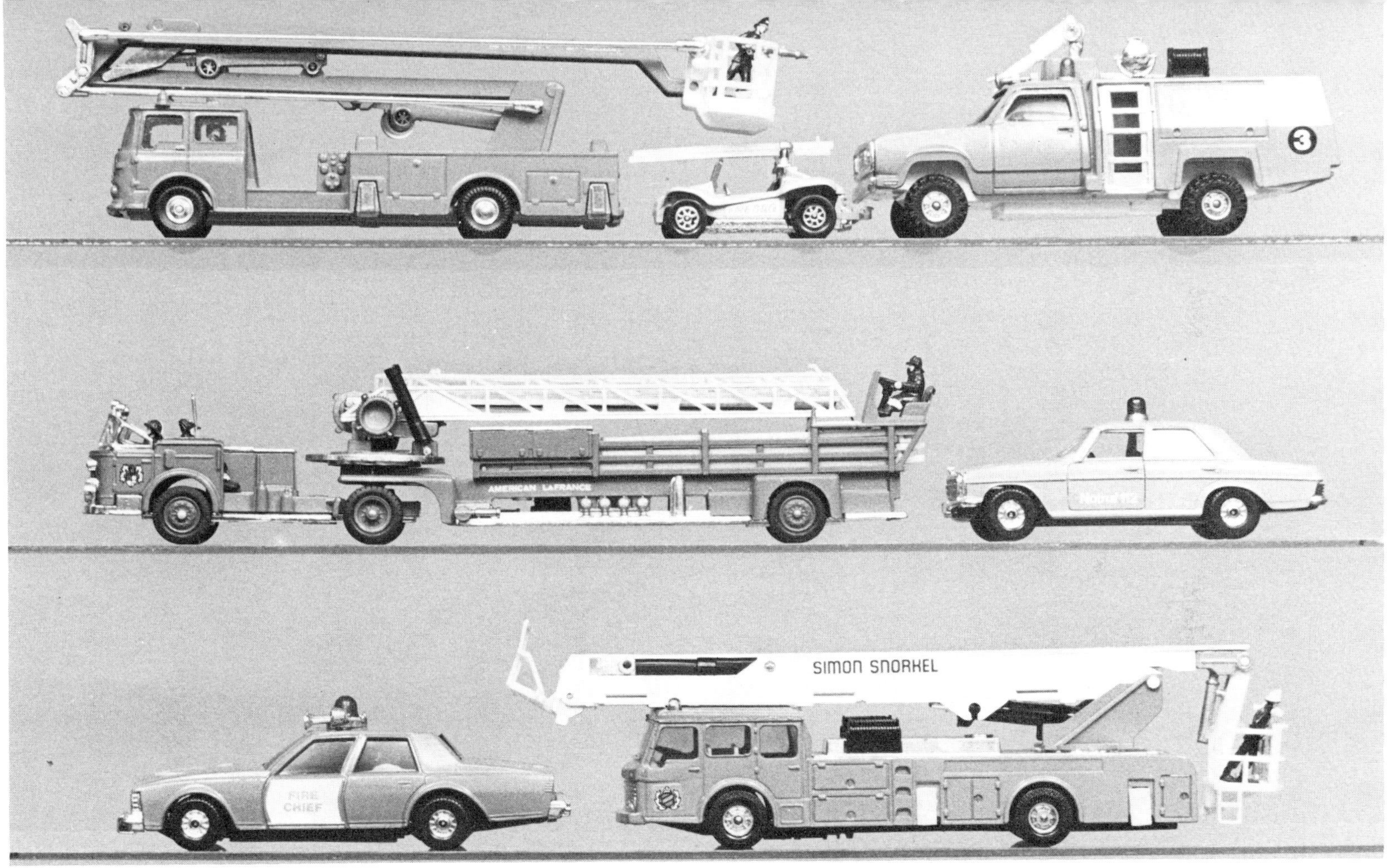

Row 1: Corgi Toys 1127 **Simon Snorkel** (type 1), 395 **Fire Bug,** 1001 **Angus Firestreak.**
Row 2: Corgi 1143 **American LaFrance Ladder Truck,** 284 **Mercedes-Benz Fire Chief.**
Row 3: Corgi 1008 **Chevrolet Caprice Fire Chief,** 1126 **Simon Snorkel** (type 2).

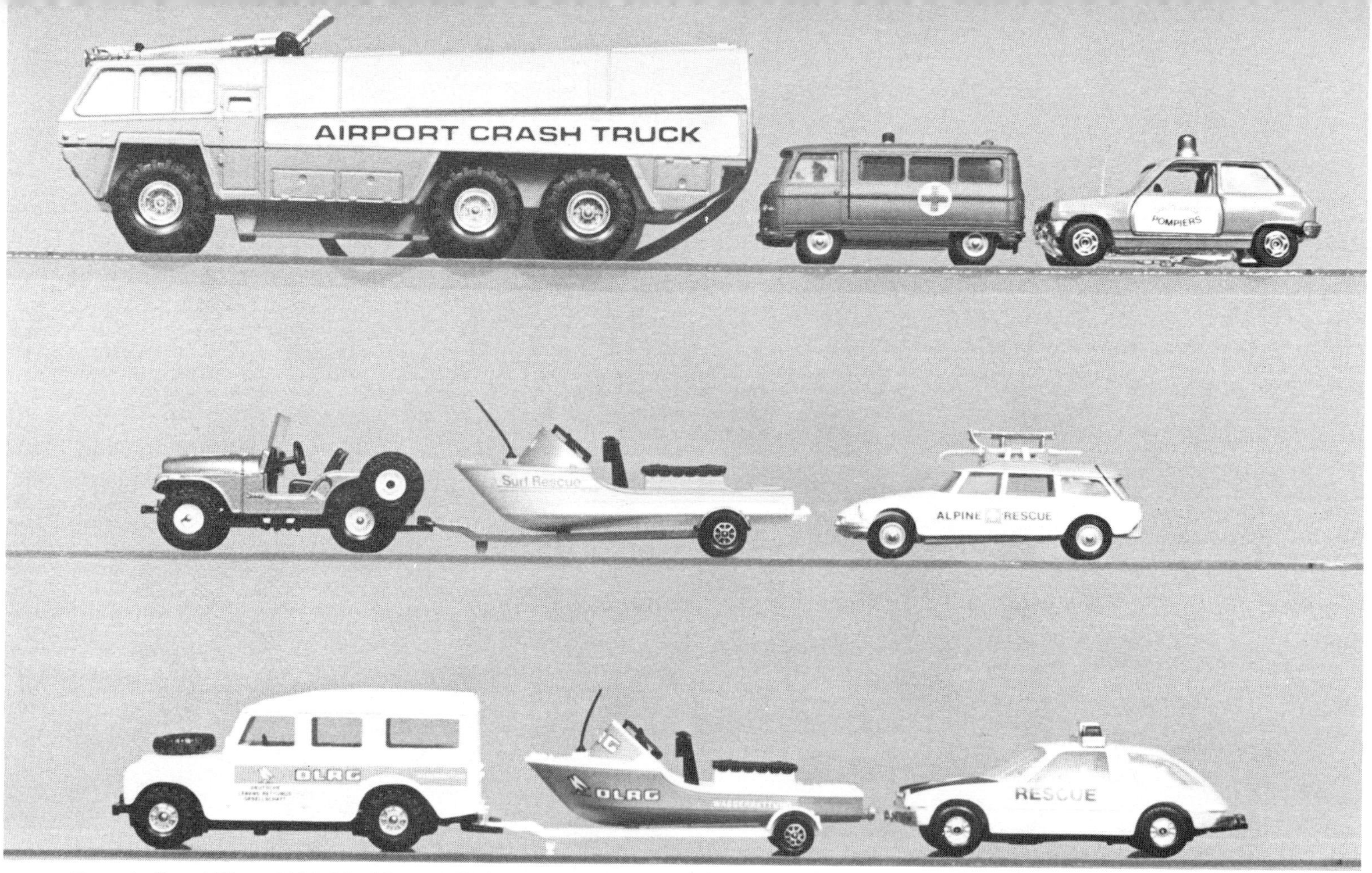

Row 1: Corgi Toys 1103 **Chubb Pathfinder Crash Truck,** 354 **Commer Military Ambulance,** 295 **Renault 5TS Pompiers.**
Row 2: Corgi 35 **Surf Rescue Set,** 513 **Citroen ID19 Alpine Rescue.**
Row 3: Corgi 33 **Deutsche Lebensrettungsgesellschaft Set,** 484 **Pacer Rescue Car.**

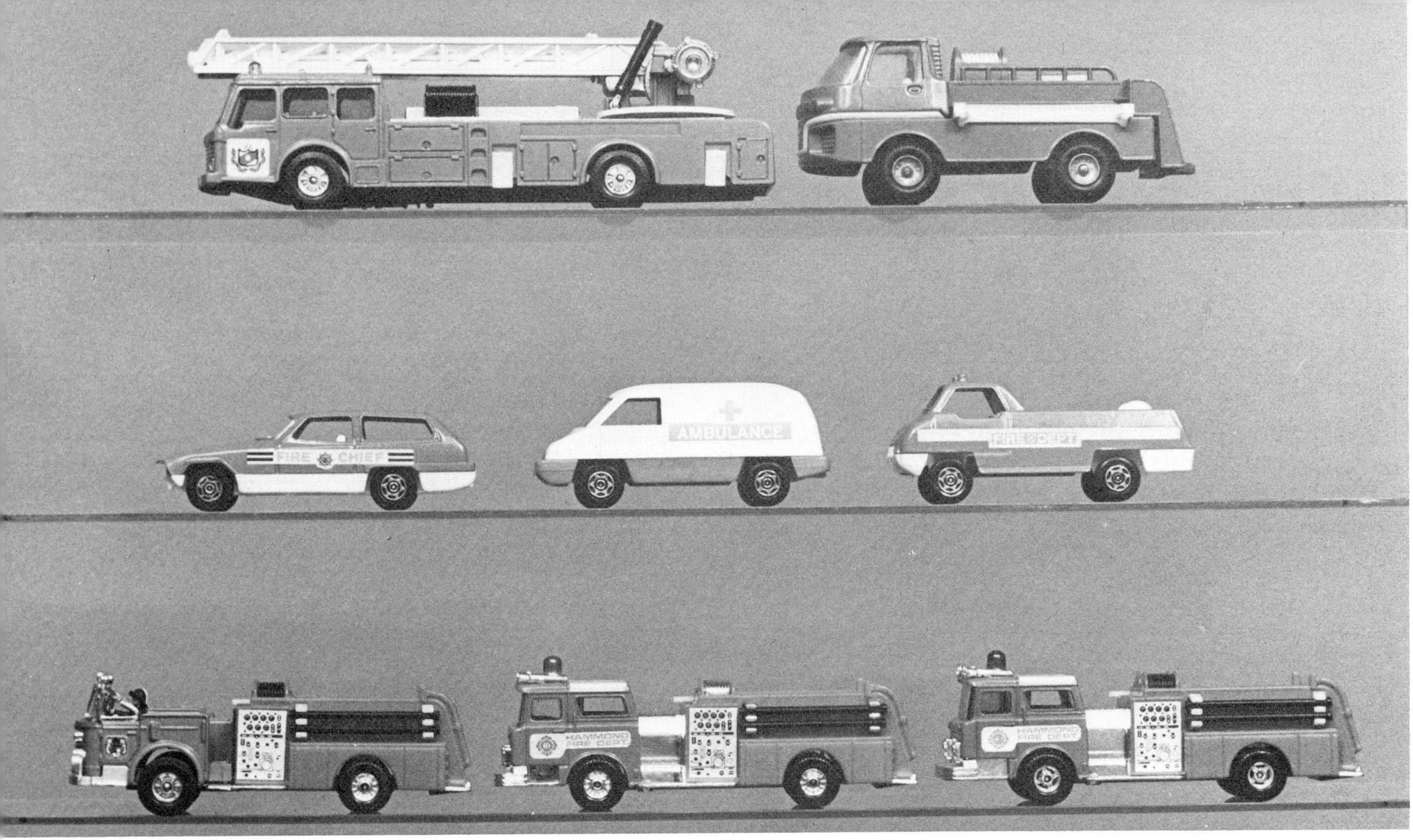

Row 1: Corgi Toys 1120 **Dennis Ladder Truck**, Qualitoys 707 **Fire Engine.**
Row 2: Corgi Cubs 505 **Fire Chief**, 511 **Ambulance**, 510 **Fire Truck.**
Row 3: Corgi Junior 2029 **Mack Fire Pumper** (open and closed cab types), Corgi 1185 **Mack Fire Pumper.**

Row 1: Husky 4-1 and 4-2 **Jaguar Fire Chief,** Corgi Junior 79 **Land Rover Military Ambulance,** 22 **Chevrolet Paramedic Van,** Husky 6 **Citroen Safari Ambulance,** 22 **Citroen Safari Military Ambulance.**
Row 2: Husky and Corgi Junior 30 **Studebaker Ambulance,** Corgi Junior 1 **Mercedes-Benz Ambulance** (all white and red roof types), 36 **Healer Wheeler** (two label types).
Row 3: Corgi Junior 56 **Ford Capri Fire Chief** (two label types), 42 **Rescue Range Rover,** 123 **Chubb Pathfinder Crash Tender,** 70 **Mercury Cougar Fire Chief,** 70 **Ford Gran Torino Fire Chief.**
Row 4: Corgi Junior 36 **Simon Snorkel,** 29 **Simon Snorkel** (two types), 26 ERF **Fire Engine** (two types).

Rows 1 & 2: Corgi Junior 3022 **Rescue Set.**
Row 3: Corgi Junior 253 **Mercedes-Benz Falck Ambulance,** 250 **Falck Simon Snorkel,** 252 **Ford Falck Wrecker,** 251 **ERF Falck Fire Engine,** 254 **Mercedes-Benz Falck Emergency Car.**
Row 4: Corgi Junior 193 **Arabian Chubb Pathfinder Crash Tender,** 192 **Mercedes-Benz Arabian Ambulance,** 255 **Chevrolet Falck Fire Van,** 208 **Ford Sierra German Doctor's Car,** 119 **Chubb Pathfinder German Crash Tender.**

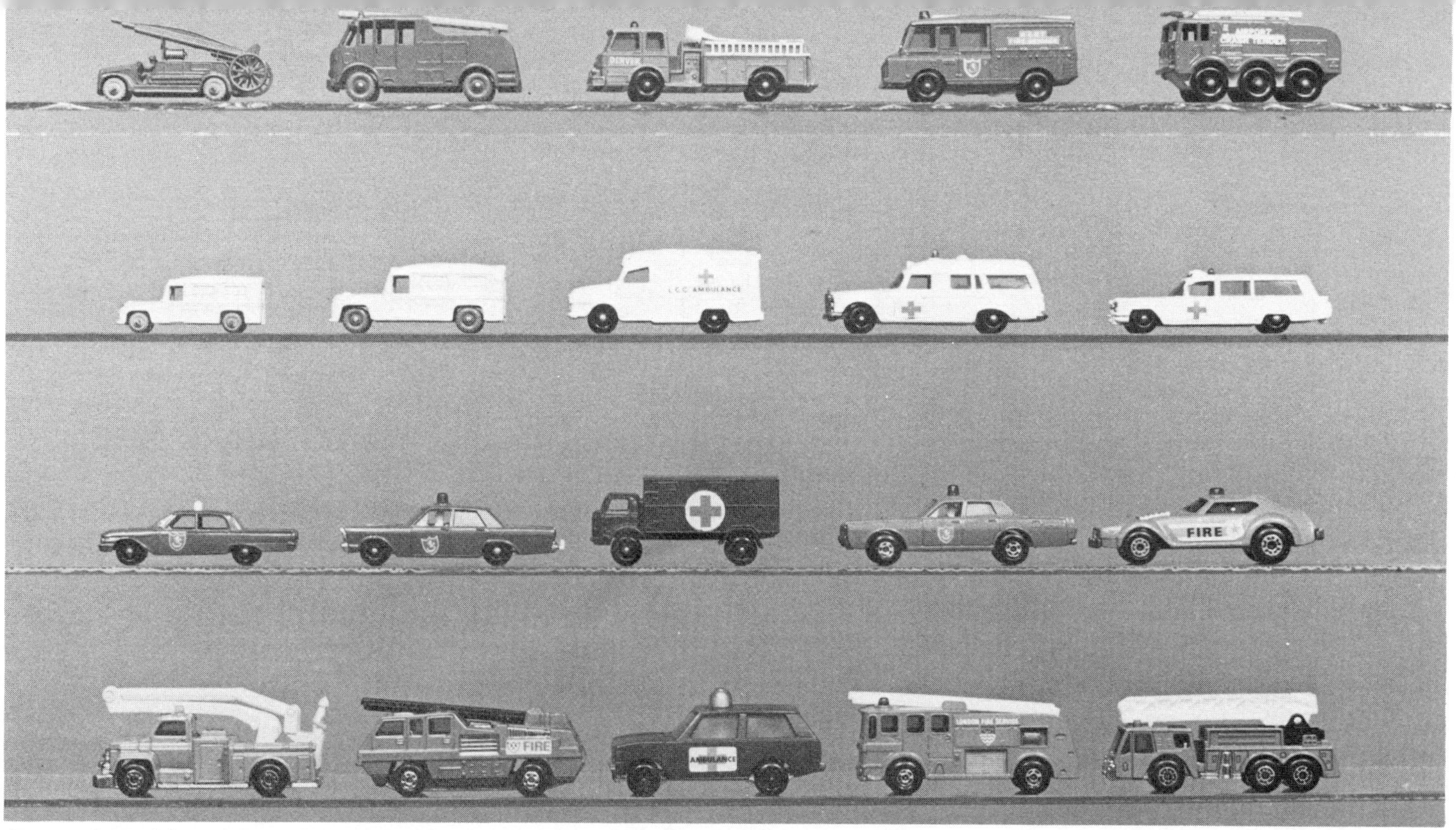

Row 1: Matchbox 9 **Dennis Fire Escape,** 9 **Merryweather Fire Engine,** 29 **Fire Pumper,** 57 **Land Rover Fire Truck,** 63 **Airport Crash Tender.**

Row 2: Matchbox 14-1 & 14-2 **Daimler Ambulances,** 14 **Lomas Ambulance,** 3 **Mercedes-Benz Ambulance,** 54 **Cadillac Ambulance.**

Row 3: Matchbox 59-1 & 59-2 **Ford Fairlane** and **Galaxie Fire Chiefs,** 63 **Military Ambulance,** 59 **Mercury Fire Chief,** 64 **Fire Chief.**

Row 4: Matchbox 13 **Snorkel Fire Engine,** 22 **Blaze Buster,** 20 **Range Rover Army Ambulance,** 35 **Merryweather Fire Truck,** 18 **Aerial Ladder Truck.**

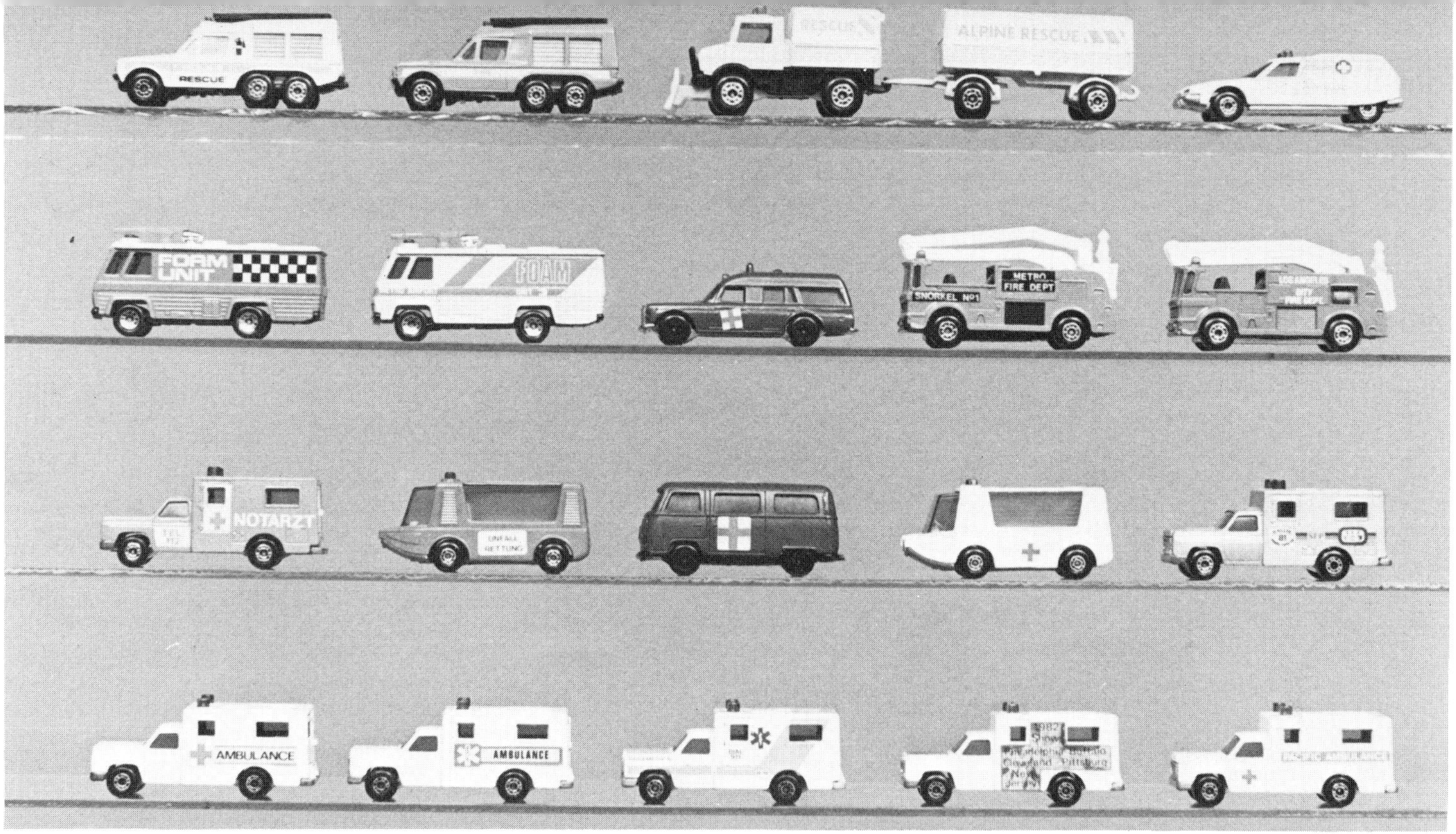

Row 1: Matchbox 57 **Carmichael Rescue** and **Fire Vehicles,** TP112 **Mercedes-Benz Unimog Rescue Truck** (48)) and **Trailer,** 12 **Citroen Ambulance.**
Row 2: Matchbox 64 Red & Yellow **Foam Monitors,** 3 **Mercedes-Benz Army Ambulance,** 63 **Snorkel Fire Truck** (two types).
Row 3: Matchbox 41 **Chevrolet Notarzt Ambulance,** 46 **Unfall Rettung Ambulance,** 23 **Volkswagen Army Ambulance,** 46 **Stretcha-Fetcha,** 41 **Paris-Dakar Ambulance.**
Row 4: Matchbox 41 **Chevrolet Ambulance:** three regular types & toy show promotional, 99 **Chevrolet Pacific Ambulance.**

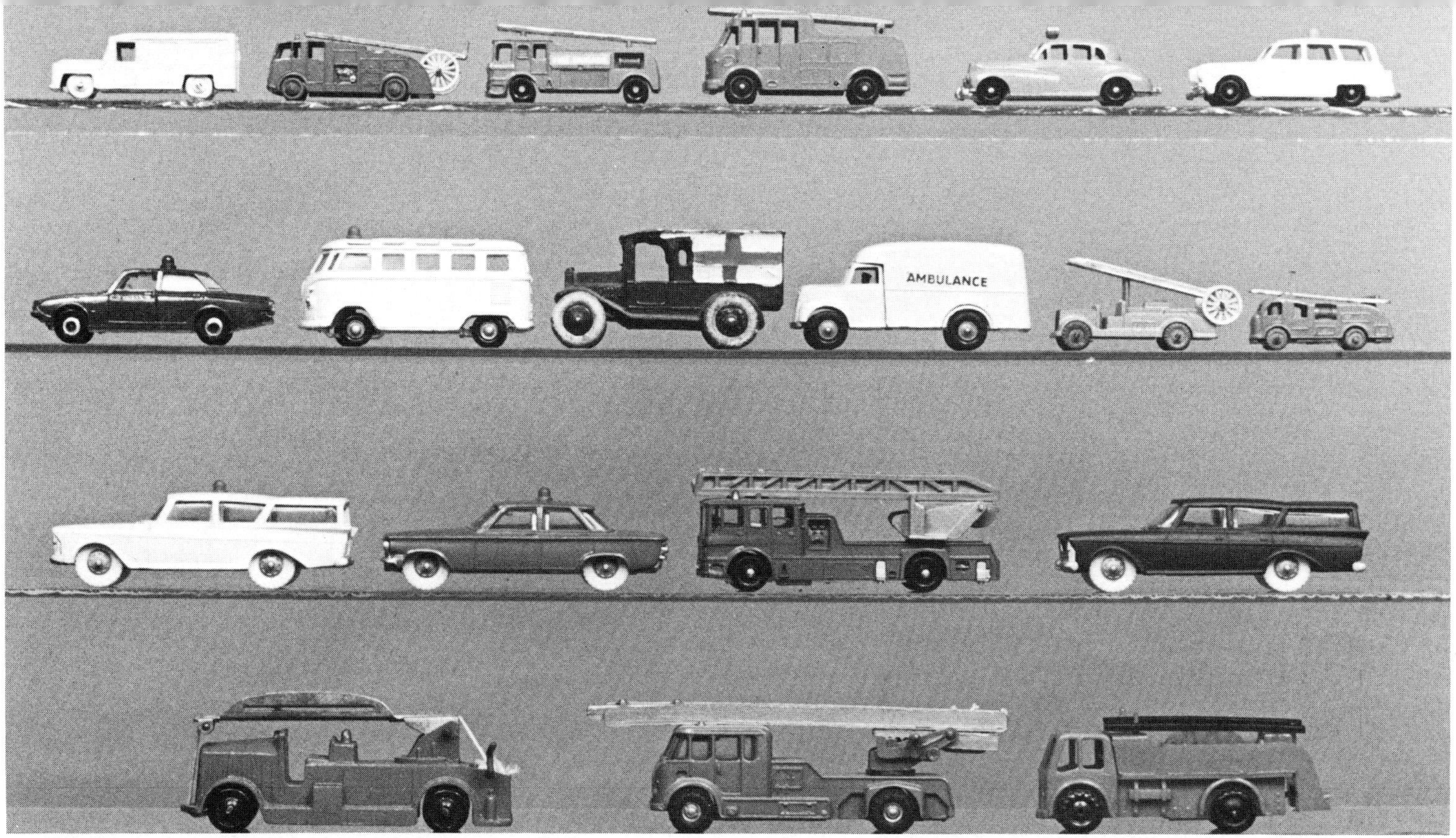

Row 1: Benbros 38 **Daimler Ambulance** & 9 **Fire Engine,** Lone Star 624 **Fire Engine,** Budgie 59 **Fire Engine,** 27 **Wolseley Fire Chief,** 20 **Austin Countryman Ambulance.**
Row 2: Lone Star 32 **Ford Corsair Fire Chief,** 20 **Volkswagen Ambulance, Britains Army Ambulance,** 617 **Ambulance,** Charbens OC26 **Fire Engine,** Unknown **Fire Engine.**
Row 3: Lone Star 1478 **Rambler Ambulance,** 1479 **Corvair Fire Chief,** 30 **Merryweather Ladder Truck,** 1481 **Rambler Military Ambulance.**
Row 4: Charbens-DCMT **Ladder Truck,** Budgie 254 **Merryweather Ladder Truck,** Tri-Ang plastic **Fire Truck.**

Row 1: Fun Ho **Ladder Truck.**
Row 2: Londontoys 56 **Fire Truck,** Fun Ho **Fire Chief's Roadster.**
Row 3: Lone Star Top Boy **Fire Truck,** Tri-Ang Minic plastic **Fire Engine.**

Row 1. Fun Ho 35 **Holden Ambulance & Fire Department Ambulance,** 21 **Fire Engine,** 40 **Fire Department Tanker,** 57 **Fire Department Pickup Truck,** 62 **Holden Army Ambulance.**
Row 2: Lincoln 4301 **Fire Truck,** Fun Ho 58 **Fire Department Jeep,** Londontoys 16 **Fire Truck,** Tink E **Steam Pumper,** Herka 708 **Fire Engine.**
Row 3: Micro GB13 **Morris Fire Engine,** GB20 **International Ambulance,** Spot-On 119 **Land Rover Fire Truck,** Fun-Ho **Fire Engine.**

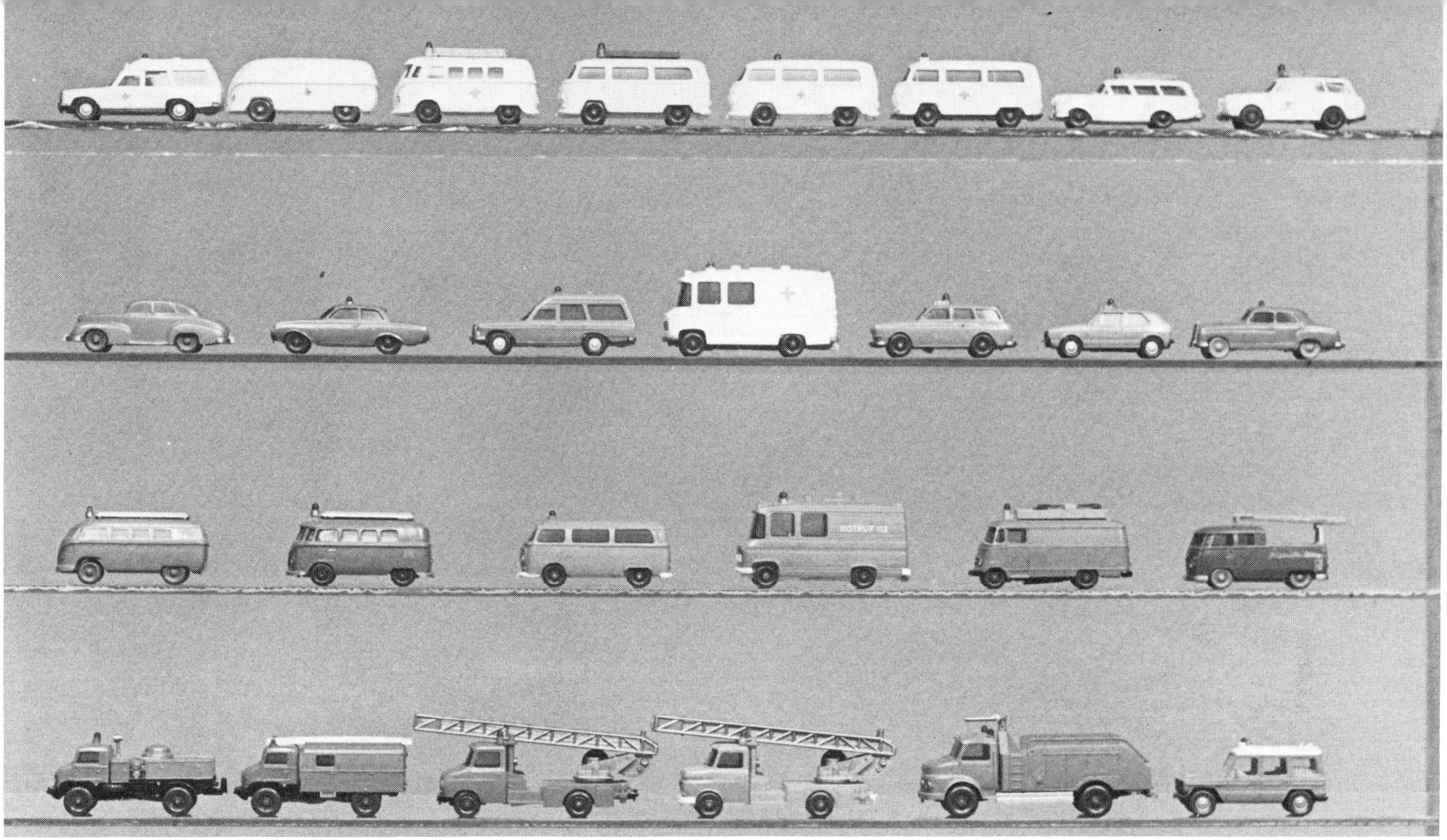

Row 1: Wiking 70 **Mercedes-Benz Ambulance,** 32 **Volkswagen 1952, 1967 and 1972 Ambulances,** 320 **Volkswagwen Ambulance** (two types), 7r **Opel Caravan & VW Variant Ambulances.**
Row 2: Wiking 60 **Opel & Ford Taunus Fire Chiefs,** 607 **Mercedes-Benz Fire Department Ambulance,** 278 **Mercedes-Benz Rescue Ambulance,** 600 **VW Variant Fire Chief,** 606 VW **Golf Fire Chief,** 60 **Mercedes-Benz 220 Fire Chief.**
Row 3: Wiking 60k **Volkswagen 1957 & 1961 Fire Vans,** 603 **Volkswagen Fire Van,** 60w & 608 **Mercedes-Benz Rescue Trucks,** 29m **Volkswagen Ladder Truck,** 609 **Mercedes-Benz Rescue Truck.**
Row 4: Wiking 60p **Mercedes-Benz Explosive Fire Truck,** 60a **Unimog Fire Truck,** 60b & 602 **Opel Ladder Trucks,** 60f **Mercedes-Benz Crash Tender,** 1344 **Mercedes-Benz 240G Fire Command Wagon.**

Row 1: Wiking 61 **Magirus & Mercedes-Benz Fire Trucks,** 610 **Magirus Fire Truck** (two types), 61n **Magirus Fire Truck.**
Row 2: Wiking 62 **Magirus Ladder Truck,** 618 **Mercedes-Benz Ladder Truck,** 622 **Unimog Fire Truck,** 620 **Magirus Ladder Truck** (two types).
Row 3: Wiking 62n **Magirus 1962 & 1968 Ladder Trucks,** 635 **Mercedes-Benz Red Cross Truck,** 621 **Mercedes-Benz Tank Fire Truck** (two types).
Row 4: Wiking 630 **Magirus Rescue Crane,** 62r **Mercedes-Benz Fire Truck with Crane,** 629 **Mercedes-Benz First Air Truck,** 623 **Mercedes-Fiedler Rescue Truck,** 608 **Mercedes-Benz Fire Department Ambulance.**

Row 1: Wiking 2600 **Fire Set,** Herpa 7507 **Ambulance Set.**
Row 2: Wiking N61 **Fire Engine,** 9033 **Ambulance Set,** 9034 **Fire Set,** N62 **Ladder Truck.**
Row 3: Siku small **Ambulance,** 71 **Mercedes-Benz Ambulance,** 56 **Mercedes-Benz Ladder Truck,** 14 **Volkswagen Ambulance Bus,** small **Fire Truck.**

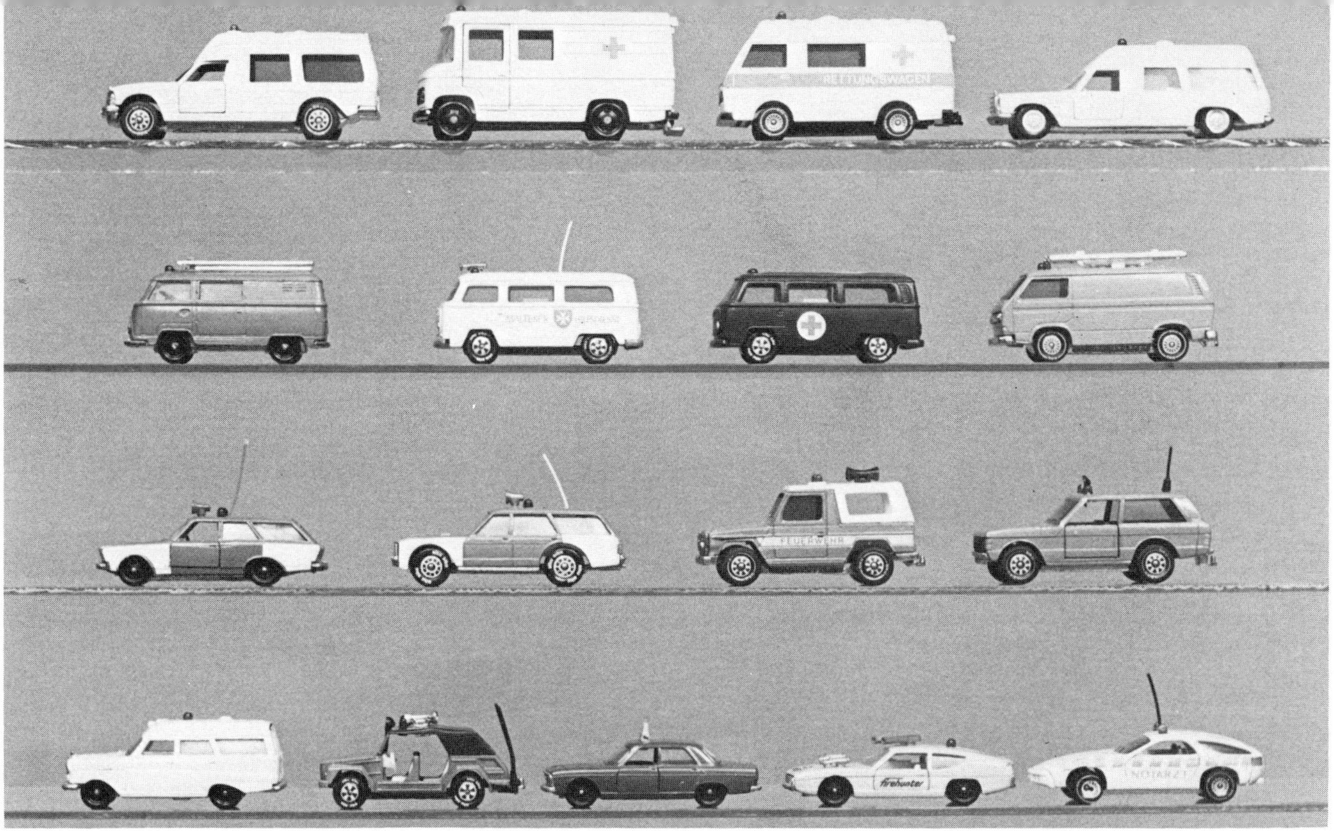

Row 1: Siku 1613 second type **Mercedes-Benz Ambulance,** 292/1911 **Mercedes-Benz Ambulance Van,** 1623 **Volkswagen Ambulance Van,** 306/1613 **Mercedes-Benz Ambulance.**
Row 2: Siku 237 **Ford Fire Van,** 356/1619 **Volkswagen Malteser Ambulance,** 1621 **Volkswagen Army Ambulance,** 1343 **Volkswagen Fire Department Van.**
Row 3: Siku 342 **Ford Taunus Fire Chief,** 1617 **Ford Granada Fire Chief,** 1344 **Mercedes-Benz Command Wagon,** 1338 **Fire Department Range Rover.**
Row 4: Siku 233 **Mercedes-Benz Ambulance,** 1335 **Fire Department Volkswagen 181,** 353/1313 **Audi Doctor's Car,** 344/1618 **Lamborghini Fire Hunter,** 1339 **Porsche Doctor's Car.**

Row 1: Gama 2604 **Magirus-Deutz Ladder Truck,** 1605 **Mercedes-Benz Ladder Truck.**
Row 2: Gama 1604 **Mercedes-Benz Rescue Crane,** 1602 **Volkswagen Rescue Truck.**
Row 3: Gama 958 **Volkswagen Ladder Truck,** 1203 **Volkswagen Ambulance.**

Row 1: Gama 1606 **Mercedes-Benz Searchlight Truck,** 2362 **Polyma Searchlight Trailer.**
Row 2: Gama 2601 **Porsche O.R.B.I.T. Fire Truck.**

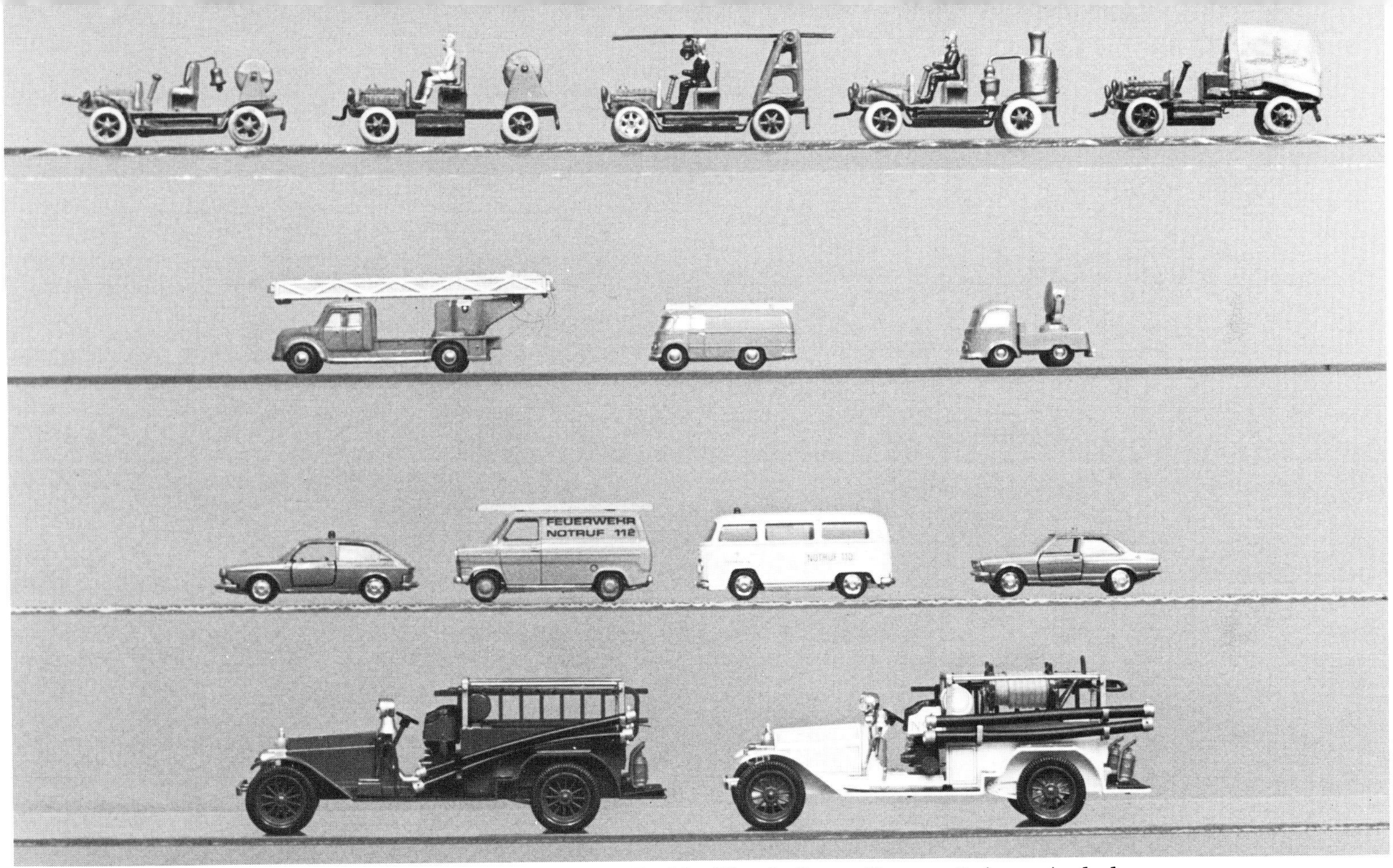

Row 1: **Ernst Plank Hose Truck** (two chassis types), **Ladder Truck, Steam Pumper & Army Ambulance.**
Row 2: Schuco Piccolo 745 **Magirus Ladder Truck,** 756 **Mercedes-Benz Fire Van,** 755 **Mercedes-Benz Searchlight Truck.**
Row 3: Schuco 824 **Volkswagen 411 Fire Chief,** 890 **Ford Fire Van,** 914 **Volkswagen Ambulance,** 876 **Audi Fire Chief.**
Row 4: Conrad 1019 (red) & 1024 (white) **American LaFrance Fire Truck.**

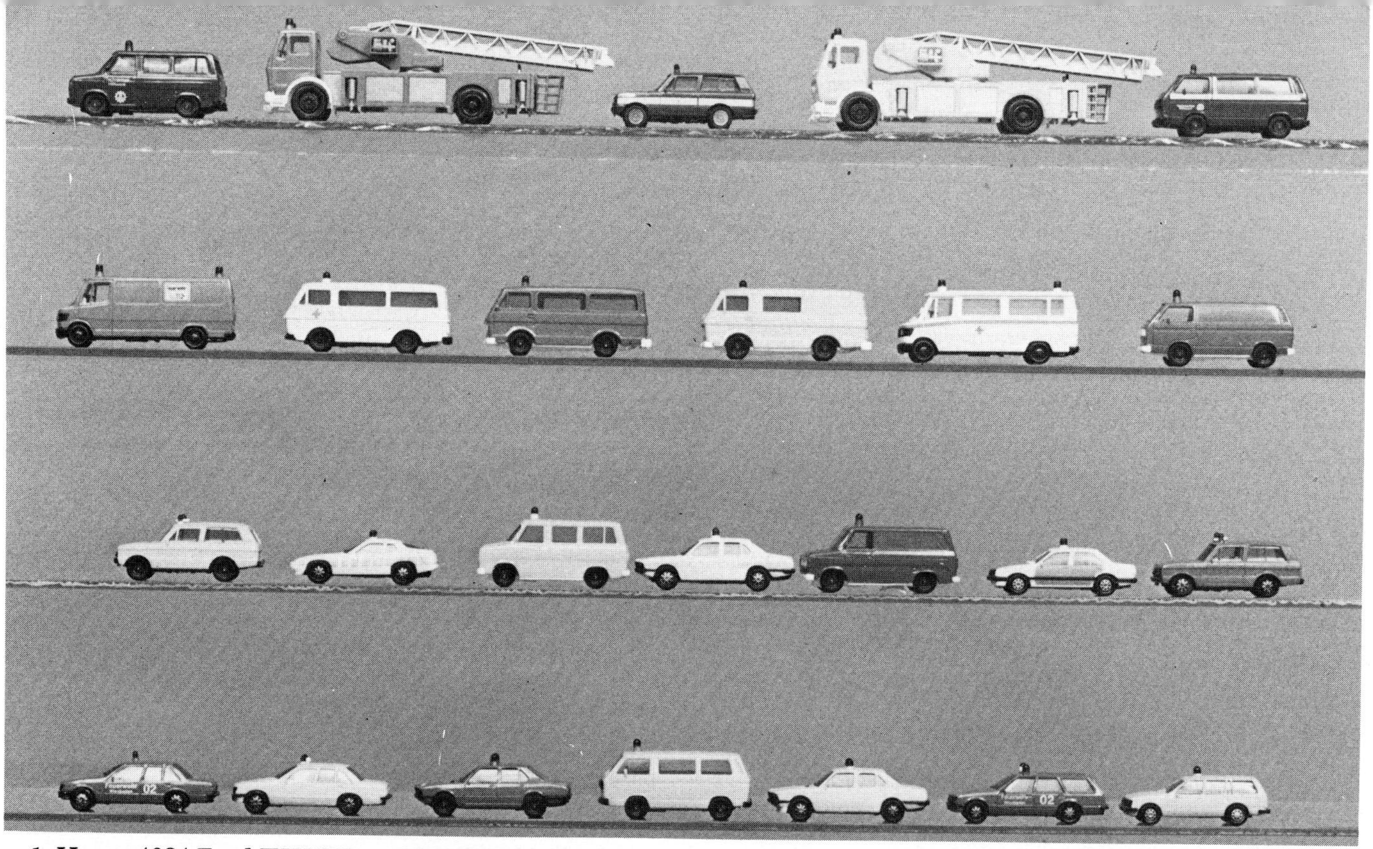

Row 1: Herpa 4024 **Ford THW Van,** 806502 **Mercedes-Benz Ladder Truck** (red), 4067 **THW Land Rover,** 806505 **Mercedes-Benz Ladder Truck** (dayglo), 4035 **Volkswagen THW Van.**
Row 2: Herpa 4073 **Mercedes-Benz Fire Van,** 4013 **Volkswagen Ambulance,** 4014 **Volkswagen Fire Department Bus,** 4016 **Volkswagen Fire Van,** 4072 **Mercedes-Benz Ambulance,** 4032 **Volkswagen Fire Van.**
Row 3: Herpa 4063 **Range Rover Fire Chief,** 4060 **Porsche Doctor's Car,** 4026 **Ford Fire Department Bus,** 4061 **BMW Doctor's Car,** 4022 **Ford Fire Van,** 4055 **Opel Ascona Fire Chief,** 4052 **Range Rover Fire Chief.**
Row 4: Herpa 4053 **Opel Rekord Fire Chief** (red), 4054 **Opel Rekord Fire Chief** (dayglo), 4051 **BMW Fire Chief,** 4034 **Volkswagen Fire Department Bus,** 4062 **BMW Fire Chief,** 4064 **Opel Rekord Fire Wagon,** 4066 **Opel Kadett Fire Wagon.**

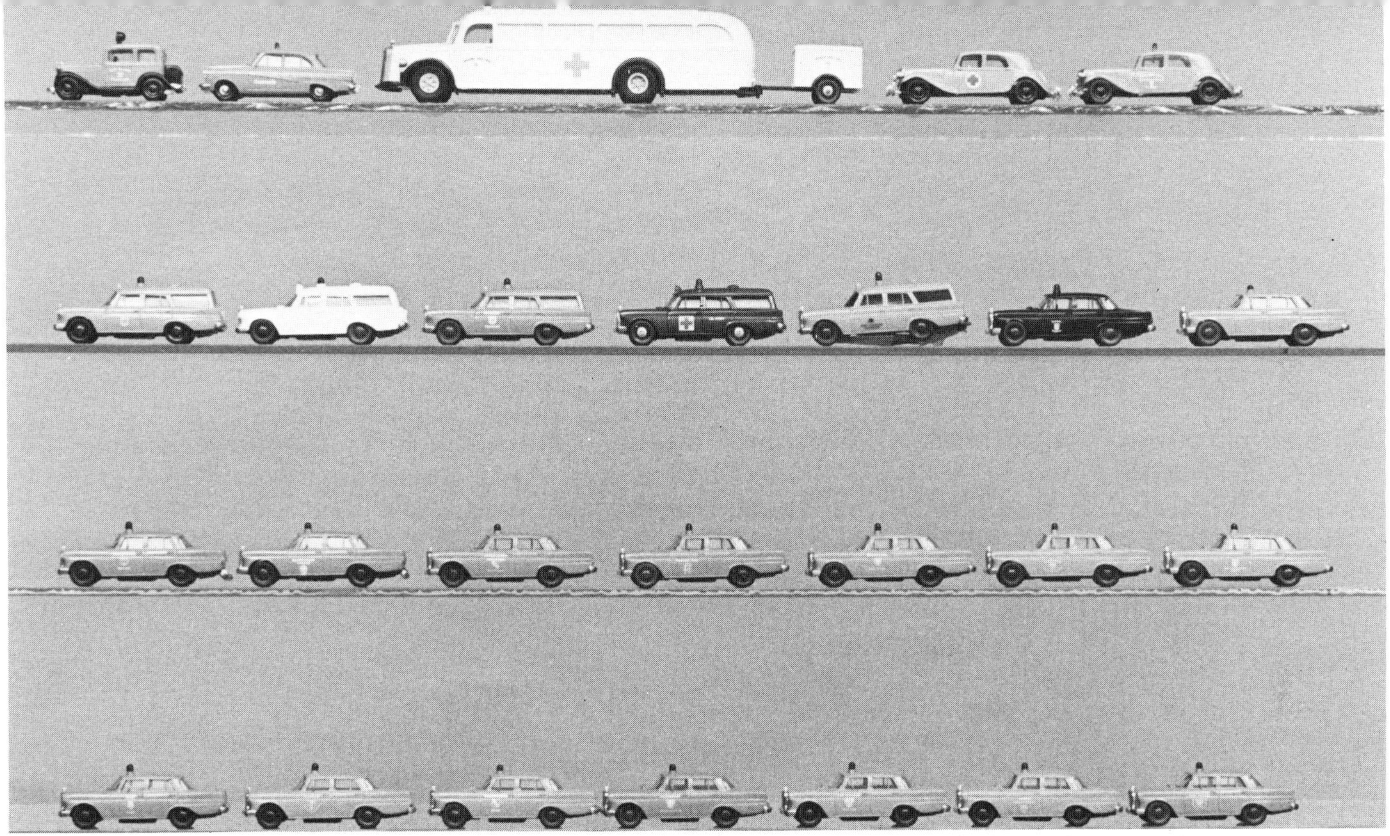

Row 1: Brekina 3031 **Opel P4 Fire Chief,** 1912 **Ford Taunus Fire Chief,** 5002 **Red Cross Bus & Trailer,** 1421 **Citroen Red Cross Car,** 1430 **Citroen Fire Chief.**
Row 2: Brekina 1873, 1870, 1871 & 1874 **Mercedes-Benz Ambulances,** 2071 electrified **Mercedes-Benz Ambulance,** 1820 **Mercedes-Benz Wuppertal** and 1821 no name **Fire Chiefs.**
Row 3: Brekina 1821 **Mercedes-Benz Büdingen, Darmstadt, Erbach, Fulda, Gelnhausen, Giessen & Hamburg Fire Chiefs.**
Row 4: Brekina 1821 **Mercedes-Benz Hanau, Kaiserslautern, Mainz, Offenbach, Reutlingen, Rodermark & Wetzlar Fire Chiefs.**

Row 1: Praline 04-15 **Mercedes-Benz Hamburg Fire Chief, 09-05 DKW Hamburg Fire Van,** 04-15 **Mercedes-Benz Frankfurt Fire Chief** (white & gray bases), 09-05 **DKW Stuttgart Fire Van,** 04-15 **Mercedes-Benz Stuttgart Fire Chief.**
Row 2: Praline 03-04 **Citroen German Red Cross Van** (white), 03-32 **Citroen French Ambulance,** 03-05 **Citroen Fire Van,** 03-07 **Citroen German Red Cross Bus,** 03-04 **Citroen German Red Cross Van** (cream).
Row 3: Roskopf 214 **Unimog Fire Truck,** 212 & 213 THW **Unimog & Trailer,** Praline 07-25 **Mercedes-Benz Rescue Van,** 09-07 **DKW Ambulance,** Roskopf 205 **Fire Department Volkswagen Iltis.**
Row 4: Roskopf 209 **MAN Covered THW Truck,** 424 & 435 **Saurer Fire Trucks,** 82 **MAN Army Ambulance Truck.**

Row 1: Preiser 1114 **Alco Fire Pump Trailer** (two types), 1100 **Faun-Krupp Rescue Crane,** 1148 **Polyma Searchlight Trailer** (two types), 2626 **Metz Airport Foam Truck,** 1112 **Ziegler Fire Pump Trailer.**
Row 2: Preiser 2631 (rèadymade) & 2632 (kit) **Metz-Faun Crash Tender,** 2628 **Faun Crash Tender.**
Row 3: Unknown **Total Crash Tender,** Preiser 1129 (readymade) & two versions of 1128 (kit) **Mercedes-Benz Fire Truck.**
Row 4: Preiser 1116 **Mercedes-Benz Fire Truck** with four bodies, 1144 **Mercedes-Ziegler Hose Truck.**

Row 1: Orobr **Fire Truck, CKO Ladder Truck,** Orobr **Steam Pumper.**
Row 2: Unknown **Ladder Truck,** Germany and U. S. Zone **Steam Pumpers,** unknown **Steam Pumper.**
Row 3: unknown **Ladder Truck,** Fischer? **Fire Truck,** unknown **Steam Pumper & Hose Truck.**

Row 1: Vilmer 657 **Volvo Ladder Truck,** 725a **Ford Falck Crane,** 857 **Mercedes-Benz Ladder Truck.**
Row 2: Vilmer 653 **Volvo Red Cross Truck,** 2722 **Volvo Falck Truck with Crane,** 853 **Mercedes-Benz Red Cross Truck.**
Row 3: Lego 655 **Mercedes-Benz Ladder Truck,** Tomte 4 **Fire Engine,** Vilmer **Dodge Searchlight Truck,** Lego 655 **Bedford Ladder Truck.**

Row 1: Best Box 503 **DAF Fire Engine,** Efsi 107 **Ford T Ambulance,** 110 **Ford T Fire Truck,** 111 **Ford T Army Ambulance,** 409 **Citroen ID19 Ambulance.**
Row 2: Efsi 206 **Citroen Red Cross Van,** 301 **Commer Army Ambulance,** 302a **Commer Ambulance,** 302c **Commer Fire Truck,** 206 **Citroen Ambulance Bus.**
Row 3: Efsi 308 & 931 **Mercedes-Benz Ladder Trucks,** 308 **Mercedes-Benz Army Ladder Truck,** 930 **Mercedes-Benz Fire Tanker,** 308 **Mercedes-Benz Ladder Truck** (Pompiers).
Row 4: Efsi 411 **Ford Ambulance Van,** 304a & 306a **Mercedes-Benz Army Red Cross Truck & Trailer,** 920 **Land Rover Blood Transfusion Unit,** 154 **Land Rover Ambulance.**

Row 1: Solido 368 **Citroen Fire Department Van, D-Day Dodge Army Ambulance,** 2001 **Saviem Fire Engine.**
Row 2: Solido 42 **Renault 4 Fire Van,** 1318 **Renault 18 Fire Chief,** 1306 **Peugeot First Aid Car,** 1325 **Renault 4 Fire Van.**
Row 3: Solido 391 **Dodge Fire Truck & Open Trailer,** 3004 **Dodge Fire Truck & Fire Pump Trailer.**

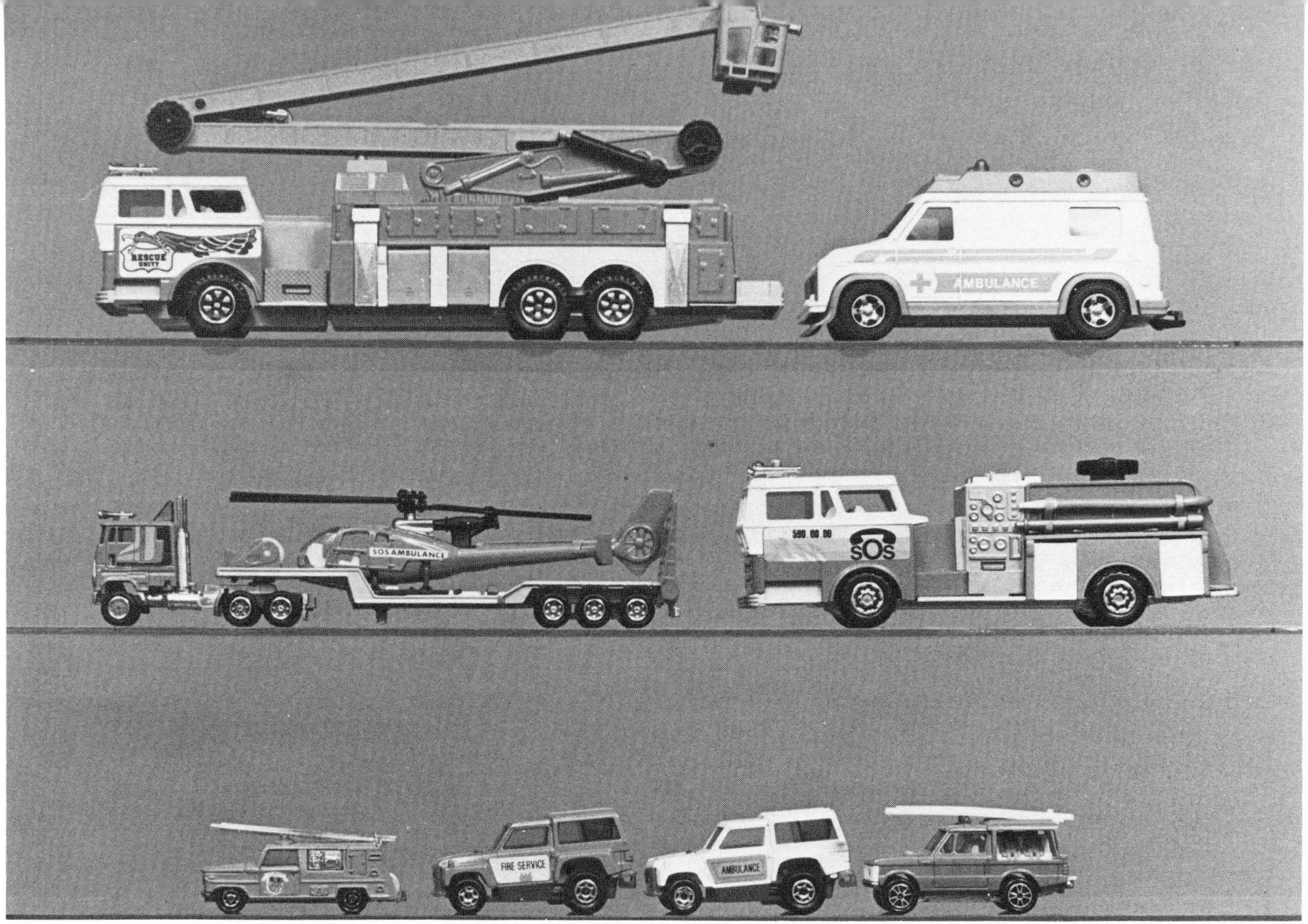

Row 1: Majorette 3091 **Rescue Unit,** 3021 **Ford Ambulance.**
Row 2: Majorette 601 **Low Loader & SOS Helicopter,** 3033 **Fire Truck.**
Row 3: Majorette 204 **Dodge Fire Truck,** #? **Range Rover Fire Car & Ambulance,** 246 **Range Rover Fire Truck.**

Row 1: Majorette 362 **Dodge Fire Truck & Trailer,** 4 **Bernard Ladder Truck,** 376 **Range Rover Fire Truck & Trailer.**
Row 2: Majorette 206 **Peugeot Ambulance,** 229 **Datsun Doctor's Car,** 264 **Alpine Doctor's Car,** 269 **Cherokee Ambulance,** 206 **Citroen Ambulance** (two types).
Row 3: Majorette 7 **Fire Jeep,** 204 **Bernard Ladder Truck,** 244 **Volkswagen Fire Department Bus,** 224 **Unimog Fire Truck,** 258 **Mercedes-Benz Fire Truck,** 230 **Renault Fire Van.**
Row 4: Majorette 244 **Volkswagen Ambulance,** 204 **Dodge Army Fire Truck,** 241 & 243 **Mercedes-Benz Army Red Cross Truck & Trailer,** 244 **Volkswagen Army & Red Cross Ambulances.**

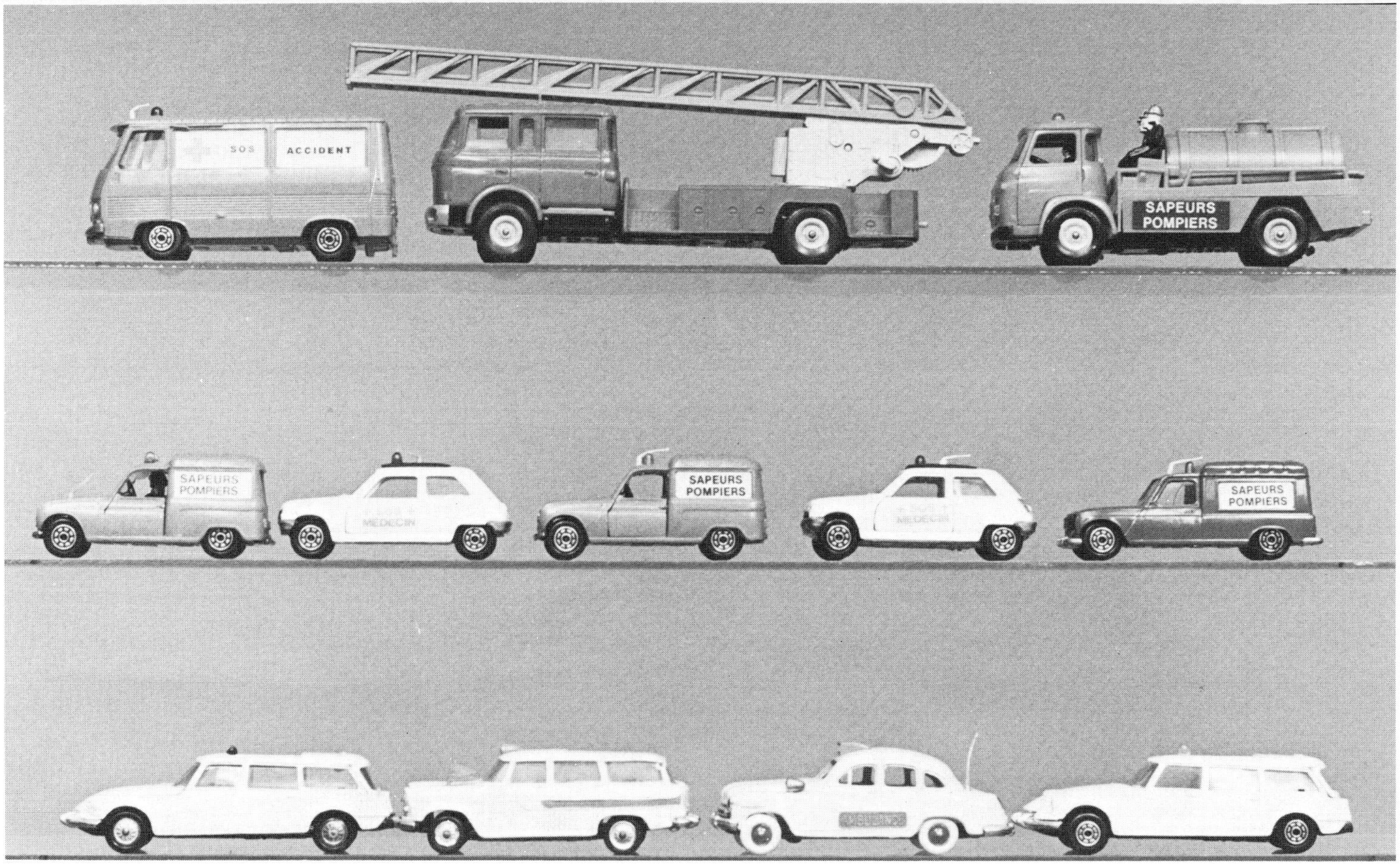

Row 1: Norev 252 **Peugeot Fire Department Ambulance,** 97 **Berliet Ladder Truck,** 220 **Saviem Fire Tanker.**
Row 2: Norev 241 **Renault 4 Fire Van,** 240 **Renault 5 Doctor's Car,** 341 **Renault 4 Fire Van,** 875 **Renault 5 Doctor's Car,** 865 **Renault 4 Fire Van.**
Row 3: Norev 40 **Citroen ID19 Ambulance,** 41 **Simca Marly Ambulance,** 14 **Ford Vedette Ambulance,** 344 **Citroen ID19 Ambulance.**

Row 1: Norev 410 **Mercedes-Benz Ambulance,** 434 **Volvo Fire Truck,** 442 **Volvo Ladder Truck,** 409 **Renault Fire Van,** 977 **Mercedes-Benz Ambulance.**
Row 2: Norev 211 **Citroen Tour de France Ambulance & Cyclists,** 210 **Peugeot Ambulance & Lifeboat Trailer.**
Row 3: Norev 461 **Fire Department Pickup Truck,** 874 **Mercdes-Benz Ambulance,** 344 **Citroen ID19 Ambulance.**

Row 1: Quiralu **Hose Reel,** Cofradis 380 **Sides Crash Truck.**
Row 2: Cofradis 01 **Citroen Fire Chief,** 03 **Citroen Ambulance,** Quiralu **Simca Marly Ambulance,** Cofradis 04 **Peugeot Fire Chief.**
Row 3: Quiralu **Peugeot D4A Army Ambulance,** Cofradis 534 **Magirus Ladder Truck,** Cofalu **Tour de France Ambulance.**

Row 1: AR **Peugeot Ambulance, Renault Army Ambulance, Peugeot Fire Truck,** KP **Ambulance,** Rhodanienne **Army Ambulance.**
Row 2: Cle **Citroen 1923 Ambulance,** 18 **Citroen Fire Van & Ambulance,** 24 **Peugeot 404 Red Cross Car,** CD **Ambulance.**
Row 3: J. P. Cars **Citroen Fire Department Ambulance, Renault Fire Engine & Fire Tanker,** Safir **Dodge Ladder Truck** (plastic).

Row 1: Safir **Renault Estafette Ambulance,** 11 **Citroen Fire Truck, Mercedes-Benz Ladder Truck & Tank Trailer,** and **Rover Army Ambulance.**
Row 2: Safir **Dodge Ambulance & Ladder Truck,** F.J. 407 **Dodge Ladder Truck & 409 Ambulance.**
Row 3: F.J. 301 **GMC Ambulance** & 507 **Fire Jeep,** Safir **Fire Jeep & Red Cross Jeep.**

Row 1: R.L. **Fire Truck,** unknown **Ladder Truck,** Emo 713 **Citroen Ambulance.**
Row 2: Unknown **Ladder Truck,** Rico **Steam Pumper & Ladder Truck,** Rai **Ladder Truck.**
Row 3: Sesame **Renault Ambulance, Army Ambulance,** Safir **Dodge Army Ambulance,** Sesame **Renault Fire Van.**

Row 1: Roco 1319 **Unimog Fire Truck,** 1311 **Steyr 91 Fire Truck** (red), 1327 **GMC Rescue Crane,** 1312 **Steyr 91 Fire Truck** (dayglo), 1315 **Steyr 680 Fire Truck.**
Row 2: Roco 1300 **DKW Fire Jeep,** 1317 & 338 **Opel Blitz Fire Trucks,** 1321, 1303 & 1310 **Pinzgauer Fire Trucks.**
Row 3: Roco 1314 **Unimog Covered Fire Truck,** 326 **Unimog Army Fire Truck,** 1313 & 1309 **THW Unimog & Trailer,** 344 & 1304 **Unimog Fire Trucks.**
Row 4: Roco 1301 **DKW THW Jeep,** 1302, 1324 & 1308 **THW Trucks,** 1323 **Volkswagen Iltis THW** & 1320 **THW Field Kitchen Trailer.**

Row 1: Ernst Plank **Hose Truck** (restored), Mattel 4225 **Firefighters Play Set,** Eko 2019 **Magirus Ladder Truck.**
Row 2: Roco 356 **Unimog Ambulance,** 323 & 1305 **Pinzgauer Ambulances,** 1306 **Unimog Ambulance,** 1318 **Steyr Red Cross Truck & Field Kitchen Trailer.**
Row 3: Roco 215 **Armored Ambulance,** 322 **Pinzgauer Army Ambulance,** 241 **Unimog Army Ambulance,** 223 **Dodge Army Ambulance** (two types).
Row 4: Roco 341 **Dodge Army Ambulance,** 274 **Opel Army Truck,** 260 **MAN Army Truck,** 325 **Unimog Army Ambulance,** 280 **M3 Army Halftrack.**

Row 1: Metalcar **Mercedes-Benz Ladder Truck,** Igra **Barkas Ambulance,** Bison 3 **Ladder Truck,** Metalcar **Mercedes-Benz Ambulance.**
Row 2: Novoexport A2 *Moskvitch Red Cross Car,* Tuzolto **Ladder Truck,** Metalcar **VW Golf Fire Department** & **Red Cross Ambulances.**
Row 3: Igra **Mercedes-Benz Ambulance,** Igra **Ladder Truck,** Novoexport A18 **RAF Ambulance Bus** & A24 **Volga Ambulance.**

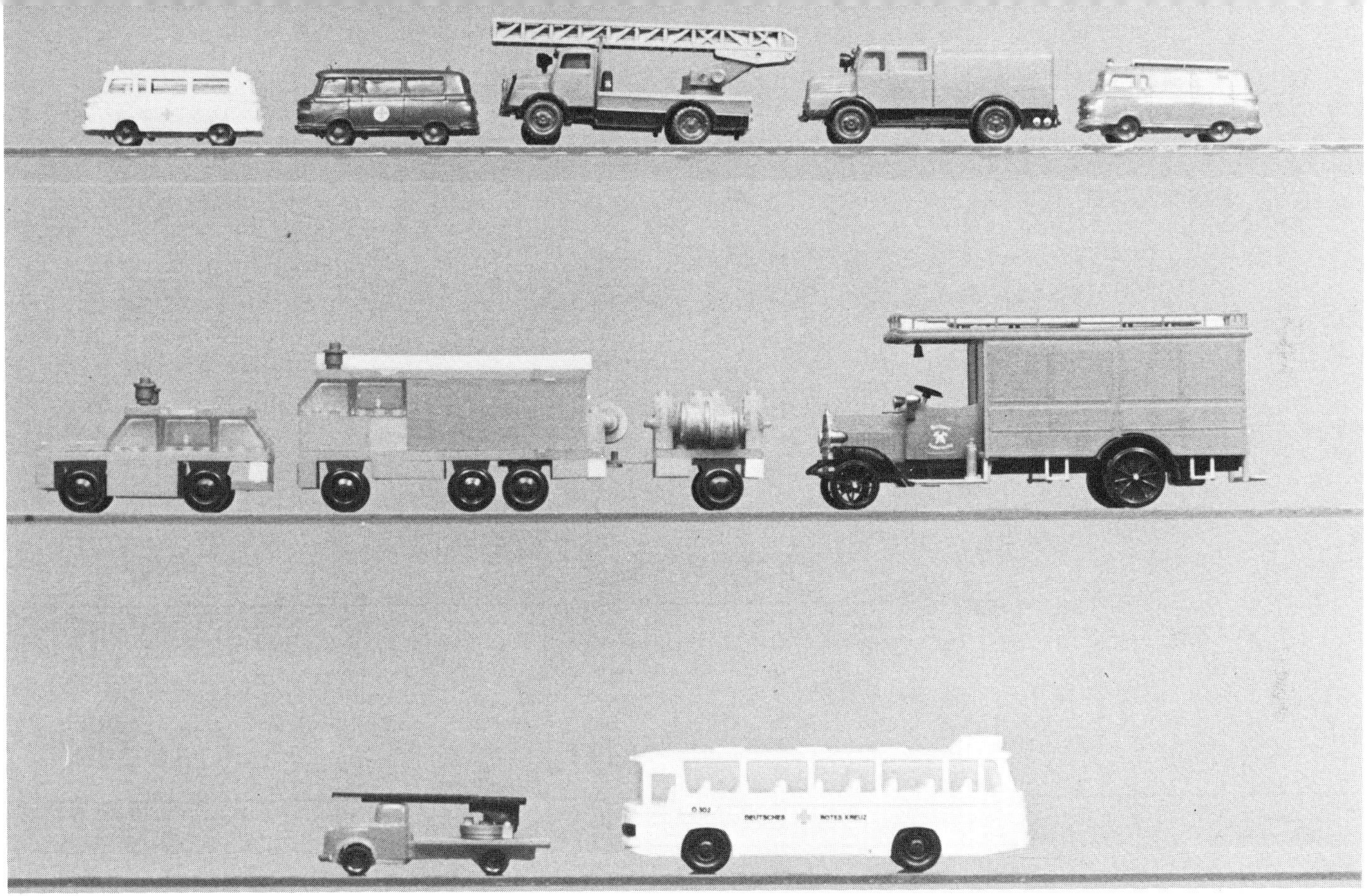

Row 1: Espewe 1013-4 **Barkas Civilian & Army Ambulances,** 1014-3 S-4000 **Ladder Truck,** 1014-2 **TLF Fire Engine,** 1013-5 **Barkas Fire Van.**
Row 2: Pebe 77 **Fire Truck Set,** VEB 143 **Daimler Fire Truck.**
Row 3: A.B. 41 **Ladder Truck** & 51 **Red Cross Bus.**

Row 1: Old Cars 305 **Fiat Campagnola Fire Tender,** 28a **Fiat LWB Army Ambulance,** 43 **Fiat LWB Fire Van.**
Row 2: Old Cars 27f **Fiat Fire Department Bus,** 24v **Fiat VVF Milano Fire Bus,** 42 **Fiat Fire Department Ambulance.**
Row 3: Old Cars 309v **Fiat Campagnola** with Fire Searchlight, 24a **Fiat Fire Department Bus,** 205v **Fiat Fire Tanker.**

Row 1: Burago 1509 **Fiat Ladder Truck** & 1511 **Fiat Fire Crane Truck,** Mercury 94c **Ciclope Ladder Truck.**
Row 2: Mebetoys 21 **Fiat Fire Chief,** 74 **Land Rover Fire Truck,** 42 **Land Rover Ambulance,** 81 **Fire Jeep.**
Row 3: Mercury 7 **Fiat Ambulance,** 4 **Fiat 131** & 9 **Fiat 128 Fire Chiefs,** Mebetoys 92 **Alfetta Fire Chief.**

Row 1: Antoine 2 **Fiat Fire Truck, PM Fire Truck & Ambulance.**
Row 2: Politoys AE14 **Alfa Romeo Giulia Ambulance** & AE16 **Fire Chief,** CE79 **Range Rover Fire Chief** & CE79b **Ambulance.**
Row 3: Politoys 117 **Lancia Fire Truck,** 300 **Romeo Ambulance Bus,** 8 **Army Ambulance.**

Row 1: Brumm 85 **Fiat 508c open Tobruk Fire Chief,** 80 **Fiat Fire Van,** 51r **Fiat Tobruk Fire Van,** 84 **Fiat 508c covered Tobruk Fire Chief.**
Row 2: Brumm 24 **Fiat 500** & 63 **Fiat 1100 Fire Chiefs,** Rampini 124 **Lancia Fire Van,** AM **Studebaker Fire Chief.**
Row 3: Sam Toys **Ladder Truck,** Ingap **Ladder Truck,** Sam Toys **Army Ambulance.**

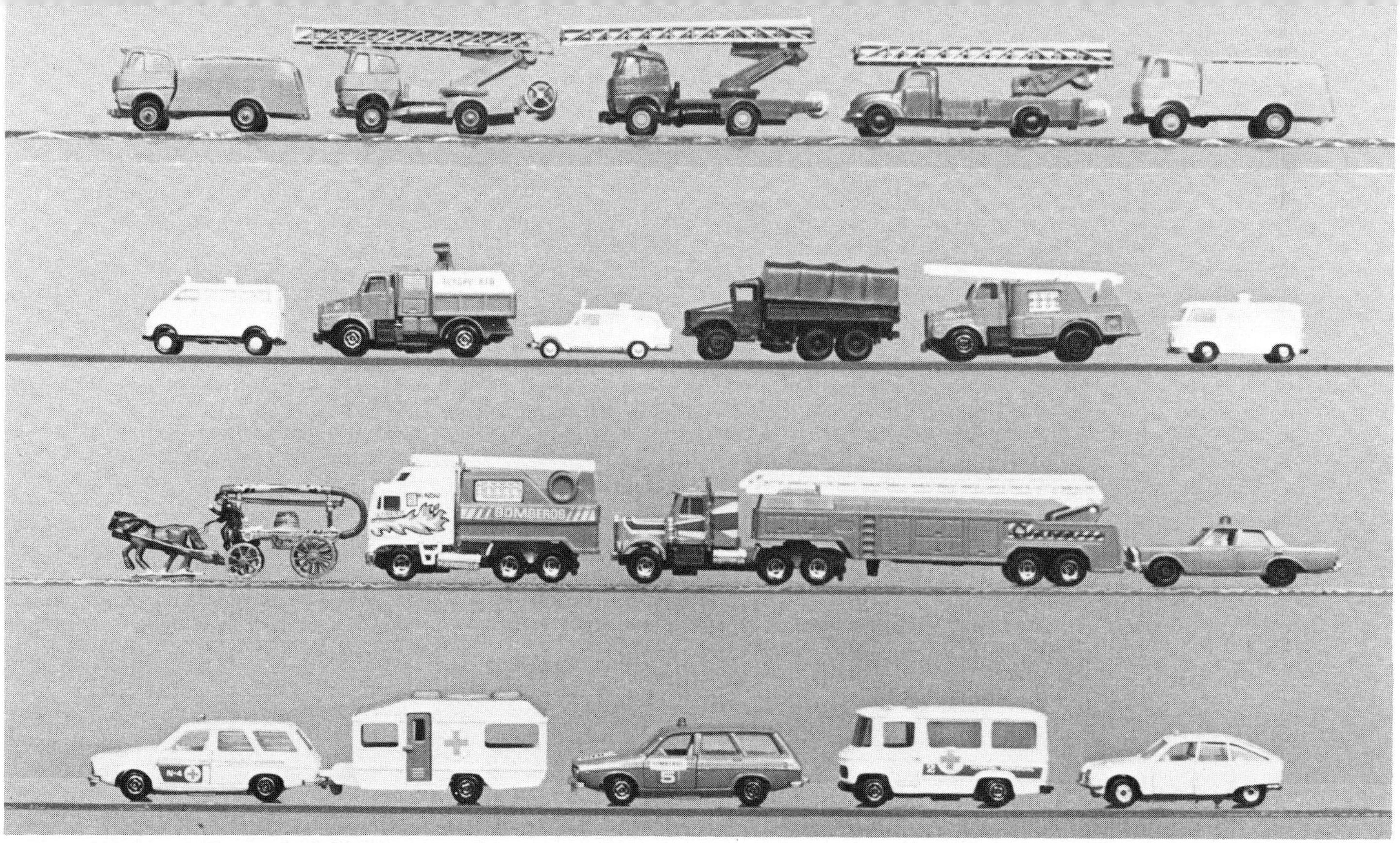

Row 1: Anguplas 74 **Pegaso Fire Engine** & 72 **Ladder Truck,** Eko 2097 **Pegaso Ladder Truck,** 2019 **Magirus Ladder Truck,** 2093 **Pegaso Fire Engine.**
Row 2: Anguplas 29 **DKW Ambulance Van,** Guisval 45 **Airport Fire Truck,** Eko 2041 **Fiat 1800 Ambulance,** 4028 **GMC Army Ambulance,** Guisval 34 **Volvo Fire Truck,** Eko 2029 **Ford Ambulance Van.**
Row 3: Aylmer 755 **Horsedrawn Fire Engine,** Guisval 72 **Fire Truck,** 663 **Ladder Truck,** Paya 2107 **Ford Fire Chief.**
Row 4: Guisval 12-2 **Renault Ambulance,** 44 **Red Cross Trailer,** 27 **Renault Fire Chief,** 37 **Mercedes-Benz Ambulance,** 21-1 **Citroen Red Cross Car.**

Row 1: Guisval 5022 **Ladder Truck**, 5026 **Mercedes-Benz Ambulance**, 114 **Volvo Fire Truck.**
Row 2: Guisval 110-1 **Ford Capri Fire Chief**, #? **Citroen SM Red Cross Car**, 110-2 **Ford Capri Fire Chief.**
Row 3: Guisval 172 **Scammell Fire Truck**, 1312 **Citroen Ambulance**, 1311 **Citroen Fire Truck**, 579 **Fire Engine.**

Row 1: Pilen 814 **Seat Fire Chief,** 815 **Fire Department Range Rover,** 807 **Renault Fire Van,** 801 **Seat Ambulance.**
Row 2: Mira 4010 **Seat Red Cross Car,** 4023 **Chrysler** 150 **Fire Chief,** Pilen 551 **Volkswagen Scirocco Red Cross Car,** Mira 4005 **Volkswagen Scirocco Fire Chief.**
Row 3: Pilen 553 **Talbot 150 Fire Chief,** 297 **Mercedes-Benz Red Cross Car,** 294 **Renault 12 Fire Chief,** Mira 4014 **Citroen CX Red Cross Car.**

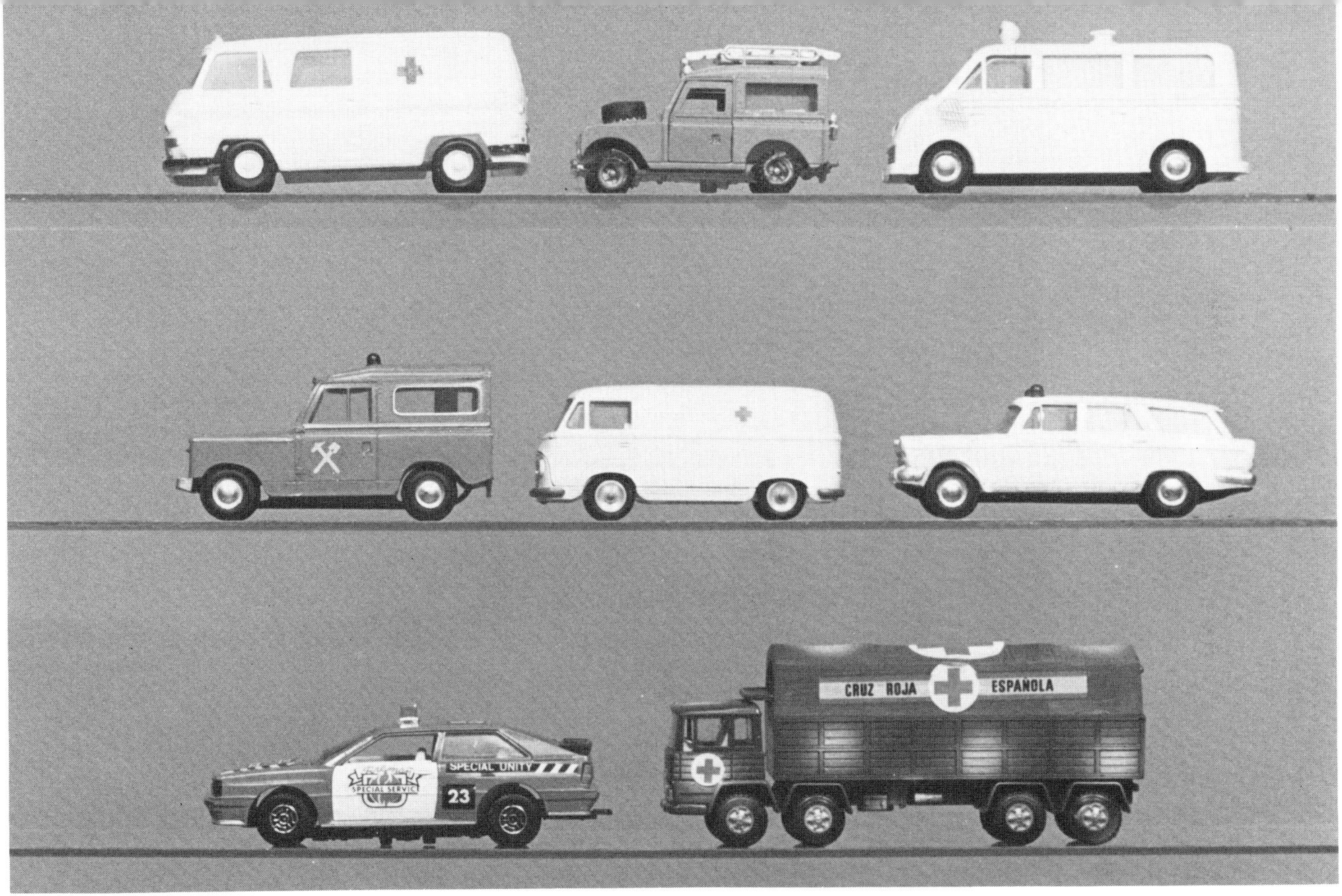

Row 1: Rico 423 **Auto Union Ambulance,** Nacoral 2028 **Fire Department Land Rover,** Rico 708 **DKW Ambulance.**
Row 2: Rico 733 **Fire Department Land Rover,** Dalia 415 **Ford Taunus Ambulance,** Rico 734 **Seat 1400c Ambulance.**
Row 3: Guisval 466 **Audi Fire Chief,** Mira 63 **Army Red Cross Truck.**

Row 1: Vitesse 161 **Mercedes-Benz Fire Chief,** Luso 13b **Citroen Ambulance** & 79 **Fire Rescue Set.**
Row 2: Metosul **Mercedes-Benz Fire Chief, Mercedes-Benz Fire Tanker & Citroen Fire Chief.**
Row 3: Pilen 296 **Citroen SM Red Cross Car,** 549 **Fire Department Range Rover,** 361 **Range Rover Ambulance,** 289b **Oldsmobile Toronado Fire Chief.**

Row 1: Buby 29 **Peugeot Fire Chief,** 118 **Opel Fire Department Ambulance,** Jet 7 **Oldsmobile Ambulance,** Roly 3a **Volkswagen Ambulance,** 2b **DKW Fire Chief,** Muky 24 **Plymouth Fire Chief.**
Row 2: Jet 17 **Chevrolet Fire Truck,** Rapitoy 6 **Ford Fire Department, Army & Red Cross Ambulances,** Muky 35 **Plymouth Fire Chief.**
Row 3: Cubas 205 **Fire Chief,** Jue 001-4 **First Aid Jeep,** Galgo 53 **Fiat Snorkel Truck,** Jue 001-3 **Fire Jeep,** Cubas 204 **Ambulance.**
Row 4: Buby 1051 **Peugeot Fire Chief,** Galgo **Renault Fire Chief and Ladder Truck,** Solido 9 **Opala Fire Chief.**

Row 1: Arpra 17f **Fire Department Bulldozer,** IVH **Ford Falcon Red Cross Car,** Fidart 120 **Dodge Fire Tanker.**
Row 2: Chico 0 **Volvo Ladder Truck,** RM **Torino Fire Chief,** Chico 20 **Mercedes-Benz Ladder Truck.**
Row 3: Motoplastic **Fire Engine,** Galgo **Volkswagen Ambulance,** McGregor 300 **Romeo Ambulance,** IVH **Ford Falcon Fire Chief.**

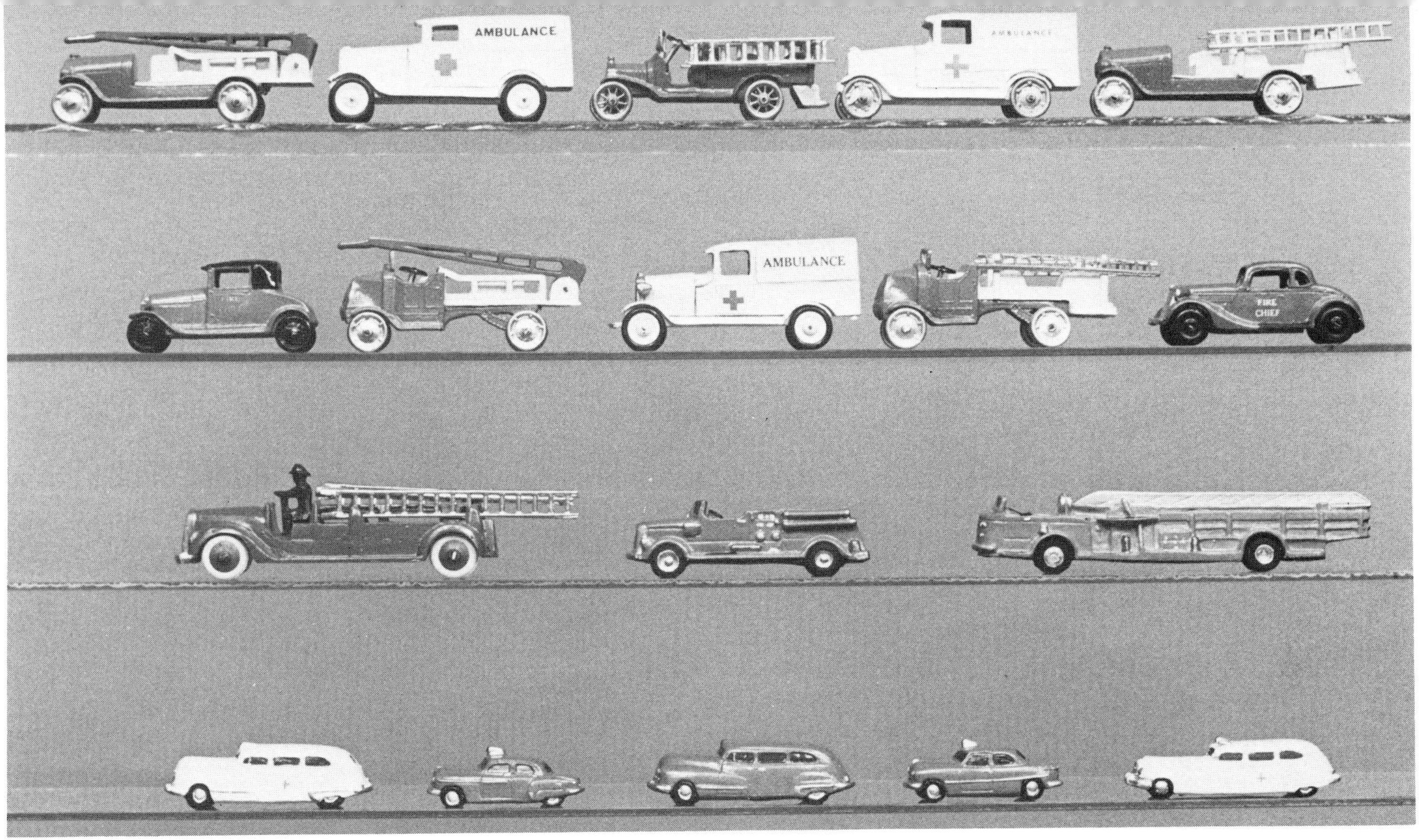

Row 1: Accucast 2023 **Water Tower,** 2034 **Cadillac Ambulance,** 2054 **Ford T Fire Truck,** 2013 **Buick Ambulance,** 204 **Ladder Truck.**
Row 2: Accucast 208f **Ford A Fire Chief,** 2062 **Mack Water Tower,** #? **Chevrolet Ambulance,** 2051 **Mack Ladder Truck,** 304f **Ford 1935 Fire Chief.**
Row 3: Accucast 301 **Mack Ladder Truck,** RCB **Fire Pumper & Ladder Truck.**
Row 4: RCB **Packard Ambulance, Chevrolet Fire Chief,** red **Buick Ambulance, Ford Fire Chief,** white **Buick Ambulance.**

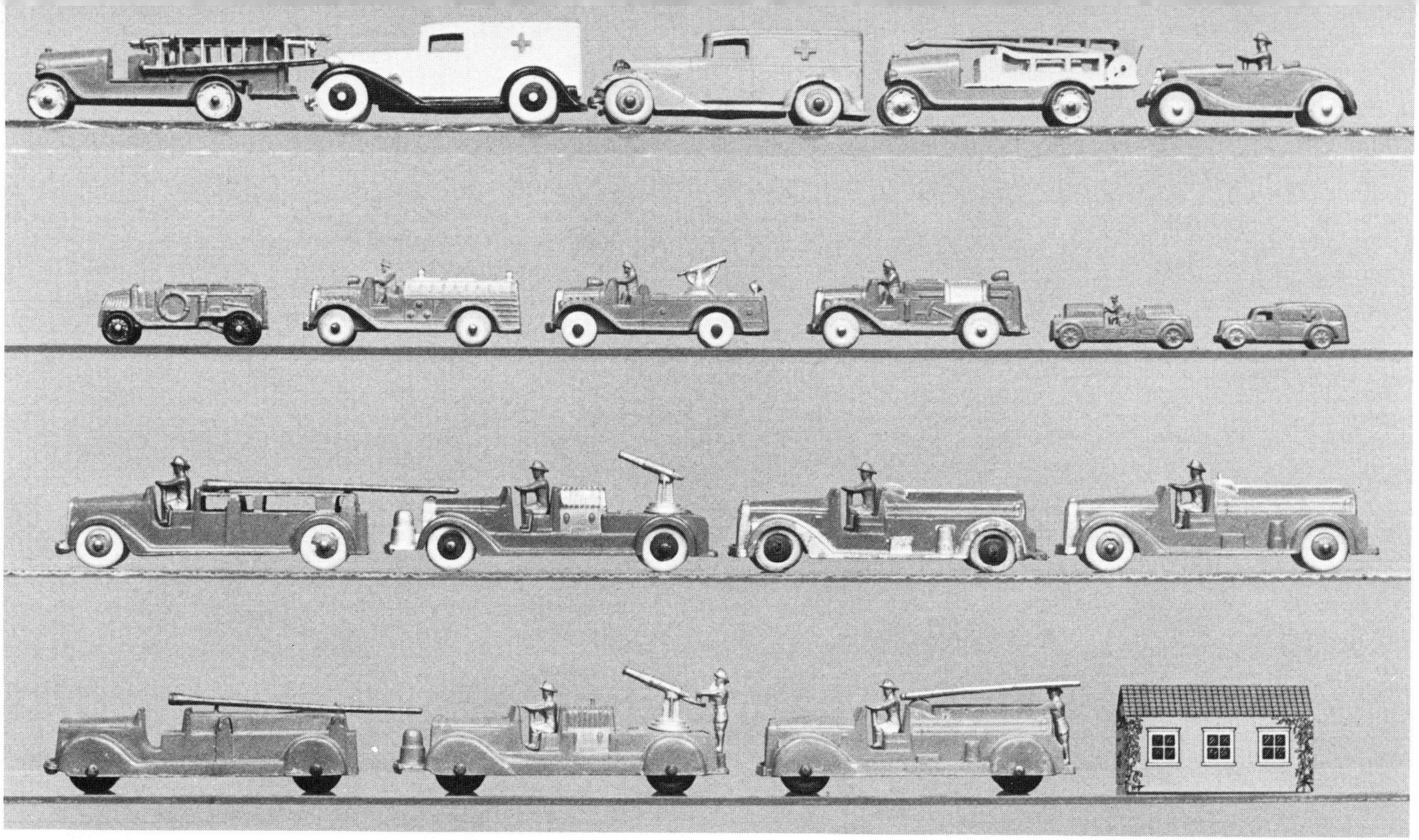

Row 1: Tootsietoy 4652 **Ladder Truck,** 809 **Graham Civilian & Army Ambulances,** 4653 **Water Tower,** 1935 **Ford Fire Chief's Roadster.**
Row 2: Tootsietoy 4658 **Mack Fire Truck,** 236 **Ladder Truck,** 237 **Hose Car,** 238 **Insurance Patrol, Midget Fire Engine & Ambulance.**
Row 3: Tootsietoy 1040 **Ladder Truck,** 1041 **Hose Car,** 1042 **Insurance Patrol** (two types).
Row 4: Tootsietoy postwar 1040 **Ladder Truck,** 1041 **Hose Car,** 1042 **Insurance Patrol, Tinplate Fire House** for 4658 Mack.

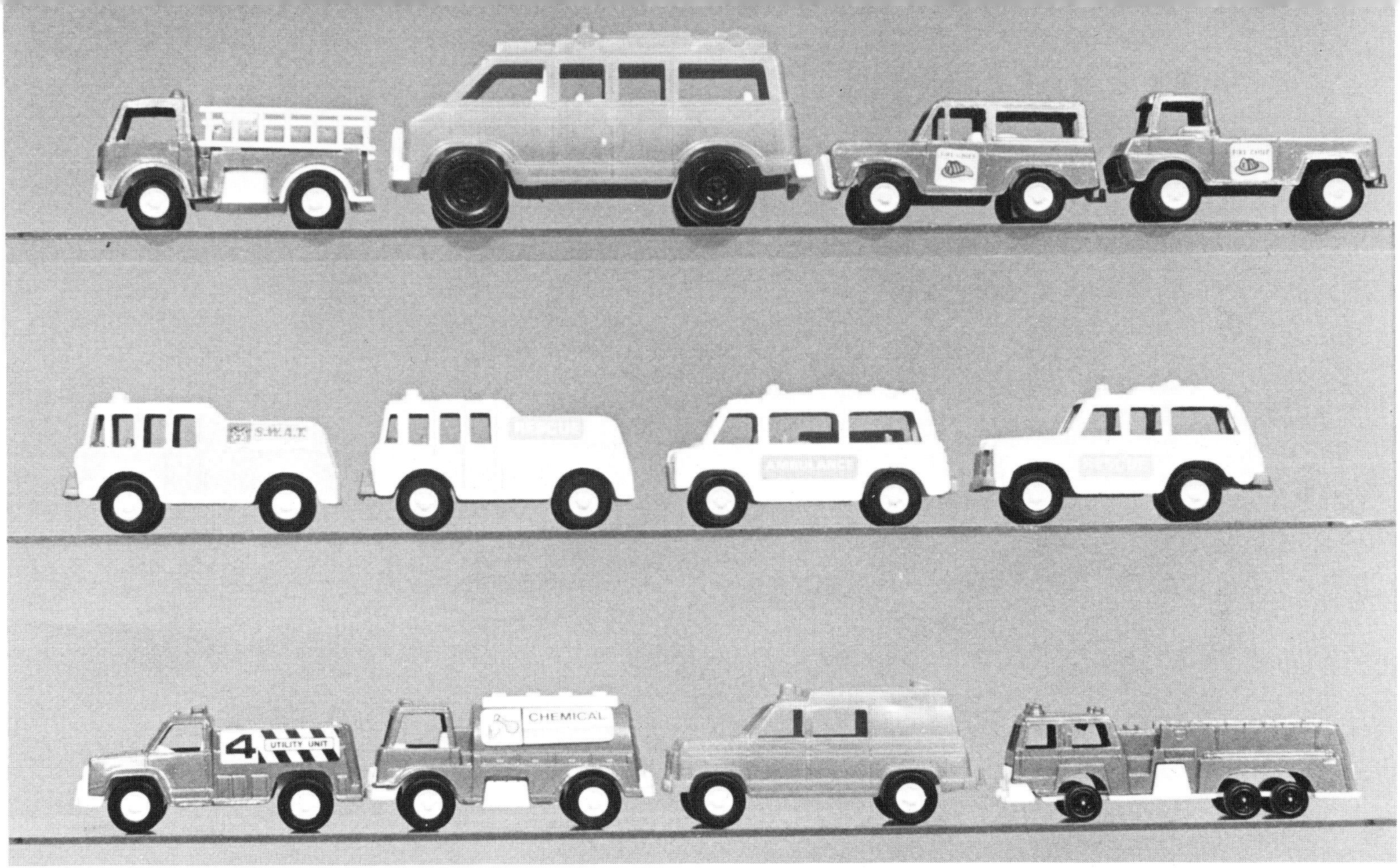

Row 1: Tootsietoy 1290 **Fire Pumper,** big plastic **Rescue Van, Fire Chief's Jeep, Fire Chief's Pickup.**
Row 2: Tootsietoy 1297 yellow and white **Emergency Rescue Trucks, Ambulance & Rescue Wagon.**
Row 3: Tootsietoy **Fire Utility Unit, Chemical Fire Truck,** small plastic **Rescue Van,** 2303 3-axle **Fire Truck.**

Row 1: Tootsietoy 2545 **Ladder Truck,** first & second types.
Row 2: Tootsietoy 2905 **Mack Ladder Truck,** 2330 **Mack Fire Engine.**
Row 3: Tootsietoy 2985 **Ladder Truck,** 2905 **International Ladder Truck.**

Row 1: Hubley Real Toys **Chevrolet Ambulance,** 306 & 307 **American LaFrance Pumper & Ladder Truck, Real Toys Chevrolet Fire Chief.**
Row 2: Hubley 404 **Fire Engine,** Tootsietoy 1249 **Snorkel Truck,** Jam-Pac **Fire Pumper** & 1249 **Ladder Truck,** Hubley 405 **Ladder Truck.**
Row 3: Tootsietoy 4652 **Ladder Truck** with wheels & tires, 3-inch American LaFrance **Fire Pumper,** postwar 237 **Hose Car** & 238 **Insurance Patrol.**
Row 4: Tootsietoy 4-inch **Mercury Fire Chief, Chevrolet Civilian & Army Ambulances, Pontiac Fire Chief.**

Row 1: Hubley 463 & 465 **Ladder Trucks.**
Row 2: Hubley **Ahrens-Fox Fire Engine** & **Steam Pumper.**
Row 3: Hubley open cab **Ahrens-Fox Fire Engine** & **Ladder Truck.**

Row 1: Hubley 306 **Steam Pumper,** 402 **Fire Engine,** 307 **Ladder Truck.**
Row 2: Hubley 437 **Packard Fire Chief, #? Steam Pumper,** 331 **Diesel Ladder Truck.**
Row 3: Hubley 1949 **Packard Fire Chief, #? Ladder Truck,** 324 **Ladder Truck.**

Row 1: Hubley 3.5-inch **Steam Pumper**, 382 **Steam Pumper**, 383 **Ladder Truck**, 3.5-inch **Ladder Truck.**
Row 2: Hubley 3.5 & 4.5-inch **Ahrens-Fox Fire Trucks**, 4.5-inch **Steam Pumper** & **Ladder Truck.**
Row 3: Hubley 7-inch **Ahrens-Fox Fire Truck**, 213 repro **Steam Pumper**, 6-inch **Steam Pumper.**

Row 1: Hubley 127mm **Steam Pumper,** 172mm **Ladder Truck,** 153mm **Steam Pumper.**
Row 2: Hubley 165mm **Steam Pumper & Ladder Truck.**
Row 3: Hubley 163 mm **Steam Pumper,** 149mm **Ladder Truck.**

Row 1: Arcade 133mm **Steam Pumper,** 125mm **Fire Chief,** 124mm **Ladder Truck.**
Row 2: Arcade 154mm **Steam Pumper,** 114mm **Steam Pumper,** 181mm **Ladder Truck.**
Row 3: Arcade 110mm **Steam Pumper,** 150mm **City Ambulance,** 120mm **Ladder Truck.**

Row 1: Dent **Fire Chief, Mack Ladder Truck** & 139mm **Ladder Truck.**
Row 2: Kenton 142mm **Steam Pumper,** 182mm **Ladder Truck,** unknown 115mm **Steam Pumper.**
Row 3: Kilgore 127mm **Steam Pumper,** 163mm & 127mm **Ladder Trucks.**

Row 1: Williams 92mm & 127mm **Steam Pumpers,** 135mm & 96mm **Ladder Trucks.**
Row 2: Williams 125mm & 158mm **Steam Pumpers,** 132mm **Ladder Truck.**
Row 3: Williams 185mm **Steam Pumper,** 194mm **Ladder Truck.**

Row 1: Williams 174mm **Steam Pumper,** 188mm **Ladder Truck.**
Row 2: Williams 137mm **Ladder Truck,** unknown 142mm **Steam Pumper,** Kenton **Ford Fire Chief.**
Row 3: Unknown 80mm **Ladder Truck,** Hubley? 177mm **Fire Truck,** unknown 131mm **Ladder Truck.**

Row 1: Barclay 79mm **Hose Truck** (2 types), 78mm **Steam Pumper,** 78mm **Ladder Truck** (2 types).
Row 2: Barclay 90mm **Ambulance** (small cross), Manoil **Ladder Truck,** unknown 85mm red **Steam Pumper,** Manoil **Steam Pumper,** Barclay **Ambulance (big cross).**
Row 3: Unknown 70 **Steam Pumper,** 70mm **Ladder Truck** (metal wheels), 85mm blue **Steam Pumper,** 70mm **Ladder Truck** (wheels & tires), 70mm **Steam Pumper.**
Row 4: Unknown 94mm **Steam Pumper,** 116mm **Ladder Truck** (unpainted without bell, painted with bell), 97mm **Steam Pumper.**

Row 1: Barclay diecast **Ladder Truck,** 125mm slushmold **Ambulance,** 157mm **Steam Pumper.**
Row 2: Savoye flat grille **Steam Pumper** (2 wheel types), **Ladder Truck,** 100mm **Steam Pumper.**
Row 3: Savoye **Water Tower,** Tommy Toy **Ambulance,** Savoye **Emergency Truck.**

Row 1: Hudson **Fire Engine & Ladder Truck,** Authenticast **Ambulance, Ladder Truck & Fire Engine.**
Row 2: Midgetoy **Emergency Wrecker,** 73mm **Fire Engine,** 2 Authenticast **Fire Chiefs,** Midgetoy **Fire Department Ambulance** and 63mm **Fire Chief.**
Row 3: Renwal 8040 **Steam Pumper,** Midgetoy 89mm **Fire Engine** (regular & army), 90mm **Fire Chief,** Renwal 8022 **Ladder Truck.**
Row 4: It's A Beaut 4 **Fire Chief,** Barclay **Fire Chief & Ambulance Truck,** Goodee 3-inch **Fire Engine & Ford Fire Chief.**

Row 1: Metal Masters **Fire Department Pickup** with diecast ladder rack, Winross **White 3000 Fire Truck,** Metal Masters **Fire Department Pickup** with sheet metal ladder rack.
Row 2: Metalcraft **Hose Truck,** Manoil 709 **Fire Engine,** Renwal **Steam Pumper.**
Row 3: Midgetoy **Fire Engine** (largest size), Winross **White 1500 Fire Truck,** Goodee 8-inch **Fire Engine.**

Row 1: Mattel First Wheels **Fire Chief, Fire Truck & Rescue Van,** Slik Toys 9700 Hose Truck.
Row 2: Midgetoy **Ambulance Van** (red & white) & **Ambulance Bus** (white & red).
Row 3: Midgetoy 110mm **Fire Engine, Army Ambulance Van,** Ralstoy 1 **Fire Truck.**

Row 1: American plaster **Buick Ambulance, Hose Truck, Ladder Truck & Mack Fire Engine.**
Row 2: Ralstoy **Chevrolet Seymour, Ambulance, Hickman & Army Ambulance Vans.**
Row 3: Ralstoy **Chevrolet Ralston, Bruno & Omaha** (red/white & all red) **Fire Vans.**

Row 1: Ertl 1361 **Red Cross Van,** Hallmark **Fiery Fred,** Ertl 1461 **Smurf Ladder Truck** & 1865 **Ford Transcon Ambulance.**
Row 2: Mattel 7665 **Chief's Special** (2 types), 7068 **Fire Smasher,** 2639 **Fire Chaser,** 1510 **Fire Chief Car.**
Row 3: Mattel 7666 **Ranger Rig,** 7650 **Emergency Squad,** 1695 **Old Number 5,** 7661 white & yellow **Paramedic.**
Row 4: Mattel 1699 **Airport Rescue,** 6454 **Fire Truck,** 6469 **Fire Chief Cruiser,** 9640 **Fire Eater,** 6451 **Ambulance.**

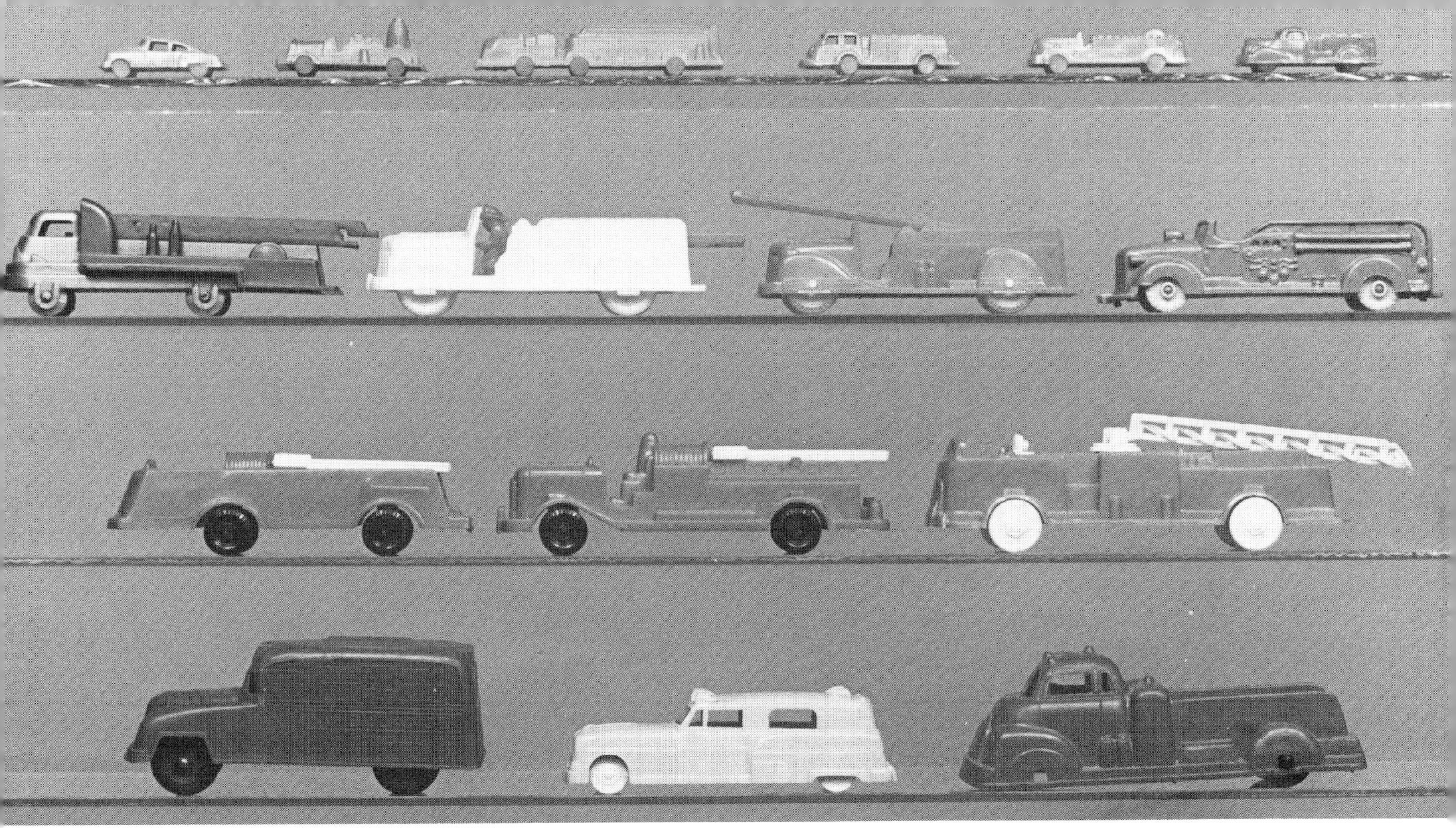

Row 1: Empire **Fire Chief, Steam Pumper, Ladder Truck, Fire Engine, Hose Truck & Rescue Truck.**
Row 2: Gilmark **Ladder Truck**, Renwal 105 & Hasbro **Fire Trucks**, Banner 1 **Hose Truck.**
Row 3: Wannatoy **Fire Truck & Ladder Truck**, Plasticville **Ladder Truck.**
Row 4: Unknown **Daimler Army Ambulance,** Plasticville **Ambulance,** unknown gray **Fire Truck.**

Row 1: Renwal 57 & 179 **Ladder Trucks.**
Row 2: Zimmerman **Cap'n Crunch Fire Truck,** unknown green **Rescue Van,** Banner 7 **Fire Truck.**
Row 3: Banner 219 **Army Ambulance,** unknown 120mm **Fire Truck,** Banner 219 **Ambulance Truck.**

Row 1: Ideal Motorific **Fire Truck**, Nosco **Fire Engine.**
Row 2: California **Fire Engine,** Pyro **Fire Control Truck,** California **Steam Pumper.**
Row 3: California **Ladder Truck** (earlier red & later blue types).

Row 1: BW **Ladder Truck,** Jordan 221 **Ahrens-Fox Fire Truck,** BKC **Steam Pumper.**
Row 2: Ideal 1-1729 **City Hospital Ambulance,** unknown green glass **Steam Pumper,** Ideal 1-1729 **Army Ambulance.**
Row 3: Keystone **Chrysler Fire Chief, Fire Engine & Ladder Truck,** Wheel Works **Fire Truck.**

Row 1: F & F **Ford Fire Chief & Ambulance,** Lido 10 **Fire Engine,** BW **Ladder Truck** (2 types).
Row 2: W.G. 10 & 8 **Fire Engines,** unknown 80mm **Fire Engine,** Renwal 145 **Steam Pumper** & 146 **Ladder Truck.**
Row 3: Marx? **Hose Truck** (cast-in wheels), Marx **Hose Truck & Fire Engine,** Wyandotte **Ladder Truck.**
Row 4: Acme 133 **Buick Fire Chief,** Thomas 183 **Ford Fire Chief** & 140 **Fire Tanker,** Kilgore **Hupmobile Fire Chief.**

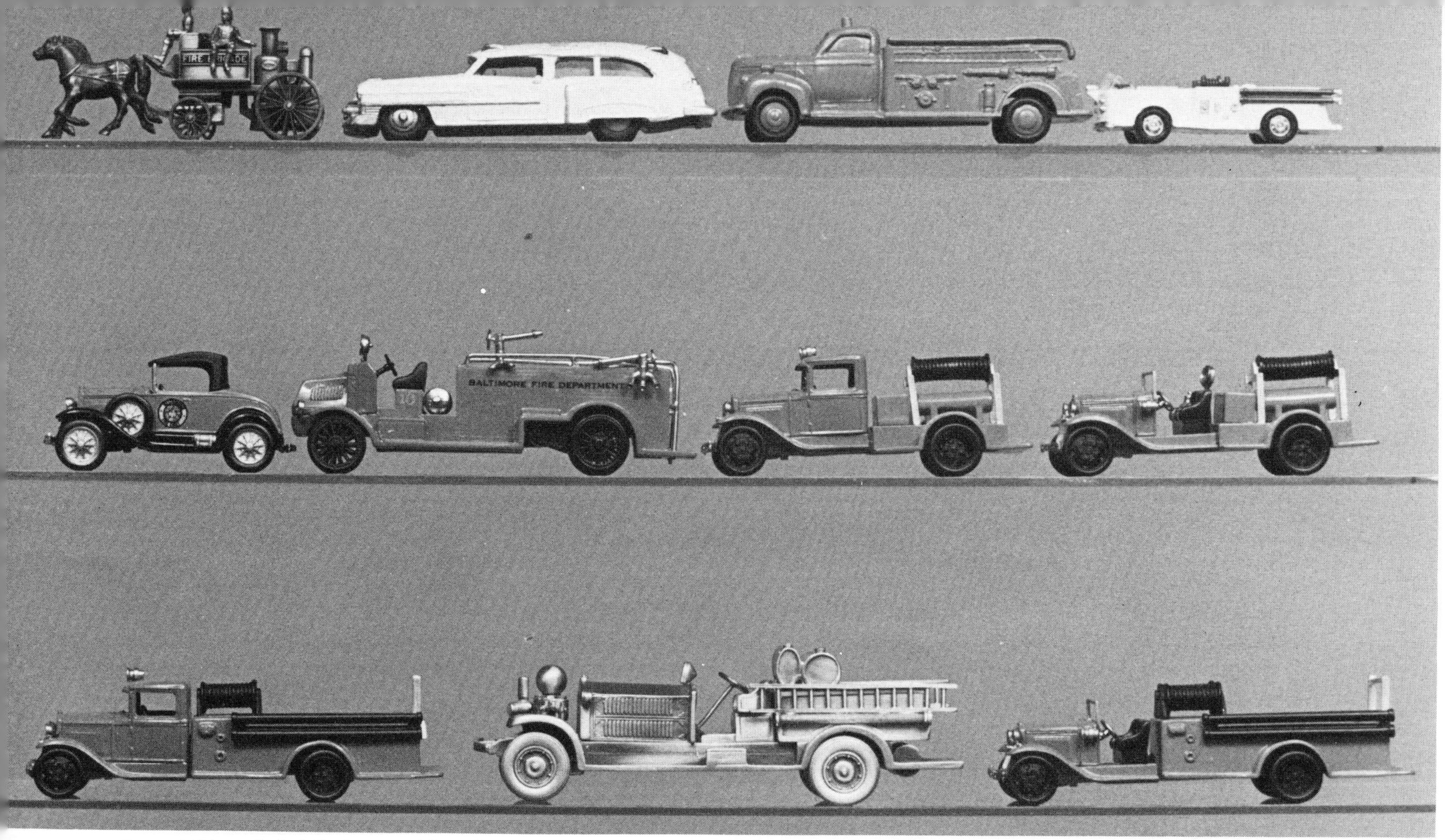

Row 1: Nostalgic Miniatures **Shand-Mason Steamer,** Jurgens **Cadillac Ambulance,** Miller **Studebaker Fire Truck,** Lindy 10 **Fire Engine.**
Row 2: Nostalgic 203 **Ford Fire Chief,** 237 **Mack Pumper,** 258 **Ford Chemical Truck,** 250 **Ford Open Cab Pumper.**
Row 3: Nostalgic 253 **Ford Chemical Truck,** 269 **Ahrens-Fox Fire Pumper,** 256 **Ford Twin Hose Pumper.**

Row 1: Auburn 4-inch rubber **Fire Engine,** 8-inch **Fire Engine,** 4-inch plastic **Fire Engine.**
Row 2: Auburn **Ambulance, Emergency Truck & Ahrens-Fox Fire Engine.**
Row 3: Two Auburn 8-inch **Steam Pumpers.**

Row 1: Sun Rubber **Mickey Mouse Fire Truck**, green **Fire Truck & Donald Duck Fire Truck.**
Row 2: Sun Rubber **Ambulance**, Auburn 8-inch **Fire Truck,** Sun Rubber **Army Ambulance.**
Row 3: Unique **Fire Truck,** unknown **Ambulance,** Auburn plastic **Rescue Truck.**

Row 1: Tonka 6150 **Fire Squad Van,** 675 **Ladder Truck, & Paramedic Van** from Fire Set.
Row 2: Argo **Hudson Ambulance,** Tonka 1100 & 086 **Fire Trucks,** Argo **Hudson Fire Chief.**
Row 3: Tonka **Fire Chief's Van, Ambulance Van** & 6-inch **Fire Truck.**

Row 1: Buddy L **Code Red Fire Engine & Ladder Truck.**
Row 2: Buddy L plastic **Fire Truck,** metal **Rescue Van** & short **Fire Truck,** & plastic **Ambulance.**
Row 3: Wyandotte **Ladder Truck,** Marx **Ambulance** & **Fire Department Bus** from Fire Set.

Row 1: Plasticville **Fire House.**
Row 2: Metal Masters **Fire Engine.**
Row 3: Tru-Scale **Municipal Fire Truck.**

Row 1: Processed Plastic **Fire Truck.**
Row 2: Freeport **Ladder Truck.**
Row 3: Amloid **Fire Truck.**

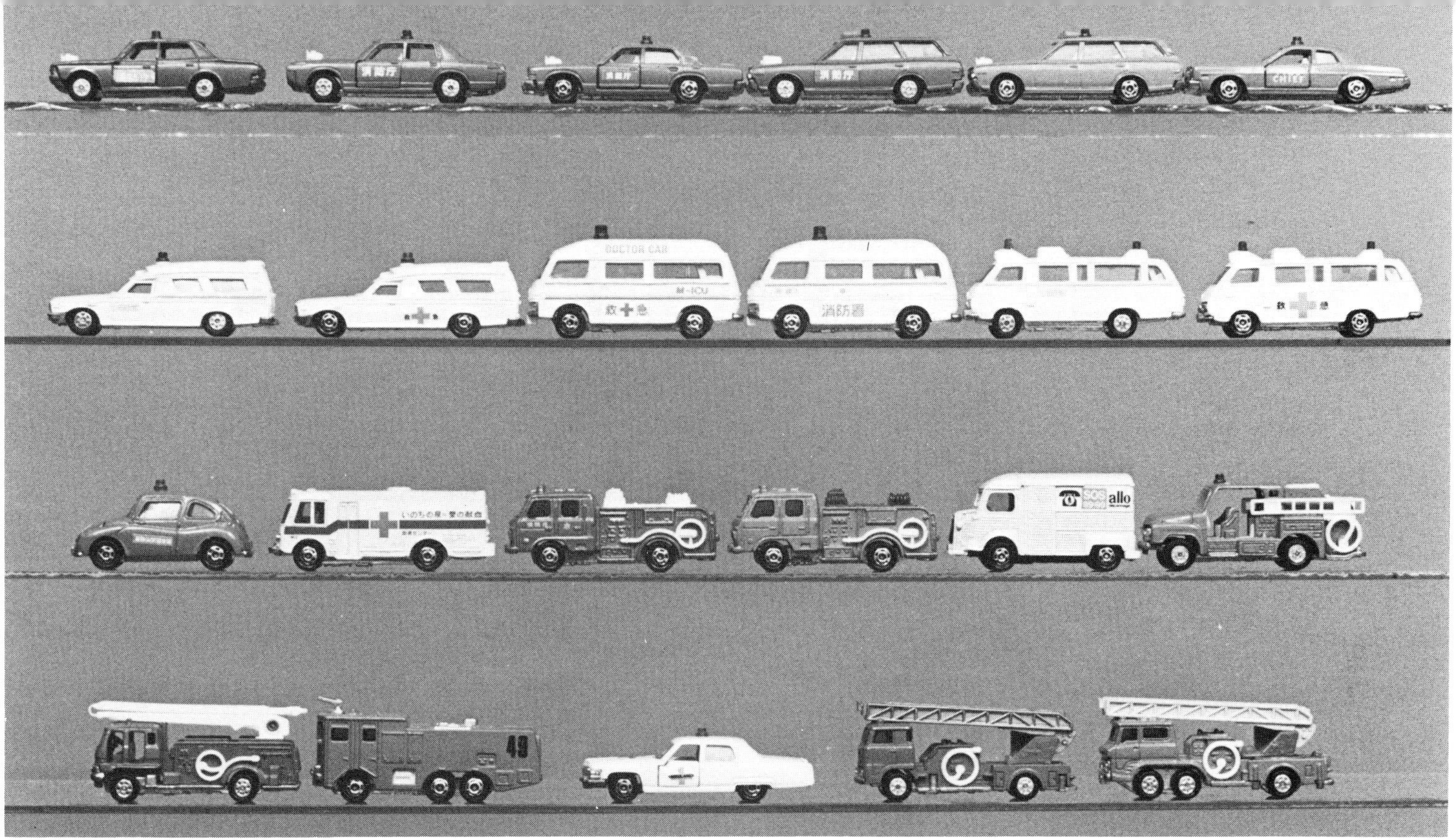

Row 1: Tomica 27-1, 27-2 & 27-3 **Toyota Crown Fire Chiefs,** 78-1 **Nissan Cedric Fire Chief** (2 types), F10-1 **Dodge Fire Chief.**
Row 2: Tomica 40-1 **Toyota Ambulance** (2 types), 36-2 **Nissan Caravan Ambulance** (2 types), 57-1 **Toyota Hiace Ambulance** (2 types).
Row 3: Tomica 21 **Subaru 360 Fire Chief,** 8-3 **Isuzu Blood Bank Van,** 22-2 & 94-2 **Condor Chemical Fire Engine,** F17-2 **Citroen SOS Van,** 68-1 **Isuzu Fire Engine.**
Row 4: Tomica 3-2 **Isuzu Squirt Snorkel,** 94-1 **Tokyu Airport Fire Truck,** F19-1 **Cadillac Red Cross Car,** 29-1 & 29-2 **Hino Fire Engines** with ladders.

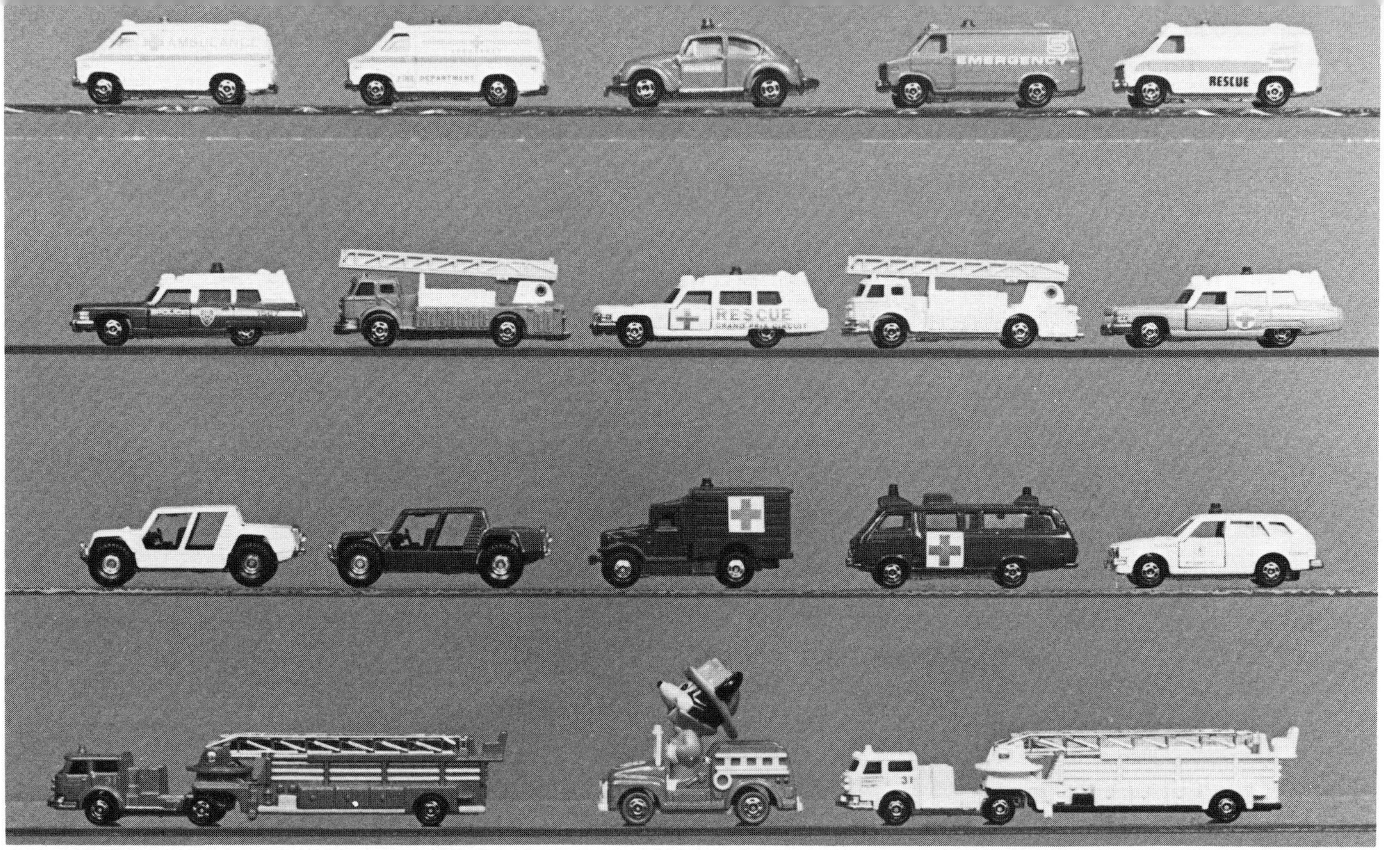

Row 1: Tomica F22-1 **Chevrolet Ambulance Van** (2 types), F20-1 **Volkswagen Fire Chief,** F22-1 **Chevrolet Rescue & Emergency Vans.**
Row 2: Tomica F60-1 **Cadillac Police Ambulance,** F33-1 red **Ladder Chief,** F60-1 **Cadillac Grand Prix Rescue Ambulance,** F33-1 yellow **Ladder Chief,** F60-1 **Cadillac Ambulance.**
Row 3: Tomica F65 **Cheetah Civilian & Army Red Cross Cars,** 67-2 **Toyota Army Red Cross Truck,** 57-1 **Toyota Army Ambulance,** 34-3 **Honda Emergency Car.**
Row 4: Tomica L10 red **American LaFrance Ladder Truck,** PD2 **Mickey Mouse Fire Truck,** L10 yellow **American LaFrance Ladder Truck.**

Row 1: Tomica D45 **Isuzu Fire Engine,** D37 **Hino Snorkel Truck,** D25 **Hino Ladder Truck,** D42 **Mitsubishi Fire Jeep.**
Row 2: Tomica D20 **Datsun Gloria Fire Chief,** D12-1 **Toyota Ambulance Bus,** D12-2 **Nissan Caravan Ambulance,** D9 **Toyota Crown Fire Chief.**
Row 3: Tomica DF23 **Volkswagen Fire & THW Vans,** D42 **Isuzu Ambulance,** D5 **Nissan Fire Engine.**

Row 1: Tomica Dandy **Emergency Set.**
Row 2: Tomica Dandy D2 **Hino Ladder Truck,** DF20 **Volkswagen Fire Chief.**

Row 1: Diapet P55 **Toyota Hiace Ambulance,** P4 **Datsun Caravan Ambulance,** P43 **Toyota Hiace Ambulance.**
Row 2: Diapet 239 **Prince Red Cross Car,** 238 **Prince Fire Chief,** 151 **Toyota Emergency Car,** #? **Mazda Cosmo Red Cross Car.**
Row 3: Diapet 319 **Toyota Hiace Ambulance,** 203 **Toyota Ambulance,** 0264 **Toyota Hiace Fire Department Bus.**

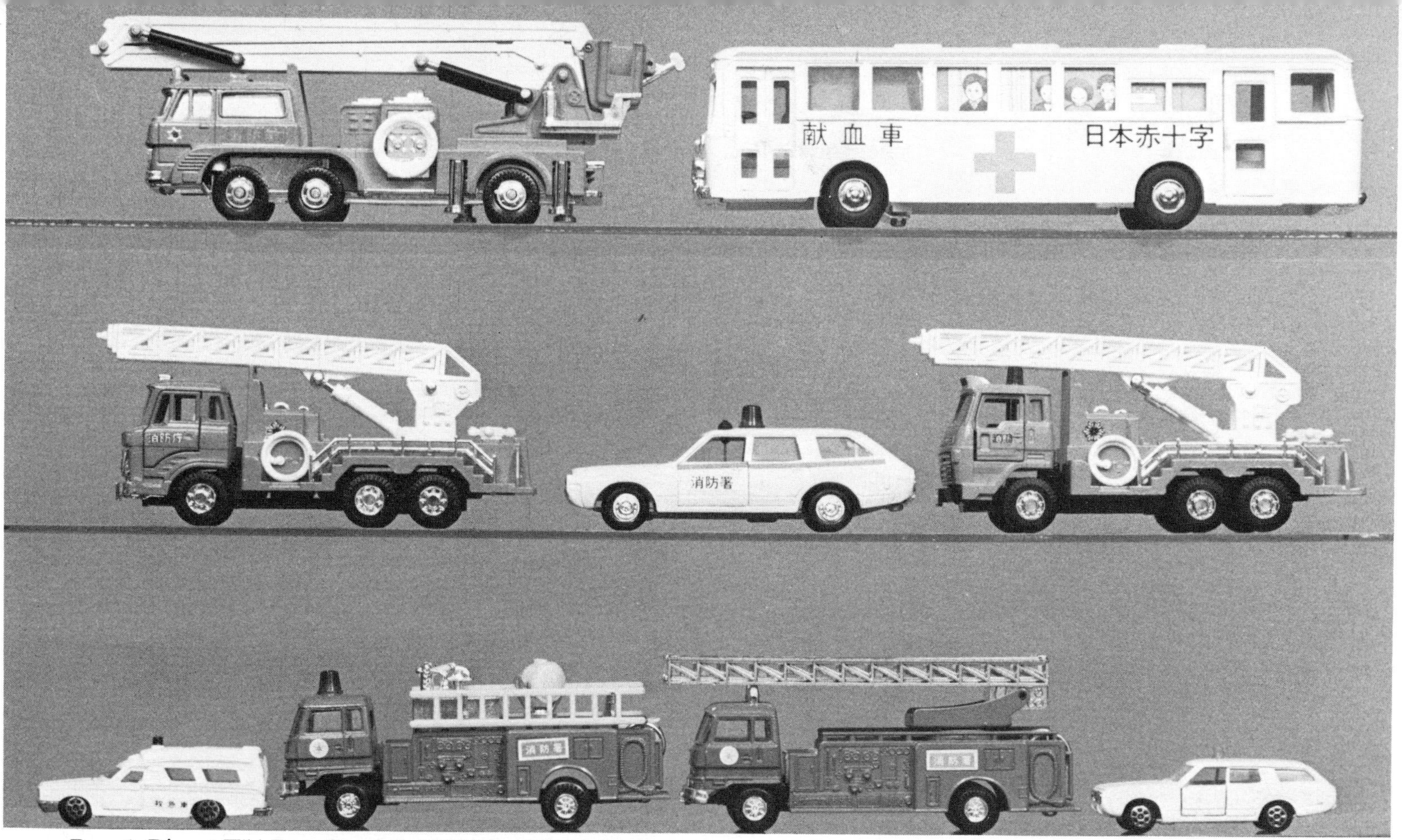

Row 1: Diapet T54 **Fuso Snorkel,** 0232 **Blood Bank Bus.**
Row 2: Diapet T87 **Hino Ladder Truck,** 296 **Toyota Crown Ambulance,** T20 **Isuzu Ladder Truck.**
Row 3: Diapet 0464 **Toyota Ambulance,** D15 **Isuzu Chemical Fire Truck,** 291 **Isuzu Fire Truck,** 0412 **Toyota Ambulance Wagon.**

Row 1: Shinsei 4108 **Fuso Chemical Fire Truck,** 4104 **Fuso Snorkel Truck,** 4109 **Fuso Snorkel Fire Engine.**
Row 2: Sakura 603 & 2 **Isuzu Fire Pumpers,** Shinsei 4101 **Ladder Truck,** Sakura 601 **Toyota Corona Red Cross Car.**
Row 3: Sakura 610 **Nissan Skyline Fire Chief,** 611 **Nissan Skyline Ambulance,** 100 **Nissan Cedric Red Cross Car,** 4071 **Nissan Cedric Fire Chief.**

Row 1: Sakura 106 **Fire Department Land Cruiser,** L13 **Suzuki Red Cross Jeep,** L11 **Suzuki Fire Jeep.**
Row 2: Sakura 4086 **Nissan Caravan Fire Bus,** Aviva 700 **Snoopy's Fire Engine,** Sakura 4087 **Nissan Caravan Ambulance.**
Row 3: Marusan 8503 **Daimler Ambulance,** Yone 2133 **Ladder Truck,** ATC Model Pet 21 **Toyopet Masterline Ambulance.**

Row 1: Aviva 1 **Snoopy Snorkel,** 20 **Snoopy Fire Engine,** 72044-3 **Snoopy Fire Truck,** Bandai 12 **Chemical Fire Truck,** 13 **Nissan Ambulance.**
Row 2: Unknown small **Fire Engine, Fire Engine** with whistle, **Fire Engine** with pencil sharpener, **Steam Pumper** with whistle & small horsedrawn **Steam Pumper.**
Row 3: Eidai 12 **Hino Ladder Truck,** 43 **Nissan Caravan Ambulance,** Madmax 14 **Nissan Caravan Ambulance,** Eidai 16 **Hino Snorkel Truck.**
Row 4: Unknown **Ladder Truck,** Tonka **Go-Bots Fire Truck & Ambulance,** unknown **Daimler Ambulance.**

Row 1: Y 110 **Fire Chief,** unknown 100mm **Fire Chief & Ambulance, Studebaker Fire Chief.**
Row 2: Unknown 47 **Fire Chief Wagon,** 6544 **Fire Chief & Ambulance,** 47 **Ambulance Wagon.**
Row 3: Unknown 2540 **Mercedes-Benz Ambulance,** 11-1410 **Fire Chief,** 1375 **Mercedes-Benz Fire Chief.**
Row 4: Unknown 7237 **Ambulance,** MTH 7530 **Ambulance,** 7237 **Fire Chief.**

Row 1: Unknown yellow **Ambulance Truck,** Yone 2038 **Ladder Truck,** unknown 184 **Fire Emergency Van,** red **Fire Department Truck.**
Row 2: Unknown cream **Ambulance,** open cab **Fire Engine, Fire Jeep** with ladder, F260 **Fire Chief.**
Row 3: Unknown long nose **Ladder Truck,** S-2023 **Ladder Truck,** 108mm **Fire Truck,** Kanto **Fire Engine.**

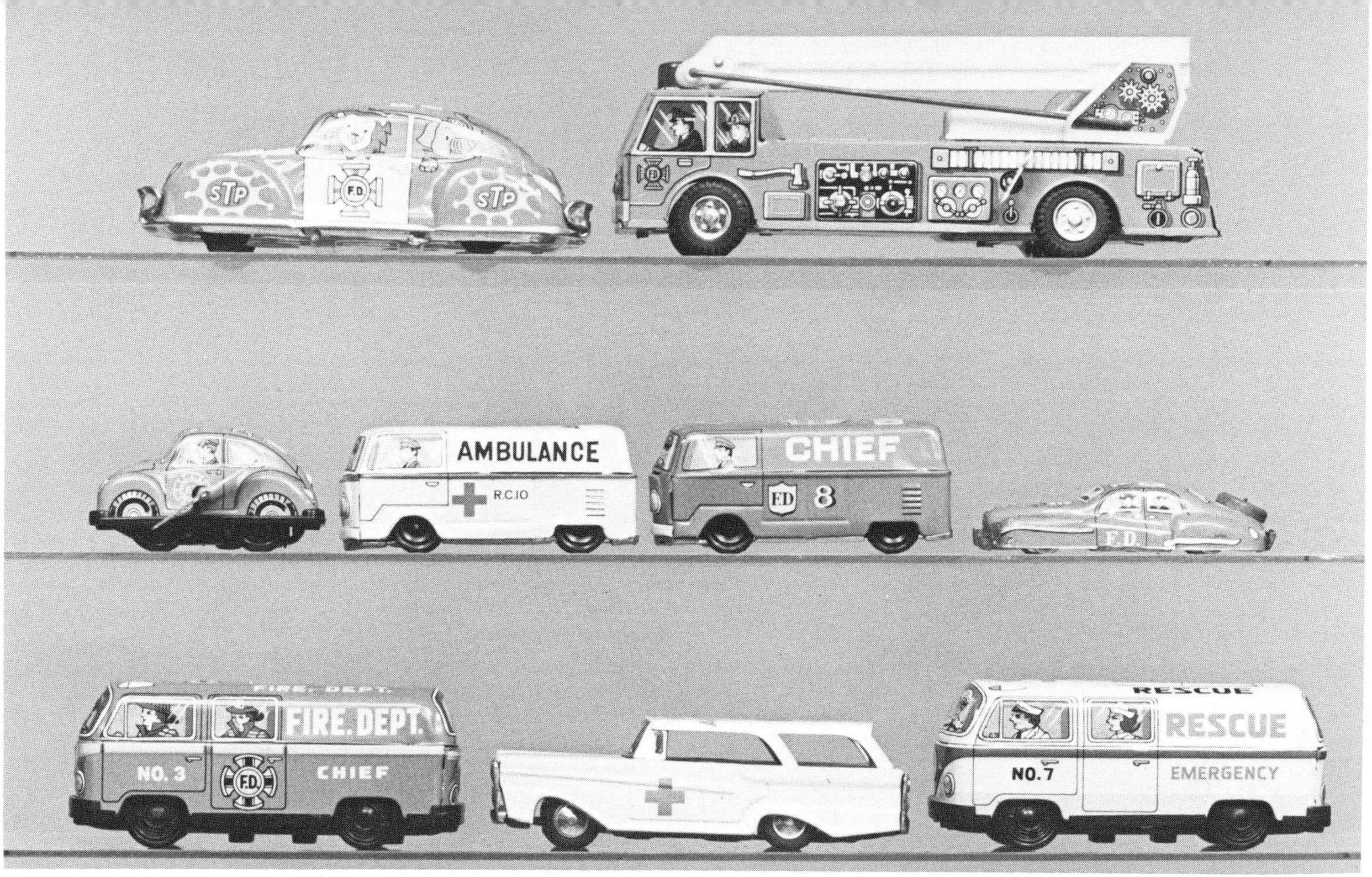

Row 1: K **Volkswagen Fire Chief** with animals, Yone 2100 **Fire Engine.**
Row 2: Y 1190 **Volkswagen Fire Chief,** RC 10 **Volkswagen Ambulance,** FD 8 **Volkswagen Fire Chief's Van,** 110 **Fire Chief's Car** with whistle.
Row 3: Unknown **Volkswagen 3 Fire Van, Ambulance Wagon, Volkswagen 7 Rescue Van.**

Row 1: TN **Ambulance Car,** MF 183 6-wheel **Fire Engine,** K **Porsche Fire Chief.**
Row 2: Remote control **Ladder Truck,** T.N. **Ladder Truck.**
Row 3: SAN **Ladder Truck,** T.N. 24670 **Ladder Truck,** Y 3-inch **Fire Truck.**

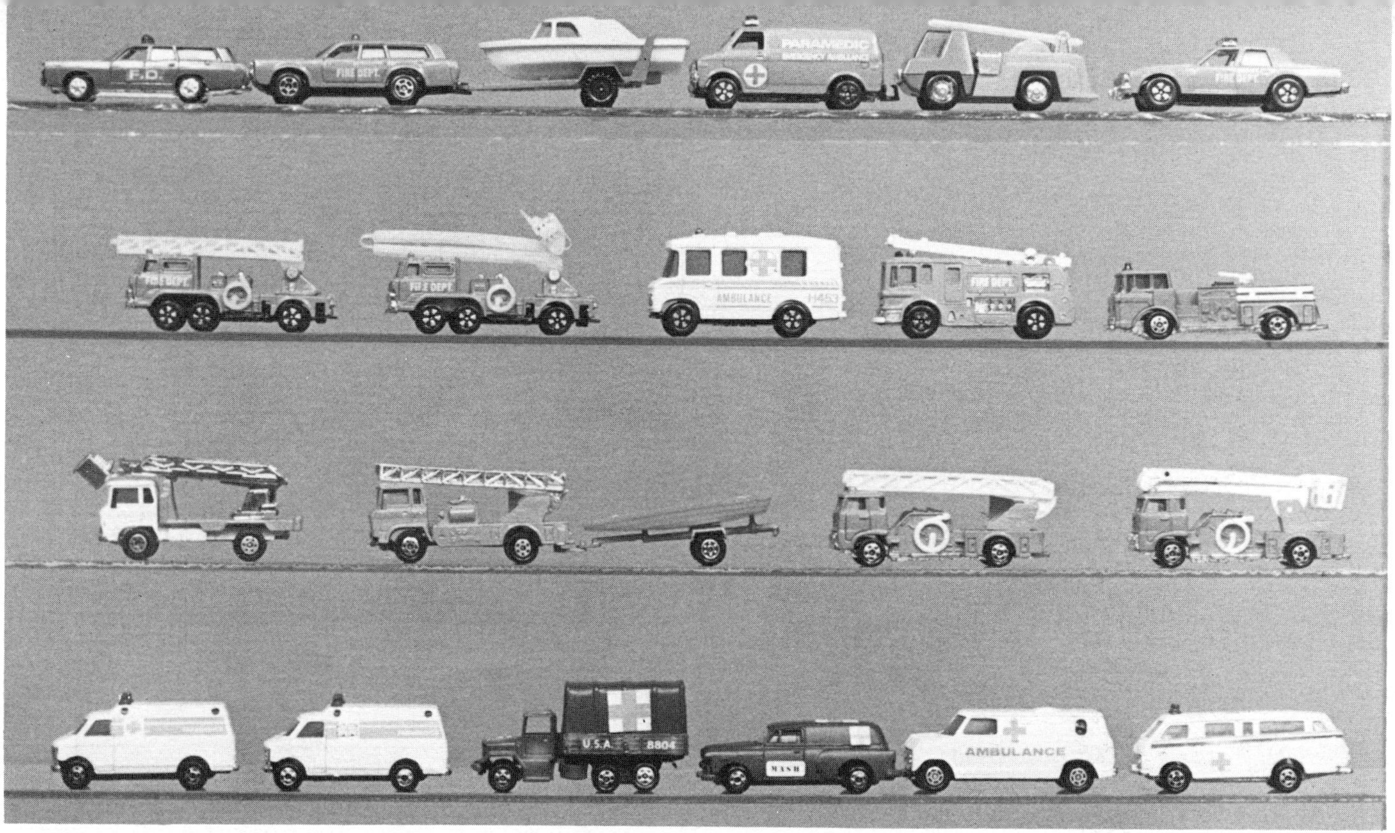

Row 1: Playart 7118 **Mercury Fire Chief**, 7716 **Fire Chief & Boat Trailer**, 7209 **Ford Paramedic Van**, 7130 **Fire Truck**, 7218 **Chevrolet Fire Chief.**

Row 2: Playart 7183 **Ladder Truck**, 7184 **Snorkel Truck**, 7167 **Mercedes-Benz Ambulance**, 7168 **Fire Tender**, Zylmex 337 **Fire Engine.**

Row 3: Yatming 1355 **Snorkel Truck**, 261 **Ladder Truck** (1356) & **Lifeboat Trailer**, Zylmex 312 **Ladder Truck**, 313 **Snorkel Truck.**

Row 4: Zylmex 346 **Paramedic Ambulance** (U. S. & Canadian), 433 **MASH Red Cross Truck**, 439 **MASH Chevrolet Ambulance**, Yatming 1501 **Ambulance**, Zylmex 333 **Toyota Ambulance.**

Row 1: Kidco 155-7 **Ladder Truck, Mini-Roller Fire Engine,** Universal **Ladder Truck.**
Row 2: Kidco 40770-2 **MASH Medical Corps Jeep,** 40770-1 **MASH Semi-Trailer Truck,** 40770-4 **MASH Ambulance,** 40770-5 **Medical Corps Supply Truck.**
Row 3: Kidco 166-2 **Dodge Fire Chief,** DTC T220 **Fire Trucks** (cab-over and long nose types), Kidco 166-4 **Blazer Rescue Car,** 166-3 **Blazer Emergency Car.**
Row 4: S.M. 8116 **Toyota Fire Engine,** 8114 **Ladder Truck,** 8113 **ERF Fire Tender,** 8115 **Fuso Chemical Fire Engine.**

Row 1: Imperial 8280 **Emergency Team:** 8213 **Fire Chief,** 8285 **Emergency Car,** 828 **Helicopter,** 8211 **Ladder Truck,** 8212 **Fire Rescue Truck.**
Row 2: Imperial 8212 white and **Army Ambulances,** 8183 **CHiPs Ambulance,** 8340-D **Army Ambulance,** Lido 7901-2A **Bedford Ambulance.**
Row 3: LJN 2000 **Rescue & Fire Trucks,** Larami 201-4 **Land Rover Ambulance,** 8222 **Fire Truck,** Welly 2222-B **Chevrolet Fire Truck.**
Row 4: Wul 808 **Army Ambulance,** 1110 **Rescue Van,** Maxwell **Ladder Truck,** S.M. 8306 **Ford Army Rescue Van.**

Row 1: Universal 805 **Chevrolet Paramedic Van, Merryweather Fire Truck, Dodge Rescue Truck,** Kidco 1610 **Transcon Ambulance Van.**
Row 2: Hasbro 72223 **Snoopy Fire Engine,** 7004 **Ernie's Fire Truck,** YDC 8787 **Hand Pumper,** Holly 8348 **Gas Up Fire Truck.**
Row 3: **Marx Fire Truck** with base, **Arco Army Red Cross Truck, Marx Fire Truck** without base.

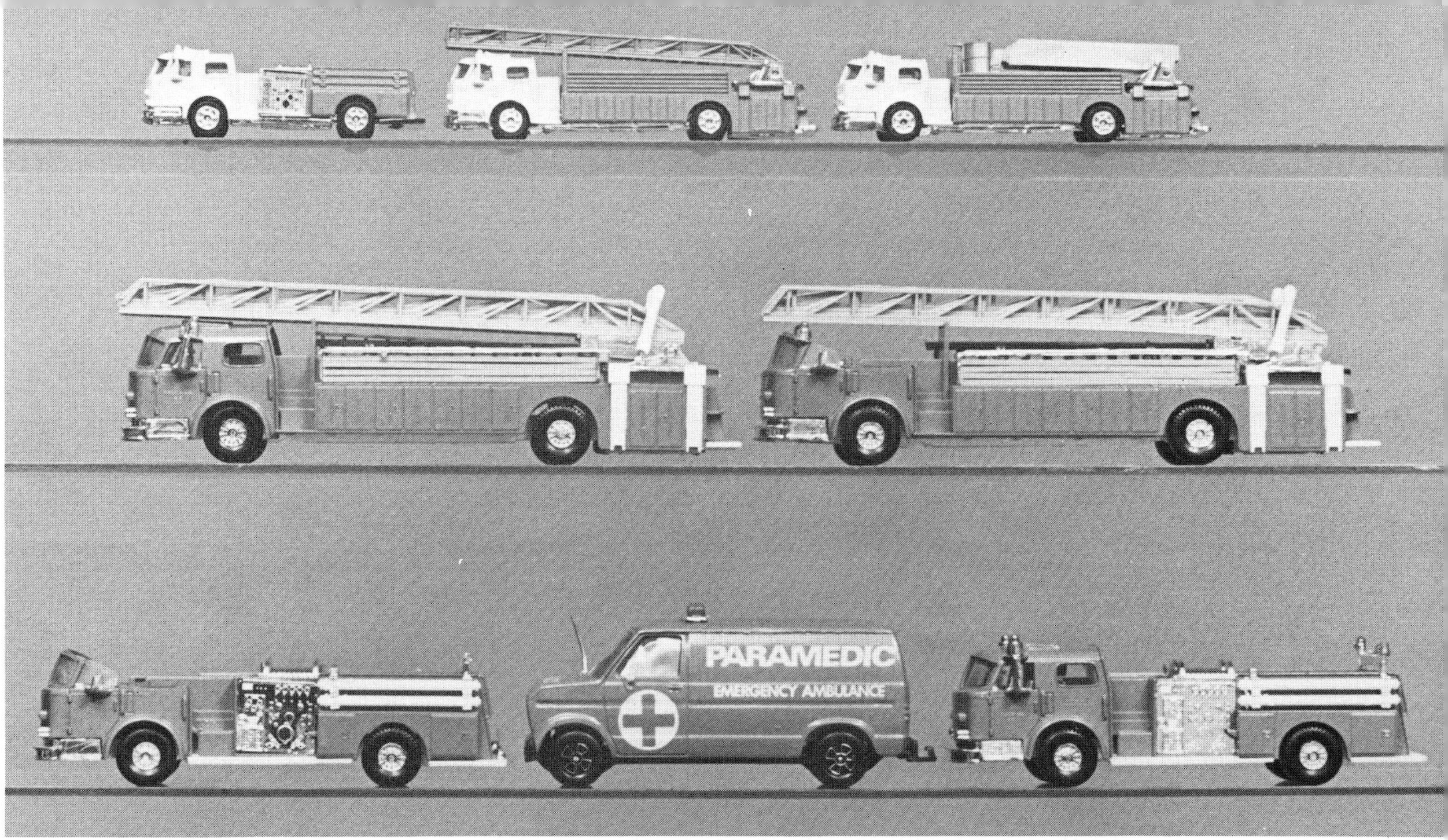

Row 1: Playart 7766 **American LaFrance Pumper,** 7767 **Ladder Truck,** 7768 **Ladder Truck** with bucket.
Row 2: Playart 1/48 scale **American LaFrance Ladder Truck** and open cab version.
Row 3: Playart 1/48 **American LaFrance Pumper,** open cab, 7902 **Paramedic Van,** 1/48 **American LaFrance Pumper,** closed cab.

Row 1: Bachmann 7019 **Fire Truck,** Gordy 834 **Cadillac Ambulance,** 833 **Fire Pumper,** Nucor **Fire Pumper & Cadillac Ambulance,** F **Ambulance Van & Fire Engine.**
Row 2: JakPak **Ambulance,** Gordy 836 **Ford Fire Chief,** Nucor **Helicopter,** JakPak **Fire Chief,** Wallace Berrie **Fire Truck.**
Row 3: Unknown tin **Ambulance, Ladder Truck,** Larami 9320-4, 8109-0 & #? **Army Red Cross Trucks,** unknown **Red Cross Jeep.**
Row 4: Unknown 301-3 **Fire Truck & Ambulance,** Steven **Fire Truck,** Larami 1131-0 **Ambulance & Fire Engine.**

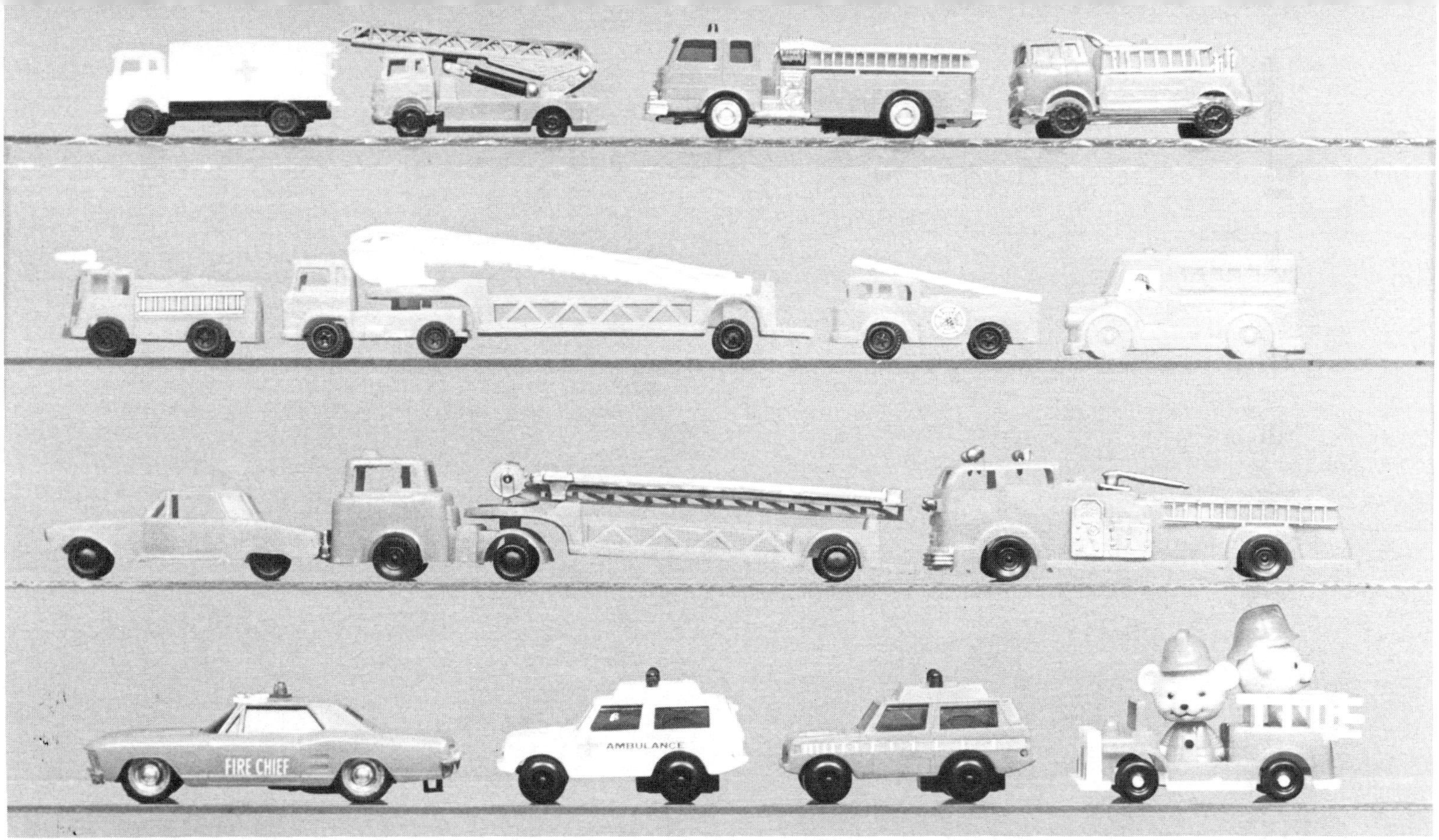

Row 1: Blue Box **Ambulance & Fire Truck,** Gordy 918 **Fire Engine,** Zylmex **Fire Engine.**
Row 2: Azrak-Hamway 7096 **Cracker Jack Set** (3 trucks), United Features **Snoopy Fire Truck** with pencils & sharpener.
Row 3: Gordy 600 **Fire Fighters Set** (chief's car & 2 trucks).
Row 4: Gordy **Buick Fire Chief,** unknown 86mm **Range Rover Ambulance & Fire Department Car,** Fleetwood 203-76 **Huggables Fire Truck.**

Row 1: Day-Ran 1155 **Fire Tender,** 1154 **Snorkel Truck,** unknown 7178 **Ladder Truck.**
Row 2: Imco 3108 **Fire Chief's Pickup Truck** & 3109 **Ambulance,** Azrak-Hamway 6263 **Fire Chief.**
Row 3: Madison 833 **Fire Department Set** (truck + Azrak 6427), Mak's 2009 **Jaguar Fire Chief.**

Row 1: Unknown 106mm **Emergency Vehicle,** Cragstan 1145 **Pumper,** Arco **Ladder Truck,** Ideal **Fire Engine.**
Row 2: Kidco 206 **Fire Engine,** E.W. 7404 **Ladder Truck,** T.P. tin **Fire Chief,** Nasta **Fire Engine.**
Row 3: Ocean 20 **Ambulance & Fire Van,** Remco **Ladder Truck,** A rubber **Fire Truck,** Jimson 302 **Porsche Fire Chief.**

Row 1: Knickerbocker **Mickey Mouse Fire Truck,** Illco 7532 **Snorkel Fire Engine.**
Row 2: Durham 8212 **Disneyland Fire Truck,** Arco 134mm **Fire Truck,** Free Wheeling **Fire Engine.**
Row 3: Lucky 7128 **Volkswagen Fire Chief & Ladder Truck.**

Row 1: Unknown 312 **Fire Engine,** Day-Ran 13103 **Fire Engine.**
Row 2: Unknown T102 **Range Rover Ambulance & Emergency Squad,** Wind Up 8201 **Ford Rescue Car.**
Row 3: Foundation 7841 **Ladder Truck,** Symbol of Quality 2146 **Airport Fire Engine.**

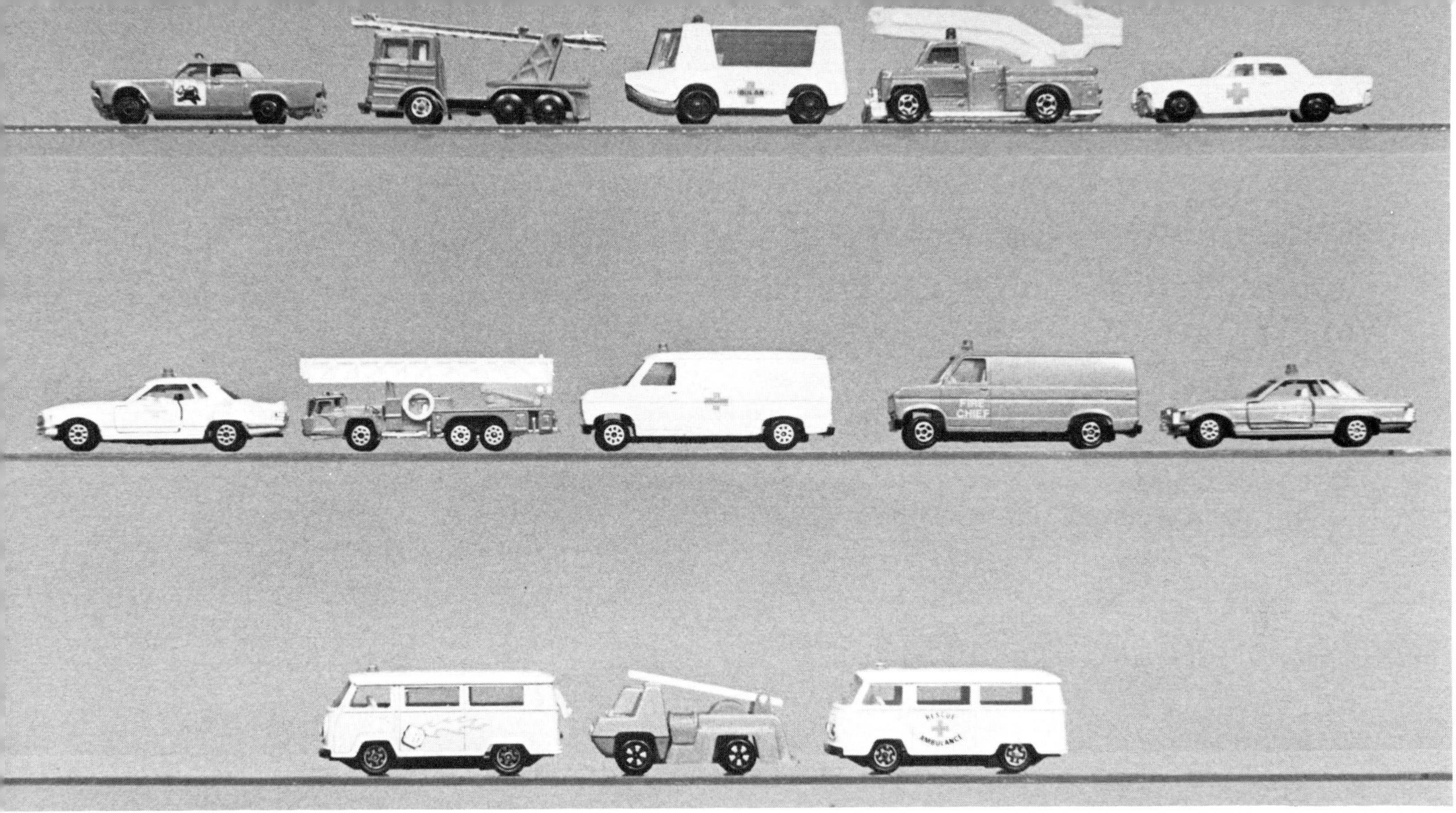

Row 1: Maxwell 514 **Lincoln Fire Chief,** Milton 344 **Ladder Truck,** 348 **Ambulance,** Mattel 1007 **Snorkel Truck,** Maxwell 515 **Lincoln Red Cross Car.**
Row 2: Kingstar 205A **Mercedes-Benz Red Cross Car,** 273 **Hino Ladder Truck,** 206 **Ford Ambulance & Fire Department Vans,** 205C **Mercedes-Benz Fire Chief.**
Row 3: Mandarin 502 **Volkswagen Fire Chief's Bus, 901 Fire Truck,** 502 **Volkswagen Ambulance Bus.**

Row 1: Milton 807 **Plymouth Fire Chief,** 307 **Plymouth Ambulance,** Maxwell 560 & Milton 309 **Chevrolet Impala Fire Chiefs' Cars.**
Row 2: Maxwell 520 **Ambassador Fire Chief,** Milton 321 **Commer Army** & 320 **Civilian Ambulances,** 832 **Commer Fire Truck.**
Row 3: Maxwell 608 **Fire Chief's Jeep,** Nicky 295 **Standard Ambulance,** Maxwell 533 **Tate Red·Cross Bus,** 551 **Red Cross Jeep,** 606 **Fire Department Jeep.**

Row 1: Sabra 8102 **Chevelle Fire Chief,** Clover 94 **Kenworth Snorkel Truck,** Sabra 8102-1 **Israeli Fire Chief** (2 types).
Row 2: Sabra 8101 **Chevelle Ambulance,** Clover 13 **Mazda Red Cross & Green Cross Cars,** Sabra 8101-1 **Chevelle Israeli Ambulance.**
Row 3: Sabra 8101-2 **Chevelle Army Ambulance,** Clover 17 **Kiamaster Ambulance,** Gamda 11 **Ambulance,** 2 **Army Ambulance Truck.**

Row 1: Talbot **Pink Panther Fire Truck,** Illco **Mickey Mouse Fire Truck,** Stomper **Fire Truck,** NTI **Fire Brigade Truck.**
Row 2: Taiwan diecast **Fire Truck,** Chinese tinplate **Fire Chief,** MF **Ambulance,** Chinese tinplate **Ambulance.**
Row 3: Taiwan rubber **Ambulance,** Turkish **Fire Jeep,** Korean tinplate **Fire Truck,** Taiwan rubber **Fire Truck.**

Row 1: Rajah **Fire Engine**, MF 718 **Ladder Truck.**
Row 2: KY **Steel Roder Set: Ladder Truck, Helicopter & Snorkel Truck.**
Row 3: Hess **Fire Engine.**

Row 1: Lone Star 000 Scale **Fire Engine,** Praline 17-05 **Pontiac Trans-Am Fire Chief,** Roco 1330 green **Opel Blitz Fire Truck,** Ibertren **Mercedes-Benz Fire Van,** Brekina 4020 **Mercedes-Benz L311 Fire Truck,** Maxwell 531 **Fire Department Jeep.**
Row 2: YDF 9627 **Hodge Steamer,** Diapet P69 **Subaru Leone Fire Department Car,** Banner 4 yellow **Fire Pumper,** Diapet P5 **Toyota Carib Fire Department Car.**
Row 3: Vitesse 291 **Mercedes-Benz 170 Fire Van,** Solido 92 **Ladder Truck** (long-nose cab), Vilmer **Dodge Ladder Truck.**

Dinky Toys

To many collectors of my generation, Dinky Toys were THE diecast miniature cars and trucks of our early days. They were produced in Britain from 1934 to 1980, in France for almost as long, and for brief periods elsewhere, and in their heyday they set the standard for other manufacturers to aim at. Dinky Toys include numerous models of emergency vehicles, beginning with such classics as the 25h Streamlined Fire Engine, its 25k version with firemen inside, and the 24a/30f Ambulance, originally with open rear windows. These were followed by a number of more modern vehicles, including the 30h/253 Daimler Ambulance, the 555/955 Fire Engine and the French 32f/899 Delahaye Ladder Truck of the early postwar years and the giant 266 E.R.F. and 285 Merryweather fire trucks of more recent times. The last major French Dinky fire truck, the 568 Berliet, became the second British 956 issue, completing the link between the two Dinky branches that had begun with such models as 25h many years before. In recent years several models were also prepared for the Danish market, wearing the red and white colors of the Falck organization. The scale of Dinky Toys has grown over the years from approximately 1/48 to 1/43, and later to 1/36, while the catalog numbering system was changed during the Fifties from the old number-and-letter system to one of three-digit numbers. We begin with the old numbering system, which was in use through 1953 in Britain and 1958 in France.

24a Ambulance, more or less generic except for its Bentley grille, in red and gray, with open side windows, 100 mm, 1/48 scale, 1934; later renumbered 30f.
25d Citroen 2cv Fire Engine, a familiar little French van in red, with Paris coat of arms decals on its doors, 84 mm, 1/43 scale, 1958; later renumbered 562.
25h Streamlined Fire Engine, with blunt nose and flowing lines, equipped with ladder and bell, plus a cast-in pump at the rear, 100 mm, 1/48 scale or smaller, 1936; issued in both Britain and France and later renumbered 250 in Britain.
25k Streamlined Fire Engine, the same casting as 25h, but with six tinplate firemen inside, 100 mm, 1/48 or smaller, 1938; issued only prewar and only in Britain.
25y Fire Department Jeep, shown in C-R Vol. II, p. 16, but never issued in this form by Dinky-France; a conversion.
30f Ambulance, the 24a casting, complete with open windows, now with either cream or gray body and black chassis, 100 mm, 1/48 scale, 1935; the postwar version was:
30f Ambulance, still in cream and black, but with the previously open side windows now filled in; 100 mm, 1/48 scale, 1946.
30h Daimler Ambulance, another classic Dinky Toy, originally in cream with cast-in red crosses, 96 mm, 1/48 scale, 1950; later renumbered 253, and also used for:
30hm Daimler Military Ambulance, the same model in olive drab, with red crosses on white panels, 96 mm, 1/48 scale, 1952; later renumbered 624; sold in the U. S. A.
32d Delahaye Ladder Truck, with classic grille, open cab, second seat facing the rear, and crank-operated two-section aerial ladder, 167 mm, 1/43 scale, 1955; later renumbered 899.
32e Berliet Fire Engine, as French as the Delahaye, with rear tank body, ladder on top, and two detachable hose reels, 111 mm, 1/43 scale, 1957; later renumbered 583.
80f Renault Military Ambulance, a slope-nosed van in olive drab with red crosses on white panels, plus one on its opening rear door, 85 mm, 1/55 scale, 1952; later renumbered 820, still later 807.
555 Fire Engine, a typical all-enclosed British type with bells and ladders on the roof, pump and other details at the rear, 136 mm, 1/43 scale, 1952; later renumbered 955.

New Catalog Numbers
002 Blazing Inferno, a Dinky Builda cardboard play scene, comprising a high-rise building, "Dinky House", and adjoining streets, 1978.
008 Firemen, a set of figures and a fire hose, for railroad platform accessory use, 1961.
195 Range Rover Fire Chief, in red, metallic or otherwise, with Fire Service labels and blue dome light, 108 mm, 1/36 scale, 1972.
250 Streamlined Fire Engine, the renumbered 25h originally made in 1936, 100 mm, 1/48 scale, renumbered in 1954.
253 Daimler Ambulance, ex-30h, of 1950 vintage, now painted white, 96 mm, 1/48 scale, renumbered in 1954.
257 Nash Rambler Fire Chief, a red Cross Country wagon with red dome light and yellow Fire Chief decals, 101 mm, 1/43 scale, 1961.
259 Fire Engine, modern and boxy for its time, with ladder and bell on the roof, cast-in hose reels, and Fire Brigade decals, 117 mm, 1/43 or smaller scale, 1961.
263 Superior Criterion Ambulance, with driver and attendant in front, patient on stretcher inside the opening rear door, siren and lights on top, plus cream and red paint, 125 mm, 1/43 scale, 1962; the casting was also used for #277.
263 Airport Fire Tender, the 266 (see below) E.R.F. casting painted a bright yellow and carrying one ladder, 170 mm, 1/36 scale, 1978.
266 E.R.F. Fire Tender, a big bruiser with a removable wheeled extending ladder on the roof, originally of unpainted metal and gray plastic, later all white; the interior first white, later yellow, the roof-mounted hose reels, spotlight, bell and catwalks of unpainted metal throughout, 200 mm, 1/36 scale, 1975.
266 E.R.F. Fire Tender, the Danish Falck version, 200 mm, 1/36 scale, 1979.
267 Superior Cadillac Ambulance, in white and red, with working lights, opening rear door and removable patient on stretcher, 151 mm, 1/36 scale, 1967; casting also used for #288.
267 Paramedic Truck, with roof bar and Emergency Rescue Squad labels; if it were another color, it might be a utility service truck; 119 mm, 1/36 scale, 1978.
268 Range Rover Ambulance, the 195 casting in white with roof bar, Ambulance labels and patient on stretcher, 107 mm, 1/36 scale, 1973.
271 Ford Transit Fire Engine, the second Ford van with bells and ladder on the roof and Fire Service labels, plus equipment inside, 130 mm, 1/36 scale, 1975.
271 Ford Transit Fire Engine, the same model with red and white Falck Zonen labels, for sale in Denmark, 130 mm, 1/36 scale, 1975 or later.
274 Ford Transit Ambulance, the newest of three Ford van castings, with roof bar, red labels, and the customary patient on a stretcher, 130 mm, 1/36 scale, 1977.
276 Airport Fire Tender, the 259 casting adapted for airport use with a plastic foam nozzle instead of 259's ladder, plus a flashing red light, 117 mm, 1/43 or smaller, 1962.
276 Ford Transit Ambulance, the second casting (like 271), equipped with roof bar and a stretcher, with older type grille and hood than 274, 125 mm, 1/36 scale, 1976.
277 Superior Criterion Ambulance, the 263 casting in metallic blue and white, with room inside its back door for a battery to work its roof light, 125 mm, 1/43 scale, 1962.
278 Vauxhall Victor Ambulance, a petite wagon with raised roof, blue dome light, red cross decals and patient on stretcher, 91 mm, 1/43 scale, 1964.
282 Land Rover Fire Appliance, with ladder, spotlight, hose and pump, plus dome lights and Fire Service labels, 120 mm, 1/36 scale, 1973.
282 Land Rover Fire Appliance—if they call them appliances in Denmark!—complete with Falck labels, 120 mm, 1/36 scale, 1974.
285 Merryweather Marquis Fire Tender, high, stubby and enclosed, with the usual equipment on the roof, plus a working hose, with red or unpainted panel atop the cab, 170 mm, 1/36 scale, 1969.
285 Merryweather Marquis Fire Tender, first in metallic, then non-metallic red, with Falck labels, 170 mm, 1/36 scale, 1974.
286 Ford Transit Fire Appliance, the first Transit van casting, with ladder, lights, labels, and retracting hose inside, 120 mm, 1/43 scale, 1969.
286 Ford Transit Fire Appliance, the same van with Danish Falck Zonen labels, 120 mm, 1/43 scale, 1974.
288 Superior Cadillac Ambulance, the same vehicle as 267 but with a simple red dome light instead of 267's working type, 151 mm, 1/36 scale, 1972.
288 Superior Cadillac Ambulance, white and black at first, by 1975 red and white, with Falck labels, blue dome light and windows, 151 mm, 1/36 scale, 1974.
298 Emergency Services Gift Set, including 263, 276 and 277, 1/43 scale, 1963.
302 Emergency Squad Gift Set, two types shown in catalogs, but never issued, announced in 1977.
304 Fire Rescue Gift Set, with 195, 282 and 384, plus a cardboard cutout of a burning building on the back of the box, 1/36 scale, 1977.
384 Fire Rescue Truck, part of Dinky's Convoy Series of modernistic trucks, with a simple white snorkel arm, basket and nozzle, 120 mm, 1/36 scale, 1976.
385 Los Angeles County Fire Department Truck, a covered Convoy truck with labels by John Gay, 105 mm, 1/36 scale, 1980.
410 Bedford London Fire Brigade Van, with John Gay's labels, 89 mm, about 1/43 scale, 1980 or before.
410 Bedford Manchester Fire Brigade Van, another John Day product, same details.
410 Bedford City Fire Brigade Van, ditto.
410 Bedford Metropolitan Fire Brigade Van, ditto.
410 Bedford Los Angeles County Fire Van, ditto.
412 Bedford Los Angeles County Fire Van, another John Gay labeling, the same basic van as before, now with roof bar and Rescue Squad labels, 89 mm, 1/43 scale, 1980.
416 Ford Transit Falck Van, no data except that it's an authentic Danish issue, not a conversion; Seventies.
442 Land Rover Falck Wrecker, at first in red with white doors, later all red, with blue roof sign, amber lights and red and white Falck labels, 122 mm, 1/36 scale, 1974. (All the Danish issues are sometimes cited as having the letter "d" after their catalog numbers.)
556 Citroen ID19 Ambulance, a long low wagon in gray and ivory, with dome light and Ambulance Municipale decals, 114 mm, 1/43 scale, 1962.
562 Citroen 2cv Fire Engine, the 25d van of 1958, renumbered a year later, 84 mm, 1/43 scale, 1959.
568 Berliet Ladder Truck, with four-door cab, silver rear deck and crank-operated two-section aerial ladder; this version is bright non-metallic red, unlike its 956 reincarnation, 200 mm, 1/43 scale, 1967.

570p Peugeot J7 Fire Department Van, with opening doors, amber light, antenna and coat-of-arms decals, otherwise just another van, 108 mm, 1/43 scale, 1970.
583 Berliet Fire Engine, ex-32e of 1957, 111 mm, 1/43 scale, renumbered in 1959.
624 Daimler Military Ambulance, formerly 30hm, 96 mm, 1/48 scale, renumbered in 1954.
626 Ford Military Ambulance, a rugged army truck with red crosses in white circles on its roof, sides and rear doors, 111 mm, 1/43 scale, 1956.
688 MASH Military Ambulance, announced in 1978 but never issued.
807 Renault Military Ambulance, the last incarnation of what was originally 80f, then 820, this time with plastic base and wheels, 85 mm, 1/55 scale, 1973.
820 Renault Military Ambulance, formerly 80f but not yet 807, with metal base and wheels, 85 mm, 1/55 scale, 1959.
899 Delahaye Ladder Truck, ex-32d of 1955, 167 mm, 1/43 scale, renumbered in 1959.
954 Fire Station, a plastic kit, presumably 1/43 scale, 1961.
955 Fire Engine, ex-555 of 1952, 136 mm, 1/43 scale, 1954.
956 Turntable Fire Escape, with typical British cab and the same ladder as 568—which later replaced it! 210 mm, 1/43 scale, 1958.
956 Turntable Fire Escape, two Falck versions, no other data.
956 Berliet Turntable Fire Escape, the 568 French model, now with metallic dark red cab and completely silver rear body, 200 mm, 1/43 scale, circa 1970.
956 Berliet Turntable Fire Escape, the Danish Falck issue in metallic red and black at first, later metallic red and silver gray, finally nonmetallic red and silver gray, 200 mm, 1/43 scale, 1974.
957 Fire Service Set, containing 257, 955 and the first 956, 1/43 scale, 1959.

The following projected French Dinky models were never put into production:
25br Peugeot D3A Fire Department Van.
525hc Peugeot 404 Fire Department Wagon.
810p Dodge Fire Command Car.
1416p Renault R6 Fire Chief's Car.

Conversions made from Dinky Toys will be found under the headings of the firms that made the conversions, for example Horton and Peover, in the British Kits and Specialty Models chapter.

Corgi Toys

Corgi Toys, in production since 1956, have included such longtime favorites as the 1143 American LaFrance ladder truck and the 1126 and 1127 Simon Snorkels. Corgi's first emergency vehicles were the firefighting and ambulance versions of their Bedford van and bus, while in more recent years the 427 Superior and 406 Mercedes-Benz ambulances and the 1103/1118 Chubb Pathfinder airport crash tender stand out. The Husky and Corgi Junior lines, as well as the Corgi Cubs, Qualitoys and pre-Corgi Mettoys, have also contributed to our list.
18 Emergency Set, including the 482 Range Rover Ambulance and two police vehicles, 1/36 scale, 1975.
20 Emergency Set, likewise including the 482 Range Rover Ambulance plus two police vehicles, 1/36 scale, 1980.
33 Deutsche Lebensrettungsgesellschaft Set, with a Range Rover, motorboat and trailer in German Lifesaving Society colors, 1/36 scale, 1980.
35 Chopper Squad Surf Rescue Set, a blue Jeep and trailer with the same type of boat as used in #33, 1/36 scale, 1978.
213 Jaguar 2.4 Litre Fire Chief, a familiar British sedan with roof sign, bells and shield decals, later upgraded to 213S, with suspension, 97 mm, 1/48 scale, 1959.
213S Jaguar 2.4 Litre Fire Chief, with suspension but otherwise unchanged, 97 mm, 1/48 scale, 1961.
284 Mercedes-Benz 240D Fire Chief, another red sedan, this time a German version with blue dome light and Notruf 112 (emergency phone number) labels, 136 mm, 1/36 scale, 1982.
295 Renault 5TS Fire Chief, a little French type with white and black Sapeurs Pompiers labels on the doors, plus a blue light, 96 mm, 1/36 scale, 1982.
332 Opel Senator Doctor's Car, a white sedan for a change, with chrome roof bar, Notarzt lettering and red cross labels, 142 mm, 1/36 scale, 1980.
354 Commer 15cwt Military Ambulance, a light bus in olive drab, with red cross rondels and blue dome light, same casting as 463 below, 90 mm, 1/43 scale, 1964.
395 Fire Bug, Corgi's G.P. Beach Buggy with blue lights, sirens and ladders, more novelty than fire vehicle, 83 mm, 1/43 scale, 1972.
405 Bedford Utilecon Fire Tender, Corgi's familiar van-type minibus with ladders on the roof, either in red with Fire Dept. decals or in green with A.F.S. (Auxiliary Fire Service, I believe) logo, 81 mm, 1/48 scale, 1956.
405M Bedford Utilecon Fire Tender, the red version of 405 with a flywheel motor and diecast (rather than tinplate) base, 81 mm, 1/48 scale, 1956. The M means Mechanical.
405 Chevrolet Superior Ambulance, a van-based rig in orange and white with raised roof, lights, labels, a stretcher and a medic, 119 mm, 1/36 scale, 1978.
406 Mercedes-Benz Bonna Ambulance, the white worldwide issue with red cross and stripe labels plus Ambulance lettering, 147 mm, 1/36 scale, 1981.
406 Mercedes-Benz Bonna Ambulance, this time in red and white Danish Falck colors; both versions come with stretcher and bearers; 147 mm, 1/36 scale, 1981.
4061 Mercedes-Benz Bonna Ambulance, this time in light cream with red trim for the German market, and with the figures as before, 147 mm, 1/36 scale, 1983.
407 Mercedes-Benz Bonna Ambulance again, the white version without the figures, for the British economy, 147 mm, 1/36 scale, 1981 or later.
412 Bedford Utilecon Ambulance, same casting as 405, in cream with Ambulance decals and opaque rear windows, 81 mm, 1/48 scale, 1957.
414 Bedford Utilecon Military Ambulance, the same model again, now in olive drab with red cross rondels, 81 mm, 1/48 scale, 1961.
421 Forest Fire Warden's Land Rover, in red with appropriate labels, white plastic roof rack and ladder up to it, 132 mm, 1/36 scale, 1978.
423 Bedford Utilecon Fire Tender, an updated 405 with single windshield (405 had a centerpost) and other casting changes, 81 mm, 1/48 scale, 1960.
437 Cadillac Superior Ambulance, in either red and cream or white and light blue, with battery-powered roof light, 114 mm, 1/43 scale, 1962.
439 Chevrolet Impala Fire Chief, first of two Corgi Impalas, with single body casting, either all red with shield labels on the doors, red with white front door labels bearing the shield emblems, or with all four doors painted white and the shield labels on them, 106 mm, 1/43 scale, 1963.
463 Commer 15cwt Ambulance, same casting as 354, in either white or cream, with blue rear windows and dome light and red Ambulance decals, 90 mm, 1/43 scale, 1964.
482 Chevrolet Impala Fire Chief, the second Corgi type, with red upper and white lower body castings and a chrome strip between them, plus the usual shield labels, 106 mm, 1/43 scale, 1965.
482 Range Rover Vigilant Ambulance, with raised roof, dome lights, and either a narrow blue stripe or a wide orange one, 103 mm, 1/43 scale, 1975.
484 AMC Pacer Rescue Car, improbably attired in white, black and orange, with a roof bar and Rescue labels, 124 mm, 1/36 scale, 1978.
513 Citroen ID19 Alpine Rescue Car, a white and red wagon with skis and sled on the roof, plus figures of skier and St. Bernard dog, 103 mm, 1/43 scale, 1970.
700 Motorway Ambulance, a futuristic van-type vehicle in white with blue windows and dome lights, 98 mm, 1/36 scale?, 1974.
703 Hi-Speed Fire Engine, similarly futuristic, with its ladder attached to a base that pivots out to the side, 115 mm, 1/36 scale?, 1976.
1001 HCB-Angus Firestreak Firefighter, a big red rescue van with equipment and figures; this first version has clear windows, 165 mm, 1/36 scale, 1980.
1001 HCB-Angus Firestreak Firefighter, the second version with opaque windows and no interior or figures, 165 mm, 1/36 scale, 1982; may have been renumbered 1011.
1008 Chevrolet Caprice Fire Chief, a big American sedan with roof bar and Fire Chief labels, plus a battery-operated siren, 148 mm, 1/36 scale, 1982.
1103 Chubb Pathfinder Airport Crash Truck, the first version, with operating pump and siren, 240 mm, 1/36 scale, 1975.
1118 Chubb Pathfinder Airport Crash Truck, the revised version without the siren, 240 mm, 1/36 scale, 1981.
1120 Dennis Aerial Ladder Truck, long and sleek, using the 1126 snorkel body and a forward-facing three-section ladder inherited from 1143, 195 mm, 1/36 scale, 1984.
1126 Simon Snorkel, Corgi's second type, with long Dennis cab, white plastic snorkel arms, and two hose reels, 265 mm, 1/36 scale, 1977.
1127 Bedford Simon Snorkel, first of two versions, with diecast snorkel arms and a short cab with open rear where three men sit, 252 mm, 1/43 scale, 1964.
1143 American LaFrance Aerial Ladder Truck, a real classic, with open cab, three-section yellow ladder plus shorter ladders stowed below, other equipment and figures; its decals are either white or silver, its wheels either red or silver diecast or chrome plastic, 105 mm, 1/43 scale, 1968 through 1983.
1185 Mack Fire Truck, Corgi Junior 2029 reincarnated, still with Hammond labels, 135 mm, about O gauge, 1984.

HUSKY

The Husky line was Corgi's small-scale series from 1964 through 1969; it was renamed Corgi Junior in 1970.
4 Jaguar Mark X Fire Chief, earlier and smaller of the two, in red with

a swiveling roof-mounted spotlight and Fire labels, 66 mm, S gauge, 1964.
4 Jaguar Mark X Fire Chief, a larger casting in darker red, otherwise the same, 71 mm, S gauge, 1967.
6 Citroen Safari Ambulance, in white with blue dome light, plus a red cross in a circle on the hood, 64 mm, S gauge, 1964.
22 Citroen Safari Military Ambulance, the same model in olive drab, 64 mm, S gauge, 1965.
30 Studebaker Wagonaire Ambulance, a white wagon with sliding roof panel, opening tailgate and removable stretcher, 75 mm, S gauge, 1966.
36 Simon Snorkel Fire Engine, with operating two-arm snorkel and basket, 79 mm, S gauge, 1967. Renumbered 29 in the Corgi Junior series.

CORGI JUNIOR

The name of the small series was changed to Corgi Junior in 1970; it was greatly expanded over the years, and most models were fitted with fast wheels. In the last few years many special versions have been made for various national markets.
1 Mercedes-Benz 220D Ambulance, either all white or with a red roof, plus blue windows and dome light, 76 mm, S gauge, 1977.
22 Chevrolet Paramedic Emergency Unit, a white Chevy van with red and black labels, 68 mm, S gauge, 1981.
26 ERF Fire Engine, a typical British fire truck with a ladder on top, the first version with grille, hose reels and rear details supplied by the base casting, the second much simplified, with black plastic base, 76 mm, S gauge, 1970.
29 Simon Snorkel Fire Engine, the Husky 36 type with wheels and tires, and a Corgi Juniors label on its base, later with fast wheels and the lettering cast into the base, 79 mm, S gauge, 1970.
29 ERF Simon Snorkel Fire Engine, a new casting, with an orange snorkel, originally a diecast base, later an orange plastic one, 75 and 76 mm, S gauge, 1972.
30 Studebaker Wagonaire Ambulance, basically the same model as Husky 30, first with opening tailgate and Corgi Juniors lettering along the center of the base, next with big Whizzwheels lettering on the base and wheels to match, last with smaller lettering, mag wheels and two sirens on the roof, 75 mm, S gauge, 1970.
33 Chevrolet Ambulance Van, announced in 1977 but apparently not issued; it would have used the same 68 mm casting as the #22 Paramedic Van.
36 Healer Wheeler, a futuristic van with blue dome light and either red cross rondels or labels with Ambulance lettering and a red cross, 76 mm, S gauge, 1973.
42 Rescue Team Range Rover, in tangerine orange with high roof, blue dome lights and black Rescue Team lettering on yellow stripes, 69 mm, S gauge, 1977.
56 Ford Capri Fire Chief, in red with white hood, blue light and either red Fire or black Fire Chief labels, 75 mm, S gauge, 1971.
70 Mercury Cougar Fire Chief, in red with blue lights and yellow labels, 75 mm, S gauge, 1975.
70 Ford Gran Torino Fire Chief, with opaque windows, red roof light and smaller labels than the Cougar, 75 mm, S gauge, 1977.
79 Land Rover Military Ambulance, with red cross labels on its olive plastic cover, 71 mm, S gauge, 1975.
119 Chubb Pathfinder Airport Crash Tender, a miniature 1103, this one in Flughafen-Feuerwehr form for sale in Germany, 74 mm, S gauge or smaller, 1983.
123 Chubb Pathfinder Airport Crash Tender, the worldwide issue, with Airport Rescue lettering, 74 mm, S gauge or smaller, 1982.
192 Mercedes-Benz 220D Ambulance, the Arabian version, all white with red crescent and two-language lattering, 76 mm, S gauge, 1983.
193 Chubb Pathfinder Airport Crash Tender, another Arabian issue, with decks and nozzle in cream instead of yellow, plus Arabic logo, 74 mm, S gauge or smaller, 1983.
208 Ford Sierra Doctor's Car, a German issue, in white with red trim, blue lights and Notarzt lettering, 75 mm, S gauge, 1983.
225 Chubb Pathfinder Airport Crash Tender, the Swiss version, which may be just like the German, 74 mm, S gauge or smaller, 1983.
227 Mercedes-Benz 220D Ambulance, Swiss issue, details not known, S gauge, 1983.
250 ERF Simon Snorkel Fire Engine, a Danish issue with red Brandbil lettering on the upper snorkel arm, 76 mm, S gauge, 1983; the last 29 casting.
251 ERF Fire Tender, #26 in Danish form, with white Falck emblems on the doors, 76 mm, S gauge, 1983.
252 Ford Transit Wrecker, another Danish issue, in red with Falck labels, for rescue service, 73 mm, S gauge, 1983.
253 Mercedes-Benz 220D Ambulance, in white and red with Danish Falck labels, 76 mm, S gauge, 1983.
254 Mercedes-Benz 240D Emergency Car, a white sedan with red Falck labels, 76 mm, S gauge, 1983.
255 Chevrolet Rescue Van, last of the six Danish issues, in red with white Falck labels, 68 mm, S gauge, 1983.
2029 Mack Fire Pumper, a realistic American fire truck with plenty of equipment and Hammond Fire Dept. labels, 143 mm, about O gauge, 1979.
2029 Fire Pumper, a privately made combination of the open cab from 1143 and the rest of the Mack, 135 mm, about O gauge, early Eighties.
2513 Fire Engine (26) and **Healer Wheeler (36),** packed together, 1977.
2521 Army Ambulance (79) and **Helicopter** packed together, 1977.
3013 Emergency Rescue Set, a building and three vehicles, 1977.
3022 Rescue Set, a building and five vehicles, including several nonstandard versions, 1976.
3026 Emergency Set, accessories and six vehicles, 1976.
3053 Fire Station Set, building and three vehicles, 1977.
3101 Fire Set, accessories and six vehicles, 1980.
3103 Emergency Set, accessories and six vehicles, 1980.
3110 Emergency Set, including five vehicles, 1982.

CORGI CUBS

Corgi Cubs are a series of simple, inexpensive toy vehicles made for playing. They were introduced in 1976, and include three emergency vehicles:
505 Fire Chief's Car, a red wagon with white base, 106 mm, roughly O gauge, 1976.
510 Fire Truck, a pickup with a hose reel, 98 mm, about O gauge, 1976.
511 Ambulance, a white van with red base, 99 mm, about O gauge, 1976.
600 Corgi Cubs Set, with the three vehicles listed above and a police car, 1976.

CORGI QUALITOYS

Qualitoys were a series of toy trucks intended, like the Cubs, for children to play with; they included one emergency vehicle:
707 Fire Engine, a snub-nosed red and yellow truck that carried ladders and other equipment that mine lacks, 137 mm, larger than O gauge, 1975. See C-R Vol. II, p. 15, for a fully equipped specimen.

METTOYS

Mettoys were large-scale metal toys made by another branch of the firm that made Corgi Toys. The sizes differ considerably, though all Mettoys are larger than O gauge
604a Fire Chief's Car, a Standard sedan, 100 mm, 1954.
633 Fire Engine, a light truck with ladder and hose, 125 mm, 1953.
723-1 Ambulance, a van type, 170 mm, 1957 or before.
725 Fire Engine, a closed-cab truck with ladder and working pump, 175 mm, 1954.
726 Fire Engine, with body like 725, aerial ladder and siren, 180 mm, 1954.
752 Fire Chief's Car, an Austin sedan, with siren, 160 mm, 1958.
850 Fire Engine, with three ladders on racks, 190 mm, 1948.
902 Fire Chief's Car is erroneous, it should be 909/2.
909/2 Fire Chief's Car, looking rather like a Packard sedan, with Joytown Fire Service lettering, 240 mm, 1954.
3102/2 Fire Engine, an open-cab oldtimer with two men and a tilting ladder, 300 mm, 1949.
3102/3 Fire Engine, apparently unchanged from 3102/2, 300 mm, 1952. The new number may indicate a minor change.
3104 Fire Engine, a venerable closed-cab type with tilting ladder, plus seated firemen behind the cab, 300 mm, 1948.
3110 Fire Engine, with open cab, seated firemen and aerial ladder, 380 mm, 1946.
3110/2 Fire Engine, as above, 380 mm, 1952.
3110/3 Fire Engine, with a bell in place of some of the men, 380 mm, 1954.
3307 Fire Chief's Car, perhaps a Singer or Riley sedan, probably about 160 mm, 1954.
3321 Fire Tender, a sleek van with a ladder on the roof, 160 mm, 1951.
3322 Fire Chief's Car, probably a two-door Morris, 160 mm, 1952.
3323 Ambulance, with operating siren, 160 mm, 1954.

6201/1022 Joytown Fire Station, a garage housing 3321 and 3322, 210 mm, 1951.
8287 Fire Escape, an open-cab semi-trailer with driver and aerial ladder, 560 mm, 1959, made of polythene.
8288 Pumping Fire Engine, also with open cab and driver, plus a ladder, hose reel and working pump, 405 mm, 1960, made of polythene.

Matchbox

The Matchbox Series and its relatives (Models of Yesteryear, King Size, Two-Packs etc.), made since the Fifties by Lesney Products and in the last few years by Universal International, have included many emergency vehicles, beginning with the #9 Dennis Fire Escape and #14 Daimler Ambulance and continuing through the years with a parade of newer firefighting and rescue equipment. The Yesteryear models have included the horsedrawn Shand-Mason steamer as well as the Rolls-Royce fire engine; the King Size series has offered several fire trucks and ambulances, plus more specialized models for the German, French and Danish markets; and the Code Red series resurrected several emergency vehicles that had seen service in the Matchbox Series itself, two of which became popular enough to win new places in the regular series. This interchange, the application of Superfast wheels, and the Matchbox tradition of updating models and materials have all enriched the Matchbox specialist's collection by creating an awesome array of variations. Our photographs will show some major varieties; for complete information the reader is referred to *Matchbox Toys*, by Nancy Schiffer.

MATCHBOX SERIES (Pre-Superfast)

3 Mercedes-Benz Binz Ambulance, a classic conventional design, with a stretcher inside, 73 mm, 1/69 scale, 1968.
9 Dennis Fire Escape, a typical English ladder truck with open cab, hose reel and cast-in extending ladder on wheels, 58 mm, 1/100 scale, 1955.
9 Merryweather Fire Engine, again in the English tradition but more modern, with fully enclosed body and a ladder on the roof, 63 mm, 1/93 scale, 1959.
14 Daimler Ambulance, another classic type, the earlier and smaller of two versions, 48 mm, 1/100 scale, 1956.
14 Daimler Ambulance, a somewhat larger model of the same vehicle, 58 mm, 1/86 scale, 1958.
14 Bedford Lomas Ambulance, a more modern design in the same tradition, with detailed interior and opening rear doors, 67 mm, 1/81 scale, 1982.
29 Fire Pumper, a typical American type with closed cab, hose bed and reels, ladder and suction hose, and Denver decals, 76 mm, 1/104 scale, 1965.
54 S. & S. Cadillac Ambulance, the usual American type before vans took over, with roof lights and detailed interior, 71 mm, 1/87 scale, 1965.
57 Land Rover Fire Truck, fully enclosed, with a ladder on the roof, details at the rear and Kent Fire Brigade logo, 65 mm, 1/77 scale, 1966.
59 Ford Fairlane Fire Chief, a red American sedan with white dome light. 4Fire Chief lettering, and the Kent arms as on #57, 65 mm, 1/80 scale, 1963.
59 Ford Galaxie Fire Chief, the Fairlane's replacement, much the same except for a blue dome light, 75 mm, 1/73 scale, 1966.
63 Ford 3-Ton 4 x 4 Service Ambulance, a rugged van in olive drab with red cross rondels, 63 mm, 1/100 scale, 1959.
63 Foamite Airport Crash Tender, stubby and strong, with gold nozzle, silver rear end and white hose, ladder and lettering, 58 mm, 1/93 scale, 1964.

SUPERFAST MATCHBOX SERIES

3 Mercedes-Benz Binz Ambulance, the earlier model with also used in olive drab military form in a Two-Pack, 73 mm, 1/69 scale, 1970.
12 Citroen CX Ambulance, sleek and modern, with two blue lights and red and black lettering and trim, 77 mm, S gauge, 1983.
13 Snorkel Fire Engine, with GMC cab, a pump on the front bumper, and a yellow snorkel arm with a fireman cast into the bucket, 77 mm, 1/86 scale, 1982.
18 Aerial Ladder Truck, with a wide body, six wheels and a two-section extending ladder on a swiveling base, 77 mm, S gauge or smaller, 1984.
20 Range Rover Military Ambulance, usually a police vehicle but this time in olive drab with Ambulance labels, 72 mm, 1/61 scale, circa 1980.
22 Blaze Buster, almost too modern to be true, with chrome interior, Fire labels and a plastic ladder, 77 mm, 1/90 scale, 1976.
23 Volkswagen Army Ambulance, a version of a VW bus used only in a Two-Pack, 69 mm, S gauge, 1977.
25 Chevrolet Pacific Ambulance, the #41 casting (see below) returned from the Code Red set with a new number, 75 mm, S gauge, 1981.
29 Fire Pumper, the previous model with Superfast wheels and without Denver decals, 76 mm, 1/104 scale, 1970.
35 Merryweather Marquis Fire Engine, a modern British truck with London Fire Service labels and the usual ladder on top, 76 mm, 1/86 scale, 1970.
41 Chevrolet Ambulance, a modern van-type in several versions, including the orange-striped 1984 issue, and also used as a toy show promo, plus the Code Red #99 and subsequent #25, 75 mm, S gauge, 1978.
41 Chevrolet Ambulance, a mostly red German version with Notarzt lettering, 75 mm, S gauge, 1979.
41 Chevrolet Ambulance, in silver with Rallye Paris-Dakar labels—I hope it's still an ambulance!—75 mm, S gauge, 1981.
46 Stretcha-Fetcha, a fanciful ultramodern Ambulance with blue lights and windows, red crosses and detailed interior, 70 mm, S gauge, 1972.
46 Stretcha-Fetcha, in red with German Unfall Rettung (Accident Rescue) labels, 70 mm, S gauge, Seventies. **8 Mercedes-Benz Unimog Rescue Truck,** a yellow 4 x 4 with snowplow, amber lights, white cover and red Rescue lettering, 77 mm, S gauge, 1983.
54 S. & S. Cadillac Ambulance, now with Superfast wheels, 1/87 scale, 1970.
57 Land Rover Fire Truck, Superfast now, 65 mm, 1/77 scale, 1970.
57 Carmichael Police Rescue Vehicle, a white six-wheeler with ladders on the roof and other equipment in back, plus an orange stripe, 77 mm, S gauge, 1981.
57 Carmichael Fire Rescue Vehicle, the same model in red with white trim, 77 mm, S gauge, 1983.
59 Ford Galaxie Fire Chief, with Superfast wheels, 75 mm, 1/73 sca[le,] 1970.
59 Mercury Fire Chief, a red sedan with blue dome light and Fi[re] Chief lettering; early issues still had the Kent arms on the doors, 7[?] mm, 1/72 scale, 1971.
63 Snorkel Fire Truck, a reworking of the #35 Merryweather fi[re] made for the Code Red set, then put into the regular seri[es] unchangwed, later given new labels, 76 mm, 1/86 scale, 1983.
64 Fire Chief, a sort of Javelin-Torino blend with blue windows an[d] dome light, plus Fire labels, 75 mm, 1/65 scale, 1976.
64 Airport Foam Monitor, a heavy red and white truck with a rotatin[g] nozzle on the roof, Foam Unit lettering and checkerboard trim, als[o] issued in yellow with red trim, 76 mm, S gauge or smaller, 1984.

CODE RED

93 Snorkel Fire Truck, a chopped-down #35 Merryweather with open cab and a big white snorkel including a man in the bucket, 76 mm, 1/86 scale, 1981; later #63.
95 Fire Pumper, the old #29 moved from Denver to Los Angeles, growing a big white nozzle in the process, 76 mm, 1/104 scale, 1981.
96 Mercury Fire Chief, the last #59 type with a new roof bar and Los Angeles City Fire Department lettering, 77 mm, 1/72 scale, 1981.
99 Chevrolet Ambulance, the #41 casting with the Pacific Ambulance logo that went with it to reenter the Matchbox Series as #25, 75 mm, S gauge, 1981.

TWO-PACKS

TP2 Police Car and Fire Engine (#35 Merryweather), 1979.
TP2 Police Car and Fire Engine (#22 Blaze Buster), 1980.
TP7 Fire Chief (#59 Mercury) and Ambulance (#46 Stretcha-Fetcha), 1976.
TP7 Fire Chief (#64) and Ambulance (#46 Stretcha-Fetcha), 1976.
TP10 Fire Chief (#59 Mercury) and Ambulance (#3 Mercedes), 1978.
TP12 Military Ambulance (#23 VW) and Jeep, 1977.
TP12 Military Ambulance (#23 VW) and Field Car, 1979.
TP14 Military Ambulance (#3 Mercedes) and Staff Car, 1979.
TP109 Citroen Marine Rescue Unit, #12 Ambulance pulling a boat on a trailer, no other data, 1984.
TP110 Matra Rancho Surf Rescue Unit, likewise with a boat trailer, no other data, 1984.
TP112 Rescue Unimog (#48) and Trailer, with Alpine Rescue logo, 162 mm, 1984.

CONVOY SERIES

CY13 Fire Engine, an odd-looking semi-trailer rig with an aerial ladder, 168 mm, S gauge, 1984.

MODELS OF YESTERYEAR

Y2 Model T Ford Fire Truck, a privately made 'chop' with open cab, hose reel, and racks holding a ladder longer than the Ford itself, 76 mm, 1/42 scale, Seventies.
Y4 Shand-Mason Horsedrawn Fire Engine, one of Lesney's all-time favorite models, first with white horses and Kent Fire Brigade decals, later black horses and London Fire Brigade, 89 mm, 1/63 scale, 1961.
Y5 Talbot 1927 London Fire Brigade Van, privately made, no other data, 1981.
Y6 Rolls-Royce 1920 Fire Engine, with open cab, benches for firefighters, and ladders (tan or white), most recently with a black chassis, 110 mm, 1/48 scale, 1977.
Y13 Crossley 1918 R.A.F. Red Cross Tender, in R.A.F. blue with tan covers and red cross labels, 95 mm, 1.47 scale, 1973.
Y13 Crossley 1918 Fire Truck, privately made from the above, with tanks, hose reel and ladders, 95 mm, 1/47 scale, Seventies.
Y25 Renault 1910 Ville de Paris Ambulance, in olive with white logo, a privately made conversion, no other data. Other private conversions of Yesteryears also exist.

KING SIZE

K6 Mercedes-Benz Binz Ambulance, #3 in larger scale; inside is an occupied stretcher with removable blanket; 105 mm, 1/45 scale, 1967; later K26, then K63.
K9 Fire Tender, with stylized cab, lots of amber glass, and two-section aerial ladder, plus a visible motor, 155 mm, 1/55 scale, 1973.
K11 Emergency Wrecker, just another tow truck until the red Falck-Zonen version was sold in Denmark, 127 mm, 1/35 scale, 1976.
K15 Merryweather Fire Engine, a good model of a British aerial ladder truck, with Kent Fire Brigade lettering and arms, 152 mm, 1/60 scale, 1963.
K26 Mercedes-Benz Binz Ambulance, the formerly cream K3, now in white with blue Ambulance labels, 105 mm, 1/45 scale, 1971; later K63.
K38 Dodge Ambulance, a white van with orange trim, blue emblems, amber lights, two attendants and a stretcher, 128 mm, larger than O gauge, 1980.
K38 Dodge Ambulance, the German issue, with blue lights and black Notarzt lettering, and its orange stripe lower, 128 mm, large scale, 1980.
K39 ERF Snorkel Fire Engine, a big fellow with white snorkel, red basket and ladders, black hose and firemen, County Fire Department lettering and a coat of arms that, for once, is not the Prancing Horse of Kent, 260 mm, O gauge or larger, 1980.
K40 Blaze Trailer, the K32 Shovel Nose casting in red with blue lights and yellow Fire Chief labels, 100 mm, 1/44 scale, 1972.
K49 Ambulance, in white with red raised roof, carrying the K3 patient, whose stretcher now has handles, though his blanket is faded, 110 mm, 1/45 scale, 1973.
K49 Ambulance, in red with white roof and Malteser Hilfsdienst labels, made for Germany, where the Maltese Cross has given its name to those who use it as an emblem, 110 mm, 1/45 scale, 1978.
K53 Hot Fire Engine, an antique car/hot rod with chrome boiler and bell, yellow ladder, fireman driver and Fire Chief labels, 113 mm, 1/45 mm, 1976.
K62 Citroen SM Doctor's Emergency Car, with cast-in roof bar, amber windows and dome light, red crosses and trim, and black lettering, 111 mm, 1/43 scale, 1977.
K63 Mercedes-Benz Binz Ambulance, originally K3, unchanged from K26 except that mine is whiter than new, still with K26 on the base, 105 mm, 1/45 scale, 1977.
K64 Fire Control Range Rover, a well-equipped first-strike vehicle, with yellow tailgate and lettering and two gold-helmeted black firefighters, 117 mm, O gauge, 1978.
K64 Fire Control Range Rover, the same vehicle with Falck Zonen labels for the Danish market, 117 mm, O gauge, 1978.
K65 Plymouth Emergency Rescue Truck, a covered red pickup with winch, spotlight, sirens, a patient on a stretcher and an attendant, 128 mm, O gauge, 1978.
K65 Plymouth Emergency Rescue Truck, in the green and white (so is the formerly blue attendant) of the Bergrettungswacht, for German mountain rescue service, 128 mm, O gauge, 1978.
K67 Dodge Monaco Fire Chief, an American wagon with roof bar, in two versions: County Brigade Headquarters Fire Chief, in red and white with blue roof lights, and City of Hackensack, New Jersey, in greenish yellow and white with red lights, 123 mm, O gauge, 1978.
K75 Airport Fire Tender, a yellow Plymouth pickup, its white rear top laden with equipment, a winch at the front and two firefighters, 130 mm, O gauge, 1979.
K75 Airport Fire Tender, with Flughafen-Feuerwehr lettering for the German market, 130 mm, O gauge, 1979.
K75 Airport Fire Tender, the same model with French Securite Aeroport logo, 130 mm, O gauge, 1979.
K77 Highway Rescue Truck, another Plymouth pickup, white and open in back, with a snowplow in front, 143 mm, O gauge, 1979.
K77 Highway Rescue Truck, the same model with Strassen Service labels, as a German road service truck, 143 mm, O gauge, 1979.
K77 Highway Rescue Truck, this time with Secours Routier labels, for sale in France, 143 mm, O gauge, 1979.
K94 Crash Tender, announced in 1982 but a victim of cost-cutting when the firm changed hands, it seems.
K96 Volvo Ambulance, adaptedfrom an estate car, with orange roof and interior, blue windows, red crosses and trim, and two bearers with a stretcher, 134 mm, O gauge or larger, 1983.
K104 Matra Rancho Coast Guard Car and Rescue Boat, no data, 1983.
K110 Magirus-Deutz Fire Tender, a realistic model with closed cab and two-section aerial ladder, 140 mm, O gauge, 1984.
BK112 DAF Ambulance, the only Battle King in this list, an olive drab army truck with tan rear cover and red crosses, 93 mm, O gauge, 1977.

OTHER

G-5 Fire Station Set, comprising the MF-1 Fire Station, 29 pumper, 54 Cadillac Ambulance and 59 Ford Galaxie Fire Chief, 1966.
G-7 Emergency Action Pack, no data, 1984 or before.
G-10 Fire Station Set, with the MF-1 Fire Station, 14 Lomas Ambulance, 59 Fairlane Fire Chief and two 9 Merryweathers, 1964.
MF-1 Fire Station, the red and white plastic firehouse by itself, 235 mm, 1/75 scale, 1964.
MX-6 Fire Rescue Site, with the K15 Ladder Truck, a plastic burning building, two girls and a fireman to rescue them, a roadway and electric controls, 1972.
58 01 01 Emergency Station, a garage with catapults, out of which two King Size emergency vehicles can come hurtling; made in Hong Kong, 1973.
WD-1 Mickey Mouse Fire Truck, with open cab up front filled to overflowing by himself, and a six-rung gray ladder in back, 75 mm, unknown scale, 1979.

British Kits and Specialty Models

A number of British manufacturers and enthusiasts have produced models of emergency vehicles, some in readymade form, others as kits, still others as adaptations of commercially available toys. These limited-production items include models of many fire vehicles and ambulances not otherwise available to the hobbyist. We have not been able to obtain full data on them all.

AIRFIX (Plastic kits)

A2024V R.A.F. Emergency Set, with a military crash tender and ambulance, OO gauge, Ambulance 70 mm, Crash Tender 87 mm, Postwar.

BARNES (metal kits)

#? Merryweather Musketeer Airport Fire Tender, 1/43 scale, 1984.

BROOKLIN (readymade metal)

5 Ford 1930 Fire Department Coupe, with New Orleans Fire Department lettering, 96 mm, 1/43 scale, 1983.
5 Ford 1930 Fire Department Coupe, this time as a Philadelphia Bureau of Fire chief's car, 96 mm, 1/43 scale, 1984, made for Miniature Toys Inc.
9 Ford 1940 Emergency Ambulance, in City of Springfield livery, 113 mm, 1/43 scale, 1983.
9 Ford 1940 Emergency Ambulance, with Nutmeg Ambulance lettering, 113 mm, 1/43 scale, 1983, made for Miniature Auto Sales.
9 Ford 1940 Emergency Ambulance, the Philadelphia Bureau of Fire version for M.T.I., 113 mm, 1/43 scale, 1984.
16 Dodge 1936 Fire Department Van, in Litchfield Volunteer Fire Department livery for Miniature Auto Sales, 96 mm, 1/43 scale, 1983.
16 Dodge 1936 Fire Department Van, as a Philadelphia Bureau of Fire rescue van, completing the M.T.I. set, 96 mm, 1/43 scale, 1984.

DAVE JONES (metal kits)

2 Renault K2 1924 Fire Tender, 1/43 scale, 1975.

HIGHWAY MODELS (metal kits)

Dennis F12 Fire Engine with Ladder, a 1954 truck with a wheeled extending ladder on the roof, 1/76 scale, early Eighties.

8 Leyland-Metz TL Fire Engine, an open-cab 1935 veteran dominated by its long aerial ladder, 1/76 scale, 1982.
13 AEC-Merryweather Fire Engine, a 1951 model much like the Dennis, again with a wheeled ladder on top, 1/76 scale, 1982.
15 Dennis-Metz F17 Ladder Truck, another 1954 type with the same cab as #5, with rear-mounted aerial ladder, 1/76 scale, 1983.
16 Dennis 1940 Fire Pump Trailer, with a length of suction hose on each side of the pump, 1/76 scale, 1983.
18 Leyland FT4A Fire Engine, a 1939 "Pump Escape" with open cab, hose reel and connections, and wheeled ladder, 1/76 scale, 1983.

HORTON or R.S.H. (metal kits)

T1 Bedford Fire Rescue Tender, the familiar Dinky van with ladder on top, equipment hatch on the side and Fire Rescue Unit logo, 89 mm, O gauge, 1978.
T2 Bedford Falck Tender, the same van with the same fittings and Falck logo, 89 mm, O gauge, 1978.
T3 Bedford Fire Control Unit, with roof sign and light, plus red and white checkered trim, 89 mm, O gauge, 1978.
T4 Ford Emergency Tender, a conversion kit for the Matchbox K29 van, with flashing roof light and West Yorkshire Fire Service logo, large scale, no other data, 1979.
T5 Ford Emergency Tender, the same conversion kit, this time in Shropshire Fire Brigade livery, large scale, no other data, 1979.
T6 Bedford Airport Fire Tender conversion kit, for Matchbox K26 or K28, with a big foam nozzle atop the cab, large scale, 1980.
T7 Dennis Fire Pump Trailer, 1/50 scale, 1982.
T8 Crossley 1918 Fire Tender, conversion kit for Matchbox Y13, O gauge, 1981.
T9 Ford 1930 Model A Chemical Fire Tender, conversion kit for Matchbox Y21, O gauge, 1983.
T10 Barton Pump and Ladder Kit, conversion for Eligor or Matchbox Yesteryear vans, 1/43 scale, 1983.
T11 Land Rover Angloco Emergency Tender, 1/50 scale, 1984.
T12 Renault 1920 First Aid Fire Tender, an open truck with ladder, hose reels and benches for the firemen, no other data, 1984.
#? Bedford Fire Tender, 1/50 scale, 1984.
#? Carmichael Range Rover Fire Truck, 1/50 scale, 1984.
#? Carmichael Land Rover Fire Truck, 1/50 scale, 1984.

These three models were mentioned in British magazines, but are not listed in the catalog Mr. Horton sent me; they may be one-offs, or be conversions using his spare parts.

MODEL FIRE SERVICE (presumably metal kits)

Fire Chief's Car, an open two-seater, 1/43 scale, 1984.
Fire Tender with Escape ladder, 1/43 scale, 1984.
Fire Tender with Two Ladders, 1/43 scale, 1984.
Fire Tender with Hose and Ladders, 1/43 scale, 1984.
Fire Hose Truck, 1/43 scale, 1984.

M. R. M. (presumably readymade)

#? Fire Pump Trailer, a reissue of the prewar Taylor & Barrett model, O gauge, 1983.

PEOVER MODEL PROMOTIONS (conversions)

PM1 Bedford Limerick City Fire Truck, the Dinky van in white with a red stripe, 90 mm, O gauge, 1984.
PM2 Bedford Northern Ireland Fire Truck, the same van in red with three logo types, 90 mm, O gauge, 1984. The types are:
Fire School
Hydrant Service
Breathing Apparatus
PM3 Ford Escort Northern Ireland Fire Department Van, the Corgi van in red with Fire Brigade and Hydrant Service lettering, 118 mm, 1/36 scale, 1984.
PM4 Renault 5TS Fire Department Car, the Corgi model with Service Departemental d'Incendie et de Secours logo, 95 mm, 1/36 scale, 1984.
PM5 Land Rover Fire Truck, a white Solido in Cambridgeshire Fire and Rescue Service trim, 104 mm, 1/43 scale, 1984.
PM/RSH T8 Crossley 1918 Fire Tender, based on Ralph Horton's Matchbox Yesteryear conversion, 111 mm, O gauge, 1984.
PM/RSH T9 Ford Model A Chemical Fire Engine, in three color variations, 113 mm, O gauge, 1984:
T9a Gray body, Sharon Vol. Fire Dept. logo.
T9b White body, Rockdale Park Vol. Fire Dept. logo.
T9c red body, Modesco Vol. Fire Dept. logo.
PM/RSH T10a Ford Model A Fire Tender, with Barton pump and ladder, another Yesteryear conversion, this one in white and green with Irish Hills Fire Dept. logo, 115 mm, O gauge, 1984.
PM/RSH T10b Talbot Fire Brigade Van, Yesteryear-based again, with a ladder on the roof, 93 mm, O gauge, 1984.
PM30 Peugeot Ambulance, a white Solido J7 bus with roof vent, blue lights and two similar logo types, long and short, 92 mm, 1/43 scale, 1984.
PM31 Talbot Ambulance, a Yesteryear conversion with either Stirling, Dorking or Welshpool lettering, 98 mm, O gauge, 1984.
PM32 Crossley Ambulance, likewise Yesteryear-based, in black and white finish, 95 mm, O gauge, 1984.

I assume the models with RSH included in their catalog numbers are based on Ralph Horton kits; the others are converted wholly by Dave Spencer, proprietor of Peover Model Productions.

PIRATE MODELS (metal kits)

#? Leyland London Fire Brigade Control Unit, an unusual model of an adapted bus, 1/43 scale, 1979.

SMITH

DAF Fire Tender, with red cab, red or silver body, and an aerial ladder on top, about 135 mm, O gauge, 1980 (C-R Vol. II, p. 125).

SUN MOTOR COMPANY (readymade metal models)

101F De Soto Fire Department Ambulance, 1/43 scale, 1985.
104 Mercedes-Benz 1982 Fire Truck, a Brazilian Arpra casting with rear body by Sun, 1/43 scale, 1984.
106 Leyland Lioness 1930 Fire Truck, 1/43 scale, 1985.
205 Studebaker-Heil Fire Truck, based on the familiar old Dinky Toys tank truck, 112 mm, O gauge, 1983.

TRANSPORT REPLICAS (metal kits)

#? Dennis 1914 Fire Engine with Ladder, 1/76 scale, no other data.

VETERAN & VINTAGE (presumably readymade metal models)

7015 Fire Pump Trailer, the ex-Taylor and Barrett type more recently made by M.R.M., O gauge, postwar.

Other British Models

There remain numerous other British firms which have contributed diecast, plastic or sheet metal models and toys to our list. They range from well-known manufacturers such as Budgie, Lone Star, Spot-On and Tri-Ang Minic to lesser-known firms such as Timpo, Toby, Wells Brimtoy and Castle Art. Some of their products are scale models of real emergency vehicles, while others are unrealistic but still intriguing toys with personalities all their own. The prewar products of Britains, Johillco, and Taylor and Barrett take us back to another era, and the present-day Lledo "Models of Days Gone" take us even farther back.
Arnold Fire Engine, a sheet metal toy in typical British style, with a ladder on the roof, about 175 mm, O gauge or larger, Fifties (C-R Vol. II, p. 117).

BENBROS

Benbros is short for Benson Brothers, makers of the small-scale Mighty Midgets and the O-gauge Zebra Toys, both of which are represented here.
9 Fire Engine, an enclosed Dennis truck carrying a wheeled fire

escape ladder, 61 mm, 1/100 scale, Fifties; this and the next model are Mighty Midgets.
38 Daimler Ambulance, the older, more squarish type, in cream including the wheels, with a red cross on the roof, 58 mm, HO or larger scale, Fifties. 27 Daimler Ambulance, the larger Zebra model of a newer, more rounded type, with driver, open side windows and opening rear doors, 103 mm, O gauge, Fifties; also numbered 107.

BRIMTOY

Wells Brimtoys include both diecast and sheet metal vehicles, but as far as I know, no diecast Brimtoys qualify for our list, leaving only:
537 Ambulance, a sheet metal rear box on a plastic truck chassis-cab, 85mm, no other data, Fifties.

BRITAINS

One of England's pioneer toymakers, specializing in military and agricultural models, offers one doubtful prewar product and several more recent ambulances.
#? Army Ambulance, much resembling the old Tootsietoy Federal trucks; this may be a private repaint of an originally all-olive military truck, 73 mm, about S gauge, Twenties or Thirties.
#? Army Ambulance, prewar type, big and angular, with opening doors, driver, sheet metal rear body and a patient on a stretcher inside, 152 mm, large scale, prewar (probably thirties).
#? Army Ambulance, postwar type, with more rounded lines, and painted olive rather than khaki, with the same basic details including the man on the stretcher, 157 mm, large scale, early postwar.
617 Ambulance, a van casting from the Lilliput series, in cream, 75 mm, 1/76 scale, 1956.
618 Army Ambulance, the same model in olive drab, 75 mm, 1/76 scale, 1956.

BUDGIE

The Budgie firm grew out of Morestone (Morris and Stone), then was bought by Guitermans; the line includes both small-scale models and a larger series of diecast commercial and public service vehicles.
20 Austin Countryman Ambulance, a white wagon with red dome light and Emergency lettering, plus a red diecast base, 67 mm, 1/86 scale, Sixties.
27 Wolseley Fire Chief, a typically British sedan in red with two sirens on the roof, 66 mm, 1/86 scale, Sixties.
59 Fire Engine, rather like the Matchbox #9 Merryweather, with a ladder on the roof, 63 mm, 1/86 scale, Sixties.
254 Merryweather Turntable Escape, with two-section aerial ladder controlled by crank and string, 134 mm, 1/72 scale, 1962.
258 Daimler the same type as the Zebra but slightly larger, the same casting as the Morestone but cream with a red base, 109 mm, 1/42 scale, 1962.
298 Alvis Crash Tender, a high stubby six-wheeler with ladders, bell and nozzle on the roof, Fire Service and other decals, 90 mm, 1/72 scale, Sixties.

CASTLE ART

The following truck was probably made by Castle Art, a small firm which marketed some of its diecast products as Gaiety Toys.
#? Fire Engine, a rather crude open truck, carrying a wheeled two-section ladder (or maybe three?) just as long as the truck, 110 mm, 1/50 scale, Fifties?

CHAD VALLEY

Chad Valley made its Wee-Kin series of clockwork-powered diecast trucks from 1949 through the mid-Fifties. Most of the trucks have the same chassis-cab casting that we see here. A smaller Midget Series was also made.
9231 Fire Engine, its simple rear body bearing a hose reel, two lengths of suction hose and a tilting ladder, 132 mm, 1/60 scale, 1955.
9554 Red Cross Van, a short, high van with, oddly enough, white crosses in red circles, 52 mm, about Ho gauge, Fifties.

CHARBENS

Charles Benson, one of the Benson Brothers of Benbros, made an assortment of diecast models, in a variety of scales, in early postwar days.
11 Ambulance, 1/90 scale, no other data, 1960.
15 Fire Engine, an open truck with a wheeled ladder and eight firefighter figures, about 100 mm, 1/50 scale, 1960 or earlier.
#? Fire Engine, a similar but by no means indentical truck with one or more diecast ladders carried on racks, plus the same eight men, 101 mm, 1/50 scale, 1960 or earlier.
OC26 Fire Escape, a little open truck with cast-in escape ladder and separate diecast wheels on it, 58 mm, 1/90 scale, 1958.

D.C.M.T.-CRESCENT

The name on this model suggests a link between the Crescent firm best known for its diecast models of racing cars and the D.C.M.T. firm, makers of Lone Star toys.
#? Ladder Truck, an open-cab vehicle with tinplate ladder pushed up by a spring and held down by a string; mine lacks the fireman that climbs it as it rises, 107mm, about S gauge, early Postwar.

ELMONT

#? Fire Engine, a plastic model of a typical British truck with a ladder on top, 1/50 scale, no other data.

JOHILLCO

Also called Hillco, makers of diecast toys in prewar days, best known for their speed record cars.
#? Dennis Fire Engine, with a ladder on racks, a winch to raise it, a bell and six firemen, 90 mm, 1/50 scale, 1934. The model shown lacks the winch.

L.D.C.W.

London Die Cast Works, as far as I know, makers of:
#? Fire Engine, a streamlined truck with one or more ladders on top; those on mine are probably not original, 104 mm, O gauge or smaller, postwar.

LLEDO

When Matchbox was sold, Jack Odell formed this company, spelling his name backward in the process, and produced a line of "Models of Days Gone" that recapture the nostalgic charm of the early Yesteryears and have become extremely popular among collectors.
DG5 Shand-Mason Fire Engine, a horsedrawn wagon with boiler, firemen and lettering, 107 mm, about S gauge, 1983. The following variations exist:
- **London Fire Brigade,** red with gold boiler.
- **Chicago Fire Brigade,** red with gold boiler.
- **Guildford Fire Brigade,** green with gold boiler and wheels.
- **Guildford fire Brigade,** black boiler, otherwise as above.
- **Hong Kong Fire Brigade,** cream with gold boiler, red wheels.
- **Hong Kong Fire Brigade,** red boiler, otherwise as above.
- **Philadelphia Bureau of Fire,** red with gold boiler and wheels, tan horses.
- **Great Western Railway (GWR),** chocolate body and wheels, gold boiler, tan horses.
- **BIFBAC II Convention,** red body, gold boiler and wheels, tan horses.
- **Lake City,** dark yellow body, red boiler and wheels.

DG6 City of London Police Ambulance, a special version of Lledo's Model T Ford Van, 69 mm, O to S gauge, 1983.
DG6 Philadelphia Bureau of Fire Van, two versions, 69 mm, O to S gauge, 1984:
- Ambulance, cream with black roof and gold logo.
- Rescue Company, red with black roof and gold logo.

DG8 Philadelphia Bureau of Fire Service Truck, a red Model T tanker with black roof, gold lettering and parts, 79 mm, O to S gauge, 1984.
DG9 Philadelphia Bureau of Fire Battalion Chief's Car, a red Model A Ford roadster with black interior, 78 mm, O to S gauge, 1984.
DG12 Dennis Fire Engine, Twenties vintage, with open cab and tan ladders, 82 mm, about S gauge, 1984. The following versions exist:
- **Luckhurst County Fire Brigade,** red body with green fenders.
- **Cardiff City Fire Service,** red body with white fenders.

LONE STAR

The D.C.M.T. firm has made Lone Star toys in a variety of scales from larger than O gauge to an almost microscopic OOO. Among them are the 1/50 scale diecast cars first made for Tootsietoys and

later expanded on for use as Lone Star issues, the Matchbox-size Impy series, and one representative each from the HO gauge Tuf-Tots and large-scale Top Boy series.
20 Volkswagen Ambulance, a white VW bus with opening doors and blue dome light, from the Impy series, 76 mm, 1/60 scale, 1966.
30 Merryweather Fire Engine, with two-section plastic aerial ladder, Impy series, 98 mm, S gauge or smaller, late Sixties, later reissued as #1252.
32 Ford Corsair Fire Chief, a dark red sedan with blue dome light and yellow Fire Chief lettering, Impy series, 75 mm, 1/65 scale, late Sixties.
624 Fire Engine, a typical enclosed truck with a ladder on the roof and Fire Brigade labels, from the Tuf-Tots series, 56 mm, HO gauge or smaller, late Sixties.
1252 Merryweather Fire Engine, #30 reissued, 98 mm, S gauge or smaller, 1980.
1296 Fire Engine, one version of a long British truck, with turntable and extending ladder, about 170 mm, larger than O gauge, Sixties.
1296 Fire Engine, the same basic truck with cast-in wheels for a white plastic escape ladder, 173 mm, larger than O gauge, late Sixties.
1478 Rambler Cross Country Army Ambulance, from the Roadmasters line that grew out of the Tootsietoy Classics, 96 mm, 1/50 scale, 1960.
1481 Rambler Cross Country Ambulance, or maybe a staff car, as it has no red crosses or dome light, 96 mm, 1/50 scale, 1960.
1479 Corvair Fire Chief, a red sedan with blue dome light and black Fire Chief lettering, 92 mm, 1/50 scale, 1960.
1479 Corvair Fire Chief, the German issue with Feuerwehr lettering, 92 mm, 1/50 scale, 1960.
#? Fire Engine, a big blunt toy from lone Star's Top Boy series, with tilting cab and two-section ladder, 140 mm, larger than O gauge, Seventies?
#? Fire Engine, a little model of a big truck with a ladder on top, identified by its owner as Triple O gauge, 45 mm, Seventies or earlier.
#? Fire Engine, a small single casting the same size as the model just above, 45 mm, no other data.

MORESTONE

The firm of Morris and Stone, which later adopted the Budgie name, made a variety of models, but the only two on our list are from their Modern Products line and are approximately O gauge.
#? Daimler Ambulance, the same casting as the Budgie but in white with a silver base, and without lettering, 109 mm, 1/42 scale, 1958.
#? Fire Escape, a blunt-nosed open truck with cleaner lines than the similar Castle Art vehicle, and with an escape ladder on yellow wheels, 130 mm, 1/50 scale, Fifties.

SPOT-ON

The Spot-On branch of Tri-Ang made its 1/42 scale models in Northern Ireland until 1967, when it died of financial ills; a few models were later made in New Zealand. Spot-On models were never as common as Dinky or Corgi Toys and are now quite rare.
207 Morris Wadham Ambulance, a big boxy van with driver and attendant up front and patient on stretcher in back, 109 mm, 1/42 scale, 1963.
316 Land Rover Fire Truck, a red pickup with tan rear cover, white lettering and gold emblem, 111 mm, 1/42 scale, 1966. It was also available in a gift set with a two-wheel trailer, ladder and firemen.
416 Land Rover Army Ambulance, announced in 1966 but never issued.

TAYLOR & BARRETT

Some very interesting T. & B. models were made in the Thirties. Though rather crude by today's standards, they certainly have personality, not to mention rarity.
Ambulance, a high-bodied short-chassis vehicle somewhere between a two-door sedan and a minibus, with Ambulane lettering cast into its sides and a red cross on the roof, 82 mm, about 1/50 scale, Thirties.
Ambulance, a more convincing one, with long chassis and hood, boxy rear body with side windows, and a red cross label on the roof, 100 mm, about 1/50 scale, Thirties.
Military Ambulance, different from both of the above. a high-bodied army truck with five-sided grille and red crosses in circles, 82 mm, 1/50 scale, Twenties? There may be a second army ambulance.
Fire Engine, with open cab, ladder racks and a two section ladder, of which only one piece remains on mine, if it's genuine, 83 mm, 1/50 scale, Thirties.
Fire Car, or what you will, an open vehicle with four seated firemen, 1/50 scale, Thirties.
Ladder Truck, or Fire Engine and Escape, the same vehicle as the four-seater just above, carrying a wheeled escape ladder, 1/50 scale, Thirties.
Turntable Fire Escape, somewhat like the last truck in styling, but with a single two-man seat and a three-section aerial ladder, 1/50 scale, Thirties.
Streamline Fire Engine, a fully enclosed body at last, with a ladder on the roof and cast-in Fire Brigade lettering on the sides, 1/50 scale, Thirties.
Fire Pump Trailer, a pump on two wheels, with hose and firemen, 1/50 scale, Thirties.

TIMPO

Timpo Toys are rather crude diecast vehicles, some with flywheel motors.
Dennis Fire Engine, with long tapering nose, enclosed body, and three yellow ladders in a channel on the roof, 102 mm, 1/42 scale, 1948.

TOBY TOYS

I can't tell you much about Toby Toys; I have a few of them, but alas, not this one.
863 Fire Engine, with open cab, long hood, and a touch of Tootsietoy about its rear body, but no ladder to hang on its racks or fit into its holes, about 115 mm, roughly O gauge, early postwar.

TRI-ANG MINIC

Tri-Ang products include a mixed bag of sheet metal and plastic vehicles in various sizes, including some interesting prewar Minic clockwork toys.
L.C.C. Ambulance, a tinplate van with clockwork motor, roof sign and red crosses, 122 mm, large scale, Thirties.
Fire Engine, tinplate, with streamlined body, opening hatches, windup motor and two long maroon ladders, 153 mm, large scale, 1937.
Fire Engine, a simple cab-over design in plastic with a ladder on top (mine may not be original) and a flywheel motor underneath, disguised as what might be a hose reel, 152 mm, large scale, postwar.
Fire Engine, much smaller, also plastic, with flywheel motor, various cast-in details, and a black ladder on top, 95 mm, about S gauge, postwar.

UNKNOWN MAKERS

Ambulance, a presumably British slushmold toy in gray, with a man clinging to the back, based on a Tommy Toy from America, 98 mm, O gauge or smaller, prewar.
Bentley Ambulance, a single casting with metal wheels, a recognizable Bentley grille and not much else of significance, 97 mm, O gauge, prewar.
Fire Engine, a little diecast streamliner with a slightly bent ladder riveted to its top, "Made in England" and "British Made" cast into the base, but no maker's name, 45 mm, perhaps 1/100 scale, postwar.
Fire Engine, an interesting slushmold truck with a ladder on each side, about 95 mm, perhaps S gauge, presumably prewar.

The British Commonwealth

Canada, Australia and New Zealand have produced few miniature emergency vehicles, but some of these few are quite interesting, particularly the excellent Micro (Australia/New Zealand) Morris Fire Engine and International Ambulance. The Tink E slushmold steam pumper from New Zealand is not beautiful, but it is unusual, as are the Canadian Londontoys. Canada has also contributed the rubber Viceroy, plastic Herka kit and sheet metal Lincoln Toys, while the small-scale Fun Ho and Lincoln models, the Matai Micro and Spot-On reissues, and the Hallmark oldtimers come from New Zealand.

FUN HO

Most of this New Zealand firm's products form a series of small-scale vehicles, while some larger toys, mainly reissues of early postwar American items, are also made.
5 Fire Service Kit, a boxed set of two 21 Fire Engines and one each of the 27 Bedford Articulated Tanker, 35 Holden Ambulance, 57 Pickup

Truck and 58 Jeep, all painted red, plus Fire labels for them, S to HO gauges, Seventies.
21 Fire Engine, a typical British design with fully enclosed body and a ladder on top, 58 mm, HO scale or smaller, Seventies or earlier.
27 Bedford Articulated Tanker, in red in the #5 set, otherwise not a fire vehicle, 96 mm, about HO gauge, Seventies.
35 Holden Ambulance, a modern high-roof type, in white with red crosses when sold singly, in red in the #5 set, 58 mm, larger than HO gauge, Seventies.
57 Utility Pickup, painted red for the #5 set, 68 mm, S gauge, Seventies.
58 Jeep, also red when used in #5, 60 mm, S gauge, Seventies.
62 Holden Army Ambulance, the #35 casting in olive drab with a large red roof light, 58 mm, larger than HO gauge, Seventies.
#? Fire Truck, a crude single sandcasting of an open truck with siren, hose reel and four firemen, numbers 175 and 4 cast on the bottom, 116 mm, about O gauge, postwar.
#? Fire Chief's Roadster, a fanciful sports car, with holes for a driver and heaven knows what else, and a bell on the front, 112 mm, large scale, postwar.
#? Ladder Truck, really big, with two men in its open cab, two six-rung ladders, and white plastic wheels, 236 mm not counting the ladders, large scale, postwar.

HALLMARK

These new models from New Zealand are made in silver for investors, in white metal for collectors. All are horsedrawn or hand-drawn vehicles, and portray the early history of firefighting in New Zealand.
Shand-Mason 1903 Steam Pumper, with more detail than the good old Yesteryear, 1/76 scale, no other data, 1984.
1902 Hose Carriage, 1/76 scale, no other data, 1984.
Morris Wheeled Fire Escape, 1/76 scale, no other data, 1984 or '85.
Shand-Mason 1903 Ladder Wagon, 1/76 scale, no other data, 1984 or '85.
1902 Horsedrawn Hose Reel, 1/76 scale, no other data, 1984 or '85.
61902 Ladder Carriage, 1/76 scale, no other data, 1984 or '85.

HERKA

This Canadian plastic kit is sold individually and also included in several firehouse kits.
708 Fire Engine, a venerable open-cab truck with two ladders and a big bell, 100 mm, HO gauge or larger, Eighties or before.

LINCOLN

Lincoln of New Zealand produced a Motorway Series of twelve small-scale vehicles, including:
4301 Fire Engine, a small single casting of an open truck with tiny hose reel and pins to hold a ladder—mine lacks the ladder—57 mm, smaller than HO gauge, Seventies or before.

LINCOLN TOY

This Lincoln comes from Canada and is made of pressed steel.
#? Ladder Truck, a big bulbous modern-looking cab-chassis unit and an open rear body with racks holding a ladder, about 170 mm, large scale, Forties (C-R Vol. 1, p. 62).

LONDONTOYS

Made in London, Ontario, these Canadian toys included four- and six-inch series of cars and trucks, both of which are represented here.
16 Fire Truck, a four-inch single casting with open cab, rudimentary steering wheel, generic grille, ladders and hose reel, 101 mm, O gauge or smaller, Fifties.
32 Military Ambulance, a six-inch single casting with a Ford grille, large scale, no other data, Fifties.
56 Fire Truck, a six-inch casting with closed cab, a siren on the roof, a hose reel in back, and a separate chassis, at least originally; 163 mm, large scale, Fifties. Same basic casting as the Metalcraft truck (see American Diecast).

MATAI-MICRO

In recent years some of the old Micro dies have been reused and the products sold in small numbers in New Zealand.
GB 13 Morris Fire Engine, re-issue of one of my favorite fire trucks, a pleasant and graceful model, 102 mm, smaller than O gauge, Seventies.

MICRO

The original Micro Models were, with few exceptions, made in both Australia and New Zealand; the letters GB before the catalog number are the initials of the two factory towns and indicate that the model was made in both countries.
GB 13 Morris Fire Engine, a handsome closed-cab pumper with two ladders, good detail including hose bed and reel, Morris grille and roof light, 102 mm, smaller than O gauge, 1960.
GB 20 International Ambulance, a fairly well-detailed van body with closed side windows painted silver, plus red crosses, 110 mm, O gauge, 1958.
GB 20 International Military Ambulance, the same model in olive drab instead of gray, 110 mm, O gauge, 1958.

MINI AUTO EMPORIUM

This present-day Canadian firm has contributed one unusual metal model to our list.
101F Cadillac 1959 Fire Chief's Convertible, with top up, 1/43 scale, no other data, 1984.

SPOT-ON

After production stopped at Spot-On's factory in Northern Ireland, some dies were sent to New Zealand and used for a short time.
119 Fire Land Rover, in red with tan cover and Fire Dept. decals, reissue of the British version, 111 mm, 1/42 scale, Seventies.
120 R.A.F. Fire Land Rover, the same model in R.A.F. blue, 111 mm, 1/42 scale, Seventies.

TINK E

I suspect that Tink E Toys were named in "the sincerest form of flattery" of a more famous brand, but I know nothing of their history.
#? Steam Pumper, a simple slush casting with open cab, driver and simple steam boiler, 82 mm, maybe S gauge, presumably early postwar.

VICEROY

Another firm whose history I don't know, save that it was Canadian and made rubber toys.
24 Fire Chief's Car, a large rubber toy, typical of early postwar rubber products north and south of the border, 134 mm, large scale, early postwar.

Märklin and Schuco

Two of Germany's most distinguished manufacturers of diecast miniature cars left the scene almost simultaneously in the late Seventies, when Märklin ceased production of miniature cars to concentrate exclusively on electric trains and Schuco went out of business. Neither produced many models of emergency vehicles, but both held high places in the world of miniature cars because of the excellence of their products. Märklin, a pioneer in diecast cars as well as in model trains, produced three series of miniature cars and trucks, each of which included at least one emergency vehicle.
5521/35 Krupp Ladder Truck, with long-nosed red body, black chassis, and silver ladder, mount and control tongue, a splendid old prewar model, and a rarity now, 133 mm, O gauge or smaller, 1938.
8023 Magirus Ladder Truck, with the familiar round Magirus nose and a two-section sheet metal aerial ladder held aloft by a tongue much like the prewar one, 160 mm, I3 scale, 1958.
8030 Volkswagen Ambulance, a cream VW van with blue dome light and red cross decals, 96 mm, 1/43 scale, 1960.
1807 VW Variant Fire Chief, the trusty Squareback in red with dome light and antenna on the roof, 97 mm, 1/43 scale, 1968.
1809 VW Variant Ambulance, the same model in white with dome light, red crosses and opaque rear windows, 97 mm, 1/43 scale, 1968.

Before its unfortunate demise, the Schuco firm had produced a wide variety of toy and model cars, from high-quality diecast miniatures to clockwork-powered sheet metal cars. Several Schuco

series include emergency vehicles; the 3047 Fire Engine represents the firm's tinplate products, while the 1046 VW Fire Chief comes from a line of motorized diecast cars. The 700 series trucks are part of Schuco's renowned small-scale Piccolo series, while the 1/43 scale 600 and 1/66 scale 800 and 900 series models represent Schuco's last two lines of diecast miniatures. The high cost of producing these high-quality models contributed to Schuco's financial collapse.
631 VW Passat Fire Chief, a red Variant wagon with blue dome light and black Feuerwehr and Notruf 110 lettering, 97 mm, 1/43 scale, 1972.
637 BMW 525 Doctor's Car, white with an orange stripe, blue lights, sirens, red crosses and Notarzt lettering, 116 mm, 1/43 scale, Seventies.
745 Magirus Ladder Truck, a realistic model with the traditional rounded nose and a crank-operated three-section aerial ladder, 94 mm, 1/90 scale, 1962.
755 Mercedes-Benz Searchlight Truck, short and stubby, with forward control cab, rear deck and tilting searchlight, 47 mm, 1/90 scale, 1962.
756 Mercedes-Benz Fire Department Van, with a ladder clamped onto its roof an no other signs of its profession, 49 mm, 1/90 scale, 1962.
824 Volkswagen 411 Fire Chief, one of VW's bigger cars, in red with a blue dome light, 69 mm, 1/66 scale, 1970.
876 Audi 80 Fire Chief, a smaller red car with an amber dome light, 64 mm, 1/66 scale, Seventies.
890 Ford Transit Fire Van, with a long slim ladder and the same lettering as #631, 67 mm, 1/66 scale, Seventies.
914 Volkswagen Ambulance, a cream VW bus with blue light, red crosses and black Notruf 110 and Nürnberg 18 lettering, 67 mm, 1/66 scale, Seventies.
1046 Volkswagen Fire Chief, the good old Beetle in red, with clockwork motor and adjustable steering, 100 mm, 1/43 scale, Sixties.
3047 Fire Engine, a windup sheet metal van with a ladder on each side, about 110 mm, O gauge or smaller, circa 1950 (C-R, Vol. 1, p. 106).

Wiking

Since 1948 the Berlin firm of Wiking has produced a vast array of HO gauge plastic vehicles of all kinds, for use as model railroad accessories or as toys and collectibles in their own right. Their earliest models had opaque windows cast integrally with the bodies, and some had cast-in wheels. The 1951 Wiking catalog calls their scale 1/100; the 1953 edition simply HO, while recent catalogs describe them as "approximately HO scale". We shall list them below as 1/90, as does the Greilsamer-Azema *Catalogue Mondial,* with the exceptions of a few 1/160 scale items. The Wiking firm has constantly updated its models to represent changes in the real vehicles, thus many variations exist in the numerous fire vehicles and ambulances they have made—probably more than we know of. Wiking's original number-and-letter system was changed in 1974; since then all catalog numbers have consisted of two, three or four digits without letter suffixes. We have tried to blend the two systems below. A change of another kind took place in 1984, when Wiking was bought by Siku, which had itself produced plastic miniatures at first.
TFa Fire Engine, with cast-in wheels, no other data, 1/100 scale, 1948.
TFb Ladder Truck, with cast-in wheels, no other data, 1/100 scale, 1948.
TFc Fire Department Crane, with cast-in wheels, no other data, 1/100 scale, 1948.
70 Mercedes-Benz Binz Ambulance, in light cream with red crosses, blue dome light and glass, 55 mm, 1/90 scale, 1974.
71 Mercedes-Benz Binz Ambulance, apparently a variation of 70 that was announced in 1975 but never materialized.
7r Opel Caravan 1961 Ambulance, a white wagon with a roof rack including a blue dome light, 52 mm, 1/90 scale, 1965.
7r VW Variant Ambulance, another white wagon with the same roof rack and dome light, 50 mm, 1/90 scale, 1969.
278 Mercedes-Benz Rescue Ambulance, a white van with red crosses and blue light; we'll see it later in red; 59 mm, 1/90 scale, 1974.
278 Mercedes-Benz Rescue Ambulance, now with Johanniter-Unfall-Hilfe emblems, 59 mm, 1/90 scale, 1984.
29m Volkswagen Ladder Truck, a double-cabin pickup with a tilting ladder, not necessarily a fire truck, 55 mm, 1/90 scale, 1966.
32 Volkswagen Ambulance, a cream van with red crosses and without clear windows, 50 mm, 1/90 scale, 1952.
32 Volkswagen Ambulance, with windows and blue dome light, 50 mm, 1/90 scale, 1958.
32 Volkswagen Ambulance, a bus this time, slightly newer in styling, with red cross rondels, 49 mm, 1/90 scale, 1961.
32 Volkswagen Ambulance, with a roof rack added, 49 mm, 1/90 scale, 1967.
32 Volkswagen Ambulance, with styling changes, plus the same roof rack, 50 mm, 1/90 scale, 1969.
32 Volkswagen Ambulance, with a new, more squarish body style, still with the roof rack, 52 mm, 1/90 scale, 1972.
320 Volkswagen Ambulance, with nothing new but the number, 52 mm, 1/90 scale, 1974.
320 Volkswagen Ambulance, without the roof rack, in either white or cream, 52 mm, 1/90 scale, 1977.
39 Volkswagen 181 Technisches Hilfswerk Car, "The Thing" in blue, with no THW markings, 43 mm, 1.90 scale, 1981.
60 Mercedes-Benz 220 Fire Chief, without windows, no other data, 1954, apparently issued simultaneously with:.
60 Opel Kapitän Fire Chief, without windows, with a blue dome light (missing from mine), 56 mm, 1/90 scale, 1954.
60 Opel Kapitän Fire Chief, with windows, otherwise as above, 56 mm, 1/90 scale, 1958.
60 Mercedes-Benz 220 Fire Chief, with blue roof light but, it seems, still no windows, no other data, 1958.
60 Mercedes-Benz 220 Fire Chief, with windows at last, 58 mm, 1/90 scale, 1961.
60 Mercedes-Benz 180 Fire Chief, similar to the 220, no other data, 1966.
60 Ford Taunus 17M Fire Chief, a new car under the blue dome light, 53 mm, 1/90 scale, 1969.
60 VW Variant Fire Chief, a red wagon with roof bar including sirens and a blue light, 50 mm, 1/90 scale, 1973.
600 VW Variant Fire Chief, with its new number, 50 mm, 1/90 scale, 1974.
60a Mercedes-Benz Unimog Fire Truck, a boxy-bodied 4 x 4 with a ladder on the roof and two blue lights atop the cab, 57 mm, 1/90 scale, 1972.
601 Mercedes-Benz Unimog Fire Truck, new number, 57 mm, 1/90 scale, 1972.
60b Opel Ladder Truck, with rear-mounted two-section aerial ladder, and a bracket at the rear of the cab holding the ladder and two blue lights, 82 mm, 1/90 scale, 1967.
602 Opel Ladder Truck, with a higher-nosed cab, otherwise as 60b, 82 mm, 1/90 scale, 1974.
60f Mercedes-Benz Airport Fire Truck, with a foam nozzle rising from its rear deck and a pump at the back, 80 mm, 1/90 scale, 1969.
60k Volkswagen Fire Truck, a bus without windows, with ladder, pike and blue light on its roof rack, 51 mm, 1/90 scale, 1957.
60k Volkswagen Fire Truck, with windows, a slightly less pointed nose, and the same roof rack, 49 mm, 1/90 scale, 1961.
60k Volkswagen FireTruck, a van instead of a bus, otherwise as before, 49 mm, 1/90 scale, 1969.
60k Volkswagen FireTruck, with more modern styling, otherwise unchanged, 49 mm, 1/90 scale, 1971.
603 Volkswagen Fire Truck, the new squarish body style, with roof rack, 51 mm, 1.90 scale, shown only in the 1974 catalog.
603 Volkswagen Fire Truck, the same vehicle minus the roof rack, with just a blue dome light, 51 mm, 1/90 scale, 1975.
60p Mercedes-Benz Unimog Explosive Fire Truck, with a domed cylinder flanked by two long boxes, plus a transverse tank and box ahead of it, 60 mm, 1/90 scale, 1964. (Fighting fires with explosives is why French firefighters are called Sapeurs as well as Pompiers.)
604 Mercedes-Benz Unimog Explosive Fire Truck, new number, 60 mm, 1/90 scale, 1974.
60w Mercedes-Benz Fire Rescue Truck, a panel van with a roof rack holding a life raft, 55 mm, 1/90 scale, 1968.
60w Mercedes-Benz Fire Rescue Truck, with a new body style featuring a more prominent nose, plus the same roof rack, no other data, 1972.
605 Mercedes-Benz Fire Rescue Truck, new number, no other data, 1974.
606 VW Golf Fire Chief, a red Rabbit with sirens flanking its dome light, 43 mm, 1/90 scale, 1979.
607 Mercedes-Benz Fire Department Ambulance, the #70 Binz in red, 55 mm, 1/90 scale, 1975.
60u Volkswagen Emergency Van, a VW van without windows, with blue dome light, 51 mm, 1/90 scale, 1958.
608 Mercedes-Benz Fire Rescue Truck, a red version of the #278 ambulance, with white Notruf 112 lettering, 58 mm, 1/90 scale, 1975.
608 Mercedes-Benz 408 Emergency Ambulance, the same van with small Feuerwehr 112 labels, 58 mm, 1/90 scale, 1983.
609 Mercedes-Benz Fire Rescue Vehicle, a 4 x 4 wagon with siren and dome lights on top and equipment inside, 50 mm, 1/90 scale, 1982.
61 Magirus Fire Engine, with traditional round-nose cab, blue roof bar, two ladders on the roof of its rear box, and a hose reel slung aft, 92 mm, 1/90 scale, 1954.
61 Mercedes-Benz Fire Engine, with a blunt-nosed Mercedes cab, otherwise as before, 92 mm, 1/90 scale, 1961. Mine lacks the rear-mounted hose reel.
61 Magirus LF16 Fire Engine, a modern truck with boxy four-door cab and boxier rear body, two separate ladders and a spare wheel on the roof, and the usual hose reel hanging on the back, 87 mm, 1/90 scale, 1973.
610 Magirus LF16 Fire Engine, the new number, 87 mm, 1/90 scale, 1974.
610 Magirus LF16 Fire Engine, with a slightly restyled cab and Feuerwehr 112 labels, 87 mm, 1/90 scale, 1983.
61n Magirus Fire Engine, with a longer cab than #61 but the same rounded nose, a shorter rear box, two ladders on the roof and the usual hose reel, 92 mm, 1/90 scale, 1962.
61n Magirus Fire Engine, with a shorter, very blunt nose, otherwise

as before, 89 mm, 1/90 scale, 1968.
618 Mercedes-Benz Metz DLK 23-12 Ladder Truck, with two-door cab, three-section aerial ladder, demountable cherry-picker basket, four jacks and, for once, no hose reel, 104 mm, 1/90 scale, 1982.
62 Magirus Ladder Truck, with triangular panels forming the sides of the lower half of its aerial ladder, plus the inevitable hose reel at the rear; the cab on mine looks suspiciously like a Mercedes and unlike the one in the 1955 catalog, so there may have been both versions with closed windows; 96 mm, 1/90 scale, 1954.
62 Magirus Ladder Truck, with a long flat nose and straight ladder sides, 96 mm, 1/90 scale, 1957.
62 Magirus Ladder Truck, with windows, otherwise as before, 96 mm, 1/90 scale, 1960.
62 Magirus DL30 Ladder Truck, with four-door cab, three-section aerial ladder and the usual hose reel, 92 mm, 1/90 scale, 1973.
620 Magirus DL30 Ladder Truck, renumbered, 92 mm, 1/90 scale, 1974.
620 Magirus DL30 Ladder Truck, with modernized cab and new labels, 92 mm, 1/90 scale, 1983.
62n Magirus Ladder Truck, with rounded nose, four-door cab, three-section ladder and hose reel, 89 mm, 1/90 scale, 1962.
62n Magirus Ladder Truck, with a big blunt nose, otherwise unchanged, 90 mm, 1/90 scale, 1968.
62r Henschel Rescue Crane Truck, with long-nose cab, a winch on the front, a sturdy crane atop its rear box body, and roller rests at the rear, no other data, 1965.
62r Mercedes-Benz Rescue Crane Truck, with shorter nose and low wide grille behind the winch, 83 mm, 1/90 scale, 1969.
621 Mercedes-Benz TLF 24/50 Fire Truck, in an odd light red, the well-equipped deck atop its rear box including a swiveling nozzle and a short ladder, 75 mm, 1/90 scale, 1979.
621 Mercedes-Benz TLF 24/50 Fire Truck, a new issue in a more typical shade of red, with new Feuerwehr 112 labels, 75 mm, 1/90 scale, 1983.
622 Mercedes-Benz Unimog TLF 8/18 Fire Truck, a stubbier version of 621 with no nozzle and apparently no tow hook, no other data, 1979 or 1980.
622 Mercedes-Benz Unimog TLF 8/18 Fire Truck, the above with a towing hook, 63 mm, 1/90 scale, 1981.
623 Mercedes-Benz-Fiedler Fire Rescue Truck, with the deck on its box equipped with a ladder, shovel, spare wheel and rubber boat, 81 mm, 1/90 scale, 1975.
629 Mercedes-Benz First Aid Truck, or perhaps Command Truck, with a tipping and removable container with windows as its rear body, 84 mm, 1/90 scale, 1975.
630 Magirus Rescue Crane Truck, big and brawny, with a crane to match; the boom telescopes and the hook catches under the front bumper, 89 mm, 1/90 scale, 1982.
635 Mercedes-Benz Red Cross Truck, a light cream covered truck with red crosses, 80 mm, 1/90 scale, 1976.
2600 Fire Truck Set, with re-issues of 61n and 62n and a revised 630 with black chassis instead of white, 1983.
3362 Opel Blitz 1939 Aerial Ladder Truck, a chassis-cab already used on civilian and army trucks, now carrying an aerial ladder, no other data, 1984.
9033 Red Cross Set, comprising VW Beetle, VW Bus and Mercedes-Benz Ambulance, 1/160 scale, circa 1980.
9034 Fire Set, the same three vehicles in red, 1/160 scale, circa 1980.
9061 Magirus Fire Engine, an N-gauge version of 61/610, also numbered N61, 49 mm, 1/160 scale, mid-Seventies.
9062 Magirus Ladder Truck, the 62/620 model in N gauge, also numbered N62, 59 mm, 1/160 scale, mid-Seventies.

Siku

The 1/60 and, more recently, 1/55 scale models produced by Richard Sieper & Co. of Lüdenscheid, Germany, were made of plastic from the Fifties to the middle Sixties, when the firm began to make its toys of Zamak. Siku models have long been known for their accuracy and their working parts; they include a number of well-detailed fire trucks and other emergency vehicles. The consecutive numbering system used since the plastic series began, and continued for the earlier diecast models, was replaced in 1974 by a four-digit system in which all models selling for the same price have the same first two digits. Most mmodels were equipped with fast wheels at the same time as the number change, so that models which have borne both numbers can be distinguished by their wheel types.
14 Volkswagen Ambulance, a red and black VW bus with red crosses and a siren, 68 mm, 1/60 scale plastic, Fifties.
55 Mercedes-Benz Fire Engine, with typically German enclosed body, equipment on the roof and rear-mounted hose reel, 130 mm, 1/60 scale plastic, 1957.
56 Mercedes-Benz Ladder Truck, with working three-section aerial ladder plus a hose reel, 130 mm, 1/60 scale plastic, 1957.
71 Mercedes-Benz Ambulance, with two removable stretchers, one occupied, plus dome light and siren, 72 mm, 1/60 scale plastic, 1957.
138 Mercedes-Benz Army Ambulance, an angular army truck with windows in its rear box, plus red crosses, no other data, 1/60 scale plastic, 1960.
233 Mercedes-Benz Binz Ambulance, with blue dome light, opening 79 mm, 1/60 scale diecast, 1964. All following models are of diecast Zamak.
237 Ford Transit Fire Truck, a light van with dome light and two diecast ladders on the roof, 70 mm, 1/60 scale, 1964.
261 Mercedes-Benz Metz DL30h Ladder Truck, a fine model with three-section aerial ladder, hose reel and four jacks, 155 mm, 1/60 scale, 1967; later #2815.
292 Mercedes-Benz Ambulance, a van with opening doors, detailed interior, red crosses, blue lights and Unfall-Rettung decals, 94 mm, 1/60 scale, 1969; later #1911.
306 Mercedes-Benz Binz-Europ 1200L Ambulance, successor to 233, with detailed two-stretcher interior, 97 mm, 1/60 scale, 1970; later #1613.
332 Metz Airport Crash Truck, a magnificent model with everything from a roof-mounted foam nozzle to removable hose reels, 194 mm, 1/60 scale, 1972; later #3411.
339 Mercedes-Benz Fire Rescue Van, same body as 292, with lifeboat and ladders on the roof and more equipment inside, 93 mm, 1/60 scale, 1972; later #2213.
342 Ford Taunus 17M Fire Chief, a red and white wagon with blue lights, siren, antenna, white lettering and a case of equipment, 79 mm, 1/60 scale, 1973.
344 Lamborghini Espada Fire Hunter, a speedy emergency car with swiveling roof nozzles and sirens, 78 mm, 1/60 scale, 1973; later #1618.
353 Audi 100 Doctor's Car, a green sedan with yellow roof sign and Arzt lettering on the rear window, 75 mm, 1/60 scale, 1973; later #1313.
356 VW Malteser Hilfsdienst Ambulance, a cream VW bus with red Maltese cross emblems, dome lights, sirens and antenna, 73 mm, 1/60 scale, 1973; later #1619.
357 Mercedes-Benz Fire Rescue Van, a companion to 339 with the interior from 292 and no roof rack, 95 mm, 1/60 scale, 1973; later #2214.
1313 Audi 100 Doctor's Car, ex-353, 75 mm, 1/60 scale, 1974.
1335 VW 181 Fire Department Car, "The Thing" with black top, blue lights, silver siren and spotlight, 70 mm, 1/55 scale, 1977.
1338 Fire Department Range Rover, with antenna, spotlight and dome lights, 80 mm, 1/55 scale, 1979.
1339 Porsche 928 Doctor's Car, in white with red trim and Notarzt lettering, blue lights and antenna, 79 mm, 1/55 scale, 1979.
1343 VW Fire Truck, a van with two ladders on a roof rack, plus two dome lights, 75 mm, 1/55 scale, 1982.
1344 Mercedes-Benz 240GE Fire Command Vehicle, originally a pickup, with white top, dome lights, siren and Feuerwehr lettering, 73 mm, 1/55 scale, 1983.
1613 Mercedes-Benz 1200L Ambulance, ex-306, 97 mm, 1/60 scale, 1974.
1613 Mercedes-Benz Binz Ambulance, high-roofed successor to the above, with detailed interior, dome lights and red crosses, 96 mm, 1/60 scale, 1983.
1617 Ford Taunus 17M Fire Chief, renumbering of 342, 79 mm, 1/60 scale, 1974 only, replaced by:
1617 Ford Granada Turnier Fire Chief, similarly equipped, 80 mm, 1/55 scale, 1975.
1618 Lamborghini Espada Fire Hunter, ex-344, 78 mm, 1/60 scale, 1974.
1619 VW Malteser Ambulance, ex-356, 73 mm, 1/60 scale, 1974.
1621 VW Army Ambulance, the 1619 casting in olive with red cross rondels, 71 mm, 1/60 scale, 1976.
1623 VW Rescue Ambulance, an LT28 van with red crosses and Rettungswagen lettering, plus detailed interior, 85 mm, 1/55 scale, 1979.
1911 Mercedes-Benz Ambulance, ex-292, 94 mm, 1/60 scale, 1974.
2213 Mercedes-Benz Fire Rescue Van, ex-339, the one with the roof rack, 93 mm, 1/60 scale, 1974.
2214 Mercedes-Benz Fire Rescue Van, ex-357, the one without the rack, 95 mm, 1/60 scale, 1974.
2218 Mercedes-Benz Unimog Red Cross Truck, a big bruiser of an ambulance, with a stretcher that slides out, 112 mm, 1/55 scale, 1978.
2815 Mercedes-Benz Metz Ladder Truck, ex-261, 155 mm, 1/60 scale, 1974.
2819 Mercedes-Benz Ladder Truck, a newer type of truck with the same aerial ladder but new jacks and hose reel, 170 mm, 1/55 scale, 1978.
2913 Mercedes-Benz Unimog Fire Truck and Trailer, a husky six-wheel emergency truck with foam nozzle, winch and sliding equipment case, pulling a two-wheel searchlight trailer, 195 mm, 1/55 scale, 1979.
2914 Faun Rescue Crane Truck, a massive six-wheeler with telescoping crane and Feuerwehr lettering, 170 mm, 1/55 scale, 1984.
3411 Metz-Faun Airport Crash Truck, ex-332, 194 mm, 1/60 scale, 1974.
6313 Fire Fighter Set, with 1343, 1344, 2819 and 2913, 1/55 scale, 1984.
#? Mercedes-Benz Fire Truck, a tiny plastic counterpart of #55, 33 mm, very small scale, presumably Fifties.
#? Mercedes-Benz Ambulance, an even smaller version of #71, 20 mm, very small scale, presumably Fifties.

Siku — Gama — Herpa

Note: Siku numbers are often prefixed with the letter V, meaning Verkehrsmodell (Traffic Model), i.e., motor vehicle, as opposed to the firm's other products, which have included railroad platform accessories, airplanes etc.

Gama

The firm of Georg Adam Mangold has produced some interesting models of emergency vehicles, particularly of Mercedes-Benz, Faun and Magirus-Deutz ladder trucks. The Gama range also includes Volkswagen fire tenders and ambulances, doctors' and fire chiefs' cars, and in recent years the remarkable Porsche Orbit Fire Engine. Gama models have for the most part been made to 1/42 or 1/43 scale, though others have been used, especially in the most recent years, since a new numbering system was introduced, with four-digit numbers beginning with 1, 2 or 3. The older system used three, four or five digits, and was in use until 1980; it included:
816 Volkswagen Fire Chief, a newer and bigger Beetle than its #916 predecessor, with a blue dome light, 98 mm, 1/43 scale, Seventies.
8338 Volkswagen Technisches Hilfswerk Car, in blue, no other data, one of at least a dozen THW versions of Gama models made in small quantities circa 1980.
8932 Opel Rekord Doctor's Car, a red and white sedan with roof bar, door labels and Notarzt lettering, 107 mm, 1/43 scale, 1977, later #1114.
90398 THW Jeep and Field Kitchen Trailer, in blue, no other data.
9047 Medical Corps Jeep, with plastic top, red cross rondel and German coat of arms, 81 mm, 1/42 scale, Seventies.
912 Mercedes-Benz Ladder Truck, oldest of the 912 family, with rounded cab and two-section aerial ladder, 130 mm, 1/42 or smaller scale, 1962.
912 Faun Ladder Truck, a modern angular cab painted dayglo tangerine, plus the same aerial ladder as before, 130 mm, 1/42 or smaller scale, Seventies.
9121 Faun Ladder Truck, with a less angular cab, rounded fenders, red paint and the same ladder, 130 mm, 1/42 or smaller scale, 1970.
9122 Faun Ladder Truck, with 9121»s tiltcab and chassis, the same ladder with its mount now red, and a chrome plastic rear deck, 132 mm, 1/42 or smaller scale, Seventies.
9123 Faun Ladder Truck, with white chassis, dual rear axles, red deck and three-section aerial ladder, 135 mm, 1/42 or smaller scale, Seventies.
916 Volkswagen 1200 Fire Chief, a little red Beetle with a blue dome light, 87 mm, probably smaller than 1/43 scale, 1965.
92818 Mercedes-Benz THW Crane Truck, in blue, with three axles, no other data.
928328 Mercedes-Benz THW Tank Truck, another blue three-axle job, no other data.
92888 Magirus THW Wrecker, likewise in blue, no other data.
92968 Magirus THW Covered Truck, blue, no other data.
9378 Munga THW Vehicle, a blue Jeepish sort of 4x4 machine, no other data.
94028 Faun THW Heavy Crane Truck, blue, no other data.
94048 Faun THW Heavy Dumper, blue, no other data.
9406 Krupp Fire Truck, a big boxy brute with some out-of-scale equipment on the roof, 155 mm, 1/43 scale?, Seventies.
94068 Faun THW Emergency Truck, the same model in blue, 155 mm, 1/43 scale?, no other data.
94128 THW Shovel Loader, blue, no other data.
9572 Volkswagen Fire Truck, a red pickup with chrome rear deck including a working rubber-bulb pump, plus ladders, the smaller of two VW sizes, 103 mm, 1/43 scale, 1964.
948 Volkswagen Fire Department Bus, with a yellow ladder and a siren on the roof, the same size VW as 9572, 98 mm, 1/43 scale, Sixties.
9532 Volkswagen Kombi Ambulance, a new and larger VW bus in white with blue light and red crosses, 103 mm, 1/42 scale, Seventies, later 3066 & 1203.
954 Volkswagen Red Cross Bus, the smaller, older Kombi in white with red crosses and dome light, 99 mm, 1/43 scale, 1963.
9541 Volkswagen Red Cross Van, sister to 954, with no side windows, burt with a working dome light and room for a battery, 99 mm, 1/43 scale, 1965.
9547 Volkswagen Ambulance, larger and newer, with red plastic chassis, 108 mm, 1/42 scale, Seventies.
95477 Volkswagen Army Ambulance, the same model in olive, 108 mm, 1/42 scale, Seventies.
95478 Volkswagen THW Kombi, the same model in blue, 108 mm, 1/42 scale, no other data.
9575 Volkswagen Fire Truck, the larger version, with chrome deck, yellow ladders and working bulb pump, much like 948, 112 mm, 1/42 scale, Seventies; may have been renumbered 1603.
958 Volkswagen Ladder Truck, the smaller type VW truck, with flat rear bed and raising ladder, not necessarily a fire truck, 129 mm, 1/43 scale, 1963.
9487 Volkswagen Fire Department Bus, the larger size, with light and ladder on the roof, plus lettering in English, 109 mm, 1/42 scale, Seventies.
New Numbers:
1114 Opel Rekord Doctor's Car, ex-8932, 107 mm, 1/43 scale, 1980.
1153 or 1154 VW Variant Fire Chief, 1/43 scale, 1983, no other data.
1156 BMW 528i Doctor's Car, painted, lettered and equipped like #1114, 108 mm, 1/43 scale, 1982.
1165 BMW 528i Fire Chief, the same car as 1156 in red with Feuerwehr lettering, 108 mm, 1/43 scale, 1982.
1172 Opel Ascona Fire Chief, another red sedan with Feuerwehr lettering, plus an antenna on the roof, 100 mm, 1/43 scale, 1982.
1203 Volkswagen Ambulance, ex-9532, later renumbered 3066, 103 mm, 1/43 scale, 1980.
1602 Volkswagen Rescue Truck, with a big cherry picker, not necessarily a fire truck, 118 mm, 1/43 scale, 1982, also numbered 9572 but first made after the old system was phased out, as is true of several models below.
1604 Mercedes-Benz Rescue Crane, with red chassis, cab and boom, and white rear deck, also not necessarily a fire truck, 115 mm, 1/43 scale, Eighties, also numbered 9288.
1605 Mercedes-Benz Ladder Truck, the 1604 truck with a two-section aerial ladder instead of the crane, 133 mm, 1/43 scale, Eighties, also numbered 92812.
1606 Mercedes-Benz Searchlight Truck, the same cab, deck and chassis again, with a tall rack of lights, 119 mm, 1/43 scale, Eighties, also numbered 92813.
2362 Polyma Searchlight Trailer, a huge working "light giraffe" in red, white and black, 167 mm, 1/25 scale, 1982, from a larger-scale series, also numbered 82362 and 012, also available as:
0128 Polyma THW Searchlight Trailer, in blue, 167 mm, 1/25 scale, 1982 or later.
2601 Porsche Orbit Firefighting System, a huge truck in four segments: first the cab, second a water tank and pump, third an equipment carrier, fourth a big snorkel; one or two pieces can be left behind if not needed; 305 mm, 1/40 scale, 1982, also numbered 3536.
2603 Krupp Fire Truck, ex-9406, 155 mm, 1/43?, 1980.
2604 Magirus-Deutz DL23-12 Ladder Truck, a big blunt modern design with three-section aerial ladder, a basket on the end, and jacks, 230 mm, 1/40 scale, 1981, also numbered 3546.
3066 Volkswagwen Ambulance, ex-9532, alias 1203, 103 mm, 1/43 scale, Eighties.
3536 Porsche Orbit Firefighting System, same as 2601, 305 mm, 1/40 scale, Eighties—and yes, it should properly be written O.R.B.I.T.
3546 Magirus-Deutz Ladder Truck, same as 2604, 230 mm, 1/40 scale, Eighties.
Gama has also made several emergency vehicles in 1/25 scale: 2108 Mercedes-Benz Red Cross Jeep, 2116 Mercedes-Benz 300 Ambulance and 2202 Volkswagen LT Ambulance, all made in or before 11982, and three fire pumpers, 3601, 3602 and 3603, on which we have no data, as well as the 2362 Polyma listed above.

Herpa

Among the German firms competing with Wiking for the plastic HO gauge model market is that of Fritz Wagener, located in Dietenhofen, not far from the toy-fair city of Nürnberg. This firm's Herpa models include a growing number of emergency vehicles, chiefly light fire vans and ambulances, chiefs' and doctors' cars and Technisches Hilfswerk versions, but also an excellent Mercedes-Benz ladder truck, the first of what we hope will be a goodly number of well-detailed models of German fire trucks.
4013 Volkswagen LT Ambulance, a boxy bus in cream, with red crosses, blue dome light and frosted rear windows, 57 mm, 1/87 scale, 1978.
4014 Volkswagen LT Fire Department Bus, the same model in darkish red, with a dome light, but with clear windows, 57 mm, 1/87 scale, 1979.
4016 Volkswagen Fire Department Van, in dayglo red with one pair of side windows aft of the front doors, 57 mm, 1/87 scale, 1980.
4016 volkswagen Fire Department Van, in dayglo red with one pair of side windows aft of the front doors, 57 mm, 1/87 scale, 1980.
4022 Ford Transit Fire Van, a red panel van with a blue dome light, 51 mm, 1/87 scale, 1978.
4024 Ford Transit THW Van, the same model in blue, with THW labels on the doors, 51 mm, 1/87 scale, 1981.
4026 Ford Transit Fire Department Bus, in dayglo red this time, with windows all around, 51 mm, 1/87 scale, 1978.
4032 Volkswagen Fire Department Van, a smaller vehicle than 4016, in the usual shade of red, 51 mm, 1/87 scale, 1982.
4034 Volkswagen Fire Department Bus, the same style with more windows, 51 mm, 1/87 scale, 1982.
4035 Volkswagen THW Bus, the smaller VW type again, now in dark blue with white trim and THW labels, 51 mm, 1/87 scale, 1982.
4047 Mercedes-Benz 190 Fire Chief, 1/87 scale, no other data, 1983.
4051 BMW 528i Fire Chief, a red sedan with two dome lights, a siren on the roof and Feuerwehr lettering across its nose, 53 mm, 1/87 scale, 1979.
4052 Fire Department Range Rover, with two dome lights flanking a collection of sirens, 49 mm, 1/87 scale, 1979.
4053 Opel Rekord Fire Chief, a red sedan with Feuerwehr Wiesbaden 02 lettering, 54 mm, 1/87 scale, 1979.
4054 Opel Rekord Fire Chief, this time in dayglo red, with two dome lights, a siren and white lettering, 54 mm, 1/87 scale, 1980.
4055 Opel Ascona Emergency Car, in white with red hoods and doors, 49 mm, 1/87 scale, 1983.

4060 Porsche 924 Doctor's Car, a white coupe with red trim and Notarzt lettering, 49 mm, 1/87 scale, 1979.
4061 BMW 528i Doctor's Car, with a different red stripe pattern, Notarzt lettering, a red cross, two dome lights and a siren, 53 mm, 1/87 scale, 1979.
4062 BMW 528i Fire Chief, the same car in dayglo red with no lettering, 53 mm, 1/87 scale, 1982.
4063 Fire Department Range Rover, in dayglo red but otherwise as 4052, 49 mm, 1/87 scale, 1982.
4064 Opel Rekord Fire Chief, a red wagon with Wiesbaden lettering, 53 mm, 1/87 scale, 1980.
4066 Opel Kadett Fire Chief, a lighter wagon in dayglo red, 49 mm, 1/87 scale, 1982.
4067 Technisches Hilfswerk Range Rover, in blue with white stripes and THW emblems, plus one corner dome light, 49 mm, 1/87 scale, 1983.
4072 Mercedes-Benz 207 Ambulance, a long light bus in cream with red stripes and crosses, plus diagonally opposed dome lights, 60 mm, 1/87 scale, 1983.
4073 Mercedes-Benz 207 Fire Van, in red with only cab windows, and with Feuerwehr 112 labels, 60 mm, 1/87 scale, 1983.
4078 Mercedes-Benz 209 Fire Truck, 1/87 scale, no other data, 1984.
4502 Ford Transit Army Ambulance, 1/87 scale, no other data, 1983 or '84.
#? MAN Fire Control Bus, 1/87 scale, no other data, 1983 or '84.
#? VW Falck Emergency Crane, 1/87 scale, no other data, 1984.
7501 Ambulance Set, comprising the 4060 Porsche Notarzt and two ambulances, one a Ford Transit bus, the other a big Mercedes box van, 1/87 scale, 1983.
#? Technisches Hilfswerk Set, 1/87 scale, no other data, 1983.
806502 Mercedes-Benz DL32-12 Aerial Ladder Truck, a fine model in red, white and silver gray, with a four-section ladder and detachable bucket, 117 mm, 1/87 scale, 1983.
806505 Mercedes-Benz DL32-12 Aerial Ladder Truck, the same model in dayglo red, 117 mm, 1/87 scale, 1983.
818502 M.A.N. Ladder Truck, 1/87 scale, no other data, 1984.

The Coleman-Russell Volume II shows two Herpa Mercedes-Benz Unimog Fire Trucks, one with a Rescue Boat (p.38), the other with a Pump Trailer (p.40). Neither appears in any Herpa catalog or dealers' catalog I have seen.

Some Herpa models have been adapted by the Beyer Electronic firm to have working electric lights. Beyer also offers one model apparently not Herpa-based. Having no data on these models, we can only list them:
1021 Saurer-Metz Aerial Ladder Truck, 1/87 scale, 1984.
8034 Volkswagen Fire Department Bus, 51 mm, 1/87 scale, 1984.
8035 Volkswagen THW Bus, 51 mm, 1/87 scale, 1984.
8065 Opel Rekord Fire Chief, 53 mm, 1/87 scale, 1984.
8066 Opel Kadett Fire Chief, 49 mm, 1/87 scale, 1984.
8067 THW Range Rover, 49 mm, 1/87 scale, 1984.

Other German Brands

Many other German manufacturers have produced miniature emergency vehicles. The story begins many years ago with the firm of Ernst Plank and continues today with the fine diecast models of Conrad and the plastic HO miniatures of such firms as Brekina, Praline, Preiser and Roskopf.

BREKINA

One of Germany's newer manufacturers, Brekina makes an ever-growing number of plastic cars and trucks in HO gauge, including numerous emergency vehicles.
1123 Opel P4 Fire Chief, apparently the same model as 3031 below.
1421 Citroen 11cv Red Cross Car, the classic old sedan in gray with red crosses, 51 mm, 1/87 scale, 1982.
1430 Citroen 11bl Fire Chief, the same car in red with white lettering, 51 mm, 1/87 scale, 1982.
1453 Mercedes-Benz 190D Fire Chief, no data, 1/87 scale, 1982.
1820 Mercedes-Benz 190 Fire Chief, in black, with the arms of Wuppertal on its doors, 53 mm, 1/87 scale, 1982.
1821 Mercedes-Benz 190 Fire Chief, in red with a variety of other city names; I have 15 and there may be more; 53 mm, 1/87 scale, 1982.
1870 Mercedes-Benz 190 Ambulance, a cream wagon with blue dome light, 53 mm, 1/87 scale, 1982.
1871 Mercedes-Benz 190 Fire Department Ambulance, in red with Feuerwehr Frankfurt on the doors but not on the tailgate, 53 mm, 1/87 scale, 1982.
1873 Mercedes-Benz 190 Fire Department Ambulance, with the German eagle on the doors and Feuerwehr Frankfurt on the tailgate, 53 mm, 1/87 scale, 1983.
1874 Mercedes-Benz 190 U. S. Army Ambulance, in olive with red crosses and white lettering, 53 mm, 1/87 scale, 1984.
1900 Fire Chief's Car with Light, no data, 1/87 scale, 1982.
1912 Ford Taunus 17M Fire Chief, with blue dome light and white Feuerwehr lettering, 50 mm, 1/87 scale, 1983.
2001 Mercedes-Benz 190 Fire Chief, this time with a light, 53 mm, 1/87 scale, 1983.
2070 Mercedes-Benz 190 Ambulance, with light, 53 mm, 1/87 scale, 1982.
2071 Mercedes-Benz 190 Fire Department Ambulance, with light, 53 mm, 1/87 scale, 1982.
3031 Opel P4 Fire Chief, a stubby old two-door model in Friedrichshafen livery, 43 mm, 1/87 scale, 1982.
4020 Mercedes-Benz L311 Metz Fire Pumper, with four-door cab. Compartmented rear body and equipment on the roof, 78 mm, 1/87 scale, 1984.
4030 Mercedes-Benz L311 Metz Ladder Truck, no data, 1/87 scale, 1984.
5002 Mercedes-Benz 0321 Red Cross Ambulance and Trailer, a big bus in German Red Cross livery, pulling a small box trailer, 153 mm, 1/87 scale, 1984.
#? Hanomag-Henschel F-45 Fire Pumper, no data, 1/87 scale, 1984.
9003 Stuttgart Emergency Vehicles Set, with four of the above models, no other data, 1/87 scale, 1984.
9006 Red Cross Set, with Mercedes-Benz 190 car and wagon and 321 bus, no other data, 1/87 scale, 1984.

CONRAD

The Conrad firm specializes in models of heavy trucks and earth-moving equipment. Among its products are several fine models of fire trucks old and new, from the veteran Gräf und Stift and Dennis machines to the ultramodern Emergency One trucks. A sentimental favorite is the American LaFrance truck in the colors of the Monhagen Hose Company of Middletown, New York, where I was born and raised on a diet of fire parades.
1018 Gräf und Stift Fire Truck, an Austrian veteran, long and high, with open cab, two ladders, a hose reel, and enough running boards and brass rails for the whole company, 145 mm, 1/43 scale, 1982.
1019 American LaFrance 1926 Fire Pumper, in dark red, with two ladders, a scaling ladder, two lengths of suction hose and many other details, 142 mm, 1/43 scale, 1982.
1023 American LaFrance 1926 Fire Pumper, the same model in F.D.N.Y. livery, 142 mm, 1/43 scale, 1983.
1024 American LaFrance 1926 Fire pumper, equipped with a hose reel and painted white to represent a truck still owned by the Monhagen Hose Company of Middletown, New York, 142 mm, 1/43 scale, 1983.
1025 Dennis 1914 Fire Engine, in London Fire Brigade livery and typically British, with a removable wheeled escape ladder, 120 mm not counting the big ladder, 1/43 scale, 1984.
3066 VW Fire Department Bus, unknown to me but shown in C-R Vol. II, p. 14, with Brandweer lettering—a special for Holland? About 100 mm, 1/43 scale, 1980.
3090 Mercedes-Benz-Rosenbauer Fire Rescue Truck, a very modern machine with a rear-mounted crane to lift its equipment container out, 153 mm, 1/50 scale, 1982.
3191 M.A.N.-Volkswagen Fire Rescue Truck, a shorter vehicle than the Mercedes, without the crane but with a ladder and equipment compartments, 124 mm, 1/50 scale, 1982.
3490 Steyr-Rosenbauer Fire Rescue Truck, with a more angular cab, but otherwise the same as the Mercedes, 155 mm, 1/50 scale, 1982.
5501 Rosenbauer Simba Airport Crash Truck, a mighty wedge-shaped machine with an odd-looking foam nozzle on the roof, plus a big cab with folding steps that lead up to it, 192 mm, 1/50 scale, 1982.
5502 Emergency One Ladder Truck, the two-axle type with three-section aerial ladder and bucket, 230 mm, 1/50 scale, 1983.
5503 Emergency One Ladder Truck, with two axles again, but this time with a four-section ladder and no bucket, 230 mm, 1/50 scale, 1983.
5504 Emergency One Ladder Truck, now with three axles, four-section ladder and no bucket, 234 mm, 1/50 scale, 1983.
5505 Emergency One Ladder Truck, with three axles, three-section ladder and bucket, 234 mm, 1/50 scale, 1983, last of four red Emergency One trucks.
5506 Emergency One Ladder-Pumper Truck, in white and silver, with three-section aerial ladder, four smaller ladders and hose couplings, 225 mm, 1/50 scale, 1984.
5507 Emergency One Airport Fire Truck, downright petite compared to 5501, and pale green too, 190 mm, 1/50 scale, 1984.
#? Ladder Towers Conestoga Duplex Ladder Truck, in Fort Worth #1 livery, no other data, 1/43 scale, 1984 or '85.

CURSOR

Cursor's products include both modern-day showroom models and plastic miniatures of German oldtime vehicles, including one fire engine.
470 Daimler 1896 Fire Engine, sort of a horse-drawn wagon without the horse, but with hose, bell and pump, one of the world's first self-propelled fire trucks, 108 mm, 1/43 scale, Sixties.

Other German Brands

FEIL

Richard Feil, a goldsmith by profession, has devoted his talent and skill to the making of pewter miniature masterpieces such as this one.
Shand-Mason Horsedrawn Fire Engine, reviving those thrilling days of Yesteryears, probably the prototype for the Nostalgic Miniatures model, no other data, Seventies.

OESTMANN

Oestmann kits are made of plastic, to HO gauge.
13 Mercedes-Benz 170S Fire Chief, which can also be made as a police car or taxi, no other data, 1/87 scale, early Eighties.

PLANK

Ernst Plank toys date back to the early days of this century. They are simple, but have their own personality that takes us back to the days before World War I; beyond that I won't try to date them.
Fire Engine, with open cab, bell and even a crank; body, wheels and hose reel are diecast, fenders and full-length running boards of sheet metal; 70 mm, between S and HO gauges, as are the rest.
Fire Engine, similar to the above but with short running boards and no fenders, with hose reel and driver, 70 mm.
Steam Pumper, with a gold boiler, plus the chassis with long running boards and fenders, 72 mm.
Ladder Truck, with a tilting ladder mounted at the rear, plus fenders and headlights, 78 mm.
Fire Chief's Car, an open two-seater with driver and spare tire, no other data.
Fire Truck; I've seen a photo of it and it seems to have a high wire rack in the rear, no other data.
Army Ambulance, with a red cross painted on its cloth rear cover, and with short running boards and no fenders, 70 mm.

POLA

Pola makes kits of a house and a commercial building, both on fire; no other data.

PRALINE AND PREP

These two lines of 1/87 scale plastic models, now apparently blended into one series, are made by Modell International of Waldorf, a town not far from Frankfurt Airport. Their numbering system was changed as of 1984. All models below are Praline except 167607, which is Prep.
141005 DKW Fire Department Van, a slant-nosed 1959 minibus in red with blue dome light and either Hamburg or Stuttgart lettering, 45 mm, 1/87 scale, 1983, now #09-05.
141007 DKW Ambulance, the same little bus in gray with red crosses, 45 mm, 1/87 scale, 1983, now #09-07.
141104 Fiat 242 Red Cross Van, in either white or cream, with Deutsches Rotes Kreuz logo, the cream one also naming its home town of Dietzenbach, 57 mm, 1/87 scale, 1982, now #03-04.
141105 Fiat 242 Fire Van, in red with blue lights and white lettering, 57 mm, 1/87 scale, 1982, now #03-05.
141107 Fiat 242 Red Cross Bus, in cream with lettering as on the van, 57 mm, 1/87 scale, 1983, now #03-07.
141305 Mercedes-Benz 170V Fire Kombi, no data, 1/87 scale, 1983, now #15-05.
141306 Mercedes-Benz 170V Red Cross Kombi, no data, 1/87 scale, 1983, now #15-06.
141307 Mercedes-Benz 170V Fire Department Ambulance, no data, 1/87 scale, 1983, now #15-07.
141407 Citroen H Fire Van, no data, 1/87 scale, 1983, now #19-07.
167607 Mercedes-Benz 220SE Fire Chief, in various city versions: I have Frankfurt, Hamburg and Stuttgart with white chassis and Frankfurt with silver gray; 56 mm, 1/87 scale, 1982, now #04-09.
03-04 Fiat 242 Red Cross Van, ex-141104.
03-05 Fiat 242 Fire Van, ex-141105.
03-07 Fiat 242 Red Cross Bus, ex-141107.
03-32 Fiat 242 French Ambulance, in white with blue lettering and asterisks, 57 mm, 1/87 scale, 1984.
04-09 Mercedes-Benz 220SE Fire Chief, the former Prep 167607.
04-15 Mercedes-Benz 220SE Fire Chief, with white fenders, 56 mm, 1/87 scale, 1984.
07-11 Mercedea-Benz L809 Rescue Van, a red and white box van in Feuerwehr Frankfurt livery with a big 112 phone number, 81 mm, 1/87 scale, 1984.
07-25 Mercedes-Benz L809 Oil Fire Truck, the same van with Olwehr logo, 81 mm, 1/87 scale, 1984.
09-05 DKW Fire Bus, ex-141105.
09-07 DKW Ambulance, ex-141107.
09-17 DKW Fire Van, presumably 09-05 without windows, 45 mm, 1/87 scale, 1984.
15-05 Mercedes-Benz 170V Fire Dept. Kombi, ex-141305.
15-06 Mercedes-Benz 170V Red Cross Kombi, ex-141306.
15-07 Mercedes-Benz 170V Fire Dept. Ambulance, ex-141307.
17-05 Pontiac Firebird Fire Chief, with lettering in English, 58 mm, 1/87 scale, 1984.
19-07 Citroen H French Fire Van, ex-141407.
19-08 Citroen H City of Saarbrücken Fire Van, no data, 1/87 scale, 1984. Saarbrücken is the capital of the Saarland, very near the French border of Germany.
23-04 Peugeot 403 Fire Department Pickup, no data, 1/87ec scale, 1984.
24-05 Ford Transit LWB Fire Van, no data, 1/87 scale, 1984.

PREISER

This present-day firm produces 1/87 scale plastic models, offering some of them in both kit and readymade form. Most Preiser kits can be made up in either of two, or sometimes more, variations of the basic model.
1100 Faun-Krupp 35GMT Fire Department Crane Truck, with telescopic crane boom, 131 mm, 1/87 scale kit, 1981.
1112 Ziegler Fire Pump Trailer, a little box trailer with hose reels and pump, 37 mm, 1/87 scale kit, 1982.
1113 Ziegler Fire Pump Trailer, 37 mm, 1/87 scale readymade, 1982.
1114 Alco Fire Pump Trailers, two similar types with single and dual nozzles, 46 mm, 1/87 scale kit, 1982.
1116 Mercedes-Benz Fire Truck with Containers, with a chassis-cab unit and four rear bodies, 104 mm, 1/87 scale kit, 1983.
1128 Mercedes-Benz LF16-Ziegler Fire Truck, fully enclosed, with big cab, rear compartments, and roof racks, 82 mm, 1/87 scale kit, 1983. The equipment on the roof can vary and the compartments can be open or closed.
1129 Mercedes-Benz LF16-Ziegler Fire Truck, the same model, in one of its possible forms, 82 mm, 1/87 scale readymade, 1983.
1134 Magirus-Deutz DL23 Aerial Ladder Truck, 1/87 scale kit, no hther data, 1984.
1144 Mercedes-Benz-Ziegler Hose Truck, very much like 1128, but with hose and a ladder on the roof, 79 mm, 1/87 scale kit, 1984.
1148 Polyma Searchlight Trailers, you can make one with its lights down low and the other with their telescopic pole fully extended, 36 mm, 1/87 scale kit, 1984.
2.1100 Faun-Krupp 35GMT Fire Department Crane Truck, the 1100 kit in white instead of red, 1984.
2.1128 Mercedes-Benz LF16-Ziegler, white kit, 1984.
2.1144 Mercedes-Benz-Ziegler Hose Truck, white kit, 1984.
2626 Metz Airport Foam Truck, with Mercedes cab, rear box body, and a foam nozzle on the top deck, 94 mm, 1/87 scale kit, 1983.
2628 Faun Airport Crash Tender, big and boxy, with eight wheels, a humped back and twin foam nozzles atop the cab, 127 mm, 1/87 scale kit, 1983.
2629 Faun Airport Crash Tender, the same model, 127 mm, 1/87 scale readymade, 1983.
2631 Metz-Faun FLF80-200 Crash Tender, an impressive eight-wheeler with a single big foam nozzle and silver Flughafen München logo, 127 mm, 1/87 scale readymade, 1980.
2632 Metz-Faun FLF80-200 Crash Tender, the kit version of 2631, 127 mm, 1/87 scale kit, 1980.

ROSKOPF

Roskopf has made numerous 1/87 scale plastic models of German commercial and military vehicles, but only recently did the firm produce its first fire and emergency trucks.
82 M.A.N. Five Ton Army Ambulance, a rugged truck with a first aid station cabin set into its rear body, 79 mm, 1/87 scale, early eighties.
205 VW Iltis Fire Department Car, VW's answer to the Jeep, in red with removable top, 39 mm, 1/87 scale, early eighties.
207 M.A.N. Fire Truck, no data, 1/87 scale, 198. 208 Fire Department Boat on Trailer, no data, 1/87 scale, early eighties.
209 M.A.N. Five Ton Technisches Hilfswerk Truck, a blue version of #82 with gray rear cover and white THW emblems, 79 mm, 1/87 scale, early eighties.
210 Lifeboat on Trailer, no data, 1/87 scale, early eighties.
211 VW Iltis THW Car, in blue with dark gray cover but no THW emblems, 40 mm, 1/87 scale, early eighties.
212 Mercedes-Benz THW Unimog, the stubby covered version in blue with white THW lettering on the hood, 55 mm, 1/87 scale, early eighties.
213 Technisches Hilfswerk Trailer, a blue two-wheeler with removable rounded top, 40 mm, 1/87 scale, early eighties.

214 Mercedes-Benz Uninmog Fire Truck, the same type as #212, in red with gray cover but no lettering, 55 mm, 1/87 scale, early eighties.
424 Saurer D290-330 Fire Truck, a six-wheeler with Rosenbauer box body complete with blue and amber lights and a foam nozzle, 99 mm, 1/87 scale, 1983.
435 Saurer D330N Fire Tender, also with Rosenbauer box body, but with a long-nose cab, 81 mm, 1/87 scale, 1984.
440 Mercedes-Benz-Ziegler Foam Fire Tender, no data, 1/87 scale, 1984.
442 Saurer Rescue Truck, no data, 1/87 scale, 1984.
498 Fire Truck Accessories, no data, 1/87 scale, early eighties.

SCHMIDT

The firm of E. S. Schmidt makes 1/87 scale plastic components and conversions for model vehicles, including these for emergency trucks.
11 Büssing 8000 Fire Truck Cab.
12 Büssing 8000 Fire Truck body.
13 Büssing 8000 Fire Truck Chassis.
14 Büssing 8000 Ladder Truck Cab.
31 Steyr-Rosenbauer Foam Truck.
32 Mercedes-Benz-Rosenbauer Explosive Fire Truck.
46 Krupp-Metz DL30 Fire Truck Cab.
47 Krupp-Metz DL30 Aerial Ladder.
86 Magirus 2000D DL30 4-door Fire Truck Cab.
87 Magirus 2000D Aerial Ladder.
88 Magirus 2000D Fire Truck Chassis.
89 Magirus 2000D Fire Truck box body.
91 Magirus 2000D RW3 4-door Fire Truck Cab.
92 Magirus 200D Fire Truck body.
93 Magirus 200D Fire Truck Chassis.
113 IFA S4000 Fire Truck.
114 Hanomag LF8 Fire Truck.
115 Mercedes-Benz LF3500 Fire Department bus.
116 Mercedes-Benz 311 4-door Fire Truck Cab.
130 Mercedes-Benz-Ziegler Fire Truck Cab.
132 Mercedes-Benz 1113 4-door Fire Truck Cab.
141 Mercedes-Benz 1313 Ladder Truck Cab.
142 Mercedes-Benz 1313 Aerial Ladder.
143 Mercedes-Benz 1313 Ladder Truck Chassis.
146 M.A.N. 450H 4-door Fire Truck Cab.
147 M.A.N. 450H Aerial Ladder.
148 M.A.N. 450H Fire Truck Chassis.
181 Büssing KS25 1940 Fire Truck.
183 Mercedes-Benz 1113 Foam Truck Cab.
206 Magirus-Metz TLF15 Fire Truck Body.
211 Volvo-Rosenbauer Airport Fire Truck Tank Body.
212 Volvo-Rosenbauer Airport Fire Truck Monitor.
221 Mercedes-Benz 1113 Fire Truck Cab.
222 Mercedes-Benz 1113 Fire Truck Box Body.
223 Ford FK2500 Fire Truck.
234 Magirus 125A Fire Truck Chassis.
235 Magirus 125A Fire Truck Box Body.
236 Magirus 125DL Fire Truck Double Cab.
237 Magirus 125DL Ladder Truck.
238 Magirus 125DL Fire Truck Chassis.
1410 M.A.N. 450H 4-door Fire Truck Cab.
1411 M.A.N. 450H Fire Truck Body.
2310 Ford FK2500 Fire Truck Rear Body.
2311 Opel Blitz LF8 Fire Truck.
2313 Mercedes-Benz-Ziegler Fire Truck Double Cab.
2314 Mercedes-Benz-Ziegler Fire Truck Body.
23141 Mercedes-Benz-Ziegler Fire Truck Chassis.

VOLLMER

Vollmer products include HO gauge plastic kits for three fire stations.
3751 Five-Stall Fire Station, 1/87 scale, no other data.
3752 Fire Station With Tower, 1/87 scale, no other data.
3759 Fire House, 1/87 scale, no other data, 1984.
#? House On Fire, 1/87 scale, no other data.

ZISS

The firm of Ziss, sometimes known as R.W., founded by the late Mr. Wittek, specialized in 1/43 scale promotional models, including this light van.
400 Ford Kombi Ambulance, a white minibus with opening rear door and red crosses, 110 mm, 1/43 scale, Sixties.

UNKNOWN MAKER

Airport Crash Tender, in red with white deck, foam nozzles and Total labels, apparently made as a promotional item, 115 mm, HO or smaller scale, circa 1970.

German Sheet Metal Toys

The best-known maker of sheet metal toy vehicles in Germany is G. G. Kellermann & Co. of Nürnberg, better known by its CKO monogram. There have been other German makers of sheet metal toy vehicles, and there may well be more such emergency vehicles than the few listed here.

CKO

#? Ladder Truck, a strong, businesslike German truck with firemen to be seen in its cab windows and a working aerial ladder in back, 154 mm including the ladder, large scale, late Forties, U.S. Zone.
402 Volkswagen Ambulance, no data.
410 Ladder Truck, with what seems to be a Mercedes-Benz cab, plus a working two-section aerial ladder, about 150 mm, large scale, late Fifties.
439 Ladder Truck, with a more modern cab, a longer rear deck and a new ladder design, about 190 mm, large scale, Seventies.

OROBR

Like CKO, this may be a firm's monogram.
#? Fire Engine, with driver and two other men, rear side rails and a windup key, 147 mm, large scale, prewar.
#? Steam Pumper, with the same grille and hood, cab and chassis as the above, a driver but no other men, and a boiler in the rear, 147 mm, large scale, prewar.

UMIS FRANK

#? Ladder Truck, with slanting grille, rugged cab, and a tower of sort on the rear of the chassis, carrying a single ladder, about 170 mm, nc other data, Thirties (C-R Vol. I, p. 141).

UNKNOWN MAKERS

Hose Truck,with a wooden spool serving as a hose reel; was anything ever wound around it? Maker's monogram may be CF, GF, FC or FG, 78 mm, smaller than O gauge, prewar.
Ladder Truck, with driver, four other seated men facing sideways, and a ladder between them, 116 mm, about O gauge, prewar; may be made by Fischer.
Steam Pumper, with red body, silver chassis, blue driver and gold boiler, marked Made In Germany and related to the next model, 114 mm, O gauge.
Steam Pumper, much like the previous model but marked US Zone Germany, 114 mm, O gauge, late Forties; the one above may be post-Occupation.
Steam Pumper, with yellow open cab, gold boiler and radiator and silver spoked wheels, with no identifying marks, but it looks German, 106 mm, about O gauge, probably prewar.
Steam Pumper, with red hood, black chassis, gold boiler and a huge windup crank on the left, 88 mm, smaller than O gauge, prewar.
Ladder Truck, with red hood, blue body and yellow tilting ladder, 94 mm body, 107 mm with ladder, O gauge or smaller, prewar.
Ladder Truck, with a closed cab bearing a huge bell that rings as the model moves, and an aerial ladder big enough to capsize a real truck, about 190 mm, large scale, late Forties (C-R Vol. I, p. 6).
Ladder Truck, with blue body and rear-mounted tilting ladder, no identifying marks, but its workmanship resembles that of the first unknown model above, 58 mm, about S gauge, date unknown.
HS-500 Chief's Car, with a huge, baby-faced chief driving, about 100 mm, Seventies (C-R Vol. I, p. 7).
HS-510 Ladder Truck, a bit less silly-looking but still an out-and-out toy, about 100 mm, Seventies (C-R Vol. I, p. 7).

Tekno

For many years the miniature car scene in Northern Europe was dominated by the Danish firm of Tekno, whose products include many superb models of fire trucks and ambulances, often bearing the

Tekno

emblems of the Falck and Zonen organizations (which later merged), suppliers of emergency and service vehicles to many communities. Financial problems brought the Danish firm and its fine products to an untimely end; Tekno is now located in The Netherlands and produces model trucks and buses, but alas, none of those magnificent fire trucks of bygone days.
404 Volkswagen Ladder Truck, a VW pickup with a raising ladder in the rear, held up by a simple sheet metal lever, 130 mm, 1/43 scale, 1959.
404 Volkswagen Falck-Zonen Tow Truck, red, no other data, thought to be a prototype only.
405 Volkswagen Red Cross Ambulance, a van, unlike the buses below, in white, 1/43 scale, no other data.
408 Volkswagen Fire Truck, the VW pickup with hose reels and equipment box, hose couplings, trailer hitch and blue dome light, 105 mm, 1/43 scale, 1962.
408 Volkswagen Falck Fire Truck, the same model with Falck decals, 105 mm, 1/43 scale, 1962.
409 Aerial Ladder Trailer, with simple chassis, jacks so it can stand alone, and a two-section ladder controlled by two cranks, 205 mm, 1/43 scale, 1962.
411 Volkswagen Falck Ambulance, a VW bus in Falck livery, 84 mm, 1/43 scale, 1959.
412 Volkswagen Zonen Ambulance, the same in Zonen colors, 84 mm, 1/43 scale, 1959; # may be 411.
412 Volkswagen Svensk Räddningstjänst Ambulance, the silver and red Swedish issue, 84 mm, 1/43 scale, 1959.
414 Volkswagen Ambulance, in white with red crosses, 84 mm, 1/43 scale, 1959; # may be 411.
414 Volkswagen Military Ambulance, this time in olive drab, 84 mm, 1/43 scale, 1959.
415a Ford Taunus Falck-Zonen Ambulance, a van, either all red, all white or white and black, with Falck-Zonen Maltese cross emblems and a patient on a stretcher, 98 mm, 1/43 scale, 1966.
415rk Ford Taunus Red Cross Ambulance, in white with red crosses, 98 mm, 1/43 scale, 1966.
424 Packard Zonen Ambulance, painted either white or red and black, a real rarity, 107 mm, 1/43 scale, 1948.
436 Volvo Falck Tow Truck, in red with Falck decals, 176 mm, 1/43 scale, 1958.
436 Volvo Falck-Zonen Tow Truck, in red with Falck-Zonen emblems, 176 mm, 1/43 scale, after the merger.
436 Volvo Svensk Räddningstjänst Tow Truck, in yellow or blue, for Sweden's equivalent of Falck-Zonen, 176 mm, 1/43 scale, 1958.
436 Volvo Falcken Tow Truck, the Norwegian version, in blue, 176 mm, 1/43 scale, 1958.
437 Volvo Falck-Zonen Flat Trailer, in red with white lettering, 163 mm, 1/43 scale, 1958.
437 Volvo Svensk Räddningstjänst Trailer, in yellow, the Swedish issue, 163 mm, 1/43 scale, 1958.
437 Volvo Falcken Flat Trailer, the blue Norse issue, 163 mm, 1/43 scale, 1958. 436 can pull 437.
445 Scania-Vabis 76 Ladder Truck, a Tekno classic, with the aerial ladder already seen on 409 and a hose reel at the rear, 205 mm, 1/43 scale, 1959.
445 Scania-Vabis 76 Falck-Zonen Ladder Truck, the same model with Falck-Zonen Maltese cross emblems on the doors, 205 mm, 1/43 scale, 1959.
459 Volvo Fire Engine, a worthy companion for 445, a box truck with ladder and hose on top, hose reels on either side, and a pump with folding shields on the front bumper, 146 mm, 1/43 scale, 1963.
459 Volvo Falck-Zonen Fire Engine, the same model with Falck-Zonen lettering and emblems, 146 mm, 1/43 scale, 1963.
480 Ford Zonen Service Truck, a low-side open truck, either red and black or white and red, with Zonen lettering, 115 mm, 1/43 scale, 1949.
481 Ford Zonen Tow Truck, in red with black fenders and chassis, or all red, plus Zonen emblems, 115 mm, 1/43 scale, 1949.
482 Mercury Fire Chief, Tekno's beloved 1948 Mercury sedan in fire department colors, 114 mm, 1/43 scale, 1949. # may be 429.
483 Mercury Zonen Loudspeaker Car, the same sedan with loudspeakers and Zonen emblems, 114 mm, 1/43 scale, 1949. # may be 429.
485 Triangel Ladder Truck, representing a Danish body on a Ford chassis, in red and black, with a ladder like that on 404 and a yellow flag on the fender, 130 mm, 1/43 scale, 1949.
485 Triangel Zonen Ladder Truck, the same model with Zonen emblems, 130 mm, 1/43 scale, 1949.
486 Triangel Fire Engine, with enclosed body, ladder and spotlight on the roof, and two yellow warning flags, 123 mm, 1/43 scale, 1949.
486 Triangel Zonen Fire Engine, the same with Zonen emblems, 123 mm, 1/43 scale, 1949.
487 Fire Pump Trailer, a red ansd black two-wheeler with pump, hose and spotlight, 63 mm, 1/43 scale, 1949; 485 or 486 can tow it.
487 Zonen Fire Pump Trailer, with gold lettering, 63 mm, 1/43 scale, 1949.
725 Mercedes-Benz 220SE Fire Chief, in red with black roof, siren and lights, yellow pennant and appropriate decals, 117 mm, 1/43 scale, 1965.
730 Mercedes-Benz 220S Falck Ambulance, looking like a hearse in black, with yellow pennant and Falck logo, 120 1/43 scale, 1962.
730 Mercedes-Benz 220S Falck-Zonen Ambulance, black as before, 120 mm, 1/43 scale, after the merger.
730 Mercedes-Benz 220S Fire Department Ambulance, in red, 120 mm, 1/43 scale, 1962.
730 Mercedes-Benz 220S Red Cross Ambulance, the same model in white, 120 mm, 1/43 scale, 1962.
731 Buick Falck Ambulance, an earlier model than the Mercedes but just as black, with Falck emblems, 120 mm, 1/43 scale, 1949. The earliest issues bear the name of H. Langes Legetoj, a firm that merged with Tekno, on the base. The Buicks are usually called Dodges and have Dodge wheel hubs.
731 Mercedes-Benz 220S Fire Department Ambulance, in red with black roof, or all in red, 120 mm, 1/43 scale, 1962.
732 Dodge Falck Ambulance, in red with Falck emblems and lettering, 120 mm, 1/43 scale, 1949.
732 Dodge Zonen Ambulance, the same model with different decals, 120 mm, 1/43 scale, 1949.
732 Dodge Red Cross Ambulance, not confirmed.
732 Mercedes-Benz 220S Falck-Zonen Ambulance, in white with the emblem of the merged agency, 120 mm, 1/43 scale, 1962.
732 Mercedes-Benz 220S Rädningskären Ambulance, red and black, 120 mm, 1/43 scale, 1962.
732 Mercedes-Benz 220S Svensk Rädningstjänst Ambulance, silver and blue. the Swedish issue, 120 mm, 1/43 scale, 1962.
733 Dodge Ambulance, in white, with Ambulance lettering but no red crosses, 120 mm, 1/43 scale, 1949. There may also be a Red Cross type.
733 Dodge Svensk Räddningstjänst Ambulance, also white, 120 mm, 1/43 in black or yellow with a Falck emblem atop the sidecar box, 71 mm, 1/43 scale, 1950.
780 Dodge Falck Wrecker, one of a smaller-scale series of trucks, 103 mm, 1/50 scale, 1950.
814 Red Cross Jeep, in white with red cross decals and driver, 76 mm, 1/43 scale, 1958.
814 Falck Jeep, in red with Falck decals, 76 mm, 1/43 scale, 1958.
814 Falck-Zonen Jeep, still in red, 76 mm, 1/43 scale, after the merger.
814 Svensk Räddningstjänst Jeep, the blue Swedish version, 76 mm, 1/43 scale, 1958.
814p Red Cross Jeep Trailer, a white two-wheeler, 50 mm, 1/43 scale, 1958. This may actually be the white UN trailer.
814p Falck Jeep Trailer, the same open two-wheel job in red, 50 mm, 1/43 scale, 1958.
814p Falck-Zonen Jeep Trailer, still red, 50 mm, 1/43 scale, after the merger.
835b Volvo 144 Fire Chief, in red and black, with spotlight, dome lights, antenna and decals, 107 mm, 1/43 scale, 1970.
850 Volvo Red Cross Bus, in white, 152 mm, 1/43 scale, 1962.
920 Ford D800 Falck-Zonen Truck, a red flatbed with rear ramps, winch and Falck-Zonen decals, 180 mm, 1/43 scale, 1971.
952 Dodge Military Ambulance Truck, in white with cloth rear cover, red cross decals and a roof-mounted spotlight that steers it, 118 mm, 1/43 scale, 1958.
956 Dodge Fire Searchlight Truck, in red with a big adjustable searchlight, a hose reel and the same steering spotlight, 130 mm, 1/43 scale, 1958.
957 Dodge Ladder Truck, the same chassis and body, with a two-section aerial ladder and two seated firefighters, 130 mm, 1/43 scale, 1958.
#? Ford Zonen Generator Truck, an open red truck with a gas cylinder on its right side, 115 mm, 1/43 scale, 1946 or later.

In prewar and early postwar days Tekno made toy vehicles of sheet metal. Their scale is larger than O gauge, but they deserve mention all the same. The trucks are patterned after Bedford vehicles, and most of the emergency vehicles were made in both Falck and Zonen versions, and Falck and Zonen stations, with two, three or four garage doors, were also made.

311 Fire Truck, with open cab and low rear box, like 361 without its searchlight; Falck decals.
313 Falck Two-Wheel Trailer, perhaps also in Zonen colors, to be pulled by 311.
321 Fire Truck, with open cab, driver and high rear box body with an axe on the side; Falck and Zonen versions.
331 Emergency Crane Truck; Falck and Zonen versions.
341 Fire Truck, with two ladders and four hose reels; Falck and Zonen versions.
351 Ambulance, looking rather like a delivery van, with its cab open at the sides, Falck, Zonen and Red Cross versions.
361 Fire Searchlight Truck, 311 with a big light mounted in back; Falck and Zonen versions.
371 Generator Truck, an ordinary open truck with a gas cylinder slung on its right side; Falck version only.

All of these were made in or after 1935; the trucks are approximately six inches long.

Other Scandinavian Models — Netherlands and Belgium

Other Scandinavian Models

Tekno was not the only Scandinavian firm to produce miniature or toy vehicles. In prewar days K. A. Birk made cast lead miniatures. More recently, a Tekno toymaker founded the Vilmer firm, whose first products bore much resemblance to Tekno toys. Lego, though best known for its toys made of many small plastic blocks (which purists will be horrified to find on our list), once made a series of small-scale plastic vehicles, as well as some, now very rare, in 1/43 scale. Lemeco produced diecast miniatures inspired by Dinky Toys, L.K.E. and Tomte have worked in softer materials, and Heljahn makes HO scale plastic kits.

BIRK

The firm of K. A. Birk produced interesting cast lead miniatures in Denmark around 1940.
IV Ambulance, with body style and particularly grille reminiscent of the Tootsietoy Graham ambulance, O gauge, no other data, circa 1940.
VIII Fire Truck, with the same grille, an open cab, firemen, a ladder and a hose reel in back, O gauge, no other data, circa 1940.

BIRK COPY?

 # ? Ambulance, an unpainted slush casting with a red cross on a raised roof panel, said to have been based on a Birk model, 88 mm, O gauge or smaller, prewar?

HELJAHN

This present-day Danish firm makes HO scale plastic kits.
34 Ford 1931 Ambulance, 1/87 scale, no other data, early eighties.
905 U.S. 1905 Fire House, 1/87 scale, no other data, early eighties.
1778 Modern Fire Station, 1/87 scale, no other data, early eighties.

LEGO

Lego's O and HO gauge plastic miniatures are long obsolete; their construction toys, which are not scale models at all, are still current.
655 Bedford Ladder Truck, with a gray two-section aerial ladder and rear-mounted hose reel, 88 mm, 1/87 scale, Sixties or before.
655 Mercedes-Benz Ladder Truck, with shorter cab, longer rear body and the same ladder and hose reel, 90 mm, 1/87 scale, Sixties or before.
960 Chevrolet Ambulance, red plastic, 1/43 scale, no other data, 1952.
970 Chevrolet Ambulance, in black this time, 1/43 scale, no other data, 1952.
6364 Paramedic Unit, including a building, a car, and figures, current.
6382 Fire Station, with a large fire house, two trucks and figures, current.
202 Fire Unit 1, an odd-looking chief's car plus a figure, current.
6650 Fire and Rescue Van, plus a figure, current.
6680 Ambulance, plus stretcher bearers, current.
6690 Snorkel Pumper, a big semi-trailer rig, plus two firefighter figures, current.

LEMECO

This Danish firm based its products on early postwar Dinky Toys.
ML47 Red Cross Jeep, similar to the well-known Dinky #153a model, 1/48 scale, no other data, Fifties.
ML90 Red Cross Trailer, an open two-wheeler for the Jeep to pull, 55 mm, 1/48 scale, Fifties.

L.K.E.

I know only that L.K.E. made this soft vinyl toy.
#? Fire Truck, a simple, typically European design, with closed cab and ladder on top, plus suction hose on each side, 97 mm, about S gauge, postwar.

TOMTE-LAERDAL

Laerdal may well be the home town of the Tomte firm, which makes rubber toy vehicles, including one too big for our list (C-R Vol. I, p. 131), and:
4 Fire Engine, an orange rubber truck with sirens, hose reels, suction hose, a ladder, an axe and other equipment cast in, 93 mm, about S gauge, Sixties.

VILMER

Like the Tekno firm from which its founder came, Vilmer produced many interesting diecast trucks, beginning with two Tekno-like Dodges. Some later Vilmer trucks were later reissued by Chico of Colombia.
#? Dodge Ladder Truck, steered by a spare tire on the cab roof, with its aerial ladder resting on a rack over the bench for the seated firemen, 112 mm, 1/43 scale, Sixties or before.
#? Dodge Searchlight Truck, the same vehicle with an adjustable searchlight in place of the ladder, and a hose reel at the rear, 132 mm, 1/43 scale, Sixties or before.
653 Volvo Red Cross Truck, with long-nose cab, plastic rear cover and red cross decals, 135 mm, 1/43 scale, Seventies or before.
657 Volvo Ladder Truck, with a three-section aerial ladder resting between two blue dome lights, 146 mm, 1/43 scale, Seventies or before.
725A Ford Thames Falck Crane Truck, with Falck lettering on its boom and a magnet at the end, 142 mm, 1/43 scale, Seventies or before.
853 Mercedes-Benz Red Cross Truck, with stubbier nose and shorter chassis than 653, otherwise the same, 123 mm, 1/43 scale, Seventies or before.
857 Mercedes-Benz Ladder Truck, again shorter than the Volvo but with the same equipment, 135 mm, 1/43 scale, Seventies or before.
2722 Volvo Falck Truck, with a light crane just behind the cab and a hydraulic lift at the rear, 150 mm, 1/43 scale, Seventies or before.
2724 Volvo Fire Truck, 1/43 scale, no other data, Seventies or before.

The Netherlands and Belgium

All but a few of the models on this list were produced by a Netherlands government agency which employs handicapped workers; originally called Best Box, the models now appear under three names: Holland, Oto, and most frequently Efsi, a name made from the agency's F.S.I. initials. Two other firms from The Netherlands, Lion Cars and G.S.P., have also contributed to our list, as has the Gasquy-Septoy company of Belgium.

BEST BOX

503 DAF Fire Engine, the only model of a real fire truck from Holland, simple but with good detail and its own personality, 62 mm, 1/70 scale, Fifties.

EFSI

Efsi has used two or more numbering systems; this list is a compromise between them.
107 Model T Ford Ambulance, a white van with red cross labels, using what was originally a 1960 Best Box casting, 57 mm, 1/70 scale, early Seventies.
110 Model T Ford Fire Truck, the same van in red with a ladder on the roof and Fire Dept. NY rondels on the sides, 57 mm, 1/70 scale, early Seventies.
111 Model T Ford Army Ambulance, the same casting again in olive drab with red cross labels, 57 mm, 1/70 scale, early Seventies.
154 Land Rover Ambulance, with orange-brown plastic rear cover, blue dome light helping to hold it on, and red cross rondels, 75 mm, 1/63 scale, 1980, also numbered 254.
206 Citroen C35 Netherlands Red Cross Ambulance, a white van with dome light, antenna and red logo, 77 mm, 1/68 scale, 1980.
301 Citroen C35 Ambulance, a simpler version of the same van, with red crosses but no lettering, 77 mm, 1/68 scale, 1981.
301 Commer Army Ambulance, an olive drab van with red cross labels, 71 mm, 1/68 scale, Seventies; the number is from an earlier series than that of the Citroen above.
302a Commer Ambulance, civilian counterpart of the above, in white with blue dome light and red cross labels, 71 mm, 1/68 scale, Seventies.
302c Commer Fire Service Van, the same casting in dayglo red with Fire Service labels and the Model T's roof ladder, 71 mm, 1/68 scale, Seventies.

304a Mercedes-Benz Army Red Cross Truck, in olive with a lighter olive plastic cover bearing red cross labels, 74 mm, 1/90 scale, Seventies.
306a Army Red Cross Trailer, a covered four-wheeler with details much like those of the truck that pulls it, 78 mm, 1/90 scale, Seventies.
308 Mercedes-Benz Ladder Truck, with the same cab as #304a and a two-section aerial ladder in back, sometimes in darkish red with dome lights and Pompier labels, sometimes in dayglo red with neither, 77 mm, 1/90 scale, Seventies; later re-issued as #931 (see below).
308 Mercedes-Benz Army Ladder Truck, the same model in olive, 77 mm, 1/90 scale, Seventies.
409 Citroen ID19 Ambulance, a white station wagon with red cross and blue light, 77 mm, 1/70 scale, Seventies.
411 Ford Transit Ambulance, a light van in white with red crosses and blue light, 58 mm, about HO scale, Seventies.
552, a combination of the **304 Fire Service Van** and **931 Ladder Truck** in one pack, 1984.
558, the 301 Citroen Ambulance with a police Land Rover, 1984.
560, the 254 Land Rover Ambulance and a police minibus, 1984.
920 Land Rover Blood Transfusion Unit, the 154 casting all in white, with red logo and gray antenna, 75 mm, 1/63 scale, 1981.
930 Mercedes-Benz Fire Tank Truck, the familiar chassis-cab with a red plastic tank, white ladder and black Brandweer lettering, 77 mm, 1/90 scale, 1981, later #409 without and 410 with Pompier labels.
931 Mercedes-Benz Ladder Truck, #308 reissued to match 930, its ladder and mount now white, plus a Brandweer label on its nose, 77 mm, 1/90 scale, 1981.
#? Mercedes-Benz Rescue Crane Truck, the familiar chassis-cab with a crane mounted on a square flat panel at the rear, unknown to me but in C-R Vol. II, p. 21.

G.S.P.

This present-day firm from Holland makes HO scale plastic models and kits.
1013 Peugeot 203 Fire Chief, a readymade model, 1/87 scale, no other data, 1984 or before.

GASQUY-SEPTOY

This Belgian firm made two series of diecast models in the late Forties, and must have made the first model listed below at least a decade later.
026 Citroen Fire Department Van, based on a Dinky Toys casting, no other data, Fifties?
#? Mercury Ambulance, a simple van in cream with red cross decal, with or without a clockwork motor, 95 mm, O gauge, 1947.
#? Red Cross Jeep, open and white, other details not known, 73 mm, 1/43 scale, 1945.

LION CARS

Most of this firm's models represent DAF cars and trucks, but it has also made a few others, such as this miniature of a familiar British van.
Commer London Fire Control Van, a special issue in London Fire Brigade livery, for sale in a London shop, 107 mm, 1/43 scale, 1982.
Commer Rutland Fire Control Van, another version of the same model, presumably for sale in Rutland and elsewhere in England, 107 mm, 1/43 scale, 1984.

Solido

In prewar and early postwar days Solido models consisted of heavy and sometimes crude bodies attached to chassis that were made to fit a whole series of models, and to which either seats or a windup motor could be attached. Solido made several such series, of which two, the 1/35 scale Major and the 1/40 scale Junior Series, included emergency vehicles. When Solido introduced a new high-quality series of 1/43 scale diecast vehicles in 1957, there were no emergency vehicles in it. Only in 1973 did Solido again produce model fire trucks; others were added through 1980, in which year a new four-digit numbering system was introduced. A year later the firm was sold to the makers of Majorette models, who have retained and recently varied the four-digit system of catalog numbers. As a result of these changes, some models have had two and even three catalog numbers, all of which will be listed below to give you complete information.

MAJOR AND JUNIOR SERIES

43e Fire Escape Truck, Major Series, 1/35 scale, no other data, 1938.
68 Simplex Ladder Truck, Junior Series, with sloping grille, separate chassis-hood and body castings, a ladder and hose reels, 1/40 scale, no other data, 1939.
92 Fire Escape Truck, Junior Series, with an aerial ladder raised by crank and gear, plus a hose reel below, 127 mm, 1/40 scale, 1950 (one source says 1947). It can be found with either forward control or long-nose cab.
95 Fire Truck, Junior Series, with large closed cab, open rear with benches, and twelve seated firefighters, 123 mm, 1/40 scale, 1952.
96 Ladder Truck, Junior Series, the same chassis, cab and rear body as 95, with a two-section aerial ladder, 123 mm, 1/40 scale, 1952. Mine, with benches and six seated firemen, seems to be a 95-96 hybrid, with the major features of both, and the ladder mounted at the rear.
97 Crane Truck, the same truck again with crane boom and hook; one source calls it a "fire department tow truck", another simply a "break-down truck". 123 mm, 1/40 scale, 1952.
196 Ford Fairlane Ambulance, Junior Series, a white wagon with removable plastic top and Ambulance lettering, 122 mm, 1/40 scale, 1956.

THE 1/43 SCALE SERIES 1957-1979

216 Auto Union Fire Department Jeep, shown in the 1967 catalog but never issued in this form; the casting was used for a military model; 82 mm, 1/43 scale.
227 AMX 13-Ton VCI, an armored vehicle with red cross markings for use as an army ambulance, 111 mm, 1/50 scale, 1961.
255 Berliet Army Airport Fire Truck, a rugged Camiva tanker with foam nozzle and ladder, 140 mm, 1/50 scale, 1978, later #2255; same casting as #351.
259 Citroen Army Ambulance, a C35 bus in olive with red cross decals and blue dome light, 100 mm, 1/50 scale, 1978, later #2259; same casting as #368 & #371.
350 Berliet Camiva Fire Engine, with a long cab, plastic rear box, ladder, two hose reels and Ville de Paris emblems, 125 mm, 1/50 scale, 1973, later #3350.
351 Berliet Airport Fire Truck, the #255 casting in red with cream roof and Aeroport de Paris logo, 140 mm, 1/50 scale, 1973, later #3351.
352 Berliet Camiva Ladder Truck, with a cab like #350 and a two-section diecast aerial ladder, 163 mm, 1/50 scale, 1973, later #3352.
353 Richier Crane Truck, which can be a fire rescue vehicle when painted red (it was also issued in yellow), 140 mm, 1/50 scale, 1973, later #3353.
354 Berliet Camiva Forest Fire Truck and Guinard Pump Trailer, a stubby firefighting truck with a sleek little trailer issued separately as 360, 140 mm, 1/50 scale, 1973, later #3354.
360 Guinard Fire Pump Trailer, with no visible sign of containing a pump, 53 mm, 1/50 scale, 1974.
361 Mercedes-Benz Ladder Truck, a Mercedes LP1418/46 cab and the ladder from 352, 165 mm, 1/50 scale, 1974, later #3361.
362 Hotchkiss H6 G54 Fire Engine, a sleek little open-cab truck with hose reels and booster tank, 112 mm, 1/66 scale, 1975, later #3362, then #2000.
366 Saviem SG4 Wrecker, all in red as a fire department vehicle or with a white cab and SOS decals, 110 mm, 1/50 scale, 1977, later #3301.
368 Citroen C35 Fire Department Van, the 259 casting in red with a white roof and Service Departmental d'Incendie decals, 100 mm, 1/50 scale, 1977, later #3368, then #2002; also used in #371.
371 Citroen C35 Fire Van and Lifeboat, #368 pulling a rubber boat on a diecast two-wheel trailer, 190 mm, 1/50 scale, 1977, later #3371, then #3000.
375 Berliet GAK 17 Fire Engine, a boxy red truck with white roof racks, sirens, hose reels and Ville de Paris logo, 115 mm, 1/55 scale, 1978, later #3375.
377 Mercedes-Benz Snorkel, never actually made as an emergency vehicle, but released as a cherry picker for a TV station, 180 mm, 1/50 scale, 1978.
380 Peugeot J7 Fire Department Ambulance, a minibus, either all red or with a white roof, 94 mm, 1/50 scale, 1978, later #3380.
391 Dodge Fire Department Truck and Trailer, an open red 6x6 World War II veteran and open two-wheel trailer, neither with any firefighting equipment, 178 mm, 1/65 scale, 1979, later #3391.
23 Peugeot 504 Ambulance, a white wagon with a sliding stretcher, dome light, flag and Ambulance Municipale decals, 111 mm, 1/43 scale, 1974, later #1123.

23d Peugeot 504 Fire Depaertment Ambulance, the same wagon in red with Sapeurs Pompiers decals, 111 mm, 1/43 scale, 1979, later #1126.
42 Renault 4 Fire Department Van, with the Paris coat of arms, 89 mm, 1/43 scale, 1976, later #1002.

NEW CATALOG NUMBERS 1980 AND BEYOND

1002 Renault 4 Fire Department Van, ex-42, 89 mm, 1/43 scale, 1980, later #1325.
1034 Fire Department Land Rover, in red with white roof and Sapeurs Pompiers logo, 108 mm, 1/43 scale, 1980.
1123 Peugeot 504 Ambulance, ex-23, 111 mm, 1/43 scale, 1980.
1126 Peugeot 504 Fire Department Ambulance, ex-23d, 111 mm, 1/43 scale, 1980.
1306 Peugeot 504 First Aid Car, a white sedan with blue Ambulance lettering and emblems, 105 mm, 1/43 scale, 1982.
1307 Talbot Tagora may have been issued in ambulance form, 1/43 scale, no other data, 1982.
1318 Renault 18 Fire Chief, in red with Sapeur Pompier lettering and Paris arms, 99 mm, 1/43 scale, 1982.
1319 Talbot Horizon may have been issued as a fire chief's car, 1/43 scale, no other data, 1982.
1322 Fire Department Jeep, the open version, with Sapeur Pompier lettering and Paris arms, 82 mm, 1/43 scale, 1982, later issued with a plastic top.
1325 Renault 4 Fire Department Van, ex-42/1002 with Sapeurs Pompiers logo, 89 mm, 1/43 scale, 1982.
2000 Hotchkiss Fire Engine, ex-362/3362, 112 mm, 1/66 scale, 1983.
2001 Saviem Fire Engine, ex-3303, with Sapeur Pompier lettering and Paris arms, 114 mm, 1/50 scale, 1983.
2002 Citroen C35 Fire Department Ambulance, ex-380/3380, 94 mm, 1/50 scale, 1983.
2008 may be a 1983 renumbering of the 350/3350 Berliet Fire Engine.
2255 Berliet Army Airport Fire Truck, ex-255, 140 mm, 1/50 scale, 1980.
2259 Citroen C35 Army Ambulance, ex-259, 100 mm, 1/50 scale, 1980.
3000 Citroen C35 Fire Van and Lifeboat, ex-371/3371, 190 mm, 1/50 scale, 1983.
3004 Dodge Forest Fire Truck and Pump Trailer, the old 391/3391 war horse with the ex-360 Guinard trailer, which adds something, 168 mm, 1/65 scale, 1983.
3301 Saviem Fire Department Wrecker, ex-366, probably also the SOS version which was renumbered 2006 in 1983, 110 mm, 1/50 scale,

3303 Saviem Fire Engine, the SG4 wrecker body with additional rear bodywork and equipment including hose and ladder, with white Sapeurs Pompiers Var logo, 114 mm, 1/50 scale, 1980.
3304 Fire Department Jeep and Pump Trailer, with a gray plastic cover on the Jeep and the Guinard trailer tagging along, 130 mm, 1/43 scale, 1980.
3350 Berliet Fire Engine, ex-350, 125 mm, 1/50 scale, 1980, perhaps later #2008.
3351 Berliet Airport Fire Truck, ex-351, 140 mm, 1/50 scale, 1980.
3352 Berliet Ladder Truck, ex-352, 163 mm, 1/50 scale, 1980.
3353 Richier Rescue Crane, ex-353, 140 mm, 1/50 scale, 1980.
3354 Berliet Forest Fire Truck and Pump Trailer, ex-354, 140 mm, 1/50 scale, 1980.
3361 Mercedes-Benz Ladder Truck, ex-361, 165 mm, 1/50 scale, 1980.
3362 Hotchkiss Fire Engine, ex-362, 112 mm, 1/66 scale, 1980, later #2000.
3368 Citroen C35 Fire Department Ambulance, ex-368, 100 mm, 1/50 scale, 1980, later #2002.
3371 Citroen C35 Fire Van and Lifeboat, ex-371, 190 mm, 1/50 scale, 1980, later #3000.
3375 Berliet Fire Engine, ex-375, 115 mm, 1/55 scale, 1980.
3380 Peugeot J7 Fire Department Ambulance, ex-380, 94 mm, 1/50 scale, 1980.
3391 Dodge Fire Truck and Trailer, ex-391, 178 mm, 1/65 scale, 1980.
4033 Citroen 15cv Fire Chief, the classic 1939 sedan with Sapeur Pompier and Paris arms decals, 112 mm, 1/43 scale, 1980.
4038 Cadillac Ambulance, a long red sedan with, believe it or not, Manhattan Fire Brigade lettering in gold, shown in the catalog in white with red crosses and Detroit Fire Dept. logo but so far not issued in that form, 130 mm, 1/43 scale, 1984.
4403 Citroen C4 1930 Fire Engine, an open truck with ladders, hose, seats for firemen (but no firemen), and Ville d'Argeles Gazost logo, 108 mm, 1/43 scale, 1982.
4411 Citroen C4 1930 Ambulance, a white box van with red crosses and Centrale Sanitaire Internationale logo, 105 mm, 1/43 scale, 1984.
7002 Fire Vehicles Set, with the 1325 Renault Van, 2001 Saviem Fire Truck, 3352 Ladder Truck and a covered Dodge truck of the 3391 type, 1984.
No# Dodge Medical Corps Truck, a re-issue of the former #242 army truck later painted red and used in #391, this time as a covered army truck with red crosses, part of Solido's D-Day Set, 118 mm, 1/65 scale, 1984.
1 Citroen C4 Fire Department Persônnel Truck, with two men in its open cab and eight more in back, plus a ladder on the side, one of four plinth-mounted Solido Specials, 1/43 scale, no other data, 1984.
2 Citroen C4 Fire Tank Truck, with closed cab, ladders over the tank and a hose reel at the rear, 1/43 scale, no other data, 1984.
3 Citroen C4 Paris Fire Truck, a closed-cab 1200kg box van with ville de Paris logo, 1/43 scale, no other data, 1984.
4 Citroen C4 Paris Fire Pumper, 1/43 scale, no other data, 1984.
Note: not all scales given above are confirmed. As for lettering, it reads "Sapeurs Pompiers" (plural) on some vehicles, "Sapeur Pompier" (singular) on others, usually more recent issues, each as stated in the text.

Majorette

Since the Sixties the French firm of Majorette, also known in the early days as Rail-Route, has made interesting small-scale miniature vehicles. The first series was divided into the 200 and 300 lines that in the most recent years have been joined by models in larger scales. Majorette is also the present owner of the time-honored firm of Solido.
4 Bernard Ladder Truck, originally with opening plastic doors and a driver, plus a two-section aerial ladder, 82 mm, 1/100 scale, 1966.
7 Fire Department Jeep, in red with a hose reel setting in back and a green driver sitting in front, 57 mm, 1/65 scale, late Sixties.
204 Bernard Ladder Truck, now with a fully diecast cab, gray chassis and no opening doors or driver, otherwise as before, 82 mm, 1/100 scale, 1969.
204 Dodge Fire Truck, a light vehicle with hose reels and couplings, a ladder on the roof, and sometimes Fire Brigade emblems, 72 mm, 1/80 scale, 1973.
204 Dodge Army Fire Truck, the same model in olive drab, 72 mm, 1/80 scale, 1978.
206 Peugeot 404 Ambulance, a white wagon with red cross and dome light, 74 mm, 1/65 scale, 1969.
206 Citroen DS21 Ambulance, in white with amber or blue windows and dome light, blue pennants and varying lettering, 79 mm, 1/65 scale, 1973.
224 Mercedes-Benz Unimog Fire Truck, with Fire Service labels on its removable cover, blue windows and dome lights, 67 mm, 1/82 scale, 1980.
229 Datsun 260Z Doctor's Car, a sport coupe with red and green decals including an emblem that isn't quite a caduceus, 75 mm, 1/60 scale, 1979.
230 Renault 4L Fire Department Van, a typical French light van in red with unconvincing yellow decals, 71 mm, 1/55 scale, 1977.
241 Saviem Army Red Cross Truck, in olive with tan plastic cover and red crosses, 79 mm, 1/100 scale, 1978.
243 Army Red Cross Trailer, similar to the truck that pulls it, 67 mm, 1/100 scale, 1978.
244 Volkswagen Kombi Ambulance, a white bus with amber light and red cross, first issued with Ambulance lettering, 77 mm, 1/60 scale, 1974.
244 Volkswagen Red Cross Ambulance, the same model with blue Croix-Rouge Francaise logo, 77 mm, 1/60 scale, 1976.
244 Volkswagen Army Ambulance, in olive drab this time, with red crosses, 77 mm, 1/60 scale, 1978.
244 Volkswagen Fire Department Bus, now red with Fire Brigade emblems, 77 mm, 1/60 scale, 1980.
246 Range Rover Fire Truck, with six blue firemen inside and a ladder made to look like two on the roof, 76 mm, 1/60 scale, 1979.
258 Mercedes-Benz Airport Fire Truck, half of it cab, the other half with valves and gauges and a big foam nozzle, 77 mm, 1/70 scale, 1979.
264 Alpine-Renault A310 Doctor's Car, with red SOS Doctor lettering and blue windows, louvers and light, 75 mm, 1/55 scale, 1983.
269 Cherokee Ambulance, with roof bar, raised rear roof, opening rear doors and detailed interior including a patient on a stretcher, 75 mm, 1/64 scale, 1980.
362 Dodge Fire Truck and Lifeboat Trailer, #204 pulling a plastic boat on a trailer, 137 mm, 1/80 scale, 1974.
376 Range Rover Fire Truck and Tank Trailer, #246 with a red two-wheel water tank trailer with a big coat of arms, 140 mm, 1/60 scale, 1979 or 1980.
601 Low Loader and Rescue Helicopter, an American-style cab, silver lowboy and red SOS Ambulance copter, 208 mm, 1/87 scale, 1983.
3021 Ford Ambulance Van, with red chassis, raised roof, trim, interior and patient, and eight blue lights on the roof, 138 mm, 1/36 scale, 1983.
3033 U. S. Fire Truck, a typical American pumper in red and white, with yellow hose reels, darker yellow interior, chrome roof bar and lots of equipment, 173 mm, 1/47 scale, 1983.
3091 Ward LaFrance Fire Snorkel, a big red and yellow machine with snorkel arms and basket, two firemen and "Rescue Unity" (sic) labels, 244 mm, 1/48 scale, 1984.
792 Fire Department Tank Truck, a red semi-trailer rig, about 1/43

Majorette — Norev — Eligor — Other French Brands

scale, no other data, 1984.
1509 Fiat Ladder Truck, 1/43 scale, no other data, 1982.
#? Range Rover Ambulance, slightly distorted and nose-down, with Ambulance labels and pullback motor, 73 mm, roughly S gauge, 1983.
#? Range Rover Fire Service Car, the same model in red with Fire Service labels, 73 mm, roughly S gauge, 1983.

Norev

Until very recently, Norev had produced only one full-blooded fire truck, plus various other fire vehicles, ambulances and doctors' cars, mostly of them in plastic. In fact, until 1971 all Norev models were made of plastic. The numbers listed below from two digits through the 300's, plus the 500's, represent the Norev tradition of 1/43 scale plastic miniatures. Norev has also produced 1/43 scale diecast models; the three 800 series models listed are among them. Shortly before 1980 the S-gauge diecast Mini-Jet models were introduced, originally in the high 900's, now with 400 series numbers. These models include several interesting small-scale fire vehicles.
14 Ford Vedette 54 Ambulance, a plastic sedan with red Ambulance signs, siren and antenna, 106 mm, 1/43 scale, 1957.
40 Citroen ID19 Ambulance, a white wagon with a stretcher that slides out its opening rear hatch, 115 mm, 1/43 scale, 1968, later re-issued as #344 and used in the #211 set.
41 Simca Marly Ambulance, another plastic wagon, also with a removable stretcher, plus a siren and two pennants, 109 mm, 1/43 scale, 1960.
97 Berliet Ladder Truck, a realistic model with a three-section aerial ladder, a Magirus DL30H, on a Berliet GBK18 chassis, 220 mm, 1/43 scale, 1968.
210 Accident SOS Set, the Peugeot J7 fire department ambulance sold seperately as #252, pulling a rubber rescue boat on a trailer, 222 mm, 1/43 scale, 1976.
211 Citroen ID19 Tour de France Ambulance and Cyclists, the #40/344 wagon with Ambulance Norev decals and three plastic bike racers, 115 mm, 1/43 scale, 1976.
211 Peugeot J7 Tour de France Ambulance and Cyclists, presumably a white version of #252, announced for 1976. Was it ever issued? I doubt it.
220 Saviem SG4 Fire Tank Truck, with two lengths of hose, a driver, and three firemen sitting in front of the tank, 127 mm, 1/43 scale, Seventies.
240 Renault 5 Doctor's Car, white with black roof panel, blue dome light and red SOS Medecin labels, 80 mm, 1/43 scale, Seventies. The metal version of the same model is #875.
241 Renault 4 Fire Department Van, with fireman driver, antenna and Sapeurs Pompiers labels, 90 mm, 1/43 scale, Seventies, recently re-issued as #341.
252 Peugeot J7 Fire Department Ambulance, already met in #210, with red cross, Accident and SOS labels, 107 mm, 1/43 scale, Seventies.
257 Mercedes-Benz Ambulance, perhaps a plastic version of #874, no other data, Seventies.
340 Renault 5 Doctor's Car, ex-240, 80 mm, 1/43 scale, early Eighties.
341 Renault 4 Fire Department Van, ex-241, without the driver, with amber dome lights and an antenna between them, 90 mm, 1/43 scale, early Eighties.
344 Citroen ID19 Ambulance, ex-41 with red stretcher to match its new interior, plus an amber dome light, 115 mm, 1/43 scale, early Eighties.
409 Renault 4TL Fire Department Wagon, with Sapeurs Pompiers labels, from the small-scale diecast Mini-Jet series, 63 mm, S gauge, 1982.
410 Mercedes-Benz Ambulance, ex-977, with red cross label, amber windows and dome light, 69 mm, S gauge, circa 1980.
427 Renault 4 Fire Department Van, presumably a small-scale diecast counterpart of #241/341, S gauge, 1984.
434 Volvo F-89 Fire Truck, with white plastic nozzle, hose and ladder, a fairly realistic little model, 73 mm, S to HO gauge, circa 1980.
442 Volvo Ladder Truck, the same cab with detailed plastic rear deck, diecast mount and plastic ladder made to look like two, 73 mm, S to HO gauge, 1982.
461 Fire Department Pickup Truck, a 4wd job with plastic rear body, hose reel and immovable ladder, 77 mm, S to HO gauge, 1984.
524 Saviem Fire Tank Truck, same vehicle as #220, 127 mm, 1/43 scale, Seventies.
525 DAF Fire Tank Truck, different cab, same tank, 1/43 scale, no other data, Seventies.
526 Volvo Fire Tank Truck, a different cab again, 1/43 scale, no other data, Seventies.
541 Medical Assistance Set, the #874 Mercedes-Benz Ambulance flanked by police motorcycles, 124 mm, 1/43 scale, Seventies.
610 Volvo Fire Truck and Trailer, including #434, listed as 1/87 scale, which it may well be, no other data, 1984.
615 Fire Department Pickup Truck and Trailer, comprising #461 and the same trailer as in #610, S to HO gauge, no other data, 1984.
865 Renault 4 Fire Department Van, diecast version of #241/341, with the same labels but only one amber dome light, 83 mm, 1/43 scale, Seventies.
874 Mercedes-Benz Ambulance, as used in #541, with red cross and S.A.M.U. labels, stretcher and two blue dome lights, 124 mm, 1/43 scale, Seventies.
875 Renault 5 Doctor's Car, with the same details as its plastic counterpart, #240/340, 80 mm, 1/43 scale, 1978.
977 Mercedes-Benz Ambulance, later renumbered #410 and identical to it, 69 mm, S gauge, Seventies.

Eligor

In its few years of existence, Eligor has produced many fine models of antique cars and trucks, including a rapidly growing number of emergency vehicles. They include several 1934 Ford trucks that have attained much popularity, albeit some controversy, in the United States, several vintage Citroen and Renault models, an Opel fire van and several chiefs' cars. The future should bring more of the same from Eligor.
1014p Renault Juvaquatre 1938 Fire Chief, a stubby red sedan with a siren and Service Sapeurs Pompiers decals, 88 mm, 1/43 scale, 1984.
1016p Peugeot 201 1931 Fire Chief, also a veteran French sedan, 1/43 scale, no other data, 1984.
1020 Citroen 1934 Fire Truck, a red van with ladder and hose on the roof and the usual detachable hose reel at the rear, 108 mm, 1/43 scale, 1979 or '80.
1021 Citroen 1934 Ambulance, the same 500kg van in white with flag, blue crosses and Ambulance Municipale decals, 93 mm, 1/43 scale, 1979 or '80.
1028 Citroen 1934 Fire Truck, with ladder and hose slung on the right side instead of on the roof, 108 mm, 1/43 scale, 1984.
1033 Citroen 11cv 1938 Fire Chief, that familiar silhouette with Service Departemental d'Incendie & de Secours de l'Ariege logo, 100 mm, 1/43 scale, 1981.
1049 Renault KZ 1928 Fire Engine, with a ladder, hose of all kinds, sirens, seats for firemen and the same decals as 1014p, 105 mm, 1/43 scale, 1981.
1056 Citroen 5cv Fire Department Van, a little truck with a long logo ending in "du Loiret" and gold sirens, 75 mm, 1/43 scale, 1981.
1079p Ford V8 1934 Fire Truck, in the cream, red and black colors of Sir Alan Cobham's Air Display, with roof and rear equipment, 123 mm, 1/43 scale, 1984.
1081 Ford V8 1934 Ambulance, a white van with a blue cross on its flag, green crosses elsewhere and brown lettering, 107 mm, 1/43 scale, 1982.
1082 Ford V8 Trenton Fire Department Truck, a pickup with black rear cover, ladder and hose on the right side, and the usual French hose reel aft, 120 mm, 1/43 scale, 1982.
1083 Ford V8 San Francisco Fire Department Truck, a van body like 1081 with a roof rack of equipment and the inevitable hose reel, 120 mm, 1/43 scale, 1982.
1084 Ford V8 Washington Fire Department Truck, an open pickup with a high rack of equipment, plus the eternal hose reel, 120 mm, 1/43 scale, 1983.
1087p Ford V8 Washington Fire Department Wrecker—one sees why purists complain that such models represent nonexistent vehicles—125 mm, 1/43 scale, 1983.
1091a Ford V8 Trenton Fire Department Tank Truck, with black fenders and filler caps, 109 mm, 1/43 scale, 1983.
1095 Opel 4hp 1925 Fire Department Van, with Stadt Rüdesheim (a wine-producing and -consuming town on the Rhine) decals and a ladder slung at a not too sober angle, 75 mm, 1/43 scale, 1983.
1109 Renault 4cv Fire Chief, with Sapeurs Pompiers de La Rochelle decals, 83 mm, 1/43 scale, 1984.
1118 BMW 2000 Fire Chief, 1/43 scale, no other data, 1984 or '85.
1122 Citroen DS21 Fire Department Car, conventionally red, 1/43 scale, no other data, 1984 or '85.
1126 Citroen DS21 Fire Chief's Car, in black, 1/43 scale, no other data, 1984 or '85.
1140 Peugeot 404 Fire Chief, 1/43 scale, no other data, 1984 or '85.
1141 Peugeot 404 Ambulance, 1/43 scale, no other data, 1984 or '85.
3001 Magirus 1925 Ladder Truck, made by Diano, distributed by Eligor and now also by Cofradis, 207 mm, 1/43 scale, circa 1979. See Cofradis, in the next chapter, for details.
3004 Citroen 11bl Fire Chief, with La Rochelle lettering, 1/25 scale, no other data.

Other French Brands

Numerous other French manufacturers have produced miniature emergency vehicles. Their history takes us from the A.R., C.D. and C.I.J. toys of prewar days through the Fifties with their diecast C.I.J. and J.R.D. models and into the present, which offers many models of modern-day vehicles as well as those that complete the circle by taking us back to bygone days.

A. R.

This firm made diecast 1/60 scale models of French cars and trucks in the Thirties.
Latil Fire Truck, 1/60 scale, no other data, Thirties.
Peugeot 301 Ambulance, a gray truck with sheet metal rear cover and red cross labels, 83 mm, 1/60 scale, Thirties.
Peugeot 301 Fire Truck, the same chassis-cab unit with a sheet metal rear body topped by a ladder, 94 mm, 1/60 scale, Thirties.
Renault 40cv Army Ambulance, a tall thin khaki truck with red cross rondels and four-spoked metal wheels, 85 mm, 1/60 scale, Thirties.

C. D.

C.D. produced 1/43 scale diecast models in the Thirties.
Chenard-Walcker Ambulance, 1/43 scale, no other data, Thirties.
Delahaye Ambulance, 1/43 scale, no other data, Thirties.
One of the above has a black chassis, gray body and white roof, red cross and Tricolor decals, and is 95 mm long.

C. I. J.

During the Thirties this firm made toy vehicles of plaster and flour. In the Fifties the 1/45 scale diecast Europarc series began, to be joined by a few small-scale versions. The firm left the scene in the late Sixties, not long after buying some dies from J.R.D., which had failed shortly before. In recent years some of the prewar models have been revived under the J. P. Cars name.
Renault Fire Engine, plaster, with ladder and hose reels, 100 mm, 1/43 scale, Thirties.
Renault Hose Truck, plaster, with six hose reels and a ladder, 1/43 scale, no other data, Thirties.
Renault Ladder Truck, plaster, with raising ladder, 1/43 scale, no other data, Thirties.
3/30 Fire Engine, with two men overflowing its open cab and a ladder atop its boxy body, not a scale model of anything, 100 mm, 1/45 scale, 1964.
3/41 Citroen ID19 Ambulance, a blue and white wagon with Croix-Rouge Francaise decals and a blue light bulb in its roof, 115 mm, 1/45 scale, 1964.
3/46e Peugeot 403 Emergency Car, another blue bulb, this time on a pale blue Secours Routier Francais wagon with a battery inside, 103 mm, 1/45 scale, 1964.
3/53a Renault Ambulance, another wagon, blue and white, with blue crosses, antenna and opaque rear windows, 102 mm, 1/45 scale, 1958.
3/55 Renault Colorale Ambulance, a bulbous panel van in cream, with blue cross pennant and Ambulance lettering, 96 mm, 1/45 scale, 1958.
3/61 Renault 1000 kg Ambulance, a van with wedge nose and corrugated roof, opening sheet metal rear doors and Ambulance Municipale decals, 105 mm, 1/45 scale, 1959.
3/61m Renault 1000 kg Army Ambulance, the same van in olive with huge red crosses, 105 mm, 1/45 scale, 1959.
3/95 Renault 2.5 Ton Fire Truck, with a raising ladder, removable hose reel and two lengths of hose, closed cab and open-air bench behind it, 135 mm, 1/45 scale, 1963.
M6 Renault 1000 kg Ambulance, a very small version of 3/61, all in white with one red cross, 43 mm, HO scale, if that, 1957.
M10 Renault 1000 kg Army Ambulance, the small version of 3/61m, 43 mm, HO or smaller scale, 1957.

CLE

This firm makes 1/48 scale plastic miniatures of modern and antique vehicles.
18 Citroen 1200 kg Ambulance, an angular, snub-nosed white van with red cross and Ambulance labels, 89 mm, 1/48 scale, Eighties or before.
18 Citroen 1200 kg Fire Truck, the same van in red with a ladder on the top but nothing to hold it there, plus Pompiers labels, 89 mm, 1/48 scale, Eighties or before.
24 Peugeot 404 Red Cross Car, a white sedan with a red cross on the hood and a red blob on the roof, 91 mm, 1/48 scale, Eighties or before.
#? Citroen B2 Ambulance, a little white 1923 van with Ambulance Municipale labels, 73 mm, 1/48 scale, Eighties or before.

COFALU

Cofalu has made some rather crude diecast models of vehicles associated with the Tour de France bicycle race.
Tour de France Ambulance, a big white and pink van with Service Sanitaire decals that also mention the French Red Cross and the Aspro firm, 155 mm, O gauge, Sixties?

COFRADIS

This present-day firm adapts Solido models for special uses and also merchandises models made by other French firms such as Diano.
0001 Citroen CX Fire Chief, a red Solido sedan with blue dome light, plus decals for you to add, 107 mm, 1/43 scale, 1983.
0003 Citroen CX Ambulance, the same car in white with blue asterisk decals, 107 mm, 1/43 scale, 1983.
0004 Peugeot 504 Fire Chief, another red sedan with blue dome light and the same decals that come with 0001, 105 mm, 1/43 scale, 1983.
380 Sides 2000 Airport Fire Truck, a massive machine, made by C.E.F., with a huge nozzle, filler caps and muffler on the roof, 255 mm, 1/43 scale, 1982.
534 Magirus-Deutz 1925 Ladder Truck, made by Diano, an open-cab flat truck with aerial ladder, hose reel and seats for firefighters, 207 mm, 1/43 scale, 1982. This model was previously distributed by Eligor.
1156 Sides 2000 Airport Fire Truck, another number for 380. I have seen references to a Sides 2000 model made by Sijam, which may be this same model under another name.

EMO

There may have been many French makers of tinplate toys in prewar days. Emo is one of the few I know of.
713 Citroen Ambulance, with a big shield grille, orange hood with louvers, blue trim and crosses in circles on its otherwise plain body, 152 mm, large scale, presumably prewar.

FRANCE JOUETS

F.J. made several series of truck models, each using the same cab with various rear bodies. The F.J. dies were later bought and used by Safir.
301 G.M.C. Army Ambulance, a white army truck with red crosses and Ambulance lettering on its sheet metal top, 102 mm, 1/45 scale, 1961.
407 Dodge Fire Truck, an open red World War II veteran with a two-section aerial ladder resting on its folding windshield, plus blue firefighter figures, 102 mm, 1/45 scale, 1966.
409 Dodge Army Ambulance, the same truck in white with a plastic top and tiny red crosses, 102 mm, 1/45 scale, 1967.
507 Jeep Fire Truck, an open red Jeep with its folding windshield supporting the ladder from #407, 100 mm, 1/45 scale, late Sixties.

J. P. CARS

Jean Piastre has made plaster-and-flour replicas of prewar C.I.J. and other early toys.
Citroen Fire Department Ambulance, at least that's what I assume it is; it has no logo but is painted red, 106 mm, 1/43 scale, circa 1980.
Fire Tank Truck, perhaps a Citroen, with a plastic ladder, a detachable hose reel, lengths of hose and other details, 125 mm, 1/43 scale, circa 1980.
Renault 1935 Fire Engine, with one hose reel below its ladder, another in back, and two firemen in its open cab, 100 mm, 1/43 scale, Seventies; the first C.I.J. model listed above reincarnated.

J. R. D.

This firm made 1/45 scale diecast cars and trucks in the Fifties and early Sixties. When it went out of business, C.I.J. bought some of its dies.
107 Citroen 1200 kg Ambulance, with typical French corrugated-sheet-metal styling, in white with red crosses, 102 mm, 1/45 scale, 1958.
109 Citroen 2cv Fire Tender, a familiar little van in similar style, with tinplate ladders on the roof, Paris coat of arms and S P (Sapeurs Pompiers) decals, 93 mm, 1/45 scale, 1958.
117 Citroen 2cv Secours Routier Van, this time without the ladders, as a road service van and thus related to C.I.J. 3/46e, 93 mm, 1/45 scale, 1958.
133 Berliet Fire Truck, with closed cab, ladder, suction hose, the

inevitable reel at the rear, and four blue men on a bench, 125 mm, 1/45 scale, 1961.

K. P.

Ambulance, a curious old slushmold vehicle with a small hood, driver in a cab open except for a roof rounded in front, and rather featureless rear body, painted light blue and black, with rubber tires on spoked wheels, 77 mm, perhaps S gauge, prewar.

MIGNOT

This firm has made toy soldiers since 1825, and its fire vehicles appear to go back almost as far; these picturesque 1/35 scale tinplate toys portray pre-World War I fire apparatus.
1300 Self-Propelled Steam Pumper, with a driver high up on the front seat and a boiler in the rear, 1/35 scale, no other data.
1301 Horsedrawn Ladder Truck, a wagon with ladders on a rack, plus horses and driver, 1/35 scale, no other data.
1302 Hose Reel, with the axle connecting its two wheels running through it and two running men pulling it, 1/35 scale, no other data.
1303 Hand pump, another two-wheeler pulled by two men, this time with flat bed, box housing, and pump handles, 1/35 scale, no other data.
1322 Ladder Truck, self-propelled but probably much like 1301, 1/35 scale, no other data.
1323 Horsedrawn Steam Pumper, perhaps a sort of retrogression from 1300, 1/35 scale, no other data.
1304 through 1321 are figures of firemen, 1324 is an alarm box. All of the above are currently in production by C.B.G. Mignot of Paris.

MINIALUXE

This firm makes plastic cars and trucks in 1/32 and 1/43 scales; its only emergency vehicles to date are in the larger scale.
Citroen 1200 kg Fire Department Van, with dome light and Sapeurs-Pompiers logo, about 140 mm, 1/32 scale, 1959 (C-R Vol. I, p. 94).
Simca Marly Ambulance, 1/32 scale, no other data, 1959.

QUIRALU

Quiralu made some good (and now rare) diecast vehicles in the late Fifties, and at least one colorful model before that.
Firemen with Hose Reel, a simple reel like that of Mignot #1302, pulled by two pompous little men supervised by another; the number 1933 on the card may be the year this aluminum toy was made; 133 mm, no other data.
Peugeot D4A Army Ambulance, a khaki van with red cross rondels on its sides, 97 mm, 1/43 scale, 1958 or '59.
Simca Marly Ambulance, a white wagon with a blue cross on the roof, 105 mm, 1/43 scale, 1958 or '59.

R. L.

Fire Truck, a red and yellow tinplate van with Citroen-type grille, a ladder on the roof, and firemen seen in the windows, 145 mm, large scale, the number 1946 on its rear may be when it was made.

RHODANIENNE

All I know of the firm is that it made this toy—or paperweight?
Army Ambulance, a single casting, wheels included, in aluminum, painted olive with red crosses, 85 mm, smaller than O gauge, postwar?

SAFIR

After making a series of antique cars that were widely imitated, Safir made its Champion and Championnette racing and sports car series, plus metal and plastic trucks and Jeeps made from France Jouets dies.
11 Citroen 1923 Fire Truck, a high van with ladders on its roof, half a hose reel, coats of arms and Paris lettering, 84 mm, 1/43 scale, 1963.
Dodge Army Ambulance, ex-F.J. 409, in white plastic with a tan cover and U. S. Army lettering, or all in olive for the British, 100 mm, 1/45 scale, Seventies.
Dodge Fire Truck, metal and plastic versions of F.J. #407, with Baskerville lettering—does anyone know why? 103 mm, 1/45 scale, Seventies.
Jeep Fire Truck, ex-F.J. #507 with Sapeurs-Pompiers Ville de Romorantin Lanthenay lettering on the hood, 95 mm, 1/45 scale, Seventies.
Fire Department Jeep, with Fire Dept. lettering, driver and antenna, either a special issue or, more likely, a conversion, 95 mm, 1/45 scale, Seventies (C-R Vol. II, p. 24; they list it as being by F.J., which was long defunct by then).
Red Cross Jeep, white this time, with olive plastic top and Croix Rouge decals, 84 mm, 1/45 scale, Seventies. The Jeeps were made only in metal.
Mercedes-Benz Fire Truck, a flatbed with a small hose reel and the same ladder used on the Dodge and Jeep, 98 mm, 1/45 scale, Seventies.
Mercedes-Benz Fire Truck and Tank Trailer, the same truck pulling a Service Departemental d'Incendie du Var water tank trailer, 175 mm, 1/45 scale, Seventies.
Land Rover Army Ambulance, from the plastic-bodied Championnette series, in olive with military rondels and red crosses, 72 mm, S gauge, Seventies.
Renault Estafette Ambulance, another Championnette, a white minibus with red crosses and blue logo, 66 mm, S gauge, Seventies.

SESAME

This firm made tinplate and plastic toy vehicles, some with flywheel motors.
Bernard Army Ambulance, with red cross rondels on its tinplate rear body, 80 mm, about S gauge, Sixties?
Renault Ambulance, an R4 minivan with red crosses and Ambulance lettering, 88 mm, about O gauge, Sixties?
Renault Fire Truck, the same van in red with Ville de Lyon logo and arms, 88 mm, about O gauge, Sixties?

UNKNOWN MAKERS

Fire Truck, made of aluminum and looking very much like a prewar toy, it features fire hose wound around a wheel hub, plus two figures, about 160 mm, no other data, Fifties (C-R Vol. I, p. 116).
Fire Department Van, tinplate, with helmeted firemen in the windows and a coat of arms on the door, about 160 mm, large scale, circa 1930 (Catalogue, p. 4).
Steam Pumper, with back-to-back firemen in the cab and a boiler that resembles a garbage can in the rear, about 100 mm, roughly O gauge, Thirties (C-R Vol. I, p. 57, listed as "Junguete Toy" (sic), but as "Juguete" is Spanish for "toy", it may not be French at all).

French Kits and Specialty Models

In the last few years numerous small French firms have produced model emergency vehicles in white metal or polyester resin, usually in kit form but in some cases readymade. Other firms specialize in detailing and adapting the products of larger firms for specialized uses. Quantities are usually small and distribution is limited, which is why we have little or no information on most of them.

ANNECY

Laffly Fire Truck, a handmade 1/50 scale model, no other data, 1984.

AUTOMANY

Renault 18 Fire Department Wagon, converted from a Norev model, 1/43 scale, no other data, 1984.

C. C. C. P.

An odd name for a French firm! It makes 1/50 scale plastic models.
1 Hotchkiss Rodane MC49 Fire Truck, 1/50 scale, 1984.
3 Berliet PCK8 Fire Truck, 1/50 scale, 1984.

4 Berliet GLA Fire Truck, 1/50 scale, 1984.
4a Berliet GLA Paris Fire Truck, 1/50 scale, 1984.
5 Laffly PS Fire Truck, 1/50 scale, 1984.
6 Delahaye Type 140 Fire Truck, 1/50 scale, 1984.

C. J. M.

Renault Fregate Domaine Fire Chief's Wagon, 1/43 scale, no other data, 1984.

CAN AM

Berliet PCK 1952 Fire Truck, 1/50 scale resin kit, no other data, 1983.
Citroen U23 Heuliez 1968 Fire Truck, 1/50 scale resin kit, no other data, 1983. These two models are presumably numbers 1 and 2.
3 Laffly Fire Pump Trailer, 1/50 scale resin kit, no other data, 1983 or '84.

D. M.

8 Land Rover Camiva Fire Department Pickup, 1/43 scale plastic kit, no other data, Eighties.
9 Land Rover Camiva Fire Tank Truck, 1/43 scale plastic kit, no other data, Eighties.

M. DUBRAY

The Dubray firm makes high quality polyester miniatures of prewar vehicles.
4 Peugeot 402b Fire Chief, a 1938 sedan in Pompiers de Lyon trim, with the Lyon arms on the door, 111 mm, 1/43 scale, 1979.
21 Citroen 11cv Fire Chief, the familiar 1938 sedan, likewise in Pompiers de Lyon livery, 110 mm, 1/43 scale, 1979.
29a Citroen C4 1930 Fire Chief, a red sedan with Pompiers de Paris emblems, 90 mm, 1/43 scale, 1980.
29c Citroen C4 1930 Fire Department Van, the same body style minus rear windows, with Paris emblems, 90 mm, 1/43 scale, 1980.
29d Citroen C4 1930 Fire Department Van, the same model in Lyon form, 90 mm, 1/43 scale, 1980.

ELEGANCE

4 Cadillac Ambulance, 1/43 scale diecast, no other data, 1984.
#? Cadillac Army Ambulance, 1/43 scale diecast, no other data, 1984.
41 Cadillac Fire Department Ambulance, 1/43 scale diecast, no other data, 1984.

ES DO

2 Citroen CX 6-Wheel Ambulance, 1/43 scale diecast, no other data, Eighties.

IDEM

10 Citroen-Guinard Type 45 Fire Truck, 1/50 scale metal kit, no other data, 1984.

K. J. D.

This firm makes 1/43 scale metal kits of fire vehicles.
1 Citroen Fire Tanker, with ladder, 1/43 scale, 1983.
2 Citroen C4 Crew Transport, with eight firemen, 1/43 scale, 1983.
3 Citroen C4 Fire Department Van, 1/43 scale, 1983.
4 Citroen 2-Ton Fire Van, with ladder, 1/43 scale, 1983.
5 Citroen C4 Fire Truck, with canvas top, 1/43 scale, 1983.
6 Citroen C6 Fire Truck, with canvas top, 1/43 scale, 1983.
7 Citroen C4 Fire Department Ambulance, 1/43 scale, 1984.
8 Citroen C6 Fire Department Van, 1/43 scale, 1984.
9 Renault Fire Engine, 1/43 scale, 1984.
10 Citroen C4 Fire Engine, 1/43 scale, 1984.
11 Citroen C6 Open Fire Truck, 1/43 scale, 1984.
12 Citroen C6 Ladder Truck, 1/43 scale, 1984.
13 Renault Fire Crew Transporter, 1/43 scale, 1984.
14 Citroen C6 Fire Truck, Ville d'Enghien, 1/43 scale, 1984.
15 Renault Fire Truck, with canvas top, 1/43 scale, 1984.
16 Delahaye Fire Engine, 1/43 scale, 1984.
17 Renault Fire Department Van, 1/43 scale, 1984.
18 Delahaye Fire Department Van, 1/43 scale, 1984.

M. G. B. SUPER TOY

Land Rover Fire Truck and Fire Pump Trailer, no data, 1984.

MINI RACING / MINI VEHICULES INCENDIES

These two names seem to be used by the same firm. The models are 1/43 scale metal kits. I have found the following unnumbered models listed as M.V.I. products:
Renault 4x4 Rescue Truck, 1982.
Camiva Fire Pump Trailer, 1982 or '83.
Guinard Fire Truck, 1983.
Peugeot 203 Ambulance, 1983.
Peugeot 203 Army Ambulance, 1983.
Citroen C4 Ville de Cayeux Fire Tender, based on a Solido model, 1984.

The following models are listed as Mini Racing M.V.I. kits.
K1 Camiva Fire Pumper, pre-1984.
K2 Renault R2069 4x4 Fire Truck, pre-1984.
K3 Peugeot 203 Fire Department Ambulance, pre-1984.
K4 Renault R2087 Forest Fire Truck, pre-1984.
K5 Peugeot 504 Combi Ambulance, pre-1984.
K6 Peugeot 504 Fire Department Ambulance, pre-1984.
K7 Berliet GAK 4x4 Fire Truck, pre-1984.
K9 Citroen 4x4 Sinpar Forest Fire Truck, pre-1984.
K10 Thousand Liter Tank, for a fire truck, pre-1984.
K11 Fire Department 109" Land Rover, pre-1984.
K12 Peugeot 403 Fire Department Ambulance, pre-1984.
K13 Saviem-Sides SP8 4x4 Double Cab Fire Truck, pre-1984.
K14 Land Rover 110" Double Cab Fire Engine, pre-1984.
K16 Renault Master LWB Fire Van, 1984.
K17 Renault Master Double Cab Fire Van, 1984.
K18 Peugeot Dangel Forest Fire Pickup, 1984.
TK1 Ambulance Conversion Kit for Solido Citroen G, pre-1984.
TK2 Hardtop for Solido Fire Jeep, pre-1984.
TK3 Peugeot 504 Ambulance Wagon, pre-1984.

MINITRUCKS

Berliet CLCK Fire Truck, 1/43 scale resin kit, 1983.

O. K. C.

2 Delahaye 1922 Fire Engine, 1/43 scale metal kit, 1982.
Unless otherwise indicated, all following O.K.C. models are metal kits.
4f Citroen 2cv Fire Department Van, 1/43 scale, 1982.
5 Peugeot 402 Fire Chief, 1/43 scale, 1982.
6 Four Firemen Figures and Flag, 1/43 scale, 1982.
7f Renault Juvaquatre Fire Department Wagon, 1/43 scale, 1982.
8 Peugeot 203 Ambulance, 1/43 scale, 1982, reissued as a plastic kit in 1983.
10 G.M.C. 353 Fire Tank Truck, 1982 or later.

PROTO

Renault Juvaquatre Fire Engine, 1/43 scale metal kit, Eighties.

PYRACAR

101 Cournil Short Chassis Fire Van, 1/43 scale resin kit, 1983.
201 Cournil Long Chassis Fire Van, 1/43 scale resin kit, 1983.
301 Cournil Forest Fire Truck, 1/43 scale resin kit, 1983.

French Kits — Austria and Switzerland — Eastern Europe

S. T. L.

Citroen CX 6-Wheel Ambulance, 1/43 scale resin kit, 1979.
Citroen CX 6-Wheel Fire Truck, 1/43 scale resin kit, 1980.
Citroen Acadiane FireTruck, 1/43 scale resin kit, 1980.
Simca 1100VF Fire Truck, 1/43 scale resin kit, 1980.

TACOT

Schmitt Mini Jeep Fire Truck, 1/43 scale resin kit, 1983.

X. V. M.

Peugeot 203 Fire Van, 1/43 scale resin kit, 1979.
Simca Aronde Fire Van, 1/43 scale resin kit, 1976.

Austria and Switzerland

Few model cars are made in Austria and Switzerland. The Austrian firm of Roco makes many small-scale plastic military and emergency vehicles, and three Swiss companies have each contributed one model to our list.

AURORE

This Swiss firm makes 1/43 scale plastic miniatures.
22 Chevrolet Custom Fire Truck, a pickup with rear body and equipment, 1/43 scale, no other data, Eighties.

BRAENDLI

This Swiss product is an HO scale metal kit.
#? Saurer M54 Fire Truck, 1/87 scale, no other data, 1982.

ROCO

Roco's HO gauge plastic models include a growing number of fire trucks, ambulances and Technisches Hilfswerk vehicles, to add to the military emergency trucks they have made for many years.
1300 DKW Munga Fire Department Car, a Jeeplike little red vehicle with black top and blue lights, 39 mm, 1/87 scale, 1982.
1301 DKW Munga Technisches Hilfswerk Car, the same model in blue, 39 mm, 1/87 scale, 1982.
1302 M.A.N. Technisches Hilfswerk Truck, with big boxy cab, black rear cover, THW emblem and lettering, 91 mm, 1/87 scale, 1981.
1303 Pinzgauer Fire Truck, an enclosed 6x6 design with ladders and other equipment on the roof and a separate water pump, 57 mm, 1/87 scale, 1981.
1304 Mercedes-Benz Unimog Fire Truck, with blue lights above its cab, and a rear box body with non-opening doors, 63 mm, 1/87 scale, 1981.
1305 Pinzgauer Ambulance, the 6x6 van in white with red crosses and black-outlined rear doors, 55 mm, 1/87 scale, 1981.
1306 Mercedes-Benz Red Cross Unimog, in cream with red crosses and blue lights, 65 mm, 1/87 scale, 1982.
1308 M.A.N. Technisches Hilfswerk Truck, with long hood, rear box body and rounded roof, 89 mm, 1/87 scale, 1982.
1309 Technisches Hilfswerk Trailer, a blue two-wheeler with black cover, 40 mm, 1/87 scale, 1982.
1310 Pinzgauer Fire Truck, differing from 1303 in having no roof equipment or silver doors, and with Einsatzleitung lettering, 53 mm, 1/87 scale, 1982.
1311 Steyr 91 TLFA Fire Truck, a typical modern-day European truck in blood red, white and silver gray, with equipment on the roof, 84 mm, 1/87 scale, 1982.
1312 Steyr 91 TLFA Fire Truck, the same model in light dayglo red, 84 mm, 1/87 scale, 1983.
1313 Mercedes-Benz Technisches Hilfswerk Unimog, in blue with white THW lettering on the hood, charcoal gray cab roof, rear cover and chassis, 55 mm, 1/87 scale, 1983.
1314 Mercedes-Benz Unimog Fire Truck, smaller than 1304, with tan covers for its otherwise open cab and its rear body, 57 mm, 1/87 scale, 1983.
1315 Steyr 680 TLF 2000 Fire Truck, with big enclosed cab and box rear, ladders and other equipment on the roof, 70 mm, 1/87 scale, 1983.
1317 Opel Blitz TLF 15 Fire Truck, a rugged veteran of 1939 vintage, with long nose, rear tank body, a ladder, suction hose, pump and hose reel, 73 mm, 1/87 scale, 1983.
1318 Steyr 680 Red Cross Truck and Field Kitchen Trailer, in cream, with red cross rondels on the truck's light gray rear cover, 112 mm, 1/87 scale, 1983.
1319 Mercedes-Benz Unimog SWB Fire Truck, the short closed-cab version with rear cover and Stadt Linz logo, 54 mm, 1/87 scale, 1983.
1320 Technisches Hilfswerk Field Kitchen Trailer, all in blue including its stovepipe, 38 mm, 1/87 scale, 1983.
1321 Pinzgauer Fire Truck, with blue dome lights and Feuerwehr lettering, 49 mm, 1/87 scale, 1984.
1322 Dodge Cheetah Crash Tender, 1/87 scale, no other data, 1984.
1323 VW Iltis Technisches Hilfswerk Car, in blue with charcoal top and white THW lettering, 45 mm, 1/87 scale, 1984.
1324 Magirus-Deutz Technisches Hilfswerk Truck, in blue with white logo, charcoal cab roof and rear cover, 91 mm, 1/87 scale, 1984.
1327 G.M.C. KW10 Rescue Crane, a big bruiser with white cab cover and telescopic crane boom, and Dietzenbach logo, 103 mm, 1/87 scale, 1984.
1328 Steyr 91 Rescue Truck, 1/87 scale, no other data, 1984.
1329 DKW Munga Red Cross Car, 1/87 scale, no other data, 1984.
1330 Opel Blitz 1939 Fire Tender, with green body and a load of firefighting equipment, 71 mm, 1/87 scale, 1984.
1331 DKW Munga, 1/87 scale, no other data, 1984.
1332 Opel Blitz Police Department Fire Engine, 1/87 scale, no other date, 1984.

The following military models have been on the market for a number of years, except for the highest numbers, which are quite recent.
215 Hotchkiss Armored Ambulance, a short tanklike vehicle on treads, 48 mm, 1/87 scale.
223 Dodge Military Ambulance, a closed van on a typical Dodge army truck chassis, in light or dark olive, the former with red crosses, 60 mm, 1/87 scale.
241 Mercedes-Benz Unimog Military Ambulance, with S404 cab and chassis, carrying a rear box with windows, 57 mm, 1/87 scale.
260 M.A.N. 630 Military Van, which can be used as an ambulance or for other purposes, as can the next two vehicles, 86 mm, 1/87 scale.
274 Opel Blitz 3 Ton Truck, with rear cabin, 65 mm, 1/87 scale.
280 M3 Halftrack Van, with its rear cover extending forward over the cab, 65 mm, 1/87 scale.
2306 Amphibian Armored Ambulance, 1/87 scale, no other data.
322 Pinzgauer Military Ambulance, the familiar 6x6 box van in olive, with blue lights fore and aft, 54 mm, 1/87 scale, Eighties.
323 Pinzgauer United Nations Ambulance, the same vehicle in white, 54 mm, 1/87 scale, Eighties.
325 Mercedes-Benz Unimog Military Ambulance, a closed-cab 1300L type with rear box body, 63 mm, 1/87 scale, Eighties.
326 Mercedes-Benz Unimog Airport Rescue Truck, the same chassis-cab with Metz fire truck body, 63 mm, 1/87 scale, Eighties.
337 Steyr 680 Military Fire Truck, a TLF 2000 with Rosenbauer body, 1/87 scale, no other data, Eighties.
338 Opel Blitz Fire Truck, a tan 1944 chassis-cab with TLF 15 body bearing its load of firefighting equipment, 67 mm, 1/87 scale, Eighties.
341 Dodge Military Ambulance, a much newer truck than 223, basically a pickup with high-roof rear body, 60 mm, 1/87 scale, Eighties.
344 Mercedes-Benz Unimog Fire Truck, with Metz body including equipment compartments, top deck, ladders and other gear, 62 mm, 1/87 scale, Eighties.
356 Mercedes-Benz Unimog Ambulance, a white truck with rear cabin body, gray cab roof and blue dome light, 58 mm, 1/87 scale, 1984.

ZAUGG

This Swiss firm makes 1/43 scale metal kits.
5A Mercury 1950 Fire Chief, reminiscent of but not based on the old Tekno model, a handsome red sedan with F.D.N.Y. logo, 1/43 scale, no other data, 1983.

Eastern Europe

The miniature emergency vehicles made in Eastern Europe include accurate scale models made by such firms as Espewe (now called Plasticart) of the German Democratic Republic, A.B. of Greece and Novoexport of the U.S.S.R., toys from Igra and Smer of Czechoslovakia and Bison of East Germany, and even the Pebe toys that snap together in Lego style. Whether models or toys, they have personalities all their own.

CZECHOSLOVAKIA

Igra Ambulance, a simple but fairly realistic plastic toy with Mercedes-like grille and flywheel motor, 95 mm, smaller than O gauge, Sixties?
Igra Barkas Ambulance, in white plastic with red cross and lettering, flywheel motor and sparkling amber dome light, 88 mm, smaller than O gauge, circa 1980.
Igra Skoda Ladder Truck, with two-piece aerial ladder, another fairly accurate plastic friction toy, 105 mm, about S gauge, Sixties or Seventies.
Smer Ladder Truck, no data.

GERMAN DEMOCRATIC REPUBLIC

Bison 3 Ladder Truck, with squarish anonymous cab, three-piece aerial ladder and flywheel motor, 140 mm, roughly O gauge, plastic, Seventies?
Espewe 1013-4 Barkas B1000 Ambulance Van, an accurate plastic model, dark cream, with two figures inside, 50 mm, 1/87 scale, postwar.
Espewe 1013-4 Barkas Army Ambulance, the same model in olive drab, 50 mm, 1/87 scale, postwar.
Espewe 1013-5 Fire Department Van, the same body minus side windows, with a rack of suction hose on the roof, 50 mm, 1/87 scale, postwar.
Espewe 1014-2 TLF 16 Fire Engine, a typical German closed-cab truck with spotlight, hose connections, and a pump inside the rear doors, 74 mm, 1/87 scale, postwar.
Espewe 1014-3 S-4000-1 Ladder Truck, also typically German, with a four-section aerial ladder 290 mm long, 85 mm, 1/87 scale, postwar.
Pebe 77 Fire Truck Set, a snap-together plastic fire engine, pump trailer and chief's (or rescue) wagon, blockish but fun, 1/75 scale, postwar.
Veb 143 Daimler 1911 Fire Truck, a well-detailed plastic model of an oldtime open-cab van with a roof full of equipment, 129 mm, 1/43 scale, postwar. Veb is the Berlin branch of Espewe

GREECE

A.B. 41 Ladder Truck, a little plastic flatbed with ladder and mounting, not necessarily a fire truck, 65 mm, 1/82 scale, Sixties?
A.B. 51 Mercedes-Benz German Red Cross Bus, a more accurate model, in cream with German logo, 113 mm, 1/82 scale, Seventies.
A.B. products are also known as Joy Toys.

HUNGARY

Metalcar Mercedes-Benz Ambulance, a white minibus with four rows of seats, a blue dome light and red lettering, 81 mm, about 1/60 scale, 1984. There may also be a fire van version with a ladder on the roof.
Metalcar Mercedes-Benz Ladder Truck, a diecast chassis-cab unit with plastic rear deck, hose reel, aerial ladder and Ville de Paris logo-on a Mercedes? 143 mm, 1/64 scale, 1984.
Metalcar VW Golf Ambulance, with fewer seats than the Mercedes, but the patients still have to sit, 94 mm, 1/43 scale, 1984.
Metalcar VW Golf Fire Department Ambulance, the same model in red with white doors and labels, 94 mm, 1/43 scale, 1984.
Tuzoltoauto Lemezaru Ladder Truck, plastic, with sheet metal ladder, mount, rear deck and base, plus flywheel motor, 115 mm, about O gauge, Eighties or before.

U.S.S.R.

Novoexport A2 Moskvitch 412 Red Cross Car, with red cross labels, 96 mm, 1/43 scale, Seventies.
Novoexport A3 Moskvitch 426a Fire Chief, another diecast sedan with labels, 98 mm, 1/43 scale, Seventies.
Novoexport A18 RAF-2203 Ambulance, a good diecast minibus with red doors, blue roof light and appropriate labels, 114 mm, 1/43 scale, early Eighties.
Novoexport A24 Volga Gaz 24 Ambulance, a white wagon equipped, as I wish #A18 had been, with a stretcher, 109 mm, 1/43 scale, early Eighties.

Italy

Italian model emergency vehicles are for the most part light vans and buses, station wagons, sedans and Jeeps in fire department or ambulance livery. Among older models, the P.M. fire truck and ambulance stand out; the Politoys Lancia and Burago Fiat fire trucks are prominent modern models. Best of all, perhaps, are the excellent Antoine miniatures that represent Fiat fire trucks of bygone days.

A. M.

This company, also known as Ambo, made tinplate cars.
#? Studebaker Fire Chief, a four-inch tinplate coupe with a personality of its own, 98 mm, O gauge or smaller, Fifties?

ANTOINE

Antoine has made two fine diecast miniatures of vintage Fiat fire engines.
1. Fiat 1934 635 Fire Engine, no data, 1982.
2. Fiat 15 TER Fire Engine, a splendid creation evoking the spirit of bygone days, expensive but worth it, 112 mm, 1/43 scale, 1982.

BARLUX

Barlux models include several scales and types of vehicles, among them one fire truck.
705 Fiat 697 TP Fire Truck, with typical European box body topped by a snorkel, 1/43 scale, no other data, Eighties.

BRUMM

Brumm specializes in 1/43 scale diecast models of vehicles with a history.
24 Fiat 500 Fire Chief, with painted-on fabric top plus siren and Servizio Prevenzione decals, 77 mm, 1/43 scale, circa 1980.
251r Fiat 500c Fire Van, with two short ladders on the roof and Vigili del Fuoco Tobruk logo in Italian and Arabic, 79 mm, 1/43 scale, 1984.
63 Fiat 1100 Fire Chief, #24's big brother, with the same siren and decals, 95 mm, 1/43 scale, circa 1980.
80 Fiat 500 Fire Department Van, like the later #51r issue but without the Tobruk (a city in Libya) logo, 79 mm, 1/43 scale, circa 1980.
84r Fiat 508c Fire Chief's Cabriolet, with top up, a big siren and the Tobruk logo, 92 mm, 1/43 scale, 1984.
85r Fiat 508c Fire Chief's Cabriolet, this time with its top down, otherwise as before, 92 mm, 1/43 scale, 1984.

BURAGO

Burago is better known for its large-scale diecast models than for these 1/43 scale trucks.
1509 Fiat 50 NC Ladder Truck, with two-section aerial ladder, in Falck livery when sold in Denmark, 152 mm, 1/43 scale, circa 1980.
1511 Fiat 50 NC Fire Department Crane Truck, the same chassis-cab with a heavy crane, also produced in Falck livery, 160 mm, 1/43 scale, circa 1980.

GIODI

This is a large-scale diecast model, but it deserves to be mentioned.
#? Fiat Snorkel Fire Truck, a massive truck with a snorkel and other equipment, 1/32 scale, no other data, 1984.

INGAP

Ingap made plastic models in various scales. #?
Ladder Truck, a five-inch plastic toy, not necessarily a fire truck, with a single ladder attached at the rear, 130 mm, roughly O gauge, Sixties.

MEBETOYS

This firm began to produce diecast miniature cars in the Sixties. For some years it has been the Italian branch of Mattel.
21 Fiat 1500 Fire Chief, a sedan with dome light, siren, antenna and Vigili del Fuoco labels, 98 mm, 1/43 scale, 1967.

42 Land Rover Ambulance, with Croce Rossa labels and detailed interior including an occupied stretcher, 89 mm, 1/43 scale, 1970.
74 Fire Department Land Rover, with detailed plastic rear body surmounted by a two-section ladder, 96 mm, 1/43 scale, Seventies.
81 Fire Department Jeep, with plastic cover, blue dome light and Vigili del Fuoco labels, 93 mm, 1/43 scale, Seventies.
92 Alfetta Fire Chief, an Alfa Romeo sedan with the usual lights and labels, 101 mm, 1/43 scale, circa 1980.

MERCURY

Mercury was Italy's premier manufacturer of diecast miniature vehicles for many years; the firm went out of business around 1980.
4 Fiat 131 Fire Chief, a red sedan with Vigili del Fuoco logo, 100 mm, 1/43 scale, Seventies.
7 Fiat 131 Ambulance, a wagon this time, with an empty stretcher in the back, 100 mm, 1/43 scale, Seventies.
9 Fiat 128 Fire Chief, stubbier than the 131, but much like it, 85 mm, 1/43 scale, late Seventies.
30 Fiat Campagnola Fire Tender, 1/43 scale, no other data, late Seventies.
32 Fiat Campagnola Army Ambulance, 1/43 scale, no other data, late Seventies.
84 Fiat Campagnola Fire Truck, 1/35 scale, no other data, late Seventies; these last three models were issued shortly before Mercury's demise, if they were issued at all.
94c Ciclope Ladder Truck, not necessarily a fire truck but an interesting model, with two ladders that interlock and fasten onto an adjustable mount, 149 mm, 1/43 or smaller scale, 1948.

MODELLI

#? Lancia Ardea 1949 Fire Department Van, 1/43 scale, no other data, 1982.

OLD CARS

This firm began by making models of antique cars but has become better known for its diecast miniatures of Italian light vans, buses and other commercial and service vehicles.
23f Fiat Daily LWB Fire Department Van, 1/43 scale, no other data, early Eighties.
24a Fiat Iveco Fire Department bus, with Ministero dell'Inferno emblems, 103 mm, 1/43 scale, 1984.
24f and 24v Fiat Combi Fire Department Bus, two versions of a minibus in V.V.F. Milano livery, 109 mm, 1/43 scale, 1983.
27f Fiat Combi Fire Department Bus, the same basic model with two dome lights instead of just one, 109 mm, 1/43 scale, early Eighties.
28a Fiat Iveco Army Ambulance, a bus in olive drab with red crosses, 133 mm, 1/43 scale, 1984.
40 Fiat Iveco Fire Department Van, with Lagos logo, 1/43 scale, no other data, 1984.
41 Fiat Iveco Fire Department Box Van, also with Lagos logo, 1/43 scale, no other data, 1984.
42 Fiat Iveco SWB Ambulance Bus, a French fire department "Ambulance de Reanimation", in fact, 107 mm, 1/43 scale, 1984.
43 Fiat Iveco LWB Ambulance Bus, the longer version of the above, with similar details, 130 mm, 1/43 scale, 1984.
44 Fiat Iveco Fire Department Ambulance, a bus with high roof, 1/43 scale, no other data, 1984.
61 Fiat 370 Fire Department Bus, 1/43 scale, no other data, 1984.
205v Fiat 90 Fire Tank Truck, a modern cab-over tanker, 110 mm, 1/43 scale, early Eighties.
208 Fiat 90 Fire Department Van, 1/43 scale, no other data, 1984.
302 Fiat Campagnola Fire Department Wrecker, a version of Fiat's answer to the Jeep, 1/43 scale, no other data, 1984.
305 Fiat Campagnola Fire Tender, with plastic top and dome light, 90 mm, 1/43 scale, Eighties.
305f Fiat Campagnola Fire Tender, the same model with English logo, 90 mm, 1/43 scale, Eighties.
305v Fiat Campagnola Fire Tender, with V.V.F. Milano lettering, 90 mm, 1/43 scale, Eighties.
306f Fiat Campagnola Fire Tender and Trailer, 1/43 scale, no other data, Eighties.
309v Fiat Campagnola Fire Tender with Searchlight, plus Pompieri labels, 90 mm, 1/43 scale, Eighties.
1003 Fiat Cometto Low Loader with Fiat Allis Shovel Loader, for fighting forest fires, 1/43 scale, no other data, 1983.
#? Fiat LWB Hi-Top Fire Department Van, 1/43 scale, no other data, 1983 or '84; possibly the same model as one of those listed above.
#? OM Fire Tank Truck, probably similar to 205v, 1/43 scale, no other data, 1983 or '84.

P. M.

This firm made some interesting diecast models in early postwar days.
#? Fire Truck, a big rugged vehicle with two-tier open back, ladders on , and four figures that look like running soldiers, 140 mm, 0 gauge, early postwar.
#? Ambulance, a simple, conventional design with red cross decals, 103 mm, 0 gauge, early postwar.

POLITOYS

The firm of A.P.S. made 1/41 scale plastic models, later 1/43 and smaller diecast vehicles; they are now known by the name of Polistil, to avoid confusion with the British Palitoys firm.
8 Army Ambulance, a plastic military truck with red crosses, 108 mm, 1/41 scale, 1961.
300 Romeo Ambulance, a white plastic minibus with blue dome lights, 108 mm, 1/41 scale, 1964.
AE14 Alfa Romeo Giulia Ambulance, a low wide wagon with Pronto Intervento baseplate lettering, 94 mm, 1/43 scale, Seventies.
AE16 Alfa Romeo Giulia Fire Chief, the same wagon in red with Vigili del Fuoco lettering, 94 mm, 1/43 scale, Seventies.
CE79 Fire Department Range Rover, with Fire Rescue and Allen Park, Michigan labels, 97 mm, 1/43 scale, 1977.
CE79b Range Rover Ambulance, the same vehicle in white with red crosses, 97 mm, 1/43 scale, 1977. These last four models were made just after the brand name was changed to Polistil.
112 Romeo Red Cross Van, 1/66 scale, no other data, Sixties, part of the firm's diecast Penny Series.
117 Lancia Esadelta Fire Truck, a nice little modern fire truck with ladders, hose and couplings, also from the Penny Series, 97 mm, 1/66 scale, late Sixties or early Seventies.
#? Dodge Ambulance Van, with Fire Rescue logo, aobut 160 mm, no other data, 1980; unknown to me until it appeared in C-R Vol. II, p. 107; it may be a special issue or a conversion.

RAMPINI

Paolo Rampini, a well-known hobbyist, was an Italian pioneer of polyester resin models.
124 Lancia Ardea 1942 Fire Department Van, with bell and ladder, 84 mm, 1/43 scale, Seventies.
134 Mercedes-Benz 220 Fire Chief, 1/43 scale, no other data, Seventies.
138 Lancia Ardea 1949 Fire Department Ambulance, 1/43 scale, no other data, Seventies.
140 Mercedes-Benz 170V 1939 Fire Chief, 1/43 scale, no other data, Seventies.
146 Mercedes-Benz 170S 1949 Fire Chief, 1/43 scale, no other data, Seventies.

SAM TOYS

This firm made a series of plastic military and civilian trucks.
#? Army Ambulance, a truck somewhat like Politoys 8, with red crosses, 112 mm, 0 gauge, Sixties or before.
#? Ladder Truck, with the same chassis and cab, plus a two-section aerial ladder, 112 mm, 0 gauge, Sixties or before.

TRON

Tron is best known for its racing and sports car kits, but has also made one fire truck.
2 Morris Fire Department Pickup, no data, 1984.

Spain and Portugal

Spain's only thoroughly home-grown model fire vehicles are the Pegaso trucks first made by Anguplas and recently reissued by Eko. These and a handful of Seat (the Spanish branch of Fiat) emergency cars are joined by numerous models of vehicles from other countries. Spain's models include HO gauge plastic (Anguplas, Eko, Ibertren), and metal (Aylmer), larger plastic (Rico), 1/43 scale diecast (Dalia, Mira, Nacoral and Pilen) and other diecast (Paya and the Pilen 800 series in S gauge, and Guisval in scales from 1/37 to 1/90). The two Guisval reissues of Safir oldtimers are 1/43 scale plastic. The three Portuguese brands, Luso, Metosul and Vitesse, are 1/43 scale diecast—all in all, quite a variety.

ANGUPLAS

For many years Anguplas made HO gauge plastic models of a wide variety of models; some have been reissued by Eko in recent years.
29 DKW Ambulance, a white minibus with a red cross sign on the roof, 49 mm, 1/86 scale, 1959.
72 Pegaso Ladder Truck, with a three-section aerial ladder and a hose reel, 95 mm, 1/86 scale, 1962.
73 Fire Department Land Rover, 1/86 scale, no other data, 1962.
74 Pegaso Fire Engine, the same cab as #72 and a well-equipped rear body including a ladder, hose and couplings, 69 mm, 1/86 scale, 1962

AYLMER

Aside from this model, I know nothing of Aylmer's products.
755 New York Horsedrawn Fire Engine, nicknamed "Blue Boys", 95 mm, small scale, Eighties or before.

DALIA

Dalia made Solido, Tekno and other diecast models under license for the Spanish market.
62 Simca 1100 Red Cross Car, presumably based on a Solido model, 1/43 scale, no other data, Sixties.
415 Ford Taunus Ambulance, a Tekno reissue, a white van with red cross decals, 97 mm, 1/43 scale, Sixties; mine is missing its dome light.

EKO

Like Anguplas, Eko has specialized in HO gauge plastic miniatures, and has reissued some Anguplas models recently.
2019 Magirus Ladder Truck, with three-section aerial ladder and rear-mounted hose reel, 93 mm, 1/88 scale, 1964.
2029 Ford FK Ambulance, a little white van with red crosses on its opaque rear windows, 47 mm, 1/88 scale, 1964.
2041 Fiat 1800 Ambulance, a white wagon with a red cross, 49 mm, 1/88 scale, 1964.
2093 Pegaso Fire Engine, ex-Anguplas #74, 69 mm, 1/86 scale, Seventies.
2097 Pegaso Ladder Truck, ex-Anguplas #72, 95 mm, 1/86 scale, Seventies.
4028 G.M.C. M-211 Red Cross Truck, a covered army ten-wheeler, 74 mm, 1/88 scale, Seventies.
4044 B.M.C. Ambulance, van-type, 1/88 scale, no other data, Seventies.
#? Citroen Fire Van, apparently based on Eko's #2034 van, with dome light, about 40 mm, HO gauge, 1983 (C-R Vol. II, p. 21).
#? Renault Fire Chief, with its dome light atop a white block on the roof, about 40 mm, HO gauge, 1983 (C-R Vol. II, p. 22). These last two may be recent Eko issues, but no other source of information I have lists them.

GUISVAL

This firm makes a wide variery of diecast models in various scales, and once made a line of plastic oldtimers based on Safir products.
12 Citroen GS Red Cross Car, a white sedan with red cross and dome light, 49 mm, 1/66 or smaller scale, Seventies; replaced by:
12 Renault 12TS Red Cross Car, a white wagon with striped rear windows and extensive decals, 82 mm, 1/66 scale, late Seventies.
24 Go-Bug Fire Truck, a fanciful creation, no other data, Seventies.
27 Renault 12TS Fire Chief, the same wagon as the second #12, in red with Bomberos labels, 82 mm, 1/66 scale, late Seventies.
34 Volvo Fire Truck, with hose reels, couplings and raising ladder, plus a sturdy Volvo truck cab, 74 mm, 1/90 scale, late Seventies.
37 Mercedes-Benz Ambulance, a white minibus with Ambulancia and Hospital Provincial labels, 74 mm, 1/66 scale, late Seventies.
44 Red Cross Caravan, a first aid station made by putting red cross labels on a house trailer, 80 mm, perhaps 1/66 scale, 1981.
45 Volvo Airport Fire Truck, the #34 chassis and cab with a plastic rear body crowned by a foam nozzle, 70 mm, 1/90 scale, 1980.
46 Mercedes-Benz 406 Fire Department Bus, perhaps the same casting as #37, 1/66 scale, no other data, early Eighties.
72 Fire Truck, a believable rear body complete with ladder, on an unlikely American-type sleeper cab-chassis, 80 mm, 1/66 or smaller scale, 1984.
104 Renault R12 Fire Chief, probably a bigger version of #27, 1/40 scale, no other data, early Eighties.
110 Ford Capri Fire Chief, originally with an equipment rack on the roof and round emblem labels, later with roof bar, spotlight and Maltese cross labels, 115 mm, 1/37 scale, early Eighties.
114 Volvo Fire Truck, a massive six-wheeler with two-section yellow aerial ladder, 124 mm, 1/50 scale, late Seventies.
124 Jeep Fire Truck, 1/37 scale, no other data. Seventies.
134 Mercedes-Benz 406 Ambulance, 1/43 scale, no other data, early Eighties.
172 Scammell Fire Truck, with Matchbox-inspired diecast cab, red plastic rear body with an aerial ladder and other equipment, 114 mm, S gauge, early Seventies.
226 Ford Fire Truck, no data, Seventies.
466 Audi Quattro Fire Chief, in red with white doors, chrome roof bar and many labels, some reading "Fireman" and "Special Unity", 127 mm, 1/35 scale, 1984.
579 Fire Engine, with open cab, stubby body, short raising ladder and Bomberos decals, 82 mm, perhaps S gauge, early Eighties.
663 Ladder Truck, with a long-nose American cab and a semi-trailer bearing a two-section aerial ladder, 175 mm, 1/100 scale?, 1984.
1311 Citroen 1923 Fire Truck, with ladders, siren and Parque de Bomberos decals, a Safir reissue, 85 mm, 1/43 scale, early Seventies or before.
1312 Citroen 1923 Ambulance, the same plastic van in white with Ambulancia Municipal decals, 85 mm, 1/43 scale, early Seventies or before.
5022 Magirus-Deutz Ladder Truck, a rugged open-cab six-wheeler with a two-section blue aerial ladder, 135 mm, 1/50 scale, early Eighties.
5026 Mercedes-Benz Ambulance, a white bus with orange roof panel and Ambulancia decals, 111 mm, 1/43 scale, early Eighties.
#? Citroen SM Red Cross Car, in white with amber dome lights, sirens and red cross labels, 131 mm, 1/37 scale, circa 1980.

GUILOY?

Coleman and Russell list this as a "Guitoy", a name unknown to me. There is a Spanish brand named Guiloy, though.
Crash Tender, with a hose line that feeds out the side of its rear box, plus some equipment on the roof, about 70 mm, HO gauge, 1979 (C-R Vol. II, p. 35).

IBERTREN

The name has also been spelled Ibertrain, the products are 1/87 scale plastic models.
2671 Seat Ritmo Fire Chief, 1/87 scale, no other data, 1984.
2672 Mercedes-Benz 409 Fire Department Bus, with amber light and Bomberos lettering, 58 mm, 1/87 scale, no other data, 1984.
#? Mercedes-Benz 409 Ambulance, 1/87 scale, no other data, 1984.

LUSO

This Portuguese firm specializes in 1/43 scale diecast and plastic cars.
13b Citroen GS Ambulance, a white wagon with either red crosses or blue S.A.M.U. livery, 106 mm, 1/43 scale diecast, 1981.
79 Citroen GS Fire Department Wagon and Lifeboat Trailer, the #13b car with plastic trailer and boat, 176 mm, 1/43 scale, 1983.

METOSUL

Portugal's best-known maker of 1/43 scale diecast vehicles produces many versions of its basic models.
2b Citroen DS19 Fire Chief, a red sedan with dome light, antenna and Bombeiros decals, 100 mm, 1/43 scale, circa 1980.
8 Morris Mini Fire Chief, in red with antenna and spotlight, 73 mm, 1/43 scale, 1984.
10 Mercedes-Benz 200 Fire Chief, in red with an amber dome light, 102 mm, 1/43 scale, Seventies or earlier.
50 Mercedes-Benz Covered Fire Truck, 121 mm, 1/43 or smaller scale, no other data, Seventies.
51 Mercedes-Benz Fire Tank Truck, the same chassis-cab and a tank body in maroon with amber dome light and silver lettering, 121 mm, 1/43 or smaller scale, Seventies.

MIRA

Mira makes diecast cars and trucks in 1/43 and smaller scales, and seems to be related to Pilen.
63 Pegaso Army Red Cross Truck, a massive eight-wheeler with plastic cover and Cruz Roja Española decals, 150 mm, 1/64 scale, Seventies.
0109 Pegaso Aerial Ladder Truck, 1/64 scale, no other data, Eighties.

Spain and Portugal — Latin America

0144 Simca-Chrysler 150 Fire Chief, 1/64 scale, no other data, Eighties.
0145 Ford Granada Fire Chief, 1/60 scale, no other data, Eighties.
0146 Renault 18 Ambulance, a station wagon, 1/60 scale, no other data, Eighties.
0625 Pegaso Fire Engine, with ladder, 1/64 scale, no other data, Eighties.
4005 VW Scirocco Fire Chief, in metallic dark maroon, with Bomberos decals, 88 mm, 1/43 scale, early Eighties.
4010 Seat 131 Red Cross Car, a white sedan with red cross and Ambulancia labels, 99 mm, 1/43 scale, early Eighties.
4014 Citroen CX Red Cross Car, another sedan with similar labels, 104 mm, 1/43 scale, early Eighties.
4023 Simca-Chrysler 150 Fire Chief, a red sedan with Bomberos and Unidad Jefe labels, 96 mm, 1/43 scale, eaerly Eighties.

NACORAL

Nacoral hasmade numerous diecast and plastic cars and trucks, some under license from other manufacturers. Both of these Land Rovers are diecast metal.
118 Fire Department Land Rover, 1/43 scale, no other data, Seventies?
2028 Fire Department Land Rover, with roof rack, ladder and other equipment, 85 mm, 1/43 scale, Seventies or before.

PAYA

Paya's small-scale models are based on obsolete Matchbox cars.
2105 Cadillac Ambulance, based on Matchbox #54, S gauge, no other data, Sixties.
2107 Ford Galaxie Fire Chief, based on Matchbox #59, with Jefe Bomberos decal, 75 mm, S gauge, Sixties.
2115 Ambulance, perhaps based on Matchbox #3, S gauge, no other data, Sixties.

PILEN

Auto-Pilen's diecast models, like those of Mira (which much resemble them in workmanship), are made in 1/43 and smaller scales.
294 Renault 12S Fire Chief, a red sedan with Jefe Bomberos decals, 100 mm, 1/43 scale, Seventies.
296 Citroen SM Red Cross Car, with Servicio de Urgencia decals and maroon dome light, 113 mm, 1/43 scale, Seventies.
297 Mercedes-Benz 250 Red Cross Car, a white sedan equipped like #296, 113 mm, 1/43 scale, Seventies.
298B Oldsmobile Toronado Fire Chief, with Fire Brigade, Fire Chief / Detroit DEP and number 013 decals, 104 mm, 1/43 scale, 1982.
361 Range Rover Ambulance, with Servicio de Urgencia decals and dome light, 93 mm, 1/43 scale, early Eighties; also numbered 561.
549 Range Rover Fire Chief, the same casting in red with Jefe Bomberos decals but no dome light, 93 mm, 1/43 scale, 1982.
551 VW Scirocco Red Cross Car, with the usual Servicio de Urgencia decals and dome light, 85 mm, 1/43 scale, early Eighties.
801 Seat 131 Ambulance, a wagon with the usual decals, 70 mm, S gauge, early Eighties.
807 Renault 4 Fire Tender, a red minivan with Jefe Bomberos logo, 65 mm, S gauge, early Eighties.
814 Seat 814 Fire Chief, a red wagon with redesigned decals that still say Jefe Bomberos, 70 mm, S gauge, early Eighties.
815 Fire Department Range Rover, equipped like #814, 72 mm, S gauge, early Eighties.

RICO

Rico made some interesting plastic models with flywheel motors.
423 Auto Union Ambulance, a white van with red cross labels, 115 mm, larger than O gauge, Seventies or earlier.
708 DKW Ambulance, a light bus with opaque windows and a red cross on its spotlight, 98 mm, larger than O gauge, Sixties.
733 Fire Department Land Rover, with green dome light and Parque Bomberos decals, 98 mm, larger than O gauge, Sixties.
734 Seat 1400C Ambulance, a wagon with one green and one red dome light, Ambulancia decals and opaque rear windows, 115 mm, larger than O gauge, Sixties.
741 Auto Union Fire Department Bus, probably #423 in red, no other data, Sixties.

VITESSE

Vitesse models, made by Cinerius, are Portugal's newest line of diecast miniatures.
161 Mercedes-Benz 170 Fire Chief, a red sedan with special fittings and City of Porto coat of arms, 98 mm, 1/43 scale, 1984.
211 Mercedes-Benz 170V Fire Chief, a red wagon, 1/43 scale, no other data, 1984.
230 Saurer Fire Truck, 1/43 scale, no other data, 1984.
231 Renault Dauphine Fire Chief, with Pompiers de Paris logo, 1/43 scale, no other data, 1984.
253 Jaguar Mark VIII Fire Chief, 1/43 scale, no other data, 1984.
291 Mercedes-Benz 170V Fire Department Van, with a ladder on the roof and Feverwehr Frankfurt logo on the doors, 97 mm, 1/43 scale, no other data, 1984.

TINPLATE TOYS

I have no idea who made one of these, but it looks as Spanish as the others, not that I can make any promises about them either. One seems to be made by Rai, the other two by Rico, which may or may not be the Rico firm listed above.

RAI

Ladder Truck, with its hood and cab looking remarkably like what Coleman and Russell listed as a French "Junguete Toy" (see Other French Brands), with a ladder fitted to the rear body and resting on the roof, 102 mm, roughly O gauge, prewar.

RICO

Ladder Truck, solidly built, with red body, black chassis, white driver and yellow ladder, 114 mm, about O gauge, prewar.
Steam Pumper, slightly less massive, with red body and black chassis again, black driver and yellow boiler, 112 mm, about O gauge, prewar.

UNKNOWN MAKER

Ladder Truck, very simple, with primitive red chassis and cab, plus a tilting ladder mounted in the middle and sticking out behind, 102 mm, vaguely S gauge, prewar?

Latin America

The miniature car industry is growing in Latin America. In Argentina such firms as Buby, Galgo, Muky, Aguti (makers of Rapitoys) and Gillette (makers of Jet) produce diecast vehicles, while tinplate and plastic toy cars are also in production. Brazil, where Jue and Roly made diecast models in the Sixties, is now represented by Arpra, Fidart and a branch of Solido. Uruguay and Colombia are also represented, as is Mexico, where the McGregor firm offers reissues of Italian Politoys.

ARPRA

This Brazilian manufacturer specializes in diecast models of heavy equipment.
17f Caterpillar Fire Department Bulldozer, in red with Litchfield Volunteer Fire Department logo, 132 mm, 1/50 scale, 1983.

BUBY

Argentina's pioneer manufacturer of diecast miniatures has produced models in 1/43 and smaller scales.
1000 Buick Ambulance, based on a station wagon, 126 mm, 1/43 scale, late Fifties.
1000 Buick Army Ambulance, the same casting in olive, 126 mm, 1/43 scale, late Fifties.
1051 Peugeot 504 Fire Chief, a red sedan with Bomberos and Unidad Comando decals and red dome light, 106 mm, 1/43 scale, Seventies.
29 Peugeot 504 Fire Chief, a smaller version of #1051 from the Buby Mini series, with blue dome light, 72 mm, 1/64 scale, Seventies.
118 Opel Ambulance, a white station wagon, the same car as the Jet Oldsmobile below, 69 mm, 1/64 scale, 1984.
118 Opel Fire Chief, the same wagon in red, 69 mm, 1/64 scale, 1984.
122 Citroen Ami-8 Red Cross Car, in white with Cruz Roja logo, 1/64 scale, no other data, 1984.

CHICO

Chico of Colombia has reissued a series of diecast trucks originally made by Vilmer of Denmark.
0 Volvo Aerial Ladder Truck, with familiar long-nose cab and three-section ladder, 147 mm, 1/43 scale, Seventies.
20 Mercedes-Benz Aerial Ladder Truck, with a stubbier cab and the same rear deck and ladder, 138 mm, 1/43 scale, Seventies.

FIDART

The products of this Brazilian firm include a series of diecast models of Dodge trucks.
120 Dodge Fire Tank Truck, in red with Corpo de Bombeiros decals, 167 mm, 1/43 or larger scale, Seventies.

GALGO

This fast-growing Argentine firm produces many diecast models in 1/43 and smaller scales.
39 Ladder Truck, a semi-trailer rig with stylized cab, a ladder that looks as if it extended, and Bomberos decals, 87 mm, small scale, circa 1980.
53 Fiat Snorkel Fire Truck, a realistic cab, but a snorkel that doesn't do what it should, 77 mm, HO or larger scale, circa 1980.
193 Ambulance, no data, Eighties; it may be:
#? VW Ambulance, a white van with Unidad Coronaria lettering, 108 mm, 1/43 scale, 1984.
#? Renault 18 Fire Chief, a short fat red sedan with a red and yellow roof bar and Salvataje hood label, the lettering of which is upside down when the label fits the hood right, 99 mm, 1/43 scale, 1984.

GORGO

Gorgo is one of Argentina's manufacturers of sheet metal toy cars.
Chevrolet Fire Department Van, 1/50 scale, no other data, 1977.
DKW Fire Truck, 1/43 scale, no other data, 1973.
DKW Snorkel Fire Truck, 1/43 scale, no other data, 1973.

I. V. H.

This Argentine firm makes flywheel-powered sheet metal toy vehicles.
Ford Falcon Fire Chief, a red sedan with dome lights and Bomberos labels, 117 mm, 1/43 or larger scale, 1979.
Ford Falcon Red Cross Car, the same sedan in white with red cross rondels, 117 mm, 1/43 or larger scale, circa 1980.
Ford Ranchero Ambulance Van, 1/43 scale, no other data, circa 1980.
Ford Ranchero Fire Department Van, 1/43 scale, no other data, 1979.

J. CUBAS

I have no idea what country these tinplate toy cars come from.
204 Red Cross Car, a white flat sedan with Ambulancia lettering, plus painted-on siren and light, 84 mm, roughly S gauge, postwar.
206 Fire Chief, the same car in red and black, lettered Servico Incendios, 84 mm, roughly S gauge, postwar.

JET

These small-scale diecast cars are made by Gillette, presumably the Argentine branch of the renowned razor manufacturer.
7 Oldsmobile Ambulance, same car as Buby 118, in white with red cross labels, 69 mm, 1/72 scale, 1978. (The Jet scale and the Buby make, Opel, are probably correct.)
7 Oldsmobile Fire Department Ambulance, the same casting in red, 69 mm, 1/72 scale, 1978.
17 Chevrolet Fire Truck, with diecast cab and plastic rear body, mount and ladder, 77 mm, 1/64 scale, 1977.

JUE

This Brazilian firm made a series of diecast Jeep models in the Sixties.
001-3 Fire Department Jeep, in red with a rack of what seem to be gasoline cans and spare wheels, 77 mm, 1/43 scale, Sixties.
001-4 First Aid Jeep, in white with a red cross decal, 77 mm, 1/43 scale, Sixties.
001-8 Medical Corps Jeep, the same in olive drab, 77 mm, 1/43 scale, Sixties.

McGREGOR

Obsolete plastic and diecast Politoys models are reissued in Mexico by a firm with the unlikely name of McGregor.
300 Romeo Ambulance, much like the original Italian issue, with a big red cross and dome light on the roof, 111 mm, 1/41 scale, Seventies.

MINIMAC

This model looks like a re-issue of the Jue Jeep listed above.
Fire Department Jeep, with an emblem on the hood, about 75 mm, 1/43 scale, Eighties (C-R Vol. II, p. 71).

MOTOPLASTIC

This Colombian firm has re-issued plastic toys originally made in U.S.A. by Banner.
Fire Engine, a quite realistic closed-cab American pumper, 106 mm, roughly S gauge, Seventies.

MUKY

Muky is one of Argentina's manufacturers of small-scale diecast miniature cars.
24 Plymouth Fury Fire Chief, with cast-in sirens, blue dome light and Bomberos decals, 77 mm, 1/64 scale, 1976.
35 Plymouth Fury Fire Chief, apparently a renumbering of #24, 77 mm, 1/64 scale, 1976.
36 Plymouth Fury Doctor's Car, presumably the same casting in white, 77 mm, 1/64 scale, 1976.

PLOM-UR

This small firm from Uruguay makes cast lead miniatures of Chevrolets.
Chevrolet Nova Fire Chief, a red sedan, 111 mm, 1/43 scale, 1975.

R. M.

R. M. is an Argentine manufacturer of plastic toy cars.
30 Torino 380TC Fire Chief, a plastic hardtop with Bomberos, Unidad Comando and other decals, 153 mm, 1/33 scale, Eighties.

RAPITOY

Aguti of Argentina produces the 1/64 scale diecast Rapitoys.
6 Ford Ambulance, based on the Matchbox #6 Ford Pickup, but with the camper shell as part of the casting and a stretcher inside, 73 mm, 1/64 scale, 1976.
#? Ford Army Ambulance, the same model in olive with a red dome light, which #6 lacks, 73 mm, 1/64 scale, 1976.
#? Ford Fire Department Ambulance, in red this time, with matching dome light, 73 mm, 1/64 scale, 1976.

ROLY

This Brazilian firm made small-scale diecast miniatures in the Sixties.
2b DKW Fire Chief, a little red wagon with fancy fire department decals on the doors, 69 mm, 1/59 scale, Sixties.
3a Volkswagen Kombi Ambulance, a bus with red crosses and Pronto Soccoro decals, 68 mm, 1/62 scale, Sixties.

SAN MARINO

This Argentine firm has made plastic toys, including a fire truck.
Fire Engine, 1/50 scale, no other data, 1973.

SOLIDO

The Brazilian branch of Solido has made a series of diecast models including a Chevrolet Opala sedan.
9 Chevrolet Opala Fire Chief, a sedan with roof light and Corpo de Bombeiros decals, 103 mm, 1/43 scale, Sixties.

SOLIDO-BUBY

Solido and Buby have collaborated on at least one model.
Renault 4 Fire Department Van, probably based on the familiar Solido model, 1/43 scale, no other data, 1978.

Tootsietoys and Accucast

Prewar Tootsietoys, which need no introduction to the collector, include several realistic fire trucks and a classic Graham ambulance. Postwar Tootsietoys are not as well known; they include everything from re-issues of the last prewar toys to present-day ladder trucks and rescue vehicles.

In recent years the Precision Accucasting Company has produced replicas and adaptations of prewar Tootsietoys. These models, known either as Accucast or P.A.C., first appeared in the late Seventies and have been made sporadically since then; we won't try to date them more exactly. Their catalog numbers begin with 20 or 30, indicating the decade in which the originals were made.

PREWAR TOOTSIETOYS

4652 Hook and Ladder Truck, in red and blue (either way), with three gold interlocking ladders, 105 mm, 1/72 scale, 1927.
4653 Water Tower, with the same chassis-hood casting as #4652 in red or blue, plus yellow body and tower, 91 mm, 1/72 scale, 1927.
4658 Mack Insurance Patrol, actually a small open-cab fire engine with cast-in equipment, 59 mm, roughly HO gauge, 1931. It came with a tinplate garage.
809 Graham Ambulance, one of a famous series of trend-setting toy cars, with cream body and black chassis, 100 mm, 1/43 scale, 1935.
809 Graham Army Ambulance, in either khaki or camouflage colors, 100 mm, 1/43 scale, 1935.
116 Ford 1935 Fire Chief's Roadster, with a fireman driver, available only in a gift set, 76 mm, about S gauge, 1936.
#? Midget Fire Engine, a curious little single casting from a Midget Assortment, 50 mm, very small scale, 1936.
#? Midget Ambulance, a camelback van with crosses cast into its sides, also from the Midget Assortment, 47 mm, very small scale, 1936.
1040 Hook and Ladder Truck, an open-cab Mack with driver, racks and three ladders, 108 mm, 1/43 scale, 1937.
1041 Hose Car, with a block of hose and a water cannon; the first version had a man standing on a block at the rear, his hands hooked into the handle of the cannon, plus a driver; the second type had neither man, block nor handle, 115 mm, 1/43 scale, 1937.
1042 Insurance Patrol, actually (again) a fire truck with booster tank and, at first, an open rear well, later a flat rear deck; each type has a driver, 109 mm, 1/43 scale, 1937.
236 Hook and Ladder Truck, a three-inch single casting with two cast-in ladders; red and silver with white wheels, 76 mm, S gauge, 1940.
237 Insurance Patrol (again!), with a big hose reel, 78 mm, S gauge, 1940.
238 Hose Truck, with no visible hose but a big water cannon on the rear deck, 78 mm, S gauge, 1940.
262 Fire Engine, announced in the 1941 catalog but never issued. Large scale.
263 Hook and Ladder Truck, also announced in 1941 but never issued.

POSTWAR TOOTSIETOYS

1040 Hook and Ladder Truck, a postwar revision with wide fenders, skirts and axle holes in place of the prewar internal pillars, 108 mm, 1/43 scale, 1946 or just after.
1041 Hose Car, likewise with wide skirted fenders, but based on the first casting, with the rear block, 115 mm, 1/43 scale, 1946 or just after.
1042 Insurance Patrol (an obsession!), the later type without the rear well, again with wide skirted fenders, 109 mm, 1/43 scale, 1946 or just after.
236 Ladder Truck; if it was re-issued, it is all red with black wheels; I haven't seen one.
237 Insurance Patrol (for the last time), all red with black wheels, 78 mm, S gauge, 1946 or just after.
238 Hose Car, likewise all red with black rubber wheels, 78 mm, S gauge, 1946 or just after.
#? Mercury 1949 Fire Chief, a red four-inch sedan with dome light and Fire Chief lettering cast in, 110 mm, O gauge, 1949 or later.
#? Pontiac 1950 Fire Chief, with the dome light but no lettering, 105 mm, O gauge, 1950 or later.
#? Chevrolet 1950 Ambulance, a cream van with dome light and cross cast into the roof, 102 mm, O gauge, 1950 or later.
#? Chevrolet 1950 Army Ambulance, the same casting in olive drab, 102 mm, O gauge, 1950 or later.
2330 Mack Fire Engine, with long enclosed cab, a ladder on one side and two lengths of hose on the other, 159 mm, large scale, circa 1950.
905 Mack Ladder Truck, a 1940 Mack cab pulling a semi-trailer with an aerial ladder, 223 mm, large scale, circa 1950.
2905 International Ladder Truck, a 1940 International cab with the same semi, 222 mm, large scale, Fifties.
5211 Fire Department Set, with the Mack pumper, Mack or International ladder truck, Mercury chief and accessories, circa 1950. Either the Mack cab was used both before and after the International, or the two were used simultaneously for a while.
#? American LaFrance Fire Engine, a fairly realistic three-inch model, 81 mm, about S gauge, 1954.
1011 Fire Pumper, with closed cab and two hose reels, from the Jam-Pac series, 63 mm, about HO gauge, before 1972.
2545 Ladder Truck, with long red body, white plastic interior, base and three-section aerial ladder, 185 mm, O gauge or larger, 1970.
2545 Ladder Truck, the same model with a simplified single-section ladder, 185 mm, O gauge or larger, 1973.
1290 Fire Pumper, with stubby body, short ladders and two hose reels, from the Tough Trucks series, 95 mm, S gauge or larger, 1969.
#? Chemical Extinguisher Truck, a tanker with labels showing its name and a flask pouring liquid on a fire, 99 mm, S gauge or larger, 1972.
#? Fire Chief's Jeep Wagon, red and white, with Fire Chief labels, in the #1747 set in 1972 but gone by 1974, 101 mm, about O gauge, 1972.
#? Fire Chief's Pickup Truck, with the same labels as the Jeep wagon and replacing it in #1747, 97 mm, about O gauge, 1974.
1747 Fire Fighters Set, with the ladder truck, pumper, chemical truck and first the Jeep wagon, then the pickup, plus two figures taller than the trucks, 1972.
1747 Fire Fighters Set, without a vehicle for the chief, otherwise as before, 1981.
1249 American LaFrance Ladder Truck, a fairly realistic body with a fairly unreal ladder, from the Little Toughs series, 102 mm, S gauge or smaller, 1967.
1249 American LaFrance Snorkel, the same body with a snorkel arm and bucket, 100 mm, S gauge or smaller, 1967.
1297 Emergency Rescue Truck, a British-looking enclosed truck with Rescue lettering cast on its roof, either white with Rescue labels or yellow with S.W.A.T. labels, 93 mm, perhaps S gauge, 1975.
1297 Ambulance, in white with red interior and base, Ambulance labels and a cross on the roof, 99 mm, S gauge or larger, 1975.
1297 Rescue Wagon, with detailed raised roof and what may be two oxygen tanks inside, 104 mm, S gauge or larger, 1975.
1749 Rescue 1 Set, the three #1297 vehicles and a helicopter, 1975.
1830 Rescue 2 Set, the contents of the #1749 and #1747 sets minus the chemical truck, plus another helicopter, 1975.
5003 Rescue Ambulance, a six-inch plastic vehicle in red with Rescue cast into its nose and roof, plus a white interior, 142 mm, large scale, 1975.
5000 Rescue Wagon, red plastic and much like #5003, introduced as a police van in 1976, turning red only later, 114 mm, O gauge, 1984 or shortly before.
2303 Fire Truck, a long one with six wheels that are too small for it, usually found in the #1805 Interstate Set, 122 mm, O gauge, 1976.
5008 American LaFrance Fire Truck, eight inches long, announced in 1976, but was it ever issued?
1814 Paramedic Truck Set, with fire and rescue trucks, copter and accessories, 1978.
1951 Utility Unit, a red truck with white interior and equipment, with its name and #4 on labels, 95 mm, O gauge, 1979.
3154 Police-Fire-Rescue Assortment, including a 5.25 inch fire truck, a police van and a helicopter, all quite unrealistic, larger than O gauge, 1979.
1642 Emergency Set, including the three #3154 vehicles, 1979.
2985 Ladder Truck, a new model to replace #2545, in red zamak and white plastic, with a one-section aerial ladder—and Engine Co. 24 cast into the roof! 185 mm, large scale, 1984.

ACCUCAST (P.A.C.)

203 Ladder Truck, like Tootsietoy #4652, with red chassis and hood, yellow rear body and gold ladders, 92 mm, 1/72 scale.
208f Model A Ford Fire Chief's Coupe, in red, based on the Tootsietoy Model A, 69 mm, about S gauge.
2013s Buick Ambulance, the G.M. series van in white with Ambulance lettering and red crosses, 80 mm, about S gauge.
2023 Water Tower, in red and yellow, like #4653, 90 mm, 1/72 scale.
2025f Model A Ford Fire Chief's Roadster, a red companion to the coupe, 69 mm, about S gauge.
2034 Cadillac Ambulance, another white G.M. series van, 82 mm, about S gauge.
2035 Oldsmobile Ambulance, still another, about S gauge, no other data.
2051 Mack Ladder Truck, with the old Bulldog chassis cab, racks and ladders, 82 mm, about S gauge.
2054 Model T Ford Fire Truck, the old T pickup with racks and ladders, booster tank and hose reel, 81 mm, about S gauge.
2060a G.M. Ambulance, this time with the no-name chassis and the usual van body, about S gauge, no other data.
2062 Mack Water Tower, the Bulldog chassis and #4653 tower, 82 mm, about S gauge.
20 Chevrolet Ambulance, another white G.M. van, with the P.A.C. deluxe detailed chassis, 85 mm, about S gauge.
301 Hook and Ladder Truck, like Tootsietoy #1040, with blue driver and silver ladders, 1/43 scale—if the original was!
302f Ford 1935 Fire Chief's Roadster, like Tootsietoy #116, 74 mm, about S gauge.
304f Ford 1935 Fire Chief's Coupe, in red with black roof panel and running boards, 74 mm, about S gauge.
338 Ford AA Ladder Truck, no data.
339 Fire Pumper, based on Tootsietoy #1041, with water cannon, no other data.
340 Mack Ladder Truck, with early-Thirties open cab plus two ladders on part of the rear body of #301, about 115 mm (C-R Vol. II, unnumbered page)
341 Stewart Ladder Truck, no data. Could Stewart be a misprint for Seagrave?
342 Insurance Patrol, based on #1042, no data. Coleman and Russell show four other models in Vol. II, from the unnumbered pages through page 1:
Mack Fire Truck with Ahrens-Fox Pump, with the front pump of #339, an open Bulldog cab, and a simple rear body with, apparently, two lengths of suction hose, about 95 mm.
Mack Pumper, with a grille reminiscent of the late prewar 3-inch Tootsietoys, open cab with windshield, and simple rear body with two ladders, about 75 mm.
Seagrave Fire Truck, with Model A Fordish grille, open cab, the rear body from #203 and two ladders, about 90 mm.
Seagrave Water Tower, a closed cab with big flat grille, part of #301's rear body, the #2023 water tower and two ladders, about 110 mm.

Hubley Toys

The venerable Hubley firm of Lancaster, Pennsylvania, has made toy vehicles for many years, using cast iron, aluminum, zamak and plastic at various times. Hubley Toys have included a wide variety of fire vehicles, some of them accurate models, others fanciful toys. The cast iron Hubleys fall into the latter category, though they are by no means as unrealistic as some of their contemporaries. There may well be more of them, but these are the only small and medium-sized types known to me. They usually came in pairs, called "fire engine" (i.e., a steam pumper) and "hook and ladder" by Hubley.
313 Steam Pumper, 3.75 inches long, probably with a nickel-plated boiler top, no other data, prewar.
314 Ladder Truck, a single casting, similar to #313 in style, with two eight-rung ladders, no other data, prewar.
380 Steam Pumper, 5 inches long, with nickel plated boiler, no other data, prewar.
381 Ladder Truck, a five-incher with plated seven-rung ladders, no other data, prewar.
382 Steam Pumper, with silver open-cab body including the driver, bell and lower boiler, and a separate red upper boiler casting, 124 mm, O gauge or larger, prewar.
383 Ladder Truck, a single casting similar to the steamer, with ladder racks on its otherwise open rear body; mine lacks the ladders, 126 mm, O gauge or larger, prewar.
#? Steam Pumper, shorter than #382, with separate body (including driver), chassis (including grille), and boiler top castings, red, black and nickel-plated in order, 114 mm, O gauge, prewar.
#? Ladder Truck, with red body and black chassis, plus two diecast five-rung ladders, 114 mm, O gauge, prewar.
2255 Ladder Truck, larger than the above, with separate bumper-grille casting, no other data, 162 mm, large scale, prewar. Did it have a steamer companion?
213 Steam Pumper, with driver, steam dome, tall boiler and wheels all in iron, the body made of left and right halves, 122 mm, O gauge, prewar. Mine is a modern reproduction.
#? Steam Pumper, 3.5 inches long, a single casting with driver, simple boiler, and what may be a steam dome, 90 mm, S gauge, Thirties.
#? Ladder Truck, also a 3.5 inch single casting, with its racks carrying two unreal four-rung ladders, 90 mm, S gauge, Thirties.
#? Ahrens-Fox Fire Truck, with front-mounted pump, open cab, and a very short rear body that probably held a ladder, 90 mm, about O gauge, prewar.
#? Ahrens-Fox Fire Truck, longer but much like the above, with a five-rung ladder sticking out behind, 117 mm (148 mm including the ladder), O gauge or larger, prewar.
530 Ahrens-Fox Fire Truck, bigger again, with two short ladders lying on their sides, 180 mm, large scale, prewar; all three of these have red wooden wheels and white rubber tires, as do several below.
#? Ladder Truck, with conventional front end, but again two ladders standing straight up on their sides instead of slanting inward, 172 mm, large scale, prewar.
#? Steam Pumper, companion to the ladder truck above, with a tall boiler, red wooden hubs and white tires, 153 mm, large scale, prewar.
#? Steam Pumper, with separate red boiler top and plated grille-bumper castings, two men in the open cab and a bell on the hood, 165 mm, large scale, prewar.
#? Ladder Truck, companion to the above, with separate grille-bumper casting and two sheet metal ladders that interlock, 165 mm, large scale, prewar; both have red wooden wheels.
#? Steam Pumper, this time with red body, black chassis, and plated grille-bumper-headlights and boiler top castings, plus two men in the open cab, 163 mm, large scale, prewar.
#? Ladder Truck, with the same black chassis and plated grille castings as its mate, and interlocking sheet metal ladders, 149 mm, large scale, prewar. Both have red wheels.
#? Steam Pumper, painted black, with hood louvers, long thin body and yellow cast spoked wheels; the black may be a repaint over original yellow; 127 mm, large scale, prewar.
#? Steam Pumper, even more skeletal than the last, with short louvered hood, driver, and not much between him and the boiler; 150 mm, large scale, prewar. The rear disc wheels are original, the tin front ones are not.
Hubley's diecast models range from big toy fire trucks to the accurate scale models made around 1960, called Real Toys in the U.S.A. and Real Types in Canada.
428 Steam Pumper, diecast re-issue of an earlier cast iron toy, probably #382, no other data, late prewar.
429 Ladder Truck, perhaps a re-issue of #383, but with longer ladders, no other data, late prewar.
437 Packard Fire Chief, from Hubley's well-known series of 5.5 inch Packards, a handsome coupe with Fire Chief cast on its 140 mm, large scale, 1940.
#? Ladder Truck, a snub-nosed red and silver open-cab truck with two brown diecast ladders, 105 mm, O gauge or smaller, Forties?
#? Steam Pumper, likewise red and silver, with nickel-plated boiler top casting, 105 mm, O gauge or smaller, Forties?
405 Ladder Truck, a three-inch single casting including two ladders, with a hole in the rear bed, 78 mm, S gauge, Thirties.
404 Steam Pumper, another single casting with a wide boiler, steam dome and such, 76 mm, S gauge, Thirties.
463 Ladder Truck, with open cab, separate windshield and ladder mount castings, and one sheet metal ladder that sticks onto the mount and projects too far either forward or aft, 190 mm, large scale, Fifties.
465 Ladder Truck, much like #463 in general, but with a hose reel, ladder racks and two six-rung diecast ladders, 190 mm, large scale, Fifties.
#? Steam Pumper, similar to the two above, with cast-in bell, hose reel and booster tank, plus separate windshield and boiler top castings, 190 mm, large scale, Fifties.
#? Fire Engine, with short closed cab and open rear, cast water cannon and spotlight in back and a wooden steam dome over the front axle, 186 mm, large scale, Fifties.
#? Fire Engine, also of the Ahrens-Fox type, but older, with open cab and blue driver, red wheels and white tires, 185 mm, large scale, early postwar.
#? Ladder Truck, with prominent nose, open cab and blue driver as above, and two of Hubley's usual interlocking sheet metal ladders, 185 mm, large scale, early postwar.
#? Ladder Truck, with round-nosed closed cab, hose reel and ladder racks, 186 mm, large scale, Fifties.
402 Fire Engine, more modern than anything before it, with closed cab and open rear crowned by hose reels and a cast-in ladder, 148 mm, O gauge or larger, 148 mm, O gauge or larger, late Fifties.
#? Chevrolet Ambulance, a light gray Real Toys wagon with a siren on the roof, 83 mm, S gauge, circa 1960.
#? Chevrolet Fire Chief, the same wagon in red, 83 mm, S gauge, circa 1960.

There are also plastic Hubley Toys; the best of them are the smallest, though their "Tiny Toys" title should not be taken too literally.
#? Packard 1949 Fire Chief, red plastic with black and silver trim, plus Fire Chief lettering on the hood, 146 mm, large scale, circa 1950.

306 Steam Pumper, in hard red plastic with separate silver boiler top, 148 mm, O gauge or larger, Fifties.
306 Steam Pumper, re-issued in soft plastic with less silver trim, and a bit shorter, 145 mm, O gauge or larger, Sixties?
307 Ladder Truck, with the same styling as #306, silver windshield and two white ladders, 148 mm, O gauge or larger, Fifties.
307 Ladder Truck, re-issued in soft plastic, with only the grille and headlights silver, 145 mm, O gauge or larger, Sixties?
324 Ladder Truck, with short-hood closed cab that lifts to expose a green engine block, and two interlocking ladders aft, 171 mm, large scale, Fifties or later.
331 Diesel Ladder Truck, similar to the above but with a long-nose cab, Diesel lettering on the hood, a chassis including front fenders and a red engine block, plus the same interlocking white ladders, 183 mm, large scale, Fifties or later.
306? American LaFrance Pumper, with windows, headlights, hose reels, suction hose, a ladder, control panel, extinguishers and hose bed, plus a silver base, a nice little model, 104 mm, about O gauge, 1959. This and the next model also came in kit form; see C-R Vol. II, p. 43, for an open-cab version.
307 American LaFrance Aerial Ladder, with the same type of cab, diecast silver chassis (the pumper's is plastic, but these may be different production runs), and swiveling silver mount and two-section aerial ladder, 157 mm, O gauge, 1959.

American Cast Iron

Cast iron toys are not my field, and I am indebted to Nelson Adams for turning me loose in his collection, where I found great numbers of fire trucks. Their sizes vary considerably, and I have limited those listed here to lengths up to 165 mm for engines and 200 mm for ladder trucks. Most are larger than O gauge, and all were made in prewar days; I have no means of dating them more exactly. There are probably more in existence than even Mr. Adams knows of, so please do not regard this list as complete.

ARCADE

Arcade Toys often do us the courtesy of telling us who made them—a rarity among cast iron toys. The two pairs of fire trucks with Pontiac-style hood stripes stand out.
Ladder Truck, with left and right castings plus a plated piece providing bumpers, grille, headlights and hood stripes; the body includes two ladders, the left one shorter to make room for a man standing on the running board; the wheels are white rubber with their hubs painted green, 120 mm, about O gauge.
Steam Pumper, with the same third casting as its partner, but without a standing man or green hubs, and with a simple boiler, 110 mm, about O gauge.
Steam Pumper, almost the same as the one just above, but a few millimeters longer, with a slightly different boiler shape, no other data, about 0 gauge.
Steam Pumper, a bigger version of similar construction, with an Arcade decal on its lefthand door (the smaller one has no doors) and white rubber wheels, 154 mm, large scale.
Ladder Truck, without the standing man, with the same third casting and Arcade decal, plus newer black rubber wheels with the Arcade name cast in, 181 mm, large scale.
Ladder Truck, like the first one listed in having a short left ladder and standing fireman, but of left-and-right two-piece construction (no third piece), and with green-painted hubs, 124 mm, about O gauge.
Steam Pumper, an older and simpler design with high narrow body, boiler top rising to a small opening, and room under its fenders for larger wheels than its plain white rubber ones, 114 mm, about O gauge.
Steam Pumper, with a different boiler design, a bell between it and the driver, and cast spoked wheels, 133 mm, large scale; not definitely Arcade, but probably.
Fire Chief's Car, a Model A Ford coupe with a gold bell and white rubber wheels, 125 mm, large scale.
City Ambulance, with those words cast into it, red crosses, and black rubber wheels with silver-painted hubs, 150 mm, large scale.

DENT

Fire Chief's Car, longer and slimmer than the Arcade, with Chief cast on the doors and his face at the window, plus metal disc wheels, 139 mm, large scale.
Ladder Truck, with driver and tillerman, two ladders, a bell, and red wooden wheels with rubber tires, 139 mm, large scale.
Ladder Truck, with louvered Mack-type hood, driver, long ladders, skeletal body, red wooden wheels and rubber tires, 172 mm, large scale, probably made by Dent.

KENTON

Fire Chief's Car, a Model A Ford coupe with a bell on the hood, Chief on the doors, and red wooden hubs, 144 mm, large scale.
Steam Pumper, with tall driver and boiler, a few bars to connect them, red wooden wheels and white rubber tires, 142 mm, large scale.
Ladder Truck, long and handsome, with blue-painted driver and tillerman (were they always?), two long ladders, typical skeletal design, red wooden wheels and rubber tires, 182 mm, large scale.

KILGORE

Steam Pumper, with two men in its open cab, a separate grille-bumper-headlights casting, small metal hubs and rubber tires, 127 mm, large scale.
Ladder Truck, also with two men, a third casting, metal hubs and rubber tires, 127 mm, large scale.
Ladder Truck, an older design with no driver, two removable cast iron ladders, and cast disc wheels, 163 mm not counting the ladders, large scale.

WILLIAMS

A. C. Williams fire trucks almost always come in pairs. The first nine listed here are stylistically similar and consist of left and right castings riveted together. The others are made of body and chassis castings attached by a sheet metal clip. The wheels are either metal discs, solid or with slots or spokes, or red wooden hubs with white rubber tires. Some models are known to exist with both.
Steam Pumper, with driver, steam domes, boiler, rear rails and, unlike the larger versions, a siren on the left front fender; the wheels are solid discs; 92 mm, about S gauge.
Ladder Truck, with a nose like its partner's, including the siren, a taller driver, oval holes along the sides, and no man standing at the rear; solid disc wheels again; 96 mm, about S gauge.
Steam Pumper, with the really typical Williams pattern, a bell on the hood instead of a siren, slotted disc wheels, other details as before, 127 mm, about O gauge.
Ladder Truck, with the bell up front, a standing fireman at the rear, red hubs and rubber tires, 133 mm, about O gauge.
Steam Pumper, like that of the second pair but longer, with wooden hubs and rubber tires, about 145 mm, large scale (C-R Vol. I, middle of page 73, maker not identified there).
Ladder Truck, much like its counterpart in the second pair, also with wooden hubs, about 170 mm, large scale (C-R Vol. I, top of page 153).
Steam Pumper, the usual design again, with spoked cast wheels this time, 158 mm, large scale.
Ladder Truck, again the same design, with spoked wheels like its partner, 194 mm, large scale.
Steam Pumper, much as before, but with its front bumper coming to a slight point in the center (the others curve inward); wooden hubs and rubber tires; 186 mm, large scale. Has anyone found a ladder truck like it?
Steam Pumper, first of the clipped-together types, with red body, red or black chassis and red wooden hubs, 125 mm, O gauge or larger.
Ladder Truck, with tillerman at the rear of the body and the same chassis and hubs as the steamer 132 mm, O gauge or larger.
Ladder Truck, with a higher, blunter nose, longer hood, two ladders on each side and the man at the rear hanging onto them, plus wooden hubs, 139 mm. Is there a steamer like it?
Steam Pumper, with more modern body style, fenders and headlights included in the body casting, while the silver chassis supplies grille, bumper, bell, steam domes, running boards and rear rails; wooden hubs and rubber tires; 174 mm, large scale.
Ladder Truck, with similar open-cab body and silver chassis, the latter including the ladders and racks; wheels as before; 189 mm, large scale.

UNKNOWN MAKERS

Ladder Truck, an incredibly short silver creation on huge spoked wheels, with two four-rung ladders and a driver who seems to be wondering where the motor went, 80 mm, doubtful scale.
Steam Pumper, silver too, with big driver and modest boiler, front crank, and cast wheels with red spokes, 115 mm, large scale.
Steam Pumper, tall andskinny, dominated by its boiler, witha stubby hood and no body to speak of, 142 mm, large scale. The wheels are replacements.
Steam Pumper, mostly painted blue, with spoked wheels cast integrally with the body, 155 mm, large scale.
Ladder Truck, skinny and skeletal, with big hood louvers, big five-rung ladders, and metal disc wheels, 131 mm, large scale.

American Slushmold

This is another field of which I have less than thorough knowledge. At one time, nobody was an expert on it, and almost any slush toy was called a Barclay. Though this still happens today, it also happens that toys with the Barclay name on them have been attributed to other manufacturers. Most of the toys listed below have been identified (correctly, we hope) as to their manufacturer; I have no idea who made the others.

BARCLAY

The big ambulance has Barclay's name on it, the others do not, but with one exception they do have Barclay's familiar base patterns of one or more raised transverse rectangles. The one exception shows typical Barclay workmanship. All presumably date from prewar days, except for a few postwar reissues.

50 Ambulance, long and sleek, with a blue cross on each side, Barclay #50 on the left rear fender and Made USA on the right, 125 mm, large scale.
Ambulance, a smaller model, with small blue crosses, hexagonal window patterns and a spare wheel cast in, 90 mm, about S gauge.
Ambulance, similar except for bigger red crosses, 90 mm, about S gauge.
Ladder Truck, with four levels of ladders, a tillerman perched atop them, a driver, a folded life net on each side, and an arm behind the cab to hold a bell, 116 mm, about S gauge.
Ladder Truck, the same casting but sold unpainted and without a bell, and running on black bakelite wheels, 116 mm, about S gauge, early postwar.
Steam Pumper, with front end design much like the ladder truck, plus boiler, steam dome, bell arm, red wooden wheels and white rubber tires, 99 mm, O gauge or smaller.
Steam Pumper, much like the previous model, but with the steam dome now bearing a water cannon, and another dome forward of it; no marks on the base; the original wheels were bakelite; 97 mm, O gauge or smaller, early postwar. I believe I bought it unpainted.
Steam Pumper, a much more modern design, long and sleek, with a low boiler, enclosed rear end, and Fire Dept No 99 lettering cast in, 157 mm, large scale, early postwar.

MAYBE BARCLAY

These models resemble the more definite Barclays in workmanship, and each has a raised transverse rectangle on the base. All are presumably prewar.

Hose Truck, with a blue-clad driver in the cab, a hose reel behind him, an open well behind that, red wooden wheels and rubber tires, 79 mm, about S gauge.
Hose Truck, with white rubber wheels and without its driver painted blue, 79 mm, about S gauge.
Ladder Truck, with gold bell, fire extinguishers and tillerman's helmet, red wooden hubs and rubber tires, 78mm, about HO gauge.
Ladder Truck, the same casting, the same gold trim, white rubber wheels, 78 mm, about HO gauge.
Steam Pumper, with a fireman standing at the rear, gold trim, red wooden hubs and rubber tires, 78 mm, S to HO gauge.

LINCOLN

Made in Lincoln, Nebraska, with styling that looks postwar but may not be.

79 Steam Pumper, long and thin, with an impossibly long hood and small boiler, running on white rubber wheels, 96 mm, abour S gauge.

MANOIL

Manoil is best known for its diecast toys, but made some interesting slush pieces too.

Ladder Truck, with a rounded grille that looks as if it bites, ladders in back, driver and tillerman, 70 mm, about HO scale.
Steam Pumper, with a rounded silver grille, boiler in back, a man standing behind it as well as a driver, 71 mm, about HO scale. Both are either late prewar or early postwar.

SAVOYE

Savoye models may have unpierced red wooden wheels with axle ends driven into them, large spoked lead wheels more at home on a farm wagon or cannon, or black bakelite wheels like those seen on some Barclays. They have transverse base lines but no raised rectangles.

Emergency Truck, with V-shaped grille, a tank inside the rear body sides with what may be a hose coupling on it, a man at the rear, Emergency lettering and red hubs, 113 mm, about O gauge.
Ladder Truck, with a blunt squarish nose, racks holding two ladders, a man at the rear, and big spoked wheels, 97 mm, about O gauge.
Steam Pumper, with squarish front end, driver and rear man, bell, dome, boiler, gold trim and spoked wheels, 99 mm, about O gauge.
Steam Pumper, the same casting but all red, with bakelite wheels, 97 mm, about O gauge, probably an early postwar reissue.
Steam Pumper, with a different, concave grille, a bell on the hood, and a bit of hose clinging to the dome just forward of the boiler, plus red wooden wheels, 100 mm, about O gauge.
Water Tower, a six-wheeler with roofed cab, more or less Mack styling, and a raising tower, 100 mm, smaller than O gauge.
Water Tower, there may also be a four-wheel version, no other data.

TOMMY TOY

Ambulance, short and high, with green windows, red wooden wheels, and a man hanging on the rear end! 102 mm, about O gauge.

UNKNOWN MAKERS

70 Steam Pumper, with what may be a hose reel behind the driver and a big boiler at the rear; the truck has an open base, no fenders and white wheels, 58 mm, about HO gauge. Mine may be a recent reissue of a prewar toy.
Ladder Truck, with the usual stack of ladders, a tillerman atop them, a driver, and a man hanging on each side, plus red wooden hubs, 69 mm, about HO gauge.
Ladder Truck, the same casting with black metal disc wheels, 69 mm, about HO gauge.
Steam Pumper, much like the ladder truck in workmanship, with driver, rear man and black metal wheels, 59 mm, about HO gauge.
Steam Pumper, a hair bigger than the above, with red wooden hubs, 61 mm, about HO gauge.
Steam Pumper, with a long tapered and fluted hood, driver and rear man, a big boiler right behind the cab, a sort of chest in back, and black metal wheels; the truck is sometimes painted blue instead of red, 85 mm, about S gauge.

American Diecast

American diecast model and toy emergency vehicles include a wide variety of products, from simple toys to accurate scale models. The single-casting Tootsietoys of early postwar days set a pattern still followed by such firms as Midgetoys, while Authenticast and Hudson produced scale models for railroad platform use. In more modern times the fast-wheel toys of Mattel and Ertl have won much popularity. Some of them are not actually made in the U.S.A., but are listed here because the firms that produce them have their headquarters in America.

AUTHENTICAST

Authenticast made HO gauge models for use on railroad platforms.

#? Aerial Ladder Truck, a nice model if you don't expect the ladder to operate; it's for looks and it looks right; 154 mm, 1/87 scale, Fifties.
#? Fire Engine, an open-cab pumper with a bed of hose in back, 79 mm, 1/87 scale, Fifties,
#? Ambulance, a white van with two blobs on the roof, 60 mm, 1/87 scale, Fifties.
#? Fire Chief, a Chrysler Corporation car with a bell on the front bumper, 56 mm, 1/87 scale, Fifties.
#? Fire Chief, a sleeker car of similar parentage, with a roof bar, 56 mm, 1/87 scale, Fifties.

American Diecast

BARCLAY

Barclay is better known for its slushmold models, but its few diecast models deserve to be known.
Ambulance Truck, a Bottle Series army truck in white with red cross label, 49 mm, small scale, Sixties.
Fire Chief, a long slim car made in both diecast and slushmold form, usually as a police car; the red diecast version is 94 mm, about O gauge, late Thirties. There may also be a slushmold version.
Ladder Truck, with simple open cab and semi-trailer, sheet metal aerial ladder, and a fireman who climbs the ladder as it raises, 148 mm, S to HO gauge, early postwar?

ERTL

This Iowa firm makes a wide variety of model and toy vehicles, including these small-scale toys.
1361 Ford American Red Cross Van, a special Disaster Services version of Ertl's Ford van, 72 mm, 1/64 scale, 1984.
1461 Smurf Fire Truck, with blue driver in white hat, cast-in ladders, hose reel and other gear, 72 mm, small scale, 1983. Licensed by Wallace Berrie & Co.
1865 Ford Ambulance Van, the same casting as #1361 in Transcon Medi-Vac livery, one of Ertl's Cannonball Run models, 72 mm, 1/64 scale, 1981.

FREEPORT TOY

This model is a diecast reissue of a prewar Arcade cast iron piece. Both Arcade and Freeport Toy were located in Freeport, Illinois. . . .
561 Ladder Truck, an open-cab type with two men and three interlocking ladders, 207 mm, large scale, early postwar.

GOODEE

Goodee Toys were made by Excel Products of New Brunswick, New Jersey, a fact which has led to some confusion. They are single castings in the Tootsietoy tradition; both three-inch and eight-inch versions often exist.
Fire Engine, the larger one, with hose at the rear, other equipment here and there, and a big roof spotlight, 158 mm, large scale, Fifties.
Fire Engine, the smaller version without the cast-in axes but otherwise much like its big brother, 80 mm, S gauge, Fifties.
Fire Chief, a 1953 Ford sedan with cast-in dome light, 79 mm, S gauge, Fifties.
Fire Chief, the bigger version of the same car, 157 mm, large scale, Fifties.

HALLMARK

Hallmark toys include a series of blobs with wheels; this one is not too unrealistic.
Fiery Fred Fire Truck, with a coil of hose sitting like a rattlesnake atop a ladder of sorts, 61 mm, no scale, 1983.

HUDSON

Hudson Miniatures products include two HO gauge model fire trucks.
Fire Engine, a simple though fairly realistic model with open cab and high-side open rear body, 65 mm, HO gauge, Fifties.
Ladder Truck, with the same front end and a longer rear body with two black ladders on racks, 74 mm, HO gauge, Fifties.

IT'S A BEAUT

What a trade name! The Beaut Manufacturing Company was its formal name. It is best known for four versions of a 1942 Chrysler sedan.
4 Chrysler Fire Chief, a red sedan with FIRE cast across the doors and a bell on its nose, 95 mm, about O gauge, early postwar.
#? Fire Truck? I've seen one listed in a reference book, but was there really a fire truck or did somebody mistake the chief's car for one?

JURGENS

Send Mr. Jurgens a broken Dinky Toys #131 Cadillac roadster with unbroken windshield and the right amount of money and he'll make one of these for you
Cadillac Ambulance, with a new rear body added to the Dinky casting, 116 mm, O gauge, 1984.

MANOIL

This New York firm made some remarkable diecast toys, but their best-known fire truck is fairly realistic.
709 Fire Engine, a sleek modern truck with suction hose and spotlights flanking its ladder, plus a hose reel in back, 118 mm, about O gauge, late Forties.
711 Ladder Truck, larger than 709 and very prone to metal fatigue, which is why I've never seen one, no other data, circa 1950.
712 Fire Pumper, ditto, circa 1950.

MATTEL HOT WHEELS

Mattel revolutionized the diecast car industry in 1968 with its fast-wheeled products.
6451 Ambulance, with diecast futuristic cab and base, plastic rear body and opening door, and blue dome light, from the Heavyweights series, 74 mm, S gauge, 1970.
6454 Fire Truck, another Heavyweight, with the same type of cab and a semi-trailer equipped with ladders and hose, 100 mm, S gauge, 1970.
6469 Fire Chief Cruiser, a metallic red Ford sedan with dome light, sirens and white lettering, 79 mm, S gauge, 1970.
7650 Emergency Squad, with blue lights and equipment, yellow stripe and white logo, 77 mm, S gauge, 1975. See also Ranger Rig.
7661 Paramedic, a white or yellow van with Paramedic Ambulance lettering, red cross and trim, 71 mm, S gauge, 1975.
7665 Chief's Special, the first version, with Police Cruiser base lettering, blue dome light flanked by sirens above, 77 mm, S gauge, 1975.
7665 Chief's Special, the later type, with cast-in roof bar, no light, and the base lettering blocked out, 77 mm, S gauge, late Seventies.
7666 Ranger Rig, the #7650 casting in green with red plastic parts and yellow Forest Service logo, 77 mm, S gauge, 1975.
9640 Fire-Eater, a pumper with a big square cab, blue plastic roof bar and lots of cast-in equipment, 77 mm, S gauge, 1977.
2639 Fire Chaser, a red sedan with blue roof bar flanked by sirens and spotlights, and with #5 and Fire Chief lettering, 78 mm, S gauge, 1978.
1510 Fire Chief Car, similar to #2639 but with more window posts, a chrome roof bar holding two blue lights, different decals with a new coat of arms, and Scorchers base enclosing its pullback motor, 74 mm, S gauge, 1980.
1695 Old Number 5, a quite authentic Twenties Ahrens-Fox engine with a pump up front and lots of detail, 80 mm, S to HO gauge, 1981.
1699 Airport Rescue, a massive yellow eight-wheeler with swiveling foam nozzles fore and aft, 85 mm, HO gauge, 1981.
4225 Firefighters Play Set, including 2639, 7650, 9640 and cardboard scenery, 1982.
7068 Fire Smasher, a chief's car with a left-side door panel that rotates, offering either a smooth lettered door or a big dent, 74 mm, S gauge, 1984.

MATTEL FIRST WHEELS

Mattel also makes these simple toys for younger children.
1300 Fire Chief, a red blob with painted-on blue windows and dome lights, 74 mm, not scale, 1979.
1301 Fire Engine, with a five-rung white plastic ladder, 82 mm, not scale, 1979.
1304 Paramedic, a bright yellow rescue van, 83 mm, not scale, 1979.

METALCRAFT

Coleman-Russell Volume I identifies this model, which is the same basic casting as the six-inch Londontoys model from Canada, as being made in U.S.A. by Metalcraft. Since many Londontoys exist with the brand name removed, the dies may well have changed hands.
Fire Truck, shown in the Catalogue with separate chassis casting, exactly like the Londontoy, but mine has integral axle pillars and no chassis, 150 mm, large scale, Fifties.

METAL MASTERS

Some of this firm's toys, including the pickup truck below, resembled Tootsietoys of the late thirties; others were larger and more original.
300 Fire Engine, a fairly realistic big toy with driver, siren, booster tank, and ladders on wire hooks, 252 mm, large scale, early postwar.
#? Fire Department Pickup, one of two versions, with cast-in rear vertical bar which, along with a tab on the cab roof, holds a ladder, 171 mm, large scale, early postwar.
#? Fire Department Pickup, without the rear bar, but with slots that hold a tinplate ladder rack, 171 mm, large scale, early postwar.

MIDGETOY

Midgetoys continue the tradition of single-casting diecast toy vehicles begun by their Illinois neighbors, Tootsietoys.
Ambulance, a member of the Swat Pack set, with cast-in crosses, 75 mm, S gauge, 1979.
Ambulance Bus, either red or white, with blunt nose, sloping tail and windows all along the sides, plus a big redcross on the roof, 108 mm, O to S gauge, Sixties.
Ambulance Van, in red, white or military olive, the same casting minus the side windows, 108 mm, O to S gauge, Sixties.
Fire Chief, a sedan with tailfins and cast-in dome light, 90 mm, S gayuge, Sixties.
Fire Chief, a smaller Swat Pack type, with three silver blobs on the roof, 63 mm, roughly HO gauge, 1979.
Fire Engine, the biggest of three, with closed cab, silver ladders and equipment, and a hose bed, 145 mm, O gauge, Sixties.
Fire Engine, similar in design but smaller, 110 mm, O to S gauge, Sixties.
Fire Engine, a smaller closed-cab type with hose, ladders and booster tank, also sold in military olive, 89 mm, S gauge, Sixties.
Fire Engine, an open-cab hose truck with a reel on top, suction hose on the left and a ladder on the right, 73 mm, S gauge or smaller, Sixties.
Fire Department Wrecker, in red with plastic crane boom, included in the Swat Pack, 70 mm, S to HO gauge, 1979.
445 Alert Assortment, containing three small emergency vehicles, 1984. I believe there are larger Midgetoy sets of emergency vehicles too.
555 Swat Pack, with four emergency vehicles, listed as new in 1984, but mine, numbered 5507, is copyrighted 1979 and includes the Ambulance, Fire Chief's Car, Wrecker and small open-cab Fire Engine.

RALSTOY

Art Massey's firm, which takes its name from its home town of Ralston, Nebraska, makes diecast trucks, mainly for promotional uses. But the first Ralstoy was a fire truck.
1 Fire Truck, long and modern, based on a six-wheel Bohn prototype, 153 mm, about O gauge, Sixties or earlier.
22 Chevrolet Step Van Ambulance, in white with red crosses and Ambulance logo, 108 mm, O gauge or larger, 1975, plus the following ambulance and fire versions of the same Chevy Step Van casting:
Army Ambulance, olive drab with red crosses on white square panels.
Bruno Volunteer Fire Department, white above, red below, with gold lettering.
Hickman Fire Dept. 3, same colors as the Bruno version.
Omaha Fire Rescue, either white and red as above or all red, with gold lettering.
Ralston Vol. Fire Dept. Fire & Rescue Unit, all red with gold logo.
Seymour Fire Rescue Service, in dark blue with matching logo on a light blue panel, commissioned by Robert W. Shortell for his home town in Connecticut; the other towns represented above are all in Nebraska.

RENWAL

Renwal's diecast fire trucks deserve as much renown as that firm's plastic ones; and in fact two types exist in both materials.
#? Steam Pumper, a well-detailed postwar truck with lots of cast-in equipment, including the toymakers' favorite anachronism, the steam boiler, plus sheet metal base and yellow plastic driver, 153 mm, large scale, 1955.
8022 Ladder Truck, with cast-in ladders and lettering, the same model as the plastic #146, 81 mm, S gauge, Fifties.
8040 Steam Pumper, the same sort of truck with hose and boiler in the back, also made in plastic as #145, 81 mm, S gauge, Fifties.

SLIK TOYS

Slik Toys were cast in aluminum by the Kipp firm of Lansing, Iowa, and sometimes known by the name of Kipp or of Lansing.
9700 Hose Truck, remarkably short and wide, with a hose reel in back of its open cab, 92 mm, doubtful scale, Fifties.

TRU-SCALE

All I know of the firm is that it made:
Municipal Fire Department Truck, a big toy made of three castings and a sheet metal chassis; the rear body includes hose and an odd sort of chute, perhaps to hold the ladders missing from mine, 240 mm, large scale, Fifties.

WINROSS

Roger Austin's firm, located in Rochester, New York, and almost named for his ancestral home of Kinross, Scotland, is renowned for its fine promotional models of White and Autocar trucks. In the Sixties Winross made two versions of a short-chassis White emergency truck.
White 1500 Emergency Truck, with simple rear body, racks and ladders, and an angular red 1500 cab, 100 mm, 1/64 scale, Sixties.
White 3000 Emergency Truck, with a rounded gray 3000 cab, otherwise as before, 100 mm, 1/64 scale, Sixties.

American Plastic

Many U.S. firms have made plastic model and toy emergency vehicles, especially in early postwar days. Some of them did not put their names on their products, and since nobody knows the whole history of these toys, we can only list those we know of and hope we have not left out too many. They range from accurate models to fanciful toys, each with its own personality, and they take us back to the days when some of us were children playing with them.

ACME

The related firms of Acme and Thomas (see below) made plastic toy cars and trucks.
1-133 Buick Fire Chief, slim and sleek, with siren, spotlight, antenna and "Fire Chief / Co. No. 7« oval decal on the roof, 109 mm, O gauge, Fifties.

AMLOID

This firm presently makes plastic toy cars.
Ladder Truck, a long open-cab type with separate windshield, driver and two-section aerial ladder, 313 mm, large scale, Eighties.

AUBURN

There is no maker's name on these plastic versions of rubber Auburn products, so we'll take them on faith.
Fire Engine, a white plastic version of the familiar closed-cab pumper, 113 mm, about O gauge, postwar.
Emergency Truck, about an inch longer, with Rescue lettering and red crosses, 135 mm, large scale, postwar.
Steam Pumper, copying the more modern of two big rubber types, 190 mm, large scale, postwar.

BANNER

Banner products include several emergency vehicles, some of which were later reissued in South America.
1 Hose Truck, a four-inch open-cab type with hose in the rear, equipment cast into the sides, and a very breakable windshield, 111 mm, about O gauge, Fifties?
4 Fire Engine, A pleasantly realistic closed-cab pumper, later reissued by Motoplastic of Colombia, 109 mm, O gauge or smaller, Fifties.
7 Hose Truck, similar but with Cadillac hood and fenders, separate spotlight and nozzle, and windup motor, 137 mm, large scale, Fifties?
219 Ambulance, a plastic truck with tinplate rear body and cover,

Ambulance lettering and red crosses, 161 mm, large scale, early postwar.
219 Army Ambulance, the same truck in olive drab with tan rear cover, white crosses and lettering, 161 mm, large scale, early postwar.

B.K.C.

This is a homely little toy with a big wheel in the middle.
Steam Pumper, high and stubby, with a towering boiler, short ladders, and a fireman's helmet as its radiator cap, plus four cast-in phony wheels; it runs on the one big one; 58 mm, doubtful scale, 1979.

B.W.

At least that's what the trademark looks like; the large upper lobe of the B slants over the W.
Ladder Truck, a big windup toy with whitewall tires, suction hose, control panels, an aerial ladder and two other ladders that can hook onto it or be used separately, like those of the California toys below; I was told that both they and this were made by Keystone. 250 mm, large scale, postwar.
Ladder Truck, much smaller, in red or green, with F.D. on the hood, an open cab, and four cast-in ladders, and with the BW monogram underneath, 89 mm, about S gauge, early postwar.
Ladder Truck, a hair smaller, without the monogram, and with a square hole in its rear deck, otherwise the same, 87 mm, about S gauge, postwar.

CALIFORNIA

They may have been made first by Keystone, and one has been attributed to Banner as well, but my later versions were made by California Moulders. They are realistic except for the steam boiler in one of them, and I've been fond of them since my boyhood.
Fire Engine, with closed cab, two interlocking ladders, suction hose, windshield and white wheel-axle units, 158 mm, large scale, Fifties.
Steam Pumper, the same basic truck without a windshield, with one yellow ladder. Two men standing at the rear, and a blue boiler and two hose reels in back, plus individual wheels on metal axles, 158 mm, large scale, Fifties or later.
Ladder Truck, the earlier red version with aerial ladder and others that interlock, plus windshield and wheels as before, and U.S.F.D. 999 lettering on the doors, 198 mm, large scale, Fifties.
Ladder Truck, a blue later version, with a red aerial ladder, apparently just one other ladder, yellow men, a bell on the roof, no windshield, and the later wheels, as on the steamer, 198 mm, large scale, Fifties or later.

COMMONWEALTH

Okay, it isn't a toy fire truck, just a toy that includes a fire truck.
Fire Chief Siren, a clear plastic whistle with a two-dimensional red fire truck on top of it, 111 mm, doubtful scale, date unknown.

EMPIRE

Empire Plastic made this set, which includes several small one-piece emergency vehicles.
Hometown U.S.A. Set, with numerous vehicles, including these single-casting items:
Aerial Ladder Truck, with open cab, 80 mm;
Steam Pumper, also with open cab, 48 mm;
Hose Truck, likewise with open cab, 53 mm;
Fire Engine, with modern closed cab, 50 mm;
Fire Chief's Car, 40 mm;
Rescue Truck? Maybe it is, maybe not, 48 mm.

F

36 VW Fire Department Van—I can't describe it until I solve the mystery of where I got the data from, 99 mm, 1/43 scale, Eighties.

F. & F.

These are cereal-box models of 1957 Fords.
Ford Custom Fire Chief, with siren on the roof and Fire Chief lettering, 81 mm, S gauge, 1957.
Ford Police Ambulance, a red Country Squire wagon with siren, lights, crosses and lettering, 81 mm, S gauge, 1957.

GILMARK

Gilmark toys include a series of odd-looking trucks with cabs that tilt whether you want them to or not. This is one of them.
Ladder Truck, with tilting cab, chassis including an engine block, rear body with ladder racks, hose reels and an axe, and two skinny ladders that interlock, 110 mm, O to S gauge, Fifties.

HASBRO

This truck much resembles Renwal #105 (see below), but its ladder is mounted at the rear and extends forward, unlike the Renwal's.
1 Fire Truck, with open cab, Fire Dept. hood lettering, and a clip amid the hose bed to hold the ten-rung ladder, 112 mm, O gauge or smaller, Fifties or later.

HESS

This toy was made by Louis Marx in Hong Kong for the well-known gasoline company.
Fire Engine, with stylized closed cab, roof light operated by a battery, and rear body including hose reels, couplings, suction hose and ladder (missing from mine), 279 mm, large scale, 1970. Good pictures that show all the equipment can be seen in C-R Vol. II, p. 40; see also Vol. II, p. 58, Lantern, for a very similar product.

IDEAL

The Ideal Toy Company made plastic toy vehicles in early postwar days, and later made the Motorific series of interlocking bodies and chassis.
1-1729 Ambulance, in white with opening rear doors, red crosses and City Hospital logo, 155 mm, large scale, early postwar.
1-1729 Army Ambulance, the same model in olive with white U.S. Army lettering and red crosses, 155 mm, large scale, early postwar.
#? Ford Fire Engine, quite a realistic Motorific model, with Metropolitan Fire Co. lettering, Ford emblems, and a lot of detail; its chassis snaps off so you can put a battery in; 160 mm, large scale, 1966.

KEYSTONE

Keystone made a fascinating fire set and several vehicles to go with it.
K-48 Chrysler Fire Chief, a sleek fastback with opening hood, water pump, and Chief decals; the number is that of its rear license plate and probably tells when it was made; 117 mm, O gauge, 1948.
#? Fire Engine, with long hood, open cab, and a pump and hose connections in the rear, for use with the set below, 125 mm, O gauge or smaller, Forties.
#? Ladder Truck, the same basic vehicle with a short aerial ladder mounted in place of the pump, 125 mm, O gauge or smaller, Forties.
1-165 Fire Department Set, including the two trucks, a big firehouse, and a burning building including a water tank; the water is pumped out, sprayed onto the building, and falls back into the tank. The chief's car may also have been included, and the whole set may have been made in 1948.

KILGORE

Kilgore made a series of cars reminiscent of late prewar Hupmobiles, including this one.
Fire Chief, a red sedan with Fire Chief lettering and a tendency to warp, 103 mm, O gauge, late Thirties.

American Plastic — American Kits and Specialty Models

LIDO

Lido made a series of small plastic toy vehicles with one-piece wheels-and-axle units.
10 Fire Engine, in green, with closed cab and open rear, the latter including a ladder, hose and a shovel, 95 mm, S gauge, Fifties.

MARX?

I am not sure these were made by Marx, but the workmanship suggests that they were.
Fire Engine, with typical closed cab, booster tank, hose reel and axe; I have red, blue and silver specimens; 96 mm, S gauge, Fifties.
Hose Truck, with open cab, hose in the rear, Fire Dept. and F D lettering; mine is yellow with blue wheels-and-axle units; 90 mm, S gauge, Fifties.
Hose Truck, the same truck but all in one piece including cast-in wheels, 91 mm, S gauge, Fifties or later.

NOSCO

This interesting toy includes a flywheel motor and twelve extra pieces listed on the box.
Fire Engine, with aerial ladder, sitting and standing men, and various equipment, plus 24 holes into which men and tools can be inserted, 200 mm, large scale, postwar.

PLASTICVILLE

Bachmann Brothers made Plasticville kits of railroad platform buildings, plus plastic vehicles to go with them.
Ambulance, a fairly realistic toy with siren and lights on the roof, 107 mm, O gauge, Fifties.
Ladder Truck, with open cab, aerial ladder and rotating spotlight, plus cast-in hose and axes, 158 mm, O gauge, Fifties.
Fire Engine, with the same body as above and a water cannon in place of the ladder mount, 158 mm, O gauge, Fifties (C-R Vol. II, p. 105; these toys definitely predate 1965).
FH-4 Fire House Kit, a white and red building with opening doors for two vehicles, one of which, the ladder truck, came with it—or at least with the one I bought—O gauge, Fifties.

PROCESSED PLASTIC

This firm has made a variety of toy cars and trucks over the years.
5800 Fire Engine, a stylized toy with high closed cab, roof bar, cast-in hose reels and two white ladders, 226 mm, large scale, Eighties.

PYRO

This must be among the oddest of Pyro's many toy vehicles.
Pyromatic Fire Control, a bulbous blue truck looking like a spacecraft, with ladder, other equipment and name cast in, 136 mm, doubtful scale, Fifties?

RENWAL

Renwal's plastic toys include several interesting fire trucks.
57 Fire Truck, with red body, yellow seat and hose reel, light green driver and ladder, 176 mm, large scale, Fifties.
105 Ladder Truck, similar to the Hasbro toy listed above, with open cab, driver, booster tank, hose bed, and a seven-rung ladder clipped on just behind the tank; I have red, blue and cream specimens; 120 mm, O gauge, Fifties.
145 Steam Pumper, just like the metal version, 82 mm, S gauge, Fifties.
146 Ladder Truck, again like the diecast one, 81 mm, S gauge, Fifties.
179 Ladder Truck, big and long, with closed cab, aerial ladder, and two yellow firemen at the rear, 235 mm, large scale, Fifties.

THOMAS

Thomas is either the same firm as Acme or a close relative, and has made similar toy cars.
1-140 Fire Tank Truck; it's been a tanker, a PA truck with loudspeaker on top, and heaven knows what; C-R Vol. II, p. 138, shows it as a fire vehicle with a ladder in the rack; 101 mm, about S gauge, Fifties.
1-183 Ford Fire Chief, a 1950 Custom Fordor with siren, spotlight, antenna and labels, 112 mm, O gauge, 1950 or later.

W.G.

These two W.G. Inc. toys run on a central flywheel connected to a big white gear that projects well above the vehicle.
Fire Engine, fairly realistic except for the flywheel, gear and blank circles representing wheels, 80 mm, S to HO gauge, postwar.
Fire Engine, more modernistic, with sloping nose and cast-in aerial ladder, 79 mm, S to HO gauge, postwar.

WANNATOY

Wannatoys include numerous cars and trucks in varying degrees of reality (or unreality).
7 Fire Truck, with blunt nose, open cab, hose bed and reels, and ladders cast in, plus an eight-rung raising ladder, 123 mm, O gauge, Fifties.
7 Fire Truck, the same model reissued in soft plastic, 123 mm, O gauge, Fifties or later.
#? Fire Truck, with a curious boatlike body, open cab, hose bed and reels, and the same eight-rung ladder as before, 117 mm, maybe O gauge, Fifties.
#? Fire Truck, the same Bohn prototype as the diecast Ralstoy #1, in red plastic with six wheels and a white raising ladder, 148 mm, O gauge or larger, Fifties.

WYANDOTTE

The one Wyandotte Toys product on our list is quite realistic.
Ladder Truck, with closed cab, aerial ladder, and wheels-and-axle units; I'm glad it survived my childhood, 153 mm, about O gauge, Fifties.

ZIMMERMAN

J. V. Zimmerman produced this Cap'n Crunch promotional.
Cap'n Crunch Fire Truck, high and narrow, with hose bed and reels, plus two ladders missing from mine, 152 mm, large scale, 1975.

UNKNOWN MAKERS

Daimler Army Ambulance, in olive plastic, with cast-in lettering and crosses, 115 mm, O gauge, probably early postwar.
Fire Engine, also in olive, perhaps related to the ambulance, with ladder, hose and booster tank, 131 mm, O gauge or larger, postwar. It bears some resemblance to the Lido truck.
Fire Engine, with prewar styling, open cab with driver, short ladder and spoked wheels, 120 mm, about O gauge, early postwar?
Fire Engine, similar to the last one in styling, with a blob of a driver dwarfed by a big booster tank, and a squiggle of hose farther aft, 80 mm, HO to S gauge, late Forties. The same firm made midget race cars at the same time.
Fire Engine, a fairly realistic closed-cab type in white plastic, with a short red ladder attached just behind the cab, 115 mm, O gauge or smaller, postwar.
Rescue Truck, bright green, with more detail on the roof than anywhere else; the siren atop the cab marks it as an emergency truck, though I have one with a label that calls it a bank; 149 mm, large scale, postwar.
American LaFrance Fire Engine, Hose Truck, Aerial Ladder Truck and Rescue Truck: see C-R Vol. I, page 45; no other data.

American Kits and Specialty Models

American kit models of emergency vehicles are for the most part in 1/87 scale, as made by such firms as Ivers, Jordan and Lee Town. Other scales are also to be found, such as the 1/43 to 1/64 scale pewter models produced by Nostalgic Miniatures.

A. H. M.

A.H.M. produces electric trains, plus buildings and accessories to go with them.
15808 Fire House, a brick building in "classic 4-story Victorian style", accompanied by two Canadian Herka fire truck kits, 1/87 scale, Eighties or before.
10150 Fire Fox I, an emergency train set with two plastic fire trucks, 1/87 scale, 1984.
10350 Fire Fox II, a larger train set with plastic ladder truck and pumper, 1/87 scale, 1984.

BACHMANN

This well-known firm produces a wide variety of model railroad accessories, including this kit.
2574 Fire House, a simple one-story building in red and white, plus lawn, trees etc., 1/87 scale, Eighties or before.

CAMPBELL

Campbell plastic kits bring the old days of Colorado back to life.
441 Breckinridge, Colorado, Fire House, a part of Colorado history, 1/87 scale, Eighties or before.

DE HANES

John DeHanes, well-known New Jersey hobbyist, offers these four models.
1. Mack LF Type 95 Fire Pumper, 1/55 scale, 1984.
2. Mack B Closed Cab Fire Pumper, 1/55 scale, 1984.
3. Seagrave Anniversary Fire Pumper, 1/55 scale, 1984.
4. American LaFrance 700 Fire Pumper, 1/55 scale, 1984.

IVERS

Ivers HO gauge metal kits include four fire trucks.
FA-001 Chevrolet 1956 Fire Pumper, 1/87 scale, 1983.
FA-003 Ford F-850 1968 Fire Pumper, 1/87 scale, 1983.
FA-004 American LaFrance Sparton Pumper, closed cab, 1/87 scale, 1984.
FA-005 American LaFrance Sparton Pumper, open cab, 1/87 scale, 1984.

JO-HAN

I have no data on what Jo-Han has made; they may have made other plastic kits besides this one.
#? Mack 1928 Mack Ladder Truck, with open Bulldog cab and semi-trailer full of ladders, aerial and others, about 180 mm, perhaps O gauge, 1976 (C-R Vol. II, p. 46).

JORDAN

Jordan makes three popular HO scale fire truck kits.
208 Ford 1913 Model T Fire Truck, 1/87 scale, postwar.
220 Mack 1923 Aerial Ladder Truck, 1/87 scale, postwar.
221 Ahrens-Fox 1927 Fire Engine, 1/87 scale, postwar.

K-LINE

Here we have another plastic HO gauge kit.
4091 Fire House with Truck and Figures, 1/87 scale, Eighties or before.

LEE TOWN

This New Jersey firm's HO gauge metal kits include a number of American fire trucks.
3035 Mack 1950 SB61 Fire Pumper, with closed cab and lots of equipment in back, 1/87 scale, Eighties.
3136 Mack 1950 SB61 "Bermuda" Open Cab Pumper, much like #3035 aft of the cab, 1/87 scale, Eighties.
3203 Mack CF Fire Pumper, 1/87 scale, Eighties.
7002 Mack CF Fire Pumper Body, 1/87 scale, 1984.
7007 Ford LN Fire Pumper, with blunt nose, closed cab, and all the usual equipment in back, 1/87 scale, Eighties.
7017 Mack CF New York Fire Pumper, 1/87 scale, 1984.
7025 Ford LS Fire Pumper, a close relative of #7007, 1/87 scale, Eighties.
7026 Pierce Fire Pumper Body, 1/87 scale, 1984.
7027 Ford Budd Cab Fire Pumper, 1/87 scale, 1984.
7028 Ford C Cab Fire Pumper, a modern truck with almost everything enclosed, 1/87 scale, 1984.
7029 Ford LN Fire Engine with Pierce Pumper, 1/87 scale, 1984.
7030 Ford LS Fire Engine with Pierce Pumper, 1/87 scale, 1984.
7031 Ford LNT-Pierce CRV-18 Rescue Truck, 1/87 scale, 1984.
7030 Diamond-Reo-Pierce CRV-18 Rescue Truck, 1/87 scale, 1984.
7033 Ford C-Pierce CRV-18 Rescue Truck, 1/87 scale, 1984.

LIFE-LIKE

This firm's products include an HO gauge plastic fire house kit.
1390 Fire Engine House, a stately two-story edifice with hose tower, siren and flagpole on the roof, 1/87 scale, Eighties or before.

LINDY

This is one of a series of small-scale plastic kits made by Lindberg in the Sixties.
10 Fire Engine, a white open-cab pumper with ladder, hose reel and suction hose, very well detailed for its small size, 89 mm, about HO gauge, Sixties.

McFADDEN

This plastic HO gauge kit takes us back to the days of horsedrawn fire trucks.
717 Old Time Fire House With Corral, 1/87 scale, Eighties or before.

MILLER

This model encompasses all I know of Sam Miller and his resin kits.
#? Studebaker Fire Engine, a cab presumably inspired by the old Dinky Toys tankers, with a well-detailed rear body, 115 mm, 1/43 or smaller scale, Seventies?

MODEL POWER

Model Power imports some Playart diecast models, and also offers HO gauge model railroad accessories.
409 Fire Department, a three-story brick fire house with an old-fashioned belfry, plus two Herka fire trucks, three plastic kits in all, 1/87 scale, Eighties or before.

MOUNTAIN STATES

This is one of a line of HO gauge plastic kits.
520 Ford 1935 Fire Chief's Car, 1/87 scale, Eighties or before.

NATIONAL MOTOR CO.

Another Ford, this time a 1/50 scale metal kit.
1906 Ford Model T 1914 Chemical Fire Truck, a little truck with a big load of chemical tanks, ladders and hose reel, 1/87 scale, Eighties.

NOSTALGIC MINIATURES

Robert S. Brennen's series of high-quality pewter miniatures includes several interesting fire vehicles. Catalog numbers vary to indicate color and logo types; those given here are the basic numbers.

#? Shand-Mason Horsedrawn Fire Engine, inspired by the beloved Matchbox Yesteryear model, all pewter including the firemen, 90 mm, 1/63 scale, Seventies.
203 Ford Model A 1930 Fire Chief, a red roadster with black chassis and raised top, plus Westborough Fire Chief emblems, 80 mm, 1/48 scale, 1976.
229 Ford 1932 Fire Chief, 1/48 scale, no other data, 1981.
237 Mack 1927 Fire Pumper, with gold rails, nozzles and water gun above its hose bed, 125 mm, 1/50 scale, 1980.
250 Ford AA 1930 Open Cab Fire Pumper, with a big hose reel in back, plus siren, bell and spotlight, 101 mm, 1/48 scale, 1981.
253 Ford AA 1930 Open Cab Chemical Fire Truck, with hose bed, two reels, suction hose, siren and bell, 129 mm, 1/43 scale, 1981.
255 Seagrave 1930 Hose Truck, 1/64 scale, no other data, 1983.
256 Ford AA 1931 Closed Cab Twin Hose Pumper, with one reel forward of the hose bed and a siren on the roof, 130 mm, 1/43 scale, 1982.
258 Ford AA 1930 Closed Cab Chemical Fire Truck, with the same hose reel as #250 and a siren on the cab roof, 102 mm, 1/48 scale, 1982.
269 Ahrens-Fox 1925 Fire Pumper, with a big pump in front and booster tanks, hose and ladders in back, 151 mm, 1/64 scale, 1983.
280 Mack B Series Open Cab Pumper, 1/48 scale, no other data, 1984.
283 Mack B Series Closed Cab Pumper, 1/48 scale, no other data, 1984.
#? International 1954 Hose Truck, 1/43 scale?, no other data, 1983? May not have been issued.

PRECISION MINIATURES

This fine series of 1/43 scale metal kits includes a Duesenberg modeled after a car really owned by a state fire marshal in the Thirties.
C17 Duesenberg 1933 Fire Marshal's Car, 1/43 scale, no other data, 1932.

TYCO

Tyco's model railroad accessories include this plastic HO gauge fire house kit.
3214 US1 Fire Alert Set, including the electric fire truck listed just below, and a fire station, 1/87 scale, Eighties.
3911 Fire Engine, with electric motor, available separately, 1/87 scale, no other data, Eighties.
7789 Fire House, a two-story brick building with belfry on top and garage on the side, plus the ever-popular Herka fire truck kit, 1/87 scale, Eighties or before.

WHEEL WORKS

This model is one of a series of 1/160 scale metal kits.
135 Fire Truck, very small, with not too much detail, but a nice little model when you get a close look at it—and the fastest kit I ever put together, 42 mm, 1/160 scale, Seventies?

Other American Toys

RUBBER

There are few American rubber fire toys. The small field is dominated by the interesting fire trucks made by Auburn, though other firms have also contributed to our list. Warning: Auburn lengths may vary.

ARCOR

Fire Truck, with open cab, ladders and equipment cast into the sides, 195 mm, large scale, no other data.

AUBURN

Ahrens-Fox Fire Engine, with front-mounted pump, driver in the open cab, water cannon and searchlight in back, 141 mm, larger than O gauge, prewar.
Ladder Truck, or at least a truck with two ladders plus hose reel and other equipment, with Auburn F. D. on its hood, 197 mm, large scale, early postwar?
Steam Pumper, with boiler, steam dome, hose reels and other equipment, open cab, and Auburn F. D. on its wide hood, 200 mm, large scale, early postwar?
Steam Pumper, more modern, with top-hatted boiler and small steam dome, hose reel, suction hose with its name cast into it, and a fireman's hat on the seat in the open cab, 186 mm, large scale, postwar.
Hose Truck, even more modern, with three hose reels and three banks of hose, suction hose and a short ladder on the sides, 190 mm, large scale, postwar.
Emergency Truck, in red or green, with a pump in front, crosses and Rescue sign, fire and rescue equipment, 133 mm, larger than O gauge, postwar.
Ambulance, with a fierce grille, two sirens, a roof rack of equipment, three faces at the windows and #577 on its rear plate, 115 mm, O gauge, postwar.
Fire Engine, with modern closed cab, two hose reels, suction hose, a ladder and other equipment, 111 mm, about O gauge, postwar.
Fire Set, a boxed set including several fire trucks, the ambulance, and, I believe, a police motorcycle, no other data, postwar.

SUN

32 Ambulance, a familiar toy from the days when my father drove the real thing, white or light orange, 93 mm, O gauge or smaller, early postwar.
32 Army Ambulance, the same model in olive, 93 mm, O gauge or smaller, early postwar.
59 Mickey Mouse Fire Truck, a high stubby vehicle with Mickey at the wheel, ladders and hose, and a duck at the rear, 164 mm, large scale, postwar.
77 Donald Duck Fire Truck, with Donald driving, otherwise the same, 164 mm, large scale, postwar.
#? Fire Truck, high and stubby, with cab-over front end, a five-rung aerial ladder aft, and what seems to be a tillerman's seat, 96 mm, doubtful scale, more recent than the others.

UNIQUE

Fire Engine, fairly unique, with a realistic closed cab, narrow thorax, and rear body sloping up to a couple of hose reels, 122 mm, O gauge or larger, postwar.

UNKNOWN MAKER

Ambulance, a 1935 Ford delivery van in white with red crosses, 109 mm, O gauge or larger, Thirties.

SHEET METAL

The big names in American sheet metal, if one sticks to fairly small-scale toys, are Buddy L and Tonka. Marx, Argo and Lupor also enter the picture.

ARGO

Hudson Ambulance, a 1948 sedan in white with red crosses, lettering and trim, plus a bell that rings, 107 mm, about O gauge, 1948 or later.
Hudson Fire Chief, the same car in red with Chief lettering and ringing bell, 107 mm, about O gauge, 1948 or later.

BUDDY L

462 Code Red Fire Engine, with red sheet metal body, yellow interior and rear, and two chromed plastic ladders, 132 mm, large scale, 1982.
511 Code Red Hook and Ladder Truck, its cab body metal, the rest plastic, with an aerial ladder and two short ones, 245 mm, large scale, 1979.
696 Code Red Set, with the two vehicles listed above and a building, 1982.
4927 Emergency Van, a boxy white delivery truck with Rescue labels and orange plastic chassis, 109 mm, large scale, Seventies.
#? Fire Truck, a high, stubby toy with plastic ladders, 79 mm, doubtful scale, postwar.

LUPOR

110 Fire Chief's Car, with siren and friction drive, 181 mm, large scale, no other data.

MARX

Ambulance, another white van, with red grille and lettering, 158 mm, large scale, prewar.
Fire Department Set, with a big fire house and three vehicles, all painted red: a car for the chief, a small bus, presumably for the firemen, and a stakeside truck stamped with the word Patrol, about O gauge, prewar.
Tricky Fire Chief, a windup car with one real wheel that keeps it from falling off the edge, about 110 mm, large scale, 1947 (C-R Vol. I, p. 71).

TONKA

I know very little about Tonka; C-R Vol. II includes a very informative chronology.
Ambulance, a light van in white with red lettering, 124 mm, large scale, postwar.
Fire Chief, the same van in red with white lettering and gold coat of arms, 124 mm, large scale, postwar.
Fire Engine, in red with dark cream plastic hose reels and ladder racks and white ladders, 145 mm, large scale, 1975.
Fire Jeep, with ladder on top, about 175 mm, large scale, Fifties (C-R Vol. II, p. 144).
Ladder Truck, with a short two-section aerial ladder, about 140 mm, O to S gauge, 1976 (C-R Vol. II, p. 145).
086 Fire Rescue Truck, from Tonka's metal-and-plastic Scramblers line, an orange and white pickup with a rear body including hose and ladder, #086 on its base, 101 mm, O gauge or smaller, 1981.
1100 Fire Rescue Truck, the same model in red except for gray equipment, red and silver labels, 101 mm, O gauge or smaller, 1982.
675 Aerial Ladder Truck, a big semi with an aerial ladder and two smaller plastic ones, 263 mm, large scale, Seventies or before.
6150 Fire Squad Van, a little closed Jeep with a ladder painted on the roof and a flywheel motor inside, 77 mm, about S gauge, 1984 or before.
1009 Fire Department Set, with special versions of 1100 and 675, a Paramedics van that I haven't seen individually, and a rescue helicopter, large scale, 1984 or shortly before.

WYANDOTTE

Ladder Truck, with simple red body, three green ladders on racks, and rubber tires bearing the maker's name, 184 mm, large scale, prewar.

PLASTER

When I was a child I had a set of rubber molds with which, as I recall, at least two four-inch fire trucks could be made. The two biggest models listed below may have come from such molds; the other items listed below are of smaller scale and still on the market today.

R.C.B.

American LaFrance 1950 Ladder Truck, the classic open-cab design, with a spotlight just in front of the aerial ladder, 134 mm, HO gauge, Eighties.
Buick 1948 Ambulance, with Buick grille and styling, siren and red crosses, this version painted white, 71 mm, HO gauge, Eighties.
Buick 1948 Fire Department Ambulance, the same model in red, ¿perhaps also in red and white, 71 mm, HO gauge, Eighties.
Chevrolet 1951 Fire Chief, in red with silver siren and trim, 53 mm, HO gauge, Eighties.
Ford 1949 Fire Chief, in the familiar Tudor style, 54 mm, HO gauge, Eighties.
Mack 1951 Fire Pumper, with long blunt nose, open cab, ladder, suction hose and hose bed, 82 mm, HO gauge, Eighties.
Packard 1948 Ambulance, longer than the Buick, in white with two sirens, 74 mm, HO gauge, Eighties.PL-12

UNKNOWN MAKERS

Buick Ambulance, sold unfinished and without wheels, 66 mm, about S gauge, Eighties or earlier. This and the next model resemble the R.C.B. products and may well be made by the same firm.
Mack Fire Truck, also unfinished, 84 mm, about S gauge, Eighties or earlier.
Fire Engine, crude but halfway realistic, with hose beds in the rear, 89 mm, about S gauge, postwar.
Ladder Truck, with a simple aerial ladder flanked by shorter ladders, 89 mm, about S gauge, postwar.

GLASS

These glass fire trucks, of which there may be more, were made as candy containers. Except for one green one, they are uncolored, though one has painted parts. I have no idea who made them; all are presumably early postwar.
Steam Pumper, the green one, with open cab, high boiler and hose reel, 126 mm. Steam Pumper, with towering boiler,tin base and "Avor 2ozs / USA" lettering cast in, 134 mm.
Steam Pumper, even taller, with a patent number on the right, and unlike the others, with separate wheels held in by the base, 132 mm.
Steam Pumper, with driver and wheels (integral with the body, as usual) painted red, and "Avor 3/4 oz" lettering, 111 mm.
Steam Pumper, with blunt nose and high boiler, about 110 mm (C-R Vol. II, p. 70).
Steam Pumper, with metal wheels and base, and a Gothic grille design, about 125 mm (C-R Vol. II, p. 115).
Steam Pumper, low and sleek, with no lettering, 128 mm.
Steam Pumper, likewise without lettering but not as low or sleek, 122 mm.
Fire Truck, with ladders mounted diagonally on the sides and "Fire Dept. 5« lettering on top, 127 mm.
Fire Truck, much like the last but smaller, about 90 mm (C-R Vol. I, p. 39).
Ladder Truck, with a ladder mounted straight on each side, and its driver, rear man and cast-in wheels painted, about 125 mm (C-R Vol. II, p. 147).

Tomica

Since 1970 this Japanese firm has produced many high-quality diecast models of emergency vehicles, including some uniquely Japanese fire trucks, in their Pocket Cars, Long and Dandy series, not to mention what may be the most realistic Mickey Mouse fire truck ever made. The Pocket Cars and Long Series models range from about 1/60 to 1/150 scales, the Dandy line from 1/43 down. The letter F in Pocket Cars and Dandy catalog numbers indicates that the model comes from the foreign series, i.e., it is of a non-Japanese vehicle. I have added the numbers after the hyphens to indicate sequence in the use of catalog numbers

POCKET CARS

3-2 Isuzu Squirt Snorkel Fire Truck, with white plastic snorkel and suction hose, closed cab and red interior, 69 mm, 1/110 scale, 1974.
8-3 Isuzu Blood Bank Van, white with green logo and red crosses, 73 mm, 1/122 scale, 1980.
21-4 Subaru 360 Fire Chief, a little red Japanese beetle of a car with dome light and labels, 60 mm, 1/50 scale, 1984.
22-2 Condor Chemical Fire Engine, ex-94-2, with gold trim and white plastic parts, later with black deck and no trim, 70 mm, 1/90 scale, 1980.
27-1 Toyota Crown Fire Chief, first of three types, "Toyota Crown" on the base, 70 mm, 1/65 scale, 1971.
27-2 Toyota Crown Fire Chief, using a newer casting, "New Crown" on the base, 70 mm, 1/65 scale, 1972.
27-3 Toyota Crown Fire Chief, a still newer type, 73 mm, 1/65 scale, 1976.
29-1 Hino Fire Engine, with three-section gray aerial ladder, short cab and single front axle, 73 mm, 1/110 scale, 1971.
29-2 Hino Fire Engine, with the same ladder in lighter gray, a longer cab and two front axles, 77 mm, 1/125 scale, 1976.
34-3 Honda Civic Country Emergency Car, white with red roof light and trim, 68 mm, 1/59 scale, 1983; included in the Emergency Gift Set.
36-2 Nissan Caravan Ambulance, a white minibus with red Doctor Car lettering, 70 mm, 1/67 scale, 1981.
40-1 Toyota Ambulance, a conventional type with red stripe or cross and varying Japanese or English lettering, 75 mm, 1/70 scale, 1972.
57-1 Toyota Hiace Ambulance, based on a commuter bus, with stripes, crosses and lettering types much like #40-1, 74 mm, 1/68 scale, 1973.
67-2 Toyota Army Red Cross Truck, in olive drab with red cross labels and red dome light, 65 mm, 1/81 scale, 1978.
68-1 Isuzu Fire Engine, a typical Japanese type with covered cab, two rows of seats, white interior and equipment, 74 mm, 1/81 scale, 1973.
78-1 Nissan Cedric Fire Chief, in varying shades of red, with large or small siren, sometimes with yellow labels, 71 mm, 1/65 scale, 1973.
94-1 Tokyu Chemical Fire Engine, a big airport crash tender with chrome nozzle and deck, 75 mm, 1/130 scale, 1975.
94-2 Condor Chemical Fire Engine, a pumper with white suction

hose and chrome or olive rear deck, 70 mm, 1/90 scale, 1977; renumbered 22 when the series was cut back to 80 models.
109 Hino Snorkel Fire Truck, announced in 1976 but never issued. 1/125 scale.
F10-1 Dodge Coronet Fire Chief, with dome light and Fire Chief labels, 75 mm, 1/74 scale, 1976.
F17-2 Citroen H Van, in white with SOS Allo and phone number labels, red interior and opening rear doors, 64 mm, 1/71 scale, 1980.
F17-2 Citroen H Van, in fire department ambulance trim, 64 mm, 1/71 scale, no other data, 1980.
F19-1 Cadillac Fleetwood Red Cross Car, a white sedan with red crosses, blue light and black Ambulance lettering, 76 mm, 1/77 scale, 1976.
F20-1 Volkswagen 1200 Fire Chief, a red Beetle with dome light and Japanese labels, 70 mm, 1/60 scale, 1984.
F22-1 Chevrolet Ambulance Van, in various ambulance, emergency or rescue logo types, 66 mm, 1/78 scale, 1978.
F33-1 Ladder Chief, in red or yellow, with a three-section aerial ladder, 77 mm, 1/143 scale, 1978.
F60-1 Cadillac Ambulance, a real ambulance this time, in red and white or orange and white, plus AAA Rescue and New York Police Department versions, 72 mm, 1/77 scale, 1979.
F65-1 Lamborghini Cheetah, in civilian or army versions with red cross labels, 72 mm, 1/62 scale, 1979.
Emergency Gift Set, with 29-2, 34-3, 36-2 and a police car, 1983. Several other Tomica gift sets include emergency vehicles, including:
Assorted Vehicles: 29-2 Ladder Truck, 57-1 Hiace Ambulance in army olive with red cross labels, plus tank truck, bulldozer, helicopter, police car and boat.

LONG SERIES

L10 American LaFrance Ladder Truck, either all red, yellow with white or white with yellow, a semi-trailer rig with three-section aerial ladder, 144 mm, 1/110 scale, 1980.

DANDY SERIES

D2 Hino Ladder Truck, a bigger version of 29-2, with three-section aerial ladder, suction hose and jacks, 220 mm, 1/43 scale, 1981.
D5 Nissan Condor Fire Engine, much like 94-2 but with more equipment and detail, including a foam nozzle, 112 mm, 1/58 scale, 1977.
D9 Toyota Crown Fire Chief, a sedan with siren, dome light and Japanese labels, 94 mm, 1/49 scale, 1972.
D12 Toyota RH18V Ambulance, a minibus like 57-1, its interior including two bunks for patients, 98 mm, 1/52 scale, 1973.
D12 Nissan Caravan Ambulance, a camper-type bus, higher than the first D12, with red roof bar and dome light, red stripes and gold lettering, 114 mm, 1/43 scale, 1983.
D20 Nissan Gloria Fire Chief, a red wagon with dome light, sirens and labels, 94 mm, 1/49 scale, 1974.
D25 Hino Ladder Truck, bigger than 29-2, smaller than D2, 115 mm, 1/82 scale, 1974.
D37 Hino Snorkel Fire Engine, the same truck as D25, with a snorkel, basket and nozzles, 130 mm, 1/82 scale, 1975.
D42 Mitsubishi Fire Department Jeep, with plastic top, opening doors and hood, red dome light and labels, 77 mm, 1/42 scale, 1975.
D42 Isuzu Lowdecker Ambulance, a minibus with red trim and lights and detailed ambulance interior, 96 mm, 1/58 scale, 1977.
D45 Isuzu TXD23F Fire Engine, a larger version of 68-1, 101 mm, 1/58 scale, 1976.
DF20 Volkswagen 1200 Fire Chief, in red with white fenders and roof, blue dome light and German labels, 98 mm, 1/43 scale, 1984.
DF23 Volkswagen Fire Department Van, red with white roof and Notruf 112 labels, 100 mm, 1/43 scale, 1983.
DF23 Volkswagen Technisches Hilfswerk Van, blue with white lettering, 100 mm, 1/43 scale, 1983.
DF#? Citroen Fire Van, with Sapeurs Pompiers logo, dome light and antenna, 101 mm, 1/48 scale, 1981. I have other versions of this casting but have never seen this one in a catalog (C-R Vol. II, p. 140).
Dandy Fire Fighting Set, with the first D12 ambulance, D25 Ladder Truck, D37 Snorkel, a helicopter, figures and accessories, middle or late Seventies.

PUTICA SERIES

PD-2 Mickey Mouse Fire Truck, a fairly realistic open-cab truck with Mickey filling the driver's seat, 67 mm, small scale, early Eighties.

Diapet

Japan's Yonezawa firm has made numerous diecast Diapet models of emergency vehicles. It is hard to say exactly how many, as the firm has used several numbering systems, and as a result many models have been issued under two or even three catalog numbers. But the models are well-made and interesting; all represent real Japanese vehicles. We'll list each model once and give its alternate catalog numbers.
151 Toyota Crown Emergency Car, a station wagon turned ambulance, with siren, dome light, red cross and trim, 117 mm, 1/40 scale, Sixties.
203 (0144, P25) Toyota Ambulance, Japan's most familiar conventional type, with four roof lights and a siren, 139 mm, 1/40 scale, Sixties.
238 Prince Skyline 2000GTR Fire Chief, a red sedan with dome light, from a firm later absorbed by Nissan, 112 mm, 1/40 scale, Sixties.
239 (0300) Prince Skyline 2000GTR Red Cross Car, the same sedan in white with red crosses and dome light, 112 mm, 1/40 scale, Sixties.
246 Nissan Laurel Ambulance, no data.
283 (0175) Nissan Cedric Ambulance, no data.
291 (0178) Isuzu Ladder Truck, with extending aerial ladder, hose reel, and an open bench behind the closed cab, 140 mm, smaller than O gauge, Sixties?
296 (0182) Toyota Crown Ambulance, a hatchback with the trimmings of an ambulance, 116 mm, 1/40 scale, Sixties?
319 (0193) Toyota Hiace Ambulance, a camper with dome lights, red trim and lettering labels, 114 mm, 1/40 scale, Sixties or Seventies.
328 (0195) Nissan Gloria Fire Chief, no data.
#? Mazda Cosmo Red Cross Car, a sport coupe with red cross, siren and dome light, 103 mm, 1/40 scale, Sixties.
0115 (D15) Isuzu Chemical Fire Truck, almost identical to #291 but with a rear deck full of equipment, 133 mm, smaller than O gauge, Sixties or Seventies.
0129 (D29) Nissan Skyline Red Cross Car, no data.
01366 (T49) Fuso Ladder Truck, 1/60 scale, no other data, Seventies.
01505 (T87) Hino Ladder Truck, with a capstan to rotate its three-section aerial ladder, 150 mm, 1/55 scale, Seventies.
01508 (P55) Toyota Hiace Ambulance, with dome lights, sirens, red crosses and Emergency Car lettering, 150 mm, 1/35 scale, Seventies.
01571 (T20) Isuzu Ladder Truck, a different cab but otherwise the same as #01505, 150 mm, 1/55 scale, Seventies or Eighties.
01633 (P4) Nissan Caravan Ambulance, a camper with front and rear roof structures and the usual details, 135 mm, 1/35 scale, Eighties.
0232 Isuzu Blood Bank Bus, with scenes of blood donors and a nurse in the windows, 224 mm, O gauge, Seventies.
0264 Toyota Hiace Fire Department Bus, the camper in red with sirens and lettering, 102 mm, 1/40 scale, Seventies.
0281 Ambulance, no data.
0283 Ladder Truck, no data.
0288 Hospital Bus, no data.
0335 (01335, P43) Toyota Hiace Ambulance, this time with three roof structures and two dome lights, 134 mm, 1/36 scale, Seventies or Eighties.
0412 (C14) Toyota Crown Custom Ambulance, a smaller version of #296, 81 mm, S gauge, Seventies.
0415 (C17) Toyota Corona Red Cross Car, S gauge, no other data, Seventies.
0418 (C22) Toyota Crown Fire Chief, S gauge, no other data, Seventies.
0464 Toyota Ambulance, a smaller version of #203, 80 mm, S gauge, Seventies.
P5 (01658) Toyota Tercel Carib Fire Vehicle, white and red wagon with radio antenna and dome light on its roof, plus labels including a lightning bolt, 110 mm, 1/40 scale, Eighties.
P69 (01617) Subaru Leone Fire Communications Car, a red and white hardtop with siren, dome light and #954 labels, 105 mm, 1/40 scale, 1983.
T54 Fuso Snorkel Fire Truck, with three axles, a snorkel and plenty of equipment, 202 mm, O gauge, Seventies or Eighties.

Other Japanese Models

Japan's other manufacturers of diecast and plastic miniature vehicles include modern-day firms such as Sakura, Shinsei, Bandai and the company known variously as Grip Zechin, Eidai and Madmax, as well as veteran companies such as Asahi, makers of A.T.C. Model Pet, Marusan, whose models were based on Dinky Toys, and Yone, which also made tinplate toys. In addition, the Peanuts cars made by Aviva, or perhaps by Tomica for Aviva, add a few items to our list.

A.T.C.

21 Toyopet Masterline Ambulance, a white wagon with dome light and siren, 110 mm, 1/43 scale, 1965.

Other Japanese Models — Japanese Sheet Metal Toys

AVIVA

1 Snoopy in Snorkel Fire Truck, a more or less Tomica-inspired truck in magenta or red, with Snoopy in its snorkel basket, 68 mm, roughly S gauge, Seventies.
20 Snoopy in Fire Engine, a simple open-cab truck with Snoopy driving, 67 mm, about S gauge, Seventies.
72044-3 Snoopy in Fire Engine, the same truck as #20 above, with a huge Snoopy towering over the cab he sits in, 67 mm, truck about S gauge, circa 1980.
700 Snoopy's Fire Truck, a big monolithic vehicle with yellow ladders, Snoopy driving and Woodstock at the rear, 120 mm, vaguely O gauge, 1975.

BANDAI

12 Chemical Fire Truck, a small model of a big airport crash tender, from Bandai's Airport Series, 75 mm, 1/130 scale, Seventies.
13 Nissan Ambulance, a minibus for airport emergency service, 61 mm, 1/99 scale, Seventies.

EIDAI (formerly Grip Zechin)

12 Hino Ladder Truck, with three-section aerial ladder and dual front axles, 92 mm, 1/100 scale, Seventies.
16 Hino Snorkel Fire Truck, the same vehicle with a snorkel of the cherry-picker type, 92 mm, 1/100 scale, Seventies.
43 Nissan Caravan Ambulance, another minibus in emergency trim, 92 mm, 1/52 scale, Seventies.

KADO

KT20 Volkswagen 1200 Fire Chief, 1/43 scale, no other data, Eighties.
KT31 Volkswagen Technisches Hilfswerk Van, 1/43 scale, no other data, Eighties.
KT36 Volkswagen Fire Department Van, 1/43 scale, no other data, Eighties.
KT44 Volkswagen 1200 Technisches Hilfswerk car, 1/43 scale, no other data, Eighties.

MADMAX

14 Nissan Caravan Ambulance, Eidai 43 reissued with wider red stripes and a red cross on the roof, 92 mm, 1/52 scale, Eighties.

MARUSAN

8503 Daimler Ambulance, based on Dinky Toys #253, 96 mm, 1/48 scale, Sixties or earlier.

SAKURA

2 Isuzu Fire Pumper, a closed-cab, open-door pickup truck with yellow interior and rear deck, chromed nozzle and searchlights, 96 mm, 1/43 scale, Eighties.
L-11 Suzuki Fire Department Jeep, with a big working dome light mounted on a column that goes through the cab, 98 mm, 1/43 scale, Eighties.
L-13 Suzuki Red Cross Jeep, the same vehicle in white, 98 mm, 1/43 scale, Eighties.
100 Nissan Cedric Red Cross Car, a white sedan with dome light and labels, 102 mm, 1/43 scale, Eighties.
106 (4074) Toyota Fire Department Land Cruiser, with a working dome light, 106 mm, 1/43 scale, Eighties.
501 Datsun Red Cross Car, 1/43 scale, no other data.
502 Datsun Fire Chief, 1/43 scale, no other data.
601 Toyota Corona Red Cross Car, a plastic-bodied white hardtop with working dome light and red crosses, 108 mm, 1/43 scale, Eighties.
603 Isuzu Fire Pumper, the same basic truck as #2, with a diecast water tank and a working dome light (which #2 lacks), 95 mm, 1/43 scale, Eighties.
610 Nissan Skyline Fire Chief, a red wagon with dome light and labels, 97 mm, 1/43 scale, Eighties.
611 Nissan Skyline Ambulance, the same wagon in white, 97 mm, 1/43 scale, Eighties.
1001 Hino Ladder Truck, 1/50 scale, no other data.
4071 Nissan Cedric Fire Chief, the same sedan as #100 with the usual dome light, 109 mm, 1/43 scale, Eighties.
4075 Toyota Land Cruiser Ambulance, 1/43 scale, no other data, Eighties.
4086 Nissan Caravan Fire Department Bus, a sleek minibus with, for once, a non-working dome light, 98 mm, 1/43 scale, 1982.
4087 Nissan Caravan Ambulance, the same bus in white with red stripes, 98 mm, 1/43 scale, 1982.

SHINSEI

4101 Aerial Ladder truck, with low closed cab, two rear axles and four-section aerial ladder, 122 mm, 1/70 scale, Seventies.
4104 Fuso Snorkel Fire Engine, with long closed cab, long snorkel arms and red basket with nozzle, 147 mm, 1/80 scale, Seventies.
4108 Fuso Chemical Fire Engine, a big enclosed truck with two nozzle turrets and a deck full of hose, 125 mm, 1/78 scale, Seventies.
4109 Fuso Snorkel Fire Engine, with short-armed centrally-mounted snorkel ending in a two-nozzle turret, on the same truck as #4108, 125 mm, 1/78 scale, Seventies.

TONKA

The Go-Bots, which convert from a vehicle into a friendly robot, are made for Tonka in Japan.
7200 Fire Engine, a squarish six-wheeler bearing an aerial ladder with a nozzle at the upper end, 64 mm, roughly HO gauge, 1983.
7201 Ambulance, shorter and wider than the fire engine, 59 mm, small scale, 1984.

YONE

2133 Fire Engine, a metallic red plastic ladder truck with a clockwork motor that propels the truck and raises or lowers the ladder, 130 mm, about S gauge, Seventies; later reissued in Hong Kong.

UNKNOWN MAKERS

Fire Truck, a crude little replica of an English ladder truck, 48 mm, very small scale, postwar.
Daimler Ambulance, another simple toy with British antecedents, 49 mm, very small scale, postwar.
Steam Pumper, with flywheel and suction hose on the left and a tow bar up front; see C-R Vol. II, p. 126, for the model complete with horses; 47 mm without them, very small scale, postwar.
Steam Pumper, patterned after American cast iron toys, with a whistle built into its boiler, 106 mm, O gauge or smaller, prewar?
Fire Engine, tall and narrow, with what seems to be a ladder surmounted by a bell on top, and a siren whistle at the rear, 109 mm, O gauge or smaller, prewar?

Japanese Sheet Metal Toys

Their name is legion! From my own collection, that of Nelson Adams, and the Coleman-Russell volumes, I have put together a list of fifty items measuring up to about 200 millimeters. There must be many more. I have no idea who made the majority of them, and even when a manufacturer is indicated, questions can still arise: Is Marline the same firm as Line Mar? Does Y equal Yone, which equals Yonezawa? T.N. ought to be Nomura Toy, San should be Marusan, but who are K, K.S., M.T.H. and the rest? I don't know.

A1

Fire Chief's Car, with slab sides, almost flat top, and a big fireman's helmeted head, about 170 mm, large scale, 1960 (C-R Vol. II, unnumbered page).

CRAGSTAN

Studebaker Fire Chief, with Maltese cross emblem, white lettering, and recognizable styling, 95 mm, about O gauge, Fifties.

K

110 Fire Chief's Car, with early postwar styling and gold F.D. lettering, 100 mm, about O gauge, postwar.
Porsche Fire Chief, at least it looks like a 911 coupe, with Maltese crosses, Chief lettering and license number FD-2221, 103 mm, too

Japanese Sheet Metal Toys

wide to be O gauge, postwar.
Volkswagen Fire Chief, a big Beetle with lion, tiger, elephant and giraffe inside, a roadrunner on the rear end, and STP emblems, 156 mm, large scale, postwar.
Fire Truck, a flat closed-cab type with unpainted ladder, flywheel motor, and K monogram in a diamond design, 108 mm, about S gauge, postwar.

HERO TOY

VW Fire Chief, with big dome light, separate tin chassis and windup motor, about 85 mm, roughly O gauge, postwar (C-R Vol. II, p. 121).

K.S.

Chevrolet Fire Chief, with flashing dome light, wheels that steer, and flywheel motor, about 130 mm, large scale, 1955 (C-R Vol. I, p. 62).

KANTO

Fire Truck, very squarish, with lithographed details and friction or windup motor, 74 mm, roughly S gauge, 1975.

M.T.H.

Ambulance, a hardtop with Fifties styling, finished in blue and white, with A 7530 license number, 132 mm, large scale, late Fifties?

MARLINE

Fire Chief's Car, an unusual twin-boom design with short hood, cab and trunk between the booms, about 150 mm, large scale, Fifties (C-R Vol. I, p. 70).

MODERN TOY

Steam Pumper, with a big funnel-topped boiler, ladder and hose, plus a helmeted driver, about 200 mm, large scale, Fifties (C-R Vol. I, p. 95).
Steam Pumper, smaller and even odder-looking, about 110 mm, maybe O gauge, Fifties (C-R Vol. I, p. 95).

S.N.

A4234 Ladder Truck, with open cab, aerial ladder and flywheel motor, about 185 mm, O gauge or larger, Fifties (C-R Vol. II, p. 128).

SAN

Ladder Truck, a curvaceous open truck with firemen painted on, a two-section aerial ladder, and a flywheel motor and siren combined, 143 mm, O gauge or larger, postwar.

T.N.

24670 Ladder Truck, a modern open-cab style with aerial ladder, driver, and a fireman on the left waving a red flag, 204 mm, large scale, postwar.
N.Y.C.F.D. Ladder Truck, with two-section aerial ladder, hose reel, bell and three standing men, one of whom rings the bell, about 190 mm, large scale, 1954 (C-R Vol. I, p. 127).
Ladder Truck, so much like the item above that I feel safe in assuming that it a T.N. product, with two-section aerial ladder, driver and three standing men, plus a spotlight on the hood, 180 mm, large scale, Fifties?
Ambulance, vaguely like a Cadillac, blue and white, with driver, nurse and license number 6544, 89 mm, about S gauge, postwar.
Fire Chief, the same car and license number, a red and white car with the chief and his driver, 89 mm, about S gauge, postwar.

Y

1190 Volkswagen Fire Chief, short and wide, with a huge windup key and license number 1190, 80 mm, S gauge or larger, recent postwar.
Fire Engine, a little rhombus-shaped van with a ladder lithographed on the roof, 79 mm, roughly S gauge, recent postwar.
Ladder Truck, with a big European-style grille, yellow aerial ladder and windup motor, 144 mm, large scale, early postwar.

YONE

2038 Ladder Truck, with two-section aerial ladder, windup motor and blockish styling, 93 mm, about S gauge, postwar.
2100 Ladder Truck, with two-section ladder hinged in the middle like a snorkel arm, 205 mm, large scale, postwar.

UNKNOWN MAKERS

Ambulance, a cream van with opening rear door, slanting nose, red crosses and lettering, 95 mm, about S gauge, postwar.
Ambulance, a sleek fastback coupe in white with red trim, lattering and crosses, license number 7237, 130 mm, large scale, recent postwar.
Ambulance Wagon, very flat, with A.M.721 license plate, white doors and roof with red crosses, the rest blue, 117 mm, about O gauge, postwar.
Ambulance Wagon, or Wagon Ambulance according to its roof lettering, big and white with blue interior, 143 mm, large scale, postwar.
Ambulance Van, a short high truck with yellow plastic body, tinplate rear cover and grille, 91 mm, roughly S gauge, Eighties.
Mercedes-Benz Ambulance, a green and white sedan (the right colors for a German police car!) with license number 2540, 125 mm, large scale, postwar.
Volkswagen Ambulance Van, with R.C.10 license plate, red crosses and a silhouette-and-headdress trade mark, 103 mm, O gauge, Eighties.
Volkswagen Rescue Van, white with blue and yellow trim, red and black lettering and number 7, plus black plastic chassis, 136 mm, large scale, Eighties.
Fire Emergency Van, with opening rear door, Company 184 logo and Maltese cross emblems with the letter G in the middle, 125 mm, O gauge or larger, postwar.
Volkswagen Fire Van, brother to the rescue van above, in red with number 3 and Chief lettering, 136 mm, large scale, Eighties.
Volkswagen Fire Van, slightly smaller, with a big dome light and number 12, about 120 mm, large scale, Fifties (C-R Vol. I, p. 40).
Volkswagen Fire Chief's Van, with F.D.8 license plate, Fire Dept. badges, and face-and-headdress trade mark, 103 mm, O gauge, Eighties.
Fire Engine, realistic if distorted, with open cab and spotlight up front, ladder and hose in back, 103 mm, about s gauge, 1955.
Fire Truck, with nobody in the cab but two standing men on each side, a ladder on top and a hose reel under it, about 160 mm, large scale, Fifties (C-R Vol. I, p. 7).
Fire Truck, a boxy windup type with an aerial ladder that does its stuff as the truck rolls, about 100 mm, O gauge or smaller, 1965 (C-R Vol. I, p. 15).
Fire Truck, another squarish design with a ladder on the roof, about 60 mm, roughly S gauge, Seventies (C-R Vol. I, p. 59).
Fire Department Truck, with plastic body and tin rear cover like its ambulance partner, red with yellow stripes, 91 mm, roughly S gauge, Eighties.
Ladder Semi, with American-style cab including the friction motor, and semi-trailer with a white ladder and S-2023 license plate, 143 mm, about S gauge, postwar.
Ladder Truck, with closed cab crowned by a big dome light, a tilting ladder in back, and a big bell seen from above, 211 mmm, large scale, postwar.
Ladder Truck, an odd-looking beast with three equally spaced axles, two-section aerial ladder and two plastic extinguishers, 200 mm plus its rear crank, large scale, postwar.
Ladder Truck, with high front and rear body, a low midsection with a sort of box in it, and the aerial ladder going over it all, not to mention working pistons! About 175 mm, O gauge or larger, 1958 (C-R Vol. II, p. 167).
Toyota Fire Jeep, a recognizable Land Cruiser with a short tilting ladder and Fire Engine lettering, 93 mm, O gauge, Fifties.
Fire Chief, a typical American car with modest tailfins, roof light, Fire Dept. No. 12 lettering on the trunk lid and 11-1410 license number, 133 mm, large scale, Fifties?
Fire Chief, an equally typical American sedan of pre-tailfin days, with Fire Chief lettering, about 90 mm, roughly O gauge, Fifties (C-R Vol. II, p. 126).
Fire Chief, fastback twin to the red and white ambulance, in red with white lettering, Maltese cross emblems and license number 7237, 130 mm, large scale, recent postwar.
Mercedes-Benz Fire Chief, the same sedan as the green and white ambulance, all in red with Maltese crosses and license number 1375,

125 mm, largescale, postwar.
Plymouth Fire Chief, with its name on the hood, plus other lettering and number 19, about 85 mm, roughly S gauge, Sixties (C-R Vol. I, p. 20).
Volkswagen Fire Chief, with a big dome light and Fire Chief lettering, similar to Y 1190 which lacks a dome light, about 80 mm, S gauge, 1978 (C-R Vol. I, p. 31).
Fire Chief, a very flat sedan with Firelance lettering on its trunk lid, about 70 mm, roughly S gauge, Fifties (C-R Vol. I, p. 31).
Fire Chief, a squared-off American sedan in red, with Chief lettering on the roof and a bell on the hood, 97 mm, S gauge or larger, postwar.
Fire Chief, a flat wagon, the same design as the AM 721 ambulance, with FD 025 license plate and number 47 on its left side, 117 mm, about O gauge, postwar.

Hong Kong Diecast

Hong Kong has produced an incredible number and variety of toy and model motor vehicles. About half of its products that qualify for our list are diecast, and I've been able to attach a manufacturer's or at least a distributor's name to each. Some of them were made by well-known firms such as Playart, Yatming and Zylmex, others by lesser-known companies, while still others are known only by the names of their importers. Most are recognizable scale models of real vehicles, and their quality has improved in recent years.

AMSI

Amsi was an American distributor of Wheeler and other brands, and seems to have died at an early age, so I am not sure if these models actually exist.
804-2 Fire Chief's Car, S gauge, announced in 1982.
804-3 Ambulance, S gauge, announced in 1982.
804-4 Fire Engine, S gauge, announced in 1982.

ARCO

Arco products include a series of army vehicles.
2318 Red Cross Rescue, an army truck with plastic rear cover, red crosses and flywheel motor, 107 mm, abour O gauge, 1981.

AZRAK-HAMWAY

This model, originally (and perhaps still) made by Imperial, was marketed as part of Azrak-Hamway's Sergeant Rock military series.
#? Military Ambulance, see Imperial 8340-D for data, 68 mm, S gauge, 1983.

D.T.C.

The D.T.C. Tins Toys series (no, they're not made of tin) includes two fire trucks, the second of which replaced the first and kept its number.
T220 Fire Truck, with diecast cab-over chassis-cab unit and plastic rear body including two hose reels on top, 79 mm, S gauge, Seventies.
T220 Fire Truck, with a larger long-nose American cab and a new plastic rear body with bigger hose reels and yellow ladders, 95 mm, S gauge, Eighties.

HASBRO

We meet Hasbro again as the importers of Hong Kong funnies-type toys.
7004 Ernie's Fire Truck, high and stubby, with a hose reel, two short ladders, and the grinning Sesame Street kid, 67 mm, no scale, 1982.
72223 Snoopy Fire Engine, a vaguely similar but lower truck with a yellow nozzle in the rear and Snoopy driving, 62 mm, no scale, 1983.

HOLLY

The baseplate says Holly, the bubblecard says Agglo, made in Hong Kong for Elmar.
8348 Gas Up Fire Truck, barely longer than it is wide, with a ladder of similar proportions, plus the gas pump that powers it, 57 mm, no scale, 1984.

IMPERIAL

Imperial has produced series of fire, police and military models which share several vehicles.
8183 CHiPs Rescue Ambulance, a white van with portholes, red crosses and California Highway Patrol emblems, 70 mm, S gauge, 1981.
8211 Fire Truck, also issued under the L.J.N. and Larami names, now simplified, with smaller running board and no extinguishers, 71 mm, S to HO gauge, b1981, also numbered 8283.
8212 Ambulance, a white version of the 8284 Fire Rescue Truck, with a red cross on its rear deck, 73 mm, S gauge, 1981.
8213 Fire Chief's Car, a red sedan with roof bar, number 3, emblems and lettering, 74 mm, S gauge, 1981; it probably has a number in the 8280 series too.
8224 Army Rescue Truck, a military version of 8212, in khaki, 73 mm, S gauge, 1981.
8280 Emergency Team Set, composed of the Fire and Rescue Trucks, Emergency and Chief's Cars, and a red helicopter that was issued separately as number 8210, S to HO gauge, 1981.
8281 or 8282 Fire Chief's Car, same as 8213; the other number is that of the 8210 helicopter.
8283 Fire Truck, same model as 8211.
8284 Fire Rescue Truck, same casting as the Ambulance above, in red with roof bar and FD emblems, 73 mm, S gauge, 1981.
8285 4WD Emergency Car, a red Chevy Blazer with FD emblems and a red cross in a white square on the roof, 67 mm, S gauge, 1981.
8340D Medic Ambulance, a military version of the Blazer, part of Imperial's Victory Force series, 67 mm, S gauge, 1982.

JARU

One incarnation of a familiar model appeared under this importer's name.
8222 Fire Truck, the same model issued under the Imperial, Larami and L.J.N. names, 73 mm, S to HO gauge, late Seventies.

KIDCO

Kidco is the American distributor of toys made by Universal of Hong Kong.
155-7 Ladder Truck, the semi-trailer unit, with a two-section aerial ladder, from the earlier Universal issue, pulled by a more modern cab, 150 mm, 1/100 scale, 1980.
166-2 Dodge Fire Chief, a yellow two-door with roof bar, lettering, and two huge crossed axes depicted on the hood, 75 mm, S gauge, 1981.
166-3 Chevy Blazer Emergency Car, in white with red crosses, stripes and roof light, and white Emergency lettering, 69 mm, S gauge, 1981.
166-4 Chevy Blazer Rescue Car, the same model in red with yellow dome light and trim, 69 mm, S gauge, 1981.
1610 Transcon Medi-Vac Ambulance, the Cannonball Run van-type in orange and white, with two roof bars and blue lettering, 98 mm, O gauge, 1981.
40770-1 MASH Supply Carrier, a low loader semi in Medical Corps colors, 180 mm, about 1/100 scale, 1981.
40770-2 MASH Jeep, its closed body in olive with red crosses, 68 mm, 1/60 scale, 1981.
40770-4 MASH Ambulance, a van with an air scoop on the hood, a rack on the roof and four exhaust pipes, 72 mm, 1/60 scale, 1981.
40770-5 MASH Supply Truck, a stepside pickup with rear stake sides and red cross labels, 68 mm, 1/60 scale, 1981.

L.J.N.

This firm's Road Stars series, some realistic, some not, were related to popular television shows.
2000 Emergency Fire Truck, the one we've already seen under Imperial and JaRu, with boxy closed cab, gray ladders on the roof and hose reels flanking them, 73 mm, S to HO gauge, 1975.
2000 Emergency Rescue Truck, the Imperial 8212 vehicle, with a compartmented rear body, 70 mm, S gauge, 1975.

LARAMI

Larami is an American importer of various Hong Kong products.
201-4 U.S. Army Ambulance, a Land Rover with red cross labels, 68 mm, S gauge, 1982 or before. Its bubblecard is numbered 5127-6; 201-4 is the number on its baseplate.
8222 Firefighter, our old friend again, but this time with fire extinguishers on the sides and a wide running board at the rear, 73 mm, S to HO gauge, Seventies. The bubblepack number is 9611-5; 8222 is

the number on its base.

LIDO

Lido is another importer of Hong Kong toys.
7901-2A Bedford Ambulance, a van with a huge porthole on each side, red crosses, trim and lettering, 69 mm, S gauge, Eighties.

MARX

Among many Marx products is a series of small-scale cars with fast wheels, dating from the days when everybody was competing with Mattel.
#? Fire Truck, a realistic little pumper with cast-in hose, ladder and spotlight, issued with or without a baseplate, the type without having ordinary plastic wheels, 62 mm, about HO gauge, late Sixties.

MAXWELL

Maxwell is apparently the distributor; I wonder who made the model.
#? Ladder Truck, a blue cab unit much like those used by Playart and a red aerial ladder semi with Tomica Long Series overtones and a seat for the tillerman, 132 mm, about 1/100 scale, circa 1980.

MINI ROLLER

The maker put no identifying mark on this model.
#? Fire Engine, a stubby truck similar to but bigger than the Holly, with white ladder, hose reel and suction hose, 62 mm, no scale, 1983.

PLAYART

This well-known firm first appeared in America with a series of small-scale cars called Woolworth Peelers. This line, sold under many names in many stores, has grown to well over a hundred models, and the firm has recently gone into larger scales.
7118 Mercury Fire Chief, the first casting with rather squarish rear wheel wells, painted a darkish red, 69 mm, S gauge, Sixties.
7118, second casting, a hair longer, with bigger wheels, rounded wells, lighter red paint and yellow lettering and trim, 71 mm, S gauge, Seventies.
7130 Fire Truck, with modernistic cab, blue glass, and a tilting white ladder, 66 mm, S to HO gauge, Sixties.
7167 Mercedes-Benz Ambulance, a high van with blue dome light and windows, red crosses and stripes, 65 mm, S to HO gauge, Seventies.
7168 Fire Tender, a typical British design with a two-section ladder and hose reels on the roof, 67 mm, about HO gauge, Seventies.
7183 Ladder Truck, a Japanese type with two front axles and three-section aerial ladder, 79 mm, about HO gauge, late Seventies.
7184 Snorkel Truck, the same vehicle with a yellow plastic snorkel sticking out over the cab, 79 mm, about HO gauge, late Seventies.
7209 Ford Custom Paramedic Van, in red with white lettering and cross discs and a blue and silver roof bar, 69 mm, S gauge or smaller, 1981.
7218 Chevrolet Caprice Fire Chief, a sleek red sedan with roof bar and white lettering, 78 mm, S gauge, 1981.
7333 Fire Truck, a small, simple toy more or less identical to one by Wheeler, 48 mm, HO or smaller, Seventies.
7508 Fire Fighters Set, with 7118, 7167, 7168, 7183, 7209, 7218, 7716 boat trailer and helicopter, S to HO gauge, 1984.
7602 Ambulance Set, 1/40 scale, no other data, Eighties.
7716 Fire Chief's Car and Boat Trailer, the second 7118 wagon pulling a diecast trailer with a plastic boat, 150 mm, S gauge, 1980.
7766 American LaFrance Fire Pumper, one of a small family, 89 mm, 1/87 scale, 1984.
7767 American LaFrance Ladder Truck, the same cab in front, with an aerial ladder aft, 119 mm, 1/87 scale, 1984.
7767-1 American LaFrance Ladder Truck with Basket, the same except for the basket on the ladder, 119 mm, 1/87 scale, 1984.
7767-2 American LaFrance Snorkel Truck, not yet on the market as of late 1984.
7902 Paramedic Emergency Ambulance, a bigger version of the Ford van, in red with white logo, 128 mm, large scale, 1983.
7902-1 Fire Rescue Van, presumably a variation with a different logo, 128 mm, large scale, 1983.
792 Fire Department Tanker, a big red semi, O gauge, no other data, 1984.
7956 Ambulance Van, which may well be the first version of the 128 mm Ford van, no other data, 1980.
7968 American LaFrance Ladder Truck, with a three-section aerial ladder aft of its closed cab, 197 mm, 1/48 scale, 1983.
7968 American LaFrance Ladder Truck, the open-cab version sold by M.T.I., 197 mm, 1/48 scale, 1983.
7968-1 American LaFrance Ladder Truck with Bucket, a variation on the theme, 197 mm, 1/48 scale, 1983.
7968-2 American LaFrance Snorkel Truck, yet another, 197 mm, 1/48 scale, 1983.
7969 American LaFrance Fire Pumper, with hose reels, suction hose, ladder and control panel, 149 mm, 1/48 scale, 1983.
7969 American LaFrance Fire Pumper, the M.T.I. open-cab version, 149 mm, 1/48 scale, 1983.
#? Firefighters Train Set, including some of the small fire vehicles, HO gauge, 1984.
#? Firefighters Yard Set, something similar, HO gauge, 1984.

S.M.

This Hong Kong firm recently made four very good models of fire trucks.
8113 ERF Fire Tender, the typical enclosed British truck with two-section wheeled ladder, 105 mm, 1/90 scale, 1982.
8114 Aerial Ladder Truck, a Japanese type with two front axles and three-section ladder, 100 mm, 1/96 scale, 1982.
8115 Fuso Chemical Fire Engine, an airport crash tender with foam nozzle, ladders and hose, 101 mm, 1/98 scale, 1982.
8116 Isuzu TXD 23F Fire Engine, with open cab sides, ladders, hose, and a fireman in the back, 92 mm, 1/62 scale, 1982.
8306 Ford Army Rescue Van, a stubby 4wd minibus in military colors, 54 mm, HO gauge, 1983.

UNIVERSAL

These models were made before Universal acquired Kidco as its American distributor, several years before it acquired Matchbox.
#? Aerial Ladder Truck, an 18-wheel semi with two-section aerial ladder, 159 mm, 1/100 scale, Seventies, now replaced by the Kidco type with a newer cab.
805 Chevrolet Nirvana Paramedic Van, in white with orange lettering and trim, amber windows and dome lights, 99 mm, about O gauge, 1977.
805 Dodge Rescue Truck, in orange with hose reel, extinguishers and conpartments, plus door emblems that are upside down on mine, 101 mm, about O gauge, 1977.
805 Merryweather Marquis Fire Tender, with an empty ladder rack, a spotlight and a hose reel on the roof, 93 mm, about S gauge, 1977. These three models and a police car all had the same catalog number.

WELLY

One of Hong Kong's many lines of three-inch diecast miniature vehicles.
2222-B Fire Truck, a red pickup with yellow plastic rear body including hose reel and short ladders, and with Apache labels on the doors, 68 mm, S gauge, Eighties.

WHEELER

Wheeler appeares to be related to Universal and uses a circled W as its trade mark; a circled U is used by Universal.
#? Fire Truck, just like Playart 7333, 48 mm, HO or smaller scale, Seventies.

WUL

Still another line of small-scale vehicles.
808 U.S. Army Ambulance, an olive van with red crosses and U.S. Army logo, 70 mm, 1/60 scale, 1983.

Y.D.C.

Y.D.C. imports a series of miniature vehicles that serve as pencil sharpeners.
8787 Hand Pumper, a four-wheel hand-drawn and -operated antique fire pump with moving handles, 65 mm, unknown scale, Eighties.
9627 Hodge Steamer, an 1840 self-propelled steam pumper, 70 mm, unknown scale, circa 1980, C-R Vol. II. p. 126, lists this model as

made in Taiwan; the one shown here was made in Hong Kong. Anything is possible in the Mysterious East.

YATMING

Yatming is one of Hong Kong's better-known manufacturers of miniature vehicles.
261 Ladder Truck and Lifeboat Trailer, with the 1356 truck pulling a trailer bearing a plastic lifeboat, 135 mm, about HO gauge, circa 1980.
1355 Snorkel Truck, with a two-section arm and basket; it's a fire truck or not depending on the color it's painted, 75 mm, about HO gauge, Seventies.
1356 Ladder truck, the same cab with a more detailed rear body and a three-section aerial ladder mounted on it, 69 mm, about HO gauge, Seventies.
1501 Ambulance, a white van with portholes, red crosses and Ambulance lettering, 69 mm, about S gauge, 1981.

ZYLMEX

Zylmex produces a long line of three-inch and larger diecast vehicles, usually known in America as Zee Toys.
312 Ladder Truck, a typical Oriental design with three-section aerial ladder and coiled suction hose, 73 mm, about HO gauge, Seventies.
313 Snorkel Truck, the same vehicle with snorkel arm and basket on a different base, 73 mm, about HO gauge, Seventies.
333 Toyota Ambulance, a long white minibus with red crosses, blue dome light and detailed interior, 72 mm, S to HO gauge, Seventies.
337 Fire Engine, typically American, with hose, ladders and foam nozzle, 73 mm, about HO gauge, Seventies.
346 Paramedic Van, a white van with raised roof, red trim, blue lights and windows, 63 mm, about S gauge, Seventies. There is also a version made for sale in Canada, with its logo including a Canadian flag.
433 MASH Army Red Cross truck, a heavy covered army truck with red crosses, 73 mm, about HO gauge, Seventies.
439 MASH Chevrolet Ambulance, a veteran Chevy panel van in army ambulance trim, 67 mm, S to HO gauge, Seventies.
21700 Dynamights Military Set, including the 433 truck, a medical corps helicopter, Jeep, trailer and tank, S to HO gauge, 1984.
21721 Highway Patrol Set, with the 346 van and four police vehicles, S to HO gauge, 1984.

Other Hong Kong Toys

In addition to diecast miniatures, Hong Kong manufacturers have also produced many toy vehicles in plastic and other materials. They range from scale models to crude toys, and though we know the names of most of their manufacturers or at least importers, some remain anonymous.

A

Fire Truck, a short, high rubber toy with ladder, hose reel, yellow wheels and black axles, 86 mm, doubtful scale, early Eighties.

ARCO

Fire Engine, short and high, with ladders, hose reel, and a big yellow bell, 134 mm, large scale, Eighties.
Ladder Truck, with tinplate cab and base, plastic chassis, rear body and aerial ladder, 92 mm, S gauge or larger, early Eighties.

AZRAK-HAMWAY

6263 Fire Chief, a big Ford sedan with blue windows, roof bar, siren and flywheel motor, 165 mm, large scale, 1975.
6427 Fire Truck, high and narrow, with two chromed hose reels and racks for two ladders, 99 mm, about S gauge, 1976. See also Madison.
7096 Cracker Jack Fire Engines, a set of three plastic trucks, HO gauge or larger, 1981:
Crash Tender, with V-shaped front end, foam nozzle above the cab, and labels showing ladders, 71 mm, about HO gauge;
Fire Engine, with squarish cab and white plastic ladder on top, 74 mm, HO or larger; and Ladder Truck, with closed cab, semi-trailer and two-section aerial ladder, 184 mm, HO or larger.

BACHMANN

7019 Fire Truck, an open-cab American type with ladder, hose, driver and windshield, made as a railroad accessory, 48 mm, small scale, Seventies or before.

BLUE BOX

77130 Emergency Call Set, with a red helicopter and two vehicles, HO or larger, postwar:
Ambulance, a white van with black chassis, red cross labels and opening rear doors, 82 mm.
Ladder Truck, with the same cab and chassis, and a two-section aerial ladder, complete with hydraulic cylinder, 84 mm.

CRAGSTAN

1145 Fire Pumper, a fairly well-detailed plastic truck with aerial ladder, another ladder, hose reels, suction hose and more, 106 mm, about S gauge, 1968.

DAY RAN

1154B Simon Snorkel Fire Engine, with a yellow cherry picker, 124 mm, about O gauge, Eighties.
1155B Fire Tender, the same truck with two-section aerial ladder, 124 mm, about O gauge, Eighties.
13103 Fire Engine, a big Merryweather with aerial ladder, two firemen, and a water tank from which you can pump water through a hose, 227 mm, large scale, postwar.

DIAMOND TOYMAKERS

301-3 Ambulance, a little plastic windup van with sloping nose and two blue dome lights, 57 mm, HO or larger scale, early Eighties.
301-3 Fire Truck, with the same base, number and windup motor, a high stubby body and six-rung ladder, plus Fire Chief lettering, 57 mm, HO or larger scale, early Eighties.

DURHAM

5777 Disneyland Fire Truck, a closed truck with Donald and Mickey in the cab, a snorkel or ladder on top, and suction hose on the side, about 195 mm, large scale, 1977 (C-R Vol. II, p. 18).
8212 Disneyland Fire Truck, with Model T Ford front end, open cab with Mickey Mouse at the wheel, two ladders, a hose reel and a steam boiler, plus off-center rear wheels, 117 mm, larger than O gauge, postwar.

E

The first of these is shown on page 47 of Coleman-Russell Volume I, the others on page 55; all are fairly realistic.
Fire Engine, based on Dinky 955, with enclosed body and ladders on the roof, about 100 mm, roughly S gauge, late Sixties.
Merryweather Ladder Truck, another typical British design, with aerial ladder, about 100 mm, roughly S gauge, late Sixties.
Bedford Fire Department Tanker, with a very squarish tank, about 85 mm, S gauge, late Sixties.
Bedford Fire Department Wrecker, with the same cab as the tanker, plus winch and boom in back, about 80 mm, S gauge, late Sixties.
Mack Ladder Truck, with closed cab unit and semi with Aerial ladder, about 160 mm, O to S gauge, late Sixties.

E.W.

7404 Fire Engine, a plastic windup version of the Japanese Yone model, with metallic red finish and white aerial ladder, 127 mm, S gauge, early Eighties.

F

Fire Engine, a typical British design, with black-daubed windows, silver trim and a raising ladder, 46 mm, HO or smaller scale, postwar.
Trojan Army Ambulance, a little brown van with red crosses and black windows, 48 mm, HO or smaller scale, postwar.

FLEETWOOD

203-76 Huggables Fire Department, a low wide truck with a big grille, two four-rung ladders and rounded depressions to hold the two Huggables, 99 mm, doubtful scale, 1983; marked "Jumbos No. 128" on the base.

FOUNDATION

7841 Ladder Truck, a semi with three-section aerial ladder, two short ladders and a tillerman's seat, 185 mm, O gauge or larger, early Eighties.

FREE WHEELING

Fire Engine, a simple but fairly realistic closed-cab American pumper with two hose reels and two interlocking ladders, 171 mm, large scale, early Eighties.

GORDY

Some of the toys sold by Henry Gordy & Co. were made by Lucky Toys and will be listed there as well; others bear only the Gordy Mite name, and the 600 set are not marked.
600 The Fire Fighters, a three-piece plastic set, O to S gauge, Seventies, including:
Fire Engine, a slab-sided pumper with ladders, foam nozzle, siren and such, 149 mm;
Ladder Truck, a semi-trailer with a curious aerial ladder whose top half is wider than its bottom, 208 mm; and
Fire Chief, a two-door American car with badge label on the roof, 95 mm.
833 Fire Engine, much like Matchbox 29, with hose bed and reels, ladder and suction hose, 75 mm, about HO gauge, Sixties.
834 Cadillac Ambulance, the same type as Matchbox 54, in cream with blue windows and dome light, 74 mm, S to HO gauge, Sixties.
836 Ford Galaxie Fire Chief, resembling Matchbox 59, with blue windows and dome light, 75 mm, S to HO gauge, Sixties.
918 Fire Engine, a bigger version of 833, with chromed ladder, hose and other parts, 118 mm, S gauge or larger, Sixties; same model as Lucky Toys 195.
919 Buick Riviera Fire Chief, with two sets of sirens on the roof, blue dome light and windows, 132 mm, large scale, Sixties; same model as Lucky Toys 178.

IDEAL

Fire Engine, a blunt-nosed truck with hose, ladders, other equipment and holes that suggest parts now lost, 92 mm, O to S gauge, 1974.

ILLCO

7532 Snorkel Fire Engine, with a big snorkel, hose reel, suction hose, roof light, bell and space for two batteries, 186 mm, large scale, early Eighties.

IMCO

3108 Fire Chief's Pickup, a simple red and white truck with Fire Chief labels, 114 mm, roughly O gauge, early Eighties.
3108 Fire Truck, I know it exists but I've never been able to get one, as it always sells out long before the pickup, no data, early Eighties.
3109 Rescue Ambulance, a stubby van with much roof detail, perhaps part of a series of rescue vehicles, 112 mm, roughly O gauge, early Eighties.

IMPERIAL

Fire Truck, in soft vinyl, portraying a typical American closed-cab pumper, 102 mm, about S gauge, 1976.

JAK PAK

0505 Ambulance, much like the Corgi Junior Healer Wheeler, in soft plastic, 99 mm, O gauge or smaller, late Seventies.
0505 Fire Chief, apparently a Barracuda fastback, the other half of the Emergency Fire Fleet, 97 mm, O gauge, late Seventies.

JIMSON

156 Ladder Truck, an American type with aerial ladder, hose reel and bell, about 140 mm, no other data, 1957 (C-R Vol. I, p. 57).
302 Porsche Fire Chief, a distorted 911 with blue dome light and windows and windup motor, 90 mm, roughly O gauge, Eighties.

KAI YIP

These three sheet metal toys are known as Steel Roder or Steel Trucks.
3329 Fire Snorkel, sold singly as a cherry picker but painted red and included in the 4406 set with labels that say "Snorkel" including the quotation marks, 125 mm, large scale, early Eighties.
3330 Fire Truck, with clear plastic cab, three-section aerial ladder and hose reels, 133 mm, large scale, early Eighties.
4406 Rescue Set, with the two trucks listed above and a rescue helicopter, early Eighties.

KIDCO

206 Fire Engine, with American truck cab, rear body with hose reel and equipment compartments, and big exhaust stacks, 92 mm, about S gauge, 1977 (on the base) or '78 (on the box).

KNICKERBOCKER

Mickey Mouse Fire Truck, with Mickey at the wheel, a hose reel and two-piece ladder, and a bell that rings as the toy moves, 165 mm, large scale, Eighties.

LARAMI

1131-0 Rescue Heroes, with a police car and three other vehicles, S to HO gauge, early Eighties:
Ambulance, a white wagon with red roof bar and red cross label, 71 mm, about S gauge;
Crash Tender, much like the Azrak-Hamway type, with foam nozzle and ladder labels, 67 mm, about HO gauge; and
Fire Engine, also like the Cracker Jack type, with a white ladder on top, 69 mm, HO or larger scale.
8109-0 Marines Mash Unit, including figures, a helicopter labeled Army, and a covered Medical Corps truck, its cover a Conestoga type with two bows, 72 mm, HO or larger scale, early Eighties.
9230-4 Army 75th Regiment Armored Convoy Set, with a Jeep, four vehicles that cause emergencies, and a Medical Corps truck with a rigid rear box and red cross labels, 76 mm, HO or larger scale, early Eighties.
#? Army Red Cross Truck, perhaps from another set, with fully faired-in front fenders and a rear box like that of #9230-4, 76 mm, HO or larger scale, early Eighties.

LITTLE PEOPLE

Fire Truck, in plastic with a driver and two five-rung ladders, about 100 mm, O to S gauge, Seventies (C-R Vol. II, p. 59).

LUCKY TOYS

114 Ladder Truck, a typical American design, with aerial ladder, about 165 mm, roughly O gauge, 1963 (C-R Vol. I, p. 65).
178 Buick Riviera Fire Chief, same model as Gordy 919, 132 mm, large scale, Sixties.
195 Fire Engine, same model as Gordy 918, 118 mm, S gauge or

larger, Sixties.
#? Land Rover Fire Tender, perhaps inspired by Matchbox 57, about 110 mm, O gauge, early Sixties (C-R Vol. I, p. 65).
7128 Emergency Fire Service Set, including figures, road signs, the front of a fire house, and two vehicles:
3121 Berliet Ladder Truck, much like Dinky 568, with white aerial ladder and yellow British coat of arms, 171 mm, O gauge, Eighties or earlier.
3190 VW Rabbit Fire Chief, with number 3167 labels, blue dome light and windows, 125 mm, large scale, Eighties or earlier.

MADISON

833 Fire Department Set, with Azrak 6427 and a fire house with a catapult, about S gauge, Eighties.

MAK'S

2009 Jaguar Fire Chief, the 2.4 litre saloon in red plastic, with roof sign and bells, 149 mm, large scale, Sixties.

NFIC

Daimler Ambulance, much like Dinky 253, no other data, postwar.

NASTA

Fire Engine, a very short truck with what may be hose in back, 68 mm, doubtful scale, 1976.

NUCOR

Fire Fighters Set, with a red helicopter and two vehicles that look like crude copies of Gordy 833 and 834:
Ambulance, with a travesty of its original Cadillac grille, 73 mm, HO to S gauge, postwar.
Fire Engine, with parts that are reluctant to fit together; I almost wrecked mine trying to fix it; 72 mm, about HO gauge, postwar.

O.K.

Ladder Truck, much like the first Dinky 956, about 165 mm, O gauge, Sixties (C-R Vol. I, p. 98).

OCEAN

20 Ambulance, a short high white van with big black wheels, blue windows, roof panel and light, and Ambulance labels, 72 mm, vaguely S gauge, early Eighties.
20 Fire Department Van, the same vehicle in red with Fire Dept. labels, 72 mm, vaguely S gauge, early Eighties.

REMCO

Fire Truck, a blockish thing with good detail on top but little elsewhere; it must have had ladders once; 113 mm, about O gauge, 1976.

STEVEN

Fire Truck, a crude little toy with hose reels and ladders, plus a horizontal steering wheel, 64 mm, vaguely HO gauge, postwar.

SYMBOL OF QUALITY

2146 Fire Engine, with plenty of equipment, International Airport labels and space for batteries to operate its light and siren, technologically similar to the Illco truck, 179 mm, large scale, early Eighties. The symbol of quality is an old-fashioned lamp, if that enlightens you.

T.P.

Fire Chief, a tinplate creation vaguely like an excessively short Ferrari bread van, with a big red light on top, 113 mm, doubtful scale, early Eighties.

UNITED FEATURES

179-0848 Snoopy Fire Truck, actually a pencil sharpener with several very small pencils inside, 82 mm, vaguely S gauge, Eighties.

WALLACE BERRIE

Fire Engine, an amusing toy but nothing like a scale model, 60 mm, no scale, 1976.

WIND UP

8201 Rescue Car, a late prewar coupe in white with red trim and crosses, 83 Rescue lettering and siren, 159 mm, large scale, Eighties.
8201 Fire Chief, the same car in red with Fire Dept. lettering, 159 mm, large scale, Eighties.

ZYLMEX

2026 Fire Engine, a realistic model with much detail, about 140 mm, no other data, Sixties (C-R Vol. I, p. 156).
Fire Engine, a smaller truck with ladders, hose reels, extinguishers and a rotating nozzle, 87 mm, about S gauge, Sixties.

UNKNOWN MAKERS

312 Fire Engine, with rounded nose, aerial ladder, water tank, working hose and four men; the base reminds me of Lucky Toys but has no name, 205 mm, large scale, postwar.
T102 Range Rover Ambulance, in white with two big spotlights on the roof and space for batteries underneath, 133 mm, large scale, early Eighties.
T102 Fire Department Range Rover, the same car in red with F.D. labels, 133 mm, large scale, early Eighties. There's also a police Range Rover in the T102 set.
7198 Ladder Truck, somewhat like Matchbox K15, with four-door European cab, two-section aerial ladder on a chromed base, but no maker's name, 149 mm, O gauge, Seventies or earlier.
Range Rover Ambulance, in white with red windows and dome lights, plus an opening tailgate so you can see its flywheel motor, 86 mm, about S gauge, early Eighties.
Fire Department Range Rover, the same car in red with Maltese cross emblem and stripes, 86 mm, about S gauge, early Eighties.
Emergency Vehicle, somewhat like Corgi's #700 Motorway Ambulance, in red with white base and Emergency lettering, 106 mm, O gauge, Seventies.
Ladder Truck, with a truck cab and not much else except a two-section aerial ladder, 85 mm, about S gauge, postwar.
Red Cross Jeep, in white with brown driver and red crosses, plus a rear cover that lifts off, 72 mm, S gauge or smaller, postwar.
Ambulance, a little white tinplate car with red lettering and black plastic base, 49 mm, about HO gauge, Eighties.
Wheaties Fire Set, #6 Fire Chief, 15 Engine with Ladder, 18 Engine, 23 Ladder Truck and 26 Hose Truck, small scale, circa 1954 (C-R Vol. II, p. 67, which refers one also to Vol. I, p. 45). See Empire in U.S. Plastic for something similar.

Other Asian Models

From Israel to Korea, various other Asian countries have contributed models to our list. Gamda Koor of Israel, first with its British-based Gamda models and later with the Sabra line originally made for Cragstan distribution, Kingstar of Korea with its series of small-scale models, and three firms from India, Maxwell, Milton Morgan and Nicky Toys, their products largely based on Dinky, Corgi and Matchbox cars, have made most of the models listed here.

CHINA AND TAIWAN
M.F.

718 Ladder Truck, Chinese tinplate, with three firemen and a two-section aerial ladder that raises with the ringing of a bell when you push the front bumper, 259 mm, large scale, postwar.
732 Ambulance, a red and white wagon made of sheet metal in China,

with a friction motor, 141 mm, large scale, postwar.
814, a boxed set of six sheet metal cars, including:
Ambulance, a white wagon with tailfins, 106 mm, about O gauge, postwar; and
Fire Chief's Car, an equally finny red and white hardtop using the same main body as the ambulance, 106 mm, about O gauge, postwar.

SCHAPER

Ladder Tower, a battery-operated plastic truck, quite realistic, part of the Stompers series, 175 mm, O gauge or larger, 1984.

TALBOT

808 The Pink Panther Fire Engine, half hot rod, half stagecoach, with a fire-helmeted Pink Panther at the wheel, made in China, 66 mm, no scale, 1982.

UNKNOWN MAKERS

Fire Engine, a tiny diecast hose truck made in Taiwan, 47 mm, about HO scale, Eighties or before. Ambulance, a blockish rubber toy from Taiwan, 80 mm, doubtful scale, Eighties.
Fire Engine, another rubber toy from whoever made the ambulance, 92 mm, doubtful scale, Eighties.

INDIA
MATTEL

1007 GMC Snorkel Fire Engine, a crude diecast toy, apparently Matchbox-inspired, with a snorkel that works or comes apart, 75 mm, 1/64 scale, 1983, cast by Maxwell for Mattel.

MAXWELL

514 Lincoln Continental Fire Chief, based on old Matchbox 31, with dome light and silly decals, 72 mm, S gauge, Seventies.
515 Lincoln Continental Red Cross Car, the same car in white with red crosses, 72 mm, S gauge, Seventies.
520 Ambassador Fire Chief, a decent model of a car made in India—not a Nash, more like a Morris—with green roof light and Fire Service decals, 91 mm, O gauge, Seventies.
531 Fire Department Jeep, with a small aerial ladder in the back, 61 mm, 1/60 scale, Seventies.
533 Tate Red Cross/Unicef Bus, a model of an Indian vehicle, very squarish, with a blue dome light, 92 mm, O gauge or smaller, Seventies.
551 Red Cross Jeep, probably the 531 casting in white, 1/60 scale, no other data, Seventies.
560 Chevrolet Impala Fire Chief, Corgi-inspired but crude, in red and white with roof sign and decals, 104 mm, 1/43 scale, Seventies.
570 Commer Army Ambulance, perhaps Corgi-based, no other data, Eighties.
580 Commer Ambulance, probably the 570 casting in white, no other data, Eighties.
585 Fire Department Jeep, no data, Eighties.
606 Fire Service Jeep, with a crude aerial ladder that can be made to extend but not to rotate, 83 mm, O gauge, Eighties.
608 Fire Chief's Jeep, the same model minus the ladder, 83 mm, O gauge, Eighties.

MILTON MORGAN

307 Plymouth Sports Suburban Ambulance, Corgi-based, with red crosses, 107 mm, 1/43 scale, Seventies.
309 Chevrolet Impala Fire Chief, based on the first Corgi Impala (the Maxwell descended from the later type), 104 mm, 1/43 scale, Seventies.
320 Commer Ambulance, based on the familiar Corgi van, 90 mm, 1/43 or smaller scale, Seventies.
321 Commer Army Ambulance, the same casting in a very glossy olive, 90 mm, 1/43 or smaller scale, Seventies.
344 Mercedes-Benz Fire Engine, a diecast truck cab with a plastic aerial ladder at the rear, perhaps Matchbox-based, 80 mm, S to HO gauge, Seventies.
348 Ambulance, based on the Matchbox Stretcha-Fetcha, 70 mm, about S gauge, Seventies.
807 Plymouth Sports Suburban Fire Chief, Corgi-based, called Milton on the base and Maxwell on the box, 106 mm, 1/43 scale, 1983. There may be another version, numbered 804.
832 Commer Fire Truck, another Maxwell/Milton blend, the Corgi-based pickup with the ladder from #606, 92 mm, 1/43 or smaller scale, 1983.

NEW TOYS

Fire Engine, tinplate and plastic, "friction powered with sparking", 106 mm, O gauge or smaller, postwar.

NICKY TOYS

295 Standard Ambulance, a reincarnated Dinky Atlas in white, 86 mm, O gauge or smaller, Seventies.
626 Ford Army Ambulance, another ex-Dinky, 111 mm, O gauge, Seventies.

RAJ

Fire Engine, tinplate with a green plastic ladder, a picture of a better-looking fire truck on the roof and action pictures on the sides, 178 mm, large scale, postwar.

ISRAEL
GAMDA

Gamda Koor made its first diecast models from dies bought from British firms.
2 Army Ambulance, a diecast truck, with sheet metal top and Star of David decals, 102 mm, O to S gauge, Sixties.
11 Ambulance, a diecast station wagon in white with red logo, 98 mm, about O gauge, Sixties.

SABRA

Gamda's later products were made first for distribution by Cragstan and known as Detroit Seniors, then sold by Gamda itself, often with unchanged baseplate lettering, under the Sabra name. The catalog numbers did not change, but you may find the models with either name on the baseplate or the plastic garage box.
8101 Chevelle Ambulance, a white wagon with roof light and red crosses, 108 mm, 1/43 scale, circa 1970.
8101-1 Chevelle Israeli Ambulance, the same model with red Star of David and lettering in two languages, 108 mm, 1/43 scale, Seventies.
8101-2 Chevelle Israeli Army Ambulance, the same again in khaki with Star of David rondels, 108 mm, 1/43 scale, Seventies.
8102 Chevelle Fire Chief, same casting again in red with Fire Chief decals, 108 mm, 1/43 scale, circa 1970.
8102-1 Chevelle Israeli Fire Chief, with Israeli decals, two different types, unless one is something else that happens to be on a red wagon, 108 mm, 1/43 scale, Seventies.
8103-1 Chevrolet Impala Fire Chief, presumably with red paint and fire decals, though I've never seen it, 118 mm, 1/43 scale, Seventies.

KOREA
CLOVER

4413A Mazda RX7 Red Cross Car, called an Ambulance on its white nose, with crosses, dome light and pullback motor, also available in Green Cross form, 113 mm, 1/37 scale, 1983.
4417A Kiamaster Bongo Ambulance, van-type, with green crosses, dome light and pullback motor, 118 mm, 1/39 scale, 1983.
94 Kenworth Snorkel, not necessarily a fire truck, with its seemingly massive cab dwarfed by the plastic snorkel, 118 mm, about S gauge, 1983.

KINGSTAR

205a Mercedes-Benz 450SLC Red Cross Car, in white with red crosses and blue dome light, 78 mm, 1/60 scale, early Eighties.
205c Mercedes-Benz 450SLC Fire Chief, the same car in red with white lettering, 78 mm, 1/60 scale, early Eighties.
206 Ford Econoline Fire Chief, a red van with blue dome light and the same labels as 205C, 78 mm, 1/60 scale, early Eighties.
206 Ford Econoline Ambulance, the same van in white with red

crosses, 78 mm, 1/60 scale, early Eighties.
273 Mitsubishi Ladder Truck, a nice little model with three-section aerial ladder and hose reels, 80 mm, 1/125 scale, early Eighties.

M.T.U. TOY

Volkswagen Fire Chief, a red tinplate car with windup motor, about 120 mm, large scale, 1979 (C-R Vol. I, p. 96).

S.U.

F117 Fire Truck, a low wide sheet metal truck with yellow plastic ladder and wide tires, 113 mm, vaguely O gauge, Eighties.

SINGAPORE
BUDDY L

4660 Emergency Van, an odd-looking car that changes into an odd-looking first aid station, 91 mm, O to S gauge, 1983.
4660 Fire Truck, that changes into a fire house, 92 mm, about S gauge, 1983.

MANDARIN

502 Volkswagen Ambulance, a white VW bus with red crosses and Rescue Ambulance lettering, 77 mm, S gauge, circa 1980.
502 Volkswagen Fire Chief, the same van in yellow with Fire Chief 79 labels, 77 mm, S gauge, circa 1980.
901 Fire Truck, a reissue of the futuristic Playart #7130, 65 mm, doubtful scale, circa 1980.

THAILAND
ILLCO

82/8 Mickey Mouse Fire Truck, a high stubby friction-powered plastic toy truck with Mickey leaning out the window, 83 mm, no scale, 1982.

TURKEY
TURK MAII

6925 Fire Department Jeep, 93 mm, about O gauge, recent postwar.

BIBLIOGRAPHY

Adshead, Chris, "Londontoy", *Modeller's World,* Vol. 7, no. 2 (January 1978), pp. 6-7.
Azema, Bertrand, *Solido,* Paris, E.P.A., 1983.
Boyd-Camps, Mike, "Spot-On Spectacular", *Modeller's World,* Vol. 2, No. 2 (Jan. 1973), pp. 2-4, and Vol. 3, No. 2 Jan. 1974, pp. 2-3.
Bridges, Graham, "Bedfords", *Modeller's World,* Vol. 10, No. 4 (July 1981), pp. 5-7.
_____, "Dinky Transits", *Modeller's World,* Vol. 10, No. 2 (Jan. 1981), pp. 18-19.
Bull, Colin, and Graham Bridges, "Budgie Models", *Modeller's World,* Vol. 11, No. 2 (Jan. 1982), pp. 2-5.
Chick, Clive, "Tekno Tinplate Fire", *Model Auto Review,* No. 12 (Winter 1984), p. 492.
Clausager, Anders Ditlev, "Schuco", *Modeller's World,* Vol. 7, No. 2 (Jan. 1978), pp. 12-14.
Coleman, Ronny J., and Raymond M. Russell, *Fire Truck Toys For Men And Boys,* Volume I, cover title *Catalogue Of Toy Fire Apparatus,* San Clemente (CA), Phenix Technology, no date (circa 1980).
_____, *Fire Truck Toys For Men And Boys,* Volume II, San Clemente (CA), Phenix Technology, no date (1984).
Danielsen, Bent, "Tekno Fire and Rescue Vehicles", *Modeller's World,* Vol. 10, No. 2 (Jan. 1981), pp. 2-5.
Filsell, David, "Reminiscences and Oddities", *Modeller's World,* Vol. 7, No. 2 (Jan. 1978), pp. 14-15.
Force, Dr. Edward, *Corgi Toys,* Exton (PA), Schiffer Publishing Ltd., 1984.
Gibson, Dr. Cecil, *Commercial Vehicles,* London, Thomas Nelson & Sons, 1970.
_____, *History of British Dinky Toys 1934-1964,* Hemel Hempstead, Model Aeronautical Press Ltd., 1966.
Greilsamer, Jacques, and Bertrand Azema, *Catalogue Mondial Des Modeles Reduits Automobiles,* Lausanne, Edita S.A., 1967.
Hardy, Beverly and Stephen, "T.H.W.", *Model Auto Review,* No. 10 (Autumn 1984), p. 418.
Hertz, Louis H., *The Complete Book Of Building And Collecting Model Automobiles,* New York, Crown Publishers, 1970.
Horton, Ralph, "Fire", in most issues of *Model Auto Review.*
_____, and Sue Courtney, "Escape From It All", *Modeller's World,* Vol. 2, No. 1 (Oct. 1972), pp. 8-10, plus followup letter, Vol. 2, No. 3 (April 1973), p. 21.
Johansen, Dorte, and Hans Hedegard, ed., *Tekno,* Copenhagen, Forlaget Togborsen, 1984.
Jones, Dave, "Odds and Ends", *Modeller's World,* Vol. 11, No. 1 (Oct. 1981), pp. 14-15.
_____, "Taylor and Barrett", *Modeller's World,* Vol. 6, No. 3 (April 1977), pp. 2-3; Vol. 6, No. 4 (July 1977), pp. 10-12; and Vol. 7, No. 1 (Oct. 1977), pp. 2-4.
King, James P., "Schuco Piccolo", *Modeller's World,* Vol. 10, No. 2 (Jan. 1981), pp. 20-21; and Vol. 10, No. 3 (April 1981), p. 5.
Lee, C. B. C., "Small Automotive Cast Iron", Part IV, *Modeller's World,* Vol. 5, No. 4 (July 1976), pp. 22-23.
Mattingly, Larry, "Model Firehouse", in many issues of *Scale Auto Enthusiast.*

Monsted, Frits, "Danish Issues", *Modeller's World,* Vol. 10, No. 3 (April 1981), pp. 11-13.
———, Letter, *Modeller's World,* Vol. 2, No. 2 (Jan. 1973), pp. 26-27.
———, "The Lego 1/43 Series", *Modeller's World,* Vol. 3, No. 3 (April 1974), pp. 12-14.
Morgan, David, "Benbros Mighty Midgets", *Modeller's World,* Vol. 6, No. 2 (Jan. 1977), p. 12.
———, "Export Dinkies", *Modeller's World,* Vol. 6, No. 4 (July 1977), p. 13.
Newson, Robert, "Benbros", *Modeller's World,* Vol. 12, No. 3 (April 1983), pp. 18-20; and Vol. 13, No. 3 (April 1984), pp. 8-13.
O'Brien, Richard, *Collecting Toys,* 4th Edition, Florence (AL), Books Americana, 1985.
Provaznik, Jiri, and Ladislav Trhlik, *Katalog Sovetskych, Modelu A Figurek,* Prague, Klub Sberatelu, 1982.
Ramsay, John, *British Diecast Model Toys,* Felixstowe, Swapmeet Toys & Models Ltd., 1984.
Richardson, Mike, "C.I.J.", *Modeller's World,* Vol. 3, No. 2 (Jan. 1974), pp. 22-23; Vol. 3, No. 4 (July 1974), pp. 20-21; Vol. 4, No. 4 (July 1975), pp. 14-15; Vol. 5, No. 1 (Oct. 1975), pp. 10-11; and Vol. 6, No. 1 (Oct. 1976), pp. 2-5.
———, and Sue, *Dinky Toys & Modelled Miniatures,* London, New Cavendish Books Ltd., 1981.
Richardson, Sue, "Chad Valley", *Modeller's World,* Vol. 6, No. 1 (Oct. 1976), pp. 6-9.
———, "The Mysteries of Minic", Part 3, *Modeller's World,* Vol. 1, No. 4 (July 1972), pp. 6-10; and Part 7, Vol. 2, No. 4 (July 1973), pp. 6-9.
Roulet, Jean-Michel, "A.R.", *Modeller's World,* Vol. 8, No. 1 (Oct. 1978), pp. 2-6.
———, "Quiralu", *Modeller's World,* Vol. 6, No. 1 (Oct. 1976), pp. 11-14.
———, "Solido", *Modeller's World,* Vol. 5, No. 3 (April 1976), pp. 2-5.
Schiffer, Nancy, *Matchbox Toys,* Exton (PA), Schiffer Publishing Ltd., 1983.
Stewart, Carville, "Micro Models", *Modeller's World,* Vol. 4, No. 4 (July 1975), pp. 18-20.
Thompson, Graham, *Spot-on Diecast Models By Tri-ang,* Sparkford, Haynes Publishing Group, 1983.
Turner, Alan, "Six of the Best", *Modeller's World,* Vol. 3, No. 3 (April 1974), pp. 20-21.
Van Den Abeele, Alain, "Schuco", *Modeller's World,* Vol. 7, No. 4 (July 1978), pp. 8-9; and Vol. 8, No. 1 (Oct. 1978), pp. 10-12.
Viemeister, Peter, *Micro Cars,* Bedford (VA), Hamilton's, 1982.
Wicklander, Kaj, "Lemeco", *Modeller's World,* Vol. 3, No. 4 (July 1974), pp. 9-10.
Wieland, James, and Dr. Edward Force, *Detroit In Miniature,* Litchfield (CT), Miniature Auto Sales, 1983.
———, *TootsieToys,* Osceola (WI), Motorbooks International, 1980.
Williams, Guy R., *The World Of Model Cars,* London, Andre Deutsch, 1976.
Wootton, Ken, "Dinky Toys 30 Series", *Modeller's World,* Vol. 7, No. 3 (April 1978), pp. 2-3.
anonymous, "Brimtoy", *Modeller's World,* Vol. 5, No. 4 (July 1976), pp. 18-19.
anonymous, "Micro", *Modeller's World,* Vol. 11, No. 1 (Oct. 1981), pp. 6-8.
Plus many photos, announcements, etc., in such periodicals as *Model Auto Review, Modeller's World, Scale Auto Enthusiast,* etc., in many manufacturers' and dealers' catalogues, and the knowledge and data of numerous hobbyists.

PRICE GUIDE

DINKY TOYS

24a Ambulance .... 60—90
25d Citroen 2cv Fire Engine .... 40—60
25h Streamlined Fire Engine .... 50—75
25k Streamlined Fire Engine .... 75—100
25y Fire Department Jeep (conversion) .... ?
30f Ambulance .... 50—75
30f Ambulance .... 40—60
30h Daimler Ambulance .... 35—55
30hm Daimler Military Ambulance ..... 40—60
32d Delahaye Ladder Truck .... 50—75
32e Berliet Fire Engine .... 45—65
80f Renault Military Ambulance .... 35—55
555 Fire Engine .... 45—65

New Catalog Numbers

002 Blazing Inferno ....3—6
008 Firemen .... 10—20
195 Range Rover Fire Chief .... 10—15
250 Streamlined Fire Engine .... 30—45
253 Daimler Ambulance .... 30—45
257 Nash Rambler Fire Chief .... 25—35
259 Fire Engine .... 30—45
263 Superior Criterion Ambulance ...... 35—55
263 Airport Fire Tender .... 25—35
266 E.R.F. Fire Tender .... 25—35
266 E.R.F. Fire Tender (Danish version) .. 40—50
267 Superior Cadillac Ambulance ...... 30—40
267 Paramedic Truck .... 20—30
268 Range Rover Ambulance .... 10—15
271 Ford Transit Fire Engine .... 15—25
271 Ford Transit Fire Engine (Danish) ... 35—45
274 Ford Transit Ambulance .... 15—25
276 Airport Fire Tender .... 30—45
276 Ford Transit Ambulance .... 15—25
277 Superior Criterion Ambulance ...... 30—40
278 Vauxhall Victor Ambulance .... 15—25
282 Land Rover Fire Appliance .... 15—25
282 LandRoverFireAppliance(Danish).... 35—45
285 Merryweather Marquis Fire Tender ... 25—35
285 Merryweather Marquis (Danish) ..... 40—50
286 Ford Transit Fire Appliance .... 20—30
286 Ford Fire Appliance (Danish) .... 35—45
288 Superior Cadillac Ambulance ...... 30—40
288 Superior Ambulance (Danish) ...... 40—60
298 Emergency Services Gift Set .... 30—45
302 Emergency Squad Gift Set .... not issued
304 Fire Rescue Gift Set .... 30—45
384 Fire Rescue Truck .... 8—12
385 Los Angeles County Fire Department Truck ....4—8
410 Bedford London Fire Brigade Van .....4—8
410 Bedford Manchester Fire Brigade Van ...4—8
410 Bedford City Fire Brigade Van ....4—8
410 BedfordMetropolitanFireBrigadeVan ....4—8
410 Bedford Los Angeles County Fire Van ...4—8
412 Bedford Los Angeles County Fire Van ...4—8
416 Ford Transit Falck Van .... 30—40
442 Land Rover Falck Wrecker .... 25—35
556 Citroen ID19 Ambulance .... 30—40
562 Citroen 2cv Fire Engine .... 25—35
568 Berliet Ladder Truck .... 35—45
570p Peugeot J7 Fire Department Van ... 35—45
583 Berliet Fire Engine .... 45—60
624 Daimler Military Ambulance .... 35—45
626 Ford Military Ambulance .... 30—45
688 MASH Military Ambulance ...... not issued
807 Renault Military Ambulance .... 30—40
820 Renault Military Ambulance .... 35—45
899 Delahaye Ladder Truck .... 50—65
954 Fire Station .... 25—35
955 Fire Engine .... 40—50
956 Turntable Fire Escape 45-60
956 Turntable Fire Escape .... 50—70
956 Berliet Turntable Fire Escape .... 35—45
956 Berliet Fire Escape (Danish) .... 45—60
957 Fire Service Set .... 80—120
25br Peugeot D3A Fire Department Van .... not issued
525hc Peugeot 404 Fire Department Wagon ....?
810p Dodge Fire Command Car ...... not issued
1416p Renault R6 Fire Chief's Car ....?

CORGI TOYS

18 Emergency Set .... 20—30
20 Emergency Set .... 20—30
33 Deutsche Lebensrettungsgesellschaft Set .... 30—40
35 Chopper Squad Surf Rescue Set ...... 10—15
213 Jaguar 2.4 Litre Fire Chief .... 35—45
213S Jaguar 2.4 Litre Fire Chief .... 35—45
284 Mercedes-Benz 240D Fire Chief .... 8—12
295 Renault 5TS Fire Chief .... 6—10
332 Opel Senator Doctor's Car .... 10—15
354 Commer 15cwt Military Ambulance .. 25—35
395 Fire Bug .... 10—15
405 Bedford Utilecon Fire Tender .... 40—50
405M Bedford Utilecon Fire Tender ..... 45—55
405 Chevrolet Superior Ambulance ...... 10—15
406 Mercedes-Benz Bonna Ambulance .... 10—15
406 Mercedes-Benz Ambulance (Danish) .. 20—30
4061 Mercedes-Benz Bonna Ambulance ... 15—25
407 Mercedes-Benz Bonna Ambulance .... 15—20
412 Bedford Utilecon Ambulance .... 35—45
414 Bedford Utilecon Military Ambulance .... 35—45
421 Forest Fire Warden's Land Rover .... 10—15
423 Bedford Utilecon Fire Tender .... 35—45
437 Cadillac Superior Ambulance ...... 30—40
439 Chevrolet Impala Fire Chief .... 25—35
463 Commer 15cwt Ambulance .... 20—30
482 Chevrolet Impala Fire Chief .... 20—30
482 Range Rover Vigilant Ambulance .... 10—20
484 AMC Pacer Rescue Car .... 10—15
513 Citroen ID19 Alpine Rescue Car ..... 20—30
700 Motorway Ambulance .... 5—10
703 Hi-Speed Fire Engine .... 8—12
1001 HCB-Angus Firestreak (type 1) ..... 15—25
1001 HCB-Angus Firestreak (type 2) ..... 10—20
1008 Chevrolet Caprice Fire Chief ...... 10—15
1103 Chubb Pathfinder Airport Crash Truck .... 20—30
1118 Chubb Pathfinder Airport Crash Truck .... 20—25
1120 Dennis Aerial Ladder Truck .... 10—15
1126 Simon Snorkel .... 20—30
1127 Bedford Simon Snorkel .... 30—40
1143 American LaFrance Aerial Ladder Truck .... 25—45
1185 Mack Fire Truck .... 8—12

Husky

4 Jaguar Mark X Fire Chief (type 1) ...... 5—10
4 Jaguar Mark X Fire Chief (type 2) ....4—8
6 Citroen Safari Ambulance .... 5—10
22 Citroen Safari Military Ambulance ..... 5—10
30 Studebaker Wagonaire Ambulance ......4—8
36 Simon Snorkel Fire Engine ....4—8

Corgi Junior

1 Mercedes-Benz 220D Ambulance ....1—2
22 Chevrolet Paramedic Emergency Unit ....1—2
26 ERF Fire Engine 2-3
29 Simon Snorkel Fire Engine ....2—3
29 ERF Simon Snorkel Fire Engine ....1—2
30 Studebaker Wagonaire Ambulance ......3—4
33 Chevrolet Ambulance Van .... not issued
36 Healer Wheeler ....1—2
42 Rescue Team Range Rover ....2—3
56 Ford Capri Fire Chief ....3—4
70 Mercury Cougar Fire Chief ....2—3
70 Ford Gran Torino Fire Chief ....1—2
79 Land Rover Military Ambulance ....2—3
119 Chubb Pathfinder Airport Crash Tender (German) ....4—8
123 Chubb Pathfinder Airport Crash Tender ....1—2
192 Mercedes-Benz 220D Ambulance ....4—8
193 Chubb Pathfinder Airport Crash Tender (Arabian) ....4—8
208 Ford Sierra Doctor's Car ....4—8
225 Chubb Pathfinder Airport Crash Tender (Swiss) ....4—8
227 Mercedes-Benz 220D Ambulance ....4—8
250 ERF Simon Snorkel Fire Engine ....4—8
251 ERF Fire Tender ....4—8
252 Ford Transit Wrecker ....4—8
253 Mercedes-Benz 220D Ambulance ....4—8
254 Mercedes-Benz 240D Emergency Car ....4—8
255 Chevrolet Rescue Van ....4—8
2029 Mack Fire Pumper ....5—10
2029 Fire Pumper .... 10—15
2513 Fire Engine (26) & Healer Wheeler (36) ....3—5
2521 Army Ambulance (79) & Helicopter ....3—5
3013 Emergency Rescue Set ....5—10
3022 Rescue Set .... 10—20
3026 Emergency Set .... 10—20
3053 Fire Station Set .... 10—20
3101 Fire Set .... 10—20
3103 Emergency Set .... 10—20
3110 Emergency Set .... 10—20

Corgi Cubs

505 Fire Chief's Car ....3—5
510 Fire Truck ....3—5
511 Ambulance ....3—5
600 Corgi Cubs Set .... 10—15

Corgi Qualitoys

707 Fire Engine .... 10—15
Mettoys ....?

MATCHBOX

3 Mercedes-Benz Binz Ambulance .... 5—10
9 Dennis Fire Escape .... 20—30
9 Merryweather Fire Engine .... 10—25
14 Daimler Ambulance (type 1) .... 20—30
14 Daimler Ambulance (type 2) .... 10—25
14 Bedford Lomas Ambulance .... 10—20
29 Fire Pumper ....5—15
54 S. & S. Cadillac Ambulance ....5—15
57 Land Rover Fire Truck ....5—15
59 Ford Fairlane Fire Chief .... 10—20
59 Ford Galaxie Fire Chief ....5—15
63 Ford 3-Ton 4 x 4 Service Ambulance ... 10—20
63 Foamite Airport Crash Tender ....5—15

Superfast Matchbox Series

3 Mercedes-Benz Binz Ambulance ....2—4
12 Citroen CX Ambulance ....1—2
13 Snorkel Fire Engine ....1—2
18 Aerial Ladder Truck ....1—2
20 Range Rover Military Ambulance ......2—4
22 Blaze Buster ....1—2

23 Volkswagen Army Ambulance . . . . 2—4
25 Chevrolet Pacific Ambulance . . . . 1—2
29 Fire Pumper . . . . 2—4
35 Merryweather Marquis Fire Engine . . . . 2—4
41 Chevrolet Ambulance (regular) . . . . 1—2
41 Chevrolet Ambulance (German) . . . . 4—8
41 Chevrolet Ambulance (Promo) . . . . 4—8
46 Stretcha-Fetcha . . . . 2—4
46 Stretcha-Fetcha (German) . . . . 4—8
8 Mercedes-Benz Unimog Rescue Truck . . . . 1—2
54 S. & S. Cadillac Ambulance . . . . 2—4
57 Land Rover Fire Truck . . . . 2—4
57 Carmichael Police Rescue Vehicle . . . . . . 2—4
57 Carmichael Fire Rescue Vehicle . . . . 2—4
59 Ford Galaxie Fire Chief . . . . 2—4
59 Mercury Fire Chief . . . . 2—4
63 Snorkel Fire Truck . . . . 1—2
64 Fire Chief . . . . 1—3
64 Airport Foam Monitor . . . . 1—2
Code Red . . . . 2—4
Two-Packs . . . . 3—6
Convoy . . . . 3—6
Convoy Series . . . . 3—6

Models of Yesteryear

Y2 Model T Ford Fire Truck . . . . ?
Y4 Shand-Mason Horsedrawn Fire Engine . . . . 20—40
Y5 Talbot 1927 London Fire Brigade Van . . . . ?
Y6 Rolls-Royce 1920 Fire Engine . . . . 8—15
Y13 Crossley 1918 R.A.F. Red Cross Tender . . . . 10—15
Y13 Crossley 1918 Fire Truck . . . . ?
Y25 Renault 910 Ville de Paris Ambulance . . . . . . ?

King Size

K6 Mercedes-Benz Binz Ambulance . . . . 10—20
K9 Fire Tender . . . . 10—20
K11 Emergency Wrecker . . . . 15—20
K15 Merryweather Fire Engine . . . . 10—20
K26 Mercedes-Benz Binz Ambulance . . . . 10—15
K38 Dodge Ambulance . . . . 8—12
K39 ERF Snorkel Fire Engine . . . . 10—20
K40 Blaze Trailer . . . . 5—15
K49 Ambulance . . . . 5—15
K49 Ambulance (German) . . . . 15—20
K53 Hot Fire Engine . . . . 5—15
K62 Citroen SM Doctor's Emergency Car . . . . 5—15
K63 Mercedes-Benz Binz Ambulance . . . . 5—15
K64 Fire Control Range Rover . . . . 10—15
K64 Fire Control Range Rover (German) . . . 15—20
K65 Plymouth Emergency Rescue Truck . . . 10—15
K65 Plymouth Truck (German) . . . . 15—20
K67 Dodge Monaco Fire Chief . . . . 5—10
K75 Airport Fire Tender . . . . 10—15
K75 Airport Fire Tender (German) . . . . 15—20
K75 Airport Fire Tender (French) . . . . 15—20
K77 Highway Rescue Truck . . . . 10—15
K77 Highway Rescue Truck (German) . . . . . 15—20
K77 Highway Rescue Truck (French) . . . . . . 15—20
K94 Crash Tendere . . . . not issued
K96 Volvo Ambulance . . . . 5—10
K104 Matra Rancho Coast Guard Car & Rescue Boat . . . . 5—10
K110 Magirus-Deutz Fire Tender . . . . 5—10
BK112 DAF Ambulance . . . . 5—10

Others

G-5 Fire Station Set . . . . 20—30
G-8 Emergency Action Pack . . . . ?
G-10 Fire Station Set . . . . 25—35
MF-1 Fire Station . . . . 10—20
MX-6 Fire Rescue Site . . . . 20—30
58 01 01 Ermergency Station . . . . 10—15
WD-1 Mickey Mouse Fire Truck . . . . 3—8

BRITISH KITS AND SPECIALTY MODELS

Airfix (plastic kits)

A2024V R.A.F. Emergency Set . . . . 5—10

Barnes (metal kits)

#? Merryweather Musketeer Airport Fire Tender . . . . current
Brooklin (readymade metal) . . . . 30—50
Dave Jones (metal kits) . . . . ?
Highway Models (metal kits) . . . . 15—20

Horton or R.S.H. (metal kits)

T1 Rescue Tender to T3 Fire Control Unit . . . . 5—10
T4 Emergency Tender to T5 Emergency Tender . . . . 4—6
T6 Bedford Airport Fire Tender . . . . 8—10
T7 Dennis Fire Pump Trailer . . . . 5—8
T8 Crossley 1918 Fire Tender . . . . 4—6
T9 Ford 1930 Model A Chemical Fire Tender——5—8
T10 Barton Pump & Ladder Kit . . . . 2—3
T11 Land Rover Angloco Emergency Tender . . . . 10—15
T12 Renault 1920 First Aid Fire Tender . . . . 10—15
#? Bedford Fire Tender . . . . ?
#? Carmichael Range Rover Fire Truck . . . . ?
#? Carmichael Land Rover Fire Truck . . . . ?

Model Fire Service (presumably metal kits)

Fire Chief's Car . . . . current
Fire Tender . . . . current
Fire Tender . . . . current
Fire Tender . . . . current
Fire Hose Truck . . . . current

M.R.M. (presumably readymade)

#? Fire Pump Trailer . . . . ?

Peover Model Promotions (conversions)

PM1 Bedford Limerick City Fire Truck . . . . 10—12
PM2 Bedford Northern Ireland Fire Truck . . . 8—12
PM3 Ford Escort Northern Ireland Fire Department Van . . . . 6—8
PM4 Renault 5TS Fire Department Car . . . . . . 5—8
PM5 Land Rover Fire Truck . . . . 5—7
PM/RSH T8 Crossley 1918 Fire Tender . . . . 16—18
PM/RSH T9 Ford Model A Chemical Fire Engine . . . . 18—20
PM/RSH T10a Ford Model A Fire Tender . . . . 10—12
PM/RSH T10b Talbot Fire Brigade Van . . . 10—12
PM30 Peugeot Ambulance . . . . 10—12
PM31 Talbot Ambulance . . . . 9—12
PM32 Crossley Ambulance . . . . 10—12

Pirate Models (metal kits)

#? Leyland London Fire Brigade Control Unit . . . . 15—25

Smith

DAF Fire Tender . . . . ?

Sun Motor Company (readymade metal models)

101 F De Soto Fire Department Ambulance . . . . current
104 Mercedes-Benz 1982 Fire Truck . . . . current
106 Leyland Lioness 1930 Fire Truck . . . . . current
205 Studebaker-Heil Fire Truck . . . . current

Transport Replicas (metal kits)

#? Dennis 1914 Fire Engine . . . . ?

Veteran & Vintage (presumably readymade metal models)

7015 Fire Pump Trailer . . . . ?

OTHER BRITISH MODELS

Arnold

Fire Engine . . . . ?

Benbros

9 Fire Engine . . . . 5—15
38 Daimler Ambulance . . . . 5—15
27 Daimler Ambulance . . . . 15—25

Brimtoy

537 Ambulance . . . . ?

Britains

#? Army Ambulance . . . . 20—40
#? Army Ambulance . . . . 40—80
#? Army Ambulance . . . . 40—80
617 Ambulance . . . . 10—20
618 Army Ambulance . . . . 10—20

Budgie

20 Austin Countryman Ambulance . . . . 4—8
27 Wolseley Fire Chief . . . . 4—8
59 Fire Engine . . . . 4—8
254 Merryweather Turntable Escape . . . . 15—35
258 Daimler Ambulance . . . . 15—35
298 Alvis Crash Tender . . . . 15—35

Castle Art

#? Fire Engine . . . . 15—25

Chad Valley

931 Fire Engine . . . . 25—45
9554 Red Cross Van . . . . 10—20

Charbens

11 Ambulance . . . . 10—15
15 Fire Engine . . . . 10—15
#? Fire Engine . . . . 15—25
OC26 Fire Escape . . . . 5—15

D.C.M.T. Crescent

#? Ladder Truck . . . . 20—40

Elmont

#? Fire Engine . . . . ?

Johillco

#? Dennis Fire Engine . . . . 50—100

L.D.C.W.

#? Fire Engine . . . . 15—30

Lledo

DG5 Fire Engine to Fire Brigade . . . . 3—6
Guildford Fire Brigade to Hong Kong Fire Brigade . . . . 40—60
Phildelphia Bureau of Fire to Lake City . . . . . . 3—6
DG6 City of London Police Ambulance . . . . 50—70
DG6 Fire Van to Fire Service . . . . 3—6

Lone Star

20 Volkswagen Ambulance to 1252 Merryweather Fire Engine . . . . 4—8
1296 Fire Engine to #? Fire Engine . . . . 10—20
#? Fire Engine to #? Fire Engine . . . . 5—10
Morestone . . . . 15—30

Spot-On

207 Morris Wadham Ambulance . . . . 30—60
316 Land Rover Fire Truck . . . . 25—45
416 Land Rover Army Ambulance . . . . . . not issued
Taylor & Barrett . . . . 30—60
Timpo . . . . 15—25
Toby Toys . . . . 15—25

Tri-ang Minic

L.C.C. Ambulance . . . . 50—75
Fire Engine . . . . 50—75
Fire Engine . . . . 10—20
Fire Engine . . . . 10—15

Unknown Makers

Ambulance . . . . 40—60
Bentley Ambulance . . . . 40—60
Fire Engine . . . . 8—15
Fire Engine . . . . ?

THE BRITISH COMMONWEALTH

Fun-Ho

5 Fire Service Kit ....8—12
21 Fire Engine ....2—4
27 Bedford Articulated Tanker ....2—4
35 Holden Ambulance ....2—4
57 Utility Pickup ....2—4
58 Jeep ....2—4
62 Holden Army Ambulance ....2—4
#? Fire Truck..........5—15
#? Fire Chief's Roadster ....5—15
#? Ladder truck ....10—20

Hallmark

Shand-Mason 1903 Steam Pumper .... current
1902 Hose Carriage .... current
Morris Wheeled Fire Escape.......... current
Shand-Mason 1903 Ladder Wagon .... current
1902 Horsedrawn Hose Reel .... current
61902 Ladder Carriage .... current

Herka

708 Fire Engine ....2—3

Lincoln

4301 Fire Engine ....5—10

Lincoln Toy

#? Ladder Truck ....?

Londontoys

16 Fire Truck ....5—10
32 Military Ambulance..........10—15
56 Fire Truck ....10—15

Matai-Micro

GB 13 Morris Fire Engine ....10—20

Micro

GB 13 Morris Fire Engine ....25—30
GB 20 International Ambulance..........25—30
GB 20 International Military Ambulance ....25—30

Mini Auto Emporium

101F Cadillac 1959 Fire Chief's Convertible .... current

Spot-On

119 Fire Land Rover ....20—40
120 R.A.F. Fire Land Rover..........20—40

Tink E

#? Steam Pumper ....10—20

Viceroy

24 Fire Chief's Car ....10—20

MAERKLIN

5521/35 Krupp Ladder Truck ....75—125
8023 Magirus Ladder Truck..........50—75
8030 Volkswagen Ambulance ....30—50
1807 VW Variant Fire Chief..........10—15
1809 VW Variant Ambulance ....10—15

SCHUCO

631 VW Passat Fire Chief ....8—15
637 BMW 525 Doctor's Car ....8—15
745 Magirus Ladder Truck..........40—60
755 Mercedes-Benz Searchlight Truck ....35—50
756 Mercedes-Benz Fire Department Van ....35—50
824 Volkswagen 411 Fire Chief ....3—6
876 Audi 80 Fire Chief ....3—6
890 Ford Transit Fire Van ....3—6
914 Volkswagen Ambulance ....3—6
1046 Volkswagen Fire Chief..........75—100
3047 Fire Engine ....?

Wiking

TFa Fire Engine..........20—30
TFb Ladder Truck..........20—30
TFc Fire Department Crane..........20—30
70 Mercedes-Benz Binz Ambulance..........2—4
71 Mercedes-Benz Binz Ambulance..........not issued
7r Opel Caravan 1961 Ambulance ....5—10
7r VW Variant Ambulance..........4—8
287 Mercedes-Benz Rescue Ambulance ....3—6
278 Mercedes-Benz Rescue Ambulance ....2—4
29m Volkswagen Ladder Truck ....5—10
32 Volkswagen Ambulance ....15—30
32 Volkswagen Ambulance ....15—25
32 Volkswagen Ambulance ....10—20
32 Volkswagen Ambulance ....5—10
32 Volkswagen Ambulance ....4—8
32 Volkswagen Ambulance ....4—8
320 Volkswagen Ambulance ....3—6
320 Volkswagen Ambulance ....2—4
39 Volkswagen 181 Technisches Hilfswerk Car ....2—4
60 Mercedes-Benz 220 Fire Chief ....15—30
60 Opel Kapitaen Fire Chief ....15—30
60 Opel kapitaen Fire Chief..........10—20
60 Mercedes-Benz 220 Fire Chief ....10—20
60 Mercedes-Benz 180 Fire Chief ....5—10
60 Ford Taunus 17M Fire Chief ....4—8
60 VW Variant Fire Chief..........3—6
600 VW Variant Fire Chief..........3—6
60a Mercedes-Benz Unimog Fire Truck..........4—8
601 Mercedes-Benz Unimog Fire Truck..........3—6
60b Opel Ladder Truck ....4—8
602 Opel Ladder Truck..........3—6
60f Mercedes-Benz Airport Truck ....4—8
60k Volkswagen Fire Truck..........15—30
60k Volkswagen Fire Truck..........10—20
60k Volkswagen Fire Truck 5-10
60k Volkswagen Fire Truck ....3—6
603 Volkswagen Fire Truck ....3—5
603 Volkswagen Fire Truck ....2—4
60p Unimog Explosive Fire Truck..........5—10
604 Mercedes-Benz Unimog Explosive Fire Truck ....4—8
60w Mercedes-Benz Fire Rescue Truck ....5—10
60w Mercedes-Benz Fire Rescue Truck ....4—8
605 Mercedes-Benz Fire Rescue Truck ....3—6
606 VW Golf Fire Chief ....2—4
607 Mercedes-Benz Fire Department Ambulance..........2—4
60u Volkswagen Emergency Van ....15—30
608 Mercedes-Benz Fire Rescue Truck ....3—6
608 Mercedes-Benz 408 Emergency Ambulance..........2—4
609 Mercedes-Benz Fire Rescue Vehicle ....2—4
61 Magirus Fire Engine ....20—40
61 Mercedes-Benz Fire Engine ....15—30
61 Magirus LF16 Fire Engine ....4—8
610 Magirus LF16 Fire Engine ....3—6
610 Magirus LF16 Fire Engine ....3—6
61n Magirus Fire Engine ....15—30
61n Magirus Fire Engine ....10—20
618 Mercedes-Benz Metz DLK 23-12 Ladder Truck ....3—6
62 Magirus Ladder Truck..........20—40
62 Magirus Ladder Truck..........15—30
62 Magirus Ladder Truck..........15—30
62 Magirus DL30 Ladder Truck ....4—8
620 Magirus DL30 Ladder Truck ....3—6
620 Magirus DL30 Ladder Truck ....3—6
62n Magirus Ladder Truck ....15—30
62n Magirus Ladder Truck ....10—20
62r Henschel Rescue Crane Truck ....10—20
62r Mercedes-Benz Rescue Crane Truck ....8—15
621 Mercedes-Benz TLF 24/50 Fire Truck ....4—8
621 Mercedes-Benz TLF 24/50 Fire Truck ....3—6
622 Mercedes-Benz Unimog TLF 8/18 Fire Truck ....4—8
622 Mercedes-Benz Unimog TLF 8/18 Fire Truck ....3—6
623 Mercedes-Benz Fiedler Fire Rescue Truck ....4—8
629 Mercedes-Benz First Aid Truck ....4—8
630 Magirus Rescue Crane Truck..........4—6
635 Mercedes-Benz Red Cross Truck ....4—8
2600 Fire Truck Set ....15—20
3362 Opel Blitz 1939 Aerial Ladder Truck ....4—8
9033 Red Cross Set..........3—6
9034 Fire Set ....3—6
9061 Magirus Fire Engine ....3—6
9062 Magirus Ladder Truck..........3—6

Siku

14 Volkswagen Ambulance ....15—30
55 Mercedes-Benz Fire Engine ....50—75
56 Mercedes-Benz Ladder Truck ....50—75
71 Mercedes-Benz Ambulance ....20—40
138 Mercedes-Benz Army Ambulance..........30—50
233 Mercedes-Benz Binz Ambulance..........10—20
237 Ford Transit Fire Truck ....8—12
261 Mercedes-Benz DL30h Ladder Truck ....15—25
292 Mercedes-Benz Ambulance ....8—12
306 Mercedes-Benz Binz Europ 1200L Ambulance..........8—12
332 Metz Airport Crash Truck..........15—25
339 Mercedes-Benz Fire Rescue Van ....6—12
342 Ford Taunus 17M Fire Chief ....4—8
344 Lamborghini Espada Fire Hunter..........4—8
353 Audi 100 Doctor's Car ....4—8
356 VW Malteser Hilfsdienst Ambulance ....4—8
357 Mercedes-Benz Fire Rescue Van ....6—12
1313 Audi 100 Doctor's Car ....3—6
1335 VW 181 Fire Department Car ....2—4
1338 Fire Department Range Rover ....2—4
1339 Porsche 928 Doctor's Car..........2—4
1343 VW Fire Truck ....3—5
1344 Mercedes-Benz 240GE Fire Command Vehicle ....3—5
1613 Mercedes-Benz 1200L Ambulance ....3—5
1613 Mercedes-Benz Binz Ambulance..........3—5
1617 Ford Taunus 17M Fire Chief ....3—5
1617 Ford Granada Turnier Fire Chief ....3—5
1618 Lamborghini Espada Fire Hunter..........3—5
1619 VW Malteser Ambulance..........3—5
1621 VW Army Ambulance ....3—5
1623 VW Rescue Ambulance ....3—5
1911 Mercedes-Benz Ambulance ....4—6
2213 Mercedes-Benz Fire Rescue Van ....4—6
2214 Mercedes-Benz Fire Rescue Van ....4—8
2218 Mercedes-Benz Unimog Red Cross Truck ....5—8
2815 Mercedes-Benz Metz Ladder Truck ....6—12
2819 Mercedes-Benz Ladder Truck ....6—12
2913 Mercedes-Benz Unimog Fire Truck & Trailer..........8—15
2914 Faun Rescue Crane Truck..........8—15
3411 Metz-Faun Airport Crash Truck ....12—20
6313 Fire Fighter Set ....20—30
#? Mercedes-Benz Fire Truck ....?
#? Mercedes-Benz Ambulance ....?

GAMA

816 Volkswagen Fire Chief..........5—10
8338 Volkswagen Technisches Hilfswerk Car ....10—20

8932 Opel Rekord Doctor's Car ....5—10
90398 THW Jeep & Field Kitchen Trailer ....10—15
9047 Medical Corps Jeep ....5—10
912 Mercedes-Benz Ladder Truck ....10—20
912 Faun Ladder Truck ....8—15
9121 Faun Ladder Truck ....8—15
9122 Faun Ladder Truck ....8—15
9123 Faun Ladder Truck ....8—15
916 Volkswagen 1200 Fire Chief ....8—15
92818 Mercedes-Benz THW Crane Truck ....10—20
928328 Mercedes-Benz THW Tank Truck ....10—20
92888 Magirus THW Wrecker ....10—20
92968 Magirus THW Covered Truck ....10—20
9378 Munga THW Vehicle ....10—20
94028 Faun THW Heavy Crane Truck ....10—20
94048 Faun THW Heavy Dumper ....10—20
9406 Krupp Fire Truck ....8—12
94068 Faun THW Emergency Truck ....10—20
94128 THW Shovel Loader ....10—20
948 Volkswagen Fire Department Bus ....10—15
9487 Volkswagen Fire Department Bus ....10—15
9532 Volkswagen Kombi Ambulance ....8—12
954 Volkswagen Red Cross Bus ....10—15
9541 Volkswagen Red Cross Van ....10—15
9547 Volkswagen Ambulance ....8—12
95477 Volkswagen Army Ambulance ....8—12
95478 Volkswagen THW Kombi ....10—20
9572 Volkswagen Fire Truck ....10—15
9575 Volkswagen Fire Truck ....8—12
958 Volkswagen Ladder Truck ....10—15

New Numbers

1114 Opel Rekord Doctor's Car ....8—12
1153 or 1154 VW Variant Fire Chief ....8—12
1156 BMW 528i Doctor's Car ....8—12
1165 BMW 528i Fire Chief ....8—12
1172 Opel Ascona Fire Chief ....8—12
1203 Volkswagen Ambulance ....8—12
1602 Volkswagen Rescue Truck ....8—15
1604 Mercedes-Benz Rescue Crane ....8—15
1605 Mercedes-Benz Ladder Truck ....8—15
1606 Mercedes-Benz Searchlight Truck ....8—15
2362 Polyma Searchlight Trailer ....8—15
0128 Polyma THW Searchlight Trailer ....8—15
2601 Porsche Orbit Firefighting System ....40—50
2603 Krupp Fire Truck ....8—12
2604 Magirus-Deutz DL23-12 Ladder Truck ....40—50
3066 Volkswagen Ambulance ....8—15
3536 Porsche Orbit Firefighting System ....40—50
3546 Magirus-Deutz Ladder Truck ....40—50

HERPA

4013 Volkswagen LT Ambulance to #? VK Falck Emergency Crane ....2—4
7501 Ambulance Set to 818502 M.A.N. Ladder Truck ....5—10
1021 Aerial Ladder Truck to 8067 Range Rover (Beyer Electronic) ....current

OTHER GERMAN BRANDS

Brekina

1123 Opel P4 Fire Chief to 1874 U.S. Army Ambulance ....2—4
1900 Fire Chief's Car ....4—8
1912 Ford Taunus 17M Fire Chief ....2—4
2001 Mercedes-Benz 190 Fire Chief ....4—8
2070 Mercedes-Benz 190 Ambulance ....4—8
2071 Mercedes-Benz 190 Fire Department Ambulance ....4—8
3031 Opel P4 Fire Chief ....2—4
4020 Mercedes-Benz L311 Metz Fire Pumper ....3—6
4030 Mercedes-Benz L311 Metz Ladder Truck ....3—6
5002 Mercedes-Benz 0321 Red Cross Ambulance & Trailer ....4—8
#? Hanomag-Henschel F-45 Fire Pumper ....3—6
9003 Stuttgart Emergency Vehicle Set ....8—12
9006 Red Cross Set ....8—12

Conrad

1018 Gräf und Stift Fire Truck ....30—45
1019 American LaFrance 1926 Fire Pumper ....30—45
1023 American LaFrance 1926 Fire Pumper ....30—45
1024 American LaFrance 1926 Fire Pumper ....30—45
1025 Dennis 1914 Fire Engine ....30—45
3066 VW Fire Department Bus ....20—30
3090 Mercedes-Benz-Rosenbauer Fire Rescue Truck ....20—30
3191 M.A.N. Volkswagen Fire Rescue Truck ....20—30
3490 Stery-Rosenbauer Fire Rescue Truck ....20—30
5501 Rosenbauer Simba Airport Crash Truck ....30—45
5502 Emergency One Ladder Truck ....30—45
5503 Emergency One Ladder Truck ....30—45
5504 Emergency One Ladder Truck ....30—45
5505 Emergency One Ladder Truck ....30—45
5506 Emergency One Ladder-Pumper Truck ....30—45
5507 Emergency One Airport Fire Truck ....30—45
#? Ladder Towers Conestoga Duplex Ladder Truck ....30—45
Cursor ....5—10
Feil ....50—100
Oestmann ....3—5
Plank ....50—75
Pola ....current

Praline & Prep

141005 Fire Department Van to 04-15 Fire Chief ....2—4
07-11 Rescue Van to 07-25 Fire Van ....3—6
09-05 Fire Bus to 24-05 Fire Van ....2—4
Preiser ....10—20
Roskopf ....2—5
Schmidt ....current
Vollmer ....current
Ziss ....8—15
Unknown Maker ....20—40

GERMAN SHEET METAL TOYS

CKO ....?
Orobr ....?
Umis Frank ....?
Unknown Makers ....?

TEKNO

404 Volkswagen Ladder Truck ....40—60
404 Volkswagen Falck-Zonen Tow Truck ....?
405 Volkswagen Red Cross Ambulance ....40—60
408 Volkswagen Fire Truck ....40—60
408 Volkswagen Falck Fire Truck ....40—60
409 Aerial Ladder Trailer ....40—60
411 Volkswagen Falck Ambulance ....40—60
412 Volkswagen Zonen Ambulance ....40—60
412 Volkswagen Svensk Räddningstjänst Ambulance ....75—100
414 Volkswagen Ambulance ....40—60
414 Volkswagen Military Ambulance ....40—60
415a Ford Taunus Falck-Zonen Ambulance ....40—60
415rk Ford Taunus Red Cross Ambulance ....40—60
424 Packard Zonen Ambulance ....75—100
436 Volvo Falck Tow Truck ....40—60
436 Volvo Falck-Zonen Tow Truck ....40—60
436 Volvo Svensk Räddningstjänst Tow Truck ....75—100
436 Volvo Falcken Tow Truck ....75—100
437 Volvo Falck-Zonen Flat Trailer ....25—35
437 Volvo Svensk Räddningstjänst Trailer ....50—75
437 Volvo Falcken Flat Trailer ....50—75
445 Scania-Vabis 76 Ladder Truck ....50—75
445 Scania-Vabis 76 Falck-Zonen Ladder Truck ....50—75
459 Volvo Fire Engine ....50—75
459 Volvo Falck-Zonen Fire Engine ....50—75
480 Ford Zonen Service Truck ....40—60
481 Ford Zonen Tow Truck ....40—60
482 Mercury Fire Chief ....60—80
483 Mercury Zonen Loudspeaker Car ....60—80
485 Triangel Ladder Truck ....60—90
485 Tringel Zonen Ladder Truck ....60—90
486 Triangel Fire Engine ....60—90
486 Triangel Zonen Fire Engine ....60—90
487 Fire Pump Trailer ....35—45
487 Zonen Fire Pump Trailer ....35—45
725 Mercedes-Benz 220SE Fire Chief ....40—60
730 Mercedes-Benz 220S Falck Ambulance ....40—60
730 Mercedes-Benz 220S Falck-Zonen Ambulance ....40—60
730 Mercedes-Benz 220S Fire Department Ambulance ....40—60
730 Mercedes-Benz 220S Red Cross Ambulance ....40—60
731 Buick Falck Ambulance ....60—90
731 Mercedes-Benz 220S Fire Department Ambulance ....40—60
732 Dodge Falck Ambulance ....50—75
732 Dodge Zonen Ambulance ....50—75
732 Dodge Red Cross Ambulance ....50—75
732 Mercedes-Benz 220S Falck-Zonen Ambulance ....40—60
732 Mercedes-Benz 220S Rädningskären Ambulance ....40—60
732 Mercedes-Benz 220S Svensk Räddningstjänst Ambulance ....75—100
733 Dodge Ambulance ....50—75
733 Dodge Svensk Räddningstjänst Ambulance ....75—100
780 Dodge Falck Wrecker ....30—50
814 Red Cross Jeep ....30—50
814 Falck Jeep ....30—50
814 Falck-Zonen Jeep ....30—50
814 Svensk Räddningstjänst Jeep ....60—90
814p Red Cross Jeep Trailer ....20—40
814p Falck Jeep Trailer ....20—40
814p Falck-Zonen Jeep Trailer ....20—40
835b Volvo 144 Fire Chief ....30—45
850 Volvo Red Cross Bus ....50—75
920 Ford D800 Falck-Zonen Truck ....40—60
952 Dodge Military Ambulance Truck ....40—60
956 Dodge Fire Searchlight Truck ....40—60

957 Dodge Ladder Truck . . . . .40—60
#? Ford Zonen Generator Truck . . . . .40—60
311 Fire Truck . . . . .75—150
313 Falck Two-Wheel Trailer . . . . .75—150
321 Fire Truck . . . . .75—150
331 Emergency Crane Truck . . . . .75—150
341 Fire Truck . . . . .75—150
351 Ambulance . . . . .75—150
361 Fire Searchlight Truck . . . . .75—150
371 Generator Truck . . . . .75—150

OTHER SCANDINAVIAN MODELS

Birk

IV Ambulance . . . . .80—120
VIII Fire Truck . . . . .80—120

Birk Copy?

#? Ambulance . . . . .40—80

Heljahn

34 Ford 1931 Ambulance . . . . current
1778 Modern Fire Station . . . . current

Lego

655 Bedford Ladder Truck . . . . .15—25
655 Mercedes-Benz Ladder Truck . . . . .15—25
960 Chevrolet Ambulance . . . . .50—75
970 Chevrolet Ambulance . . . . .50—75
6364 Paramedic Unit . . . . current
6382 Fire Station . . . . current
202 Fire Unit 1 . . . . current
6650 Fire and Rescue Van . . . . current
6680 Ambulance . . . . current
6690 Snorkel Pumper . . . . current

Lemeco

ML47 Red Cross Jeep . . . . .50—80
ML90 Red Cross Trailer . . . . .30—60
L.K.E. . . . . .10—15
Tomte-Laerdal . . . . .5—10
Vilmer . . . . .20—40

THE NETHERLANDS AND BELGIUM

Best Box . . . . .15—25
Efsi . . . . .2—5
G.S.P. . . . . current
Gasquy-Septoy . . . . .30—50
Lion Cars . . . . .10—15

SOLIDO

Major and Junior Series

43e Fire Escape Truck to 68 Simplex Ladder Truck . . . . .75—100
92 Fire Escape Truck to 196 Ambulance . . . .50—75

The 1/43 Scale Series, 1957-1979

216 Auto Union Fire Department Jeep--not issued
227 AMX 13-Ton VCI to 255 Fire Truck . . . .20—30
259 Citroen Army Ambulance . . . . .15—25
350 Fire Engine to 354 Fire Truck . . . . .10—20
360 Guinard Fire Pump Trailer . . . . .5—10
361 Ladder Truck to 362 Fire Engine . . . . . . .10—20
366 Saviem SG4 Wrecker . . . . .8—12
368 Citroen C35 Fire Department Van . . . . . . .6—10
371 Citroen C35 Fire Van & Lifeboat . . . . . . .10—15
375 Berliet GAK 17 Fire Engine . . . . .8—12
377 Mercedes-Benz Snorkel . . . . not issued
380 Peugeot J7 Fire Department Ambulance . . . . .6—10
391 Dodge Fire Department Truck & Trailer . . . . .8—12
23 Ambulance to 42 Fire Department Van . . .6—10

New Catalog Numbers, 1980 and Beyond

1002 Renault 4 Fire Department Van . . . . .4—8
1034 Fire Department Land Rover . . . . .6—10
1123 Ambulance to 2255 Fire Truck . . . . .4—8
2259 Army Ambulance to 7002 Fire Vehicles Set . . . . .6—10
No# Dodge Medical Corps Truck . . . . .15—25
1 Personnel Truck to 2 Fire Tank Truck . . .25—30
3 Citroen C4 Paris Fire Truck . . . . .20—25
4 Citroen C4 Paris Fire Pumper . . . . .30—35

Majorette

4 Bernard Ladder Truck . . . . .4—8
7 Fire Department Jeep . . . . .4—8
204 Bernard Ladder Truck . . . . .4—8
204 Dodge Fire Truck .1—3
204 Dodge Army Fire Truck . . . . .3—5
206 Peugeot 404 Ambulance . . . . .4—8
206 Citroen DS21 Ambulance . . . . .1—3
224 Mercedes-Benz Unimog Fire Truck . . . . . . .1—3
229 Datsun 260Z Doctor's Car . . . . .1—3
230 Renault 4L Fire Department Van . . . . .1—3
241 Saviem Army Red Cross Truck . . . . .3—5
243 Army Red Cross Trailer . . . . .2—4
244 Volkswagen Kombi Ambulance . . . . .1—3
244 Volkswagen Red Cross Ambulance . . . . . . .2—4
244 Volkswagen Army Ambulance . . . . .3—5
244 Volkswagen Fire Department Bus . . . . .1—3
246 Range Rover Fire Truck . . . . .1—3
258 Mercedes-Benz Airport Fire Truck . . . . .1—3
264 Alpine-Renault A310 Doctor's Car . . . . . . .1—3
269 Cherokee Ambulance . . . . .1—3
362 Dodge Fire Truck & Lifeboat Trailer . . . . .2—4
376 Range Rover Fire Truck & Tank Trailer . . . . .2—4
601 Low Loader & Rescue Helicopter . . . . .2—4
3021 Ford Ambulance Van . . . . .3—6
3033 U.S. Fire Truck . . . . .3—6
3091 Ward LaFrance Fire Snorkel . . . . .9—12
792 Fire Department Tank Truck . . . . .9—12
1509 Fiat Ladder Truck . . . . ?
#? Range Rover Ambulance . . . . .2—3
#? Range Rover Fire Service Car . . . . .2—3

NOREV

14 Ford Vedette 54 Ambulance . . . . .10—15
40 Citroen ID19 Ambulance . . . . .5—8
41 Simca Marly Ambulance . . . . .10—15
97 Berliet Ladder Truck . . . . .5—8
210 Accident SOS Set . . . . .5—8
211 Citroen ID19 Tour de France Ambulance & Cyclists . . . . .5—8
211 Peugeot J7 Tor de France Ambulance & Cyclists . . . . .5—8
220 Saviem SG4 Fire Tank Truck . . . . .5—8
240 Renault 5 Doctor's Car . . . . .2—4
241 Renault 4 Fire Department Van . . . . .2—4
252 Peugeot J7 Fire Department Ambulance . . . . .3—5
257 Mercedes-Benz Ambulance . . . . .3—5
340 Renault 5 Doctor's Car . . . . .2—4
341 Renault 4 Fire Department Van . . . . .2—4
344 Citroen ID19 Ambulance . . . . .3—5
409 Renault 4TL Fire Department Wagon . . . .2—3
410 Mercedes-Benz Ambulance . . . . .2—3
427 Renault 4 Fire Department Van . . . . .2—3
434 Volvo F-89 Fire Truck . . . . .2—3
442 Volvo Ladder Truck . . . . .2—3
461 Fire Department Pickup Truck . . . . .2—3
524 Saviem Fire Tank Truck . . . . .4—8
525 DAF Fire Tank Truck . . . . .4—8
526 Volvo Fire Tank Truck . . . . .4—8
541 Medical Assistance Set . . . . .4—8
610 Volvo Fire Truck & Trailer . . . . .3—5
615 Fire Department Pickup Truck & Trailer . . . . .3—5
865 Renault 4 Fire Department Van . . . . .3—5
874 Mercedes-Benz Ambulance . . . . .4—6
875 Renault 5 Doctor's Car . . . . .3—5
977 Mercedes-Benz Ambulance . . . . .2—3

ELIGOR

1014p Fire Chief to 1141 Ambulance . . . . .9—15
3001 Magirus 1925 Ladder Truck . . . . .30—40
3004 Citroen 11b1 Fire Chief . . . . .15—20

OTHER FRENCH BRANDS

A.R. . . . . .30—60
C.D. . . . . .50—75

C.I.J.

Fire Engine to Ladder Truck . . . . .30—50
3/30 Fire Engine . . . . .50—75
3/41 Citroen Ambulance to 3/95 Renault Fire Truck . . . . .25—45
M6 Renault 1000 kg Ambulance . . . . .10—20
Cle . . . . .3—6
Cofalu . . . . .15—30

Cofradis

0001 Fire Chief to 0004 Fire Chief . . . . .15—25
380 Fire Truck to 1156 Fire Truck . . . . .35—55
Emo . . . . .20—40
Frances Jouets . . . . .20—40
J.P. Cars . . . . .10—15
J.R.D. . . . . .30—50
K.P. . . . . .50—75
Mignot . . . . current
Minialuxe . . . . .10—30
Quiralu . . . . .30—45
R.L. . . . . ?
Rhodanienne . . . . .15—35

Safir

11 Citroen 1923 Fire Truck . . . . .10—20
Dodge Army Ambulance . . . . .5—15
Dodge Fire Truck . . . . .5—15
Jeep Fire Truck . . . . .5—15
Fire Department Jeep .5—15
Red Cross Jeep . . . . .5—15
Mercedes-Benz Fire Truck . . . . .5—15
Mercedes-Benz Fire Truck & Tank Trailer . . . . .10—20
Land Rover Army Ambulance . . . . .3—8
Renault Estafette Ambulance . . . . .3—8

Sesame

Bernard Army Ambulance . . . . .5—10
Renault Ambulance . . . . .5—10
Renault Fire Truck . . . . .5—10

Unknown Makers

Fire Truck . . . . ?
Fire Department . . . . ?
Steam Pumper . . . . ?

FRENCH KITS AND SPECIALTY MODELS

Annecy . . . . current
Automany . . . . current
C.C.C.P. . . . . current
C.J.M. . . . . current
Can Am . . . . current
D.M. . . . . current
M. Dubray . . . . .20—30
Elegance . . . . current
Es Do . . . . current
Idem . . . . current
K.J.D. . . . . current
M.G.B. Super Toy . . . . current
Mini Racing/Mini Vehicles Incendies . . . . current
Minitrucks . . . . current
O.K.C. . . . . current
Proto . . . . current

Pyacar . . . . current
S.T.L. . . . . current
Tacot . . . . current
X.V.M. . . . . current

AUSTRIA AND SWITZERLAND

Aurore . . . . current
Braendli . . . . current
Roco . . . . 1—5
Zaugg . . . . current

EASTERN EUROPE

Czechoslovakia . . . . 5—10

German Democratic Republic

Ladder Truck to Fire Truck . . . . 5—10
Veb 143 Daimler 1911 Fire Truck . . . . 8—15

Greece

A.B. 41 Ladder Truck . . . . 2—5
A.B. 51 Mercedes-Benz German Red Cross Bus . . . . 3—6
Hungary . . . . 8—12
U.S.S.R. . . . . 5—10

ITALY

A.M. . . . . 8—15
Antoine . . . . 50—75
Barlux . . . . current
Brumm . . . . 5—10
Burago . . . . 8—15
Giodi . . . . 20—40
Ingap . . . . 5—10
Mebetoys . . . . 5—10

Mercury

4 Fire Chief to 84 Fire Truck . . . . 5—15
94c Ciclope Ladder Truck . . . . 30—50
Modelli . . . . current
Old Cars . . . . 10—20
P.M. . . . . 40—60

Politoys

8 Ambulance to 117 Fire Truck . . . . 5—10
#? Dodge Ambulance Van . . . . ?
Rampini . . . . 10—15
Sam Toys . . . . 5—10
Tron . . . . current

SPAIN AND PORTUGAL

Anguplas . . . . 4—8
Aylmer . . . . 5—10
Dalia . . . . 20—40

Eko

2019 Ladder Truck to 4044 Ambulance . . . . 1—4
#? Fire Van to #? Fire Chief . . . . ?

Guisval

12 Red Cross Car to 72 Fire Truck . . . . 2—4
104 Fire Chief to #? Red Cross Car . . . . 5—10
Guiloy . . . . ?
Ibertren . . . . 2—4

Luso

13b Citreon GS Ambulance . . . . 4—8
79 Citroen GS Fire Department Wagon . . . . 5—10
Metosul . . . . 5—10
Mira . . . . 5—10
Nacoral . . . . 5—10
Paya . . . . 4—8

Pilen

294 Fire Chief to 551 Red Cross Car . . . . 5—10
801 Ambulance to 815 Range Rover . . . . 3—6
Rico . . . . 15—35
Vitesse . . . . current
Tinplate Toys . . . . current
Rai . . . . ?
Rico . . . . ?
Unknown Maker . . . . ?

LATIN AMERICA

Arpra . . . . 10—15

Buby

1000 Ambulance to 1000 Army Ambulance . . . . 35—45
1051 Peugeot 504 Fire Chief . . . . 8—12
29 Fire Chief to 122 Red Cross Car . . . . 3—6
Chico . . . . 5—10
Fidart . . . . 5—10

Galgo

39 Ladder Truck to 53 Fire Truck . . . . 3—6
193 Ambulance to #? Fire Chief . . . . 5—10
Gorgo . . . . 5—10
I.V.H. . . . . 5—10
J. Cubas . . . . 3—6
Jet . . . . 2—5
Jue . . . . 20—40
McGregor . . . . 4—8
Minimac . . . . current
Motoplastic . . . . 4—8
Muky . . . . 2—4
Plom-ur . . . . 20—40
R.M. . . . . 6—12
Rapitoy . . . . 2—4
Roly . . . . 10—20
San Marino . . . . ?
Solido . . . . 20—30
Solido-Buby . . . . 10—20

TOOTSIETOYS AND ACCUCAST

Prewar Tootsietoys

4652 Hood and Ladder Truck . . . . 40—60
4653 Water Tower . . . . 40—60
4658 Mack Insurance Patrol . . . . 25—35
809 Ambulance to 116 Roadster . . . . 50—75
#? Fire Engine to #? Ambulance . . . . 5—10
1040 Hook & Ladder Truck to 1042 Insurance Patrol . . . . 20—40
236 Hook & Ladder Truck to 263 Hook & Ladder Truck . . . . 10—15

Postwar Tootsietoys

1040 Hook & Ladder Truck to 1042 Insurance Patrol . . . . 20—35
236 Ladder Truck to #? Army Ambulance . . . . 10—15
2330 Mack Fire Engine . . . . 15—30
905 Ladder Truck to 2905 Ladder Truck . . . . 20—40
5211 Fire Department Set . . . . 50—75
#? American LaFrance Fire Engine . . . . 3—6
1011 Fire Pumper . . . . 1—3
2545 Ladder Truck (type 1) . . . . 5—10
2545 Ladder Truck (type 2) . . . . 3—6
1290 Fire Pumper to #? Pickup Truck . . . . 1—3
1747 Fire Fighters Set . . . . 10—15
1747 Fire Fighters Set . . . . 8—12
1249 American LaFrance Ladder Truck . . . . 3—6
1249 American LaFrance Snorkel . . . . 3—6
1297 Rescue Truck to 1297 Rescue Wagon . . . . 1—3
1749 Rescue 1 Set . . . . 5—10
1830 Rescue 2 Set . . . . 10—15
5003 Rescue Ambulance . . . . 2—4
5000 Rescue Wagon . . . . 1—3
2303 Fire Truck . . . . 2—4
5008 American LaFrance Fire Truck . . . . ?
1814 Paramedic Truck Set . . . . 5—8
1951 Utility Unit . . . . 1—3
3154 Police-Fire-Rescue Assortment . . . . ?
1642 Emergency Set . . . . ?
2985 Ladder Truck . . . . 2—4
Accucast (P.A.C.) . . . . 5—10

HUBLEY TOYS

313 Steam Pumper to 429 Ladder Truck . . . . ?
437 Packard Fire Chief . . . . 10—20
#? Ladder Truck . . . . ?
405 Ladder Truck to 404 Steam Pumper . . . . 10—20
463 Ladder Truck to 402 Fire Engine . . . . 15—35
#? Ambulance to #? Fire Chief . . . . 10—20
#? Fire Chief to 307 Ladder Truck . . . . 5—10
324 Ladder Truck to 331 Diesel Ladder Truck . . . . 10—20
306? Pumper to 307 Aerial Ladder . . . . 20—25

AMERICAN CAST IRON TOYS

Arcade . . . . ?
Dent . . . . ?
Kenton . . . . ?
Kilgore . . . . ?
Williams . . . . ?
Unknown Makers . . . . ?

AMERICAN SLUSHMOLD

Barclay

50 Ambulance . . . . 20—40
Ambulance . . . . 10—15
Ladder Truck to Steam Pumper . . . . 10—30
Maybe Barclay . . . . 10—30
Lincoln . . . . 20—40
Manoil . . . . 10—20
Savoye . . . . 25—50
Tommy Toy . . . . 25—45
Unknown Makers . . . . 10—30

AMERICAN DIECAST MODELS

Authenticast

#? Aerial Ladder Truck . . . . 20—40
#? Fire Engine to #? Fire Chief . . . . 15—30

Barclay

Ambulance Truck . . . . 3—6
Fire Chief . . . . 10—20
Ladder Truck . . . . 15—35
Ertl . . . . 2—4
Freeport Toy . . . . 15—35

Goodee

Fire Engine . . . . 10—20
Fire Engine . . . . 4—8
Fire Chief . . . . 4—8
Fire Chief . . . . 10—15
Hallmark . . . . 1—3
Hudson . . . . 15—25

It's a Beaut

4 Chrysler Fire Chief . . . . 10—15
#? Fire Truck? . . . . ?
Jurgens . . . . 35—45

Manoil

709 Fire Engine . . . . 10—20
711 Ladder Truck to 712 Fire Pumper . . . . ?

Mattel Hot Wheels

6451 Ambulance . . . . 4—8
6454 Fire Truck . . . . 5—10
6469 Cruiser to 7665 Chief's Special . . . . 1—5
7666 Ranger Rig . . . . 3—6
9640 Pumper (Fire-Eater) to 1699 Airport Rescue . . . . 1—5
4225 Firefighters Play Set . . . . 4—8
7068 Fire Smasher . . . . 2—3
Mattel First Wheels . . . . 1—3
Metalcraft . . . . 5—15

Metal Masters

300 Fire Engine . . . . 15—30
#? Pickup to #? Pickup . . . . 10—20

Midgetoy

Ambulance to Wrecker . . . . 1—4
445 Alert Assortment to 555 Swat Pack . . . . 3—6

Ralstoy

1 **Fire Truck** ... 15—25
22 **Ambulance** to **Fire Rescue Service** ... 4—8

Renwal

#? **Steam Pumper** ... 15—35
8022 **Ladder Truck** to 8040 **Steam Pumper** ... 5—10
Slik Toys ... 5—10
Tru-Scale ... 10—15
Winross ... 40—60

AMERICAN PLASTIC

Acme ... 5—10
Amloid ... 3—5
Auburn ... 5—10
Banner ... 10—15
B.K.C. ... 2—5

B.W.

Ladder Truck ... 25—35
Ladder Truck to **Ladder Truck** ... 5—10
California ... 10—20
Commonwealth ... ?

Empire

Hometown U.S.A. Set ... 20—25
Aerial Ladder Truck to **Rescue Truck** ... 1—3
F ... ?
F. & F. ... 3—6
Gilmark ... 4—8
Hasbro ... 4—8
Hess ... 25—35

Ideal

1-1729 **Ambulance** to 1-1729 **Army Ambulance** ... 10—15
#? **Ford Fire Engine** ... 20—25

Keystone

K-48 **Fire Chief** to #? **Ladder Truck** ... 10—20
1-165 **Fire Department Set** ... 80—120
Kilgore ... 10—15
Lido ... 3—6
Marx (probably Ideal) ... 3—6
Nosco ... 10—20
Plasticville ... 5—10
Processed Plastic ... 2—5
Pyro ... 3—6

Renwal

57 **Fire Truck** ... 10—20
105 **Ladder Truck** to 146 **Ladder Truck** ... 5—10
179 **Ladder Truck** ... 10—20
Thomas ... 3—6
W.G. ... 2—4

Wannatoy

7 **Fire Truck** ... 6—12
7 **Fire Truck** ... 5—10
#? **Fire Truck** ... 3—6
#? **Fire Truck** ... 6—12
Wyandotte ... 5—10
Zimmerman ... 5—10
Unknown Makers ... 4—12

AMERICAN KITS AND SPECIALTY MODELS

A.H.M. to *K-Line* ... current

Lee Town

3035 **Mack 1950 SB61 Fire Pumper** ... 25
3136 **Mack 1951 SB61 "Bermuda" Open Cab Pumper** ... 27
3203 **Mack CF Fire Pumper** ... 29
7002 **Mack CF Fire Pumper Body** ... 19
7007 **Ford LN Fire Pumper** ... 20?
7017 **Mack CF New York Fire Pumper** ... 29
7025 **Ford LS Fire Pumper** ... 20
7026 **Pierce Fire Pumper Body** ... 15
7027 **Ford Budd Cab Fire Pumper** ... 16
7028 **Ford C Cab Fire Pumper** ... 18
7029 **Fire Engine** to 7030 **Fire Engine** ... 25
7031 **Rescue Truck** to 7030 **Rescue Truck** ... 20
7033 **Ford C-Pierce CRV-18 Rescue Truck** ... 18
Life-Like to National Motor Co. ... current
Nostalgic Miniatures ... 40—60
Precision Miniatures to *Tyco* ... current
Wheel Works ... 4—8

OTHER AMERICAN TOYS

Arcor ... ?

Auburn

Ahrens-Fox Fire Engine ... 20—40
Ladder Truck to **Hose Truck** ... 10—20
Emergency Truck to **Fire Engine** ... 5—10
Fire Set ... 20—40

Sun

32 **Ambulance** to 32 **Army Ambulance** ... 10—15
59 **Fire Truck** to 77 **Fire Truck** ... 25—45
#? **Fire Truck** ... 5—10
Unique ... 10—20
Unknown Maker ... 20—40
Sheet Metal ... ?
Argo ... 4—8
Buddy L ... 2—5
Lupor ... ?
Marx ... ?

Tonka

Ambulance to **Fire Engine** ... 5—10
Fire Jeep to **Ladder Truck** ... ?
086 **Rescue Truck** to 1100 **Rescue Truck** ... 2—5
675 **Aerial Ladder Truck** ... 4—8
6150 **Fire Squad Van** ... 2—4
1009 **Fire Department Set** ... 6—12
Wyandotte ... ?
Plaster ... ?
R.C.B. ... 2—5
Unknown Makers ... 2—5
Glass ... 10—30

TOMICA

Pocket Cars

3-2 **Fire Truck** to 22-2 **Fire Engine** ... 2—5
27-1 **Toyota Crown Fire Chief** ... 10—15
27-2 **Toyota Crown Fire Chief** ... 5—10
27-3 **Toyota Crown Fire Chief** ... 2—5
29-1 **Hino Fire Engine** ... 10—15
29-2 **Fire Engine** to 78-1 **Fire Chief** ... 2—5
94-1 **Tokyu Chemical Fire Engine** ... 10—15
94-2 **Fire Engine** to F65-1 **Cheetah** ... 2—5
Emergency Gift Set to **Assorted Vehicles** ... 10—20
Long Series ... 3—6

Dandy Series

D2 **Hino Ladder Truck** ... 15—25
D5 **Fire Engine** to DF23 **Hilfswerk Van** ... 5—10
DF#? **Citroen Fire Van** ... ?
Dandy Fire Fighting Set ... 20—30
Putica Series ... 5—10

Diapet

151 **Emergency Car** to 01633 **Ambulance** ... 8—15
0232 **Isuzu Blood Bank Bus** ... 10—20
0264 **Toyota Hiace Fire Department Bus** ... 8—15
0283 **Ladder Truck** to 0288 **Hospital Bus** ... ?
0335 **Ambulance** to P69 **Communications Car** ... 8—15
T54 **Fuso Snorkel Fire Truck** ... 10—20

OTHER JAPANESE MODELS

A.T.C. ... 20—40

Aviva

1 **Snorkel Fire Truck** to 20 **Fire Engine** ... 1—3
72044-3 **Snoopy in Fire Engine** ... 2—4
700 **Snoopy's Fire Truck** ... 3—6
Bandai ... 2—4
Eidai (formerly Grip Zechin) ... 3—6
Kado ... current
Madmax ... 3—6
Marusan ... 20—40
Sakura ... 5—10
Shinsei ... 5—10
Tonka ... 2—4
Yone ... 4—8

Unknown Makers

Fire Truck to **Daimler Ambulance** ... 1—3
Steam Pumper ... 3—6
Steam Pumper to **Fire Engine** ... 20—40

JAPANESE TINPLATE TOYS

A1 ... ?
Cragstan ... 10—20

K

110 **Fire Chief's Car** ... 8—12
Porsche Fire Chief ... 3—6
Fire Chief to **Fire Truck** ... 5—10
Hero Toy ... ?
K.S. ... ?
Kanto ... 6—12
M.T.H. ... 8—12
Marline ... ?
Modern Toy ... ?
S.N. ... ?
San ... 10—20

T.N.

24670 **Ladder Truck** to **Ladder Truck** ... 10—20
Ambulance to **Fire Chief** ... 5—10

Y

1190 **Fire Chief** to **Fire Engine** ... 5—10
Ladder Truck ... 10—15

Yone

2033 **Ladder Truck** ... 5—10
2100 **Ladder Truck** ... 10—15
Unknown Makers ... 5—15

HONG KONG DIECAST

Amsi ... ?
Arco ... 3—6
Azrak-Hamway ... 1—3
D.T.C. ... 2—5
Hasbro ... 2—4
Holly ... 1—3

Imperial

8183 **Rescue Ambulance** to 8224 **Army Rescue Truck** ... 1—3
8280 **Emergency Team Set** ... 4—8
8281 or 8282 **Fire Chief's Car** to 8340D **Medic Ambulance** ... 1—3
JaRu ... 2—4
Kidco ... 1—3
L.J.N. ... 2—4

Larami

201-4 **U.S. Army Ambulance** ... 1—2
8222 **Firefighter** ... 2—4
Lido ... 1—2
Marx ... 1—3
*Maxwell*4—6
Mini Roller ... 2—4

Playart

7118 **Fire Chief** to 7333 **Fire Truck** ... 1—2
7508 **Fire Fighters Set** ... 8—12
7602 **Ambulance Set** ... ?
7716 **Fire Chief's Car** ... 2—3
7766 **Fire Pumper** to 7767-2 **Snorkel Truck** ... 3—6
7902 **Ambulance** to 7902-1 **Fire Rescue Van** ... 3—5

792 Fire Department Tanker ....6—12
7956 Ambulance Van.......................3—5
7968 Ladder Truck to 7969 Fire Pumper.....6—12
#? Firefighters Train Set to #? Firefighters Yard Set............................ current
S.M. ....2—4
Universal..............................2—4
Welly ....1—2
Wheeler ....1—2
Wul....................................1—2
Y.D.C. ....1—3

Yatming

261 Ladder Truck & Lifeboat Trailer.........2—3
1355 Snorkel Truck to 1501 Ambulance ......1—2

Zylmex

312 Ladder Truck to 346 Paramedic Van .....1—2
433 Red Cross Truck to 439 Ambulance ......2—4
21700 Military Set to 21721 Patrol Set ....3—5

OTHER HONG KONG PRODUCTS

A ....1—2
Arco ....3—5

Azrak-Hamway

6263 Fire Chief to 6427 Fire Truck ....2—4
7096 Cracker Jack Fire Engine ....2—5
Crash Tender to Ladder Truck ....1—2
Bachmann...............................1—2

Blue Box

77130 Emergency Call Set...................3—6
Ambulance to Ladder Truck ....1—2
Cragstan ....3—6

Day Ran

1154B Fire Engine to 1155B Fire Tender......2—4
13103 Fire Engine ....5—10
Diamond Toymakers ....1—2
Durham ....5—10
E ....?
E.W. ....3—6
F ....2—4
Fleetwood ....1—3
Foundation ....5—10
Free Wheeling ....3—5

Gordy

600 Fire Fighters..........................2—4
Fire Engine to Fire Chief ....1—2
833 Fire Engine to 836 Fire Chief ....1—3
918 Fire Engine to 919 Fire Chief ....3—5
Ideal ....1—3
Illco ....4—8
Imco ....2—4
Imperial...............................2—4
Jak Pak ....1—2

Jimson

156 Ladder Truck..........................?
302 Porsche Fire Chief ....1—3

Kai Yip

8829 Fire Snorkel to 3330 Fire Truck ....3—5
4406 Rescue Set..........................5—10
Kidco ....2—4
Knickerbocker...........................3—5

Larami

1131-0 Rescue Heroes ....2—4
Ambulance to Fire Engine ....1—2
8109-0 Mash Unit to 9230-4 Convoy Set ......1—3
#? Red Cross Truck ....1—2
Little People ....?

Lucky Toys

114 Ladder Truck..........................?
178 Fire Chief to #? Fire Tender ....3—5
7128 Emergency Fire Service Set ....10—20
3121 Berliet Ladder Truck ....5—10
3190 VW Rabbit Fire Chief ....3—6
Madison................................5—10
Mak's ....5—10
NFIC ....?
Nasta ....1—2

Nucor

Fire Fighters Set ....2—4
Ambulance to Fire Engine ....1—2
O.K. ....?

Ocean

20 Ambulance to 20 Fire Department Van ....1—2
Remco ....1—2
Steven ....1—2
Symbol of Quality ....4—8
T.P....................................1—2
United Features ....1—2
Wallace Berrie ....1—2
Wind Up ....2—4

Zylmex

2026 Fire Engine ....?
Fire Engine ....1—3

Unknown Makers

312 Fire Engine to Ambulance ....1—3
Wheaties Fire Set ....?

OTHER ASIAN MODELS

China and Taiwan

M.F.

718 Ladder Truck..........................5—8
732 Ambulance.............................3—5
Ambulance to Fire Chief's Car ....2—3
Schaper ....3—5
Talbot ....2—4
Unknown Makers ....1—2

India

Mattel.................................1—3
Maxwell................................5—10
Milton Morgan ....5—10
New Toys ....3—6
Nicky Toys ....5—10
Raj ....4—8

Israel

Gamda ....10—20
Sabra ....8—12

Korea

Clover.................................5—10
Kingstar...............................2—5
M.T.U. Toy to *Buddy L*................2—4
Mandarin ....1—3

Thailand

Illco ....3—6

Turkey

Turk Maii ....4—8

The prices listed here are intended to give the hobbyist a general idea of what the listed models are worth. It should not be taken too literally. It is impossible to put an absolute value on any obsolete model; a walk around any toy show will make clear that prices vary according to what the seller wants to get and what the buyer wants to pay, and no two collectors or dealers may value the same model to the same degree. In addition, the author is not an authority on such items as cast iron, slushmold or sheet metal toys, and thus cannot put values on such items as lie outside his area of specialization.

A high and a low price are given for each model for which values are stated. The high price might represent what a specialist collector who needed that particular model might be willing to pay; the low price might be what a hobbyist of limited means might feel like paying for the model because he happened to like it. In some cases currently produced models are listed at approximately their current prices—though even these will vary from one dealer to another—while others are simply marked "current", particularly in cases where the models can be obtained at lower prices from their country of manufacture than elsewhere.